WALKING
the
BIBLE

WILLIAM MORROW
An Imprint of HarperCollins*Publishers*

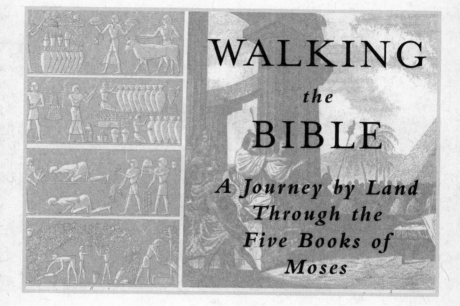

WALKING

the

BIBLE

A Journey by Land Through the Five Books of Moses

BRUCE FEILER

First Perennial edition published 2002.
First Harper Perennial edition published 2005.
First William Morrow paperback edition published 2014.

Maps by Jeffrey L. Ward
Designed by Claire Vaccaro

The Library of Congress has cataloged the hardcover edition as follows:
Feiler, Bruce S.
Walking the Bible: a journey by land through the five books
of Moses/by Bruce Feiler.
p. cm.
Includes bibliographical references and index.
ISBN 0-380-97775-3
1. Middle East—Description and travel. 2. Feiler, Bruce S.—
Journeys—Middle East. 3. Bible. O.T. Pentateuch—Geography. I. Title.
DS49.7.F45 2001
915.604'54—dc21   00-056076

ISBN 978-0-06-233650-7 (pbk.)

15   16   17   18   OV/RRD   10   9   8   7   6   5   4   3   2

FOR MY SISTER

May your descendants
be as numerous as the stars

Now the Lord said to Abram,
"Go forth from your native land
and from your father's house to the
land that I will show you."

GENESIS 12:1

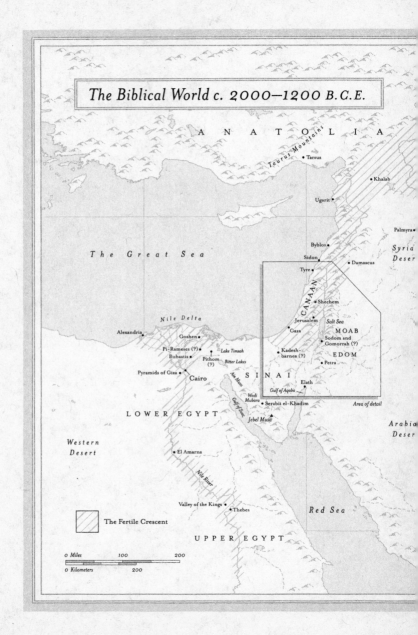

The Biblical World c. 2000–1200 B.C.E.

ANATOLIA

Taurus Mountains

• Tarsus

• Khalab

Ugarit •

Palmyra •

The Great Sea

Byblos •

Sidon •

Syria
Deser

• Damascus

Tyre •

CANAAN

• Shechem

Salt Sea

Jerusalem •

Nile Delta

• Gaza

MOAB

Alexandria •

Goshen •

Sodom and
Gomorrah (?)

Pi-Rameses (?) •

Lake Timsah

Kadesh-
barnea (?) •

EDOM

Bubastis •

Pithom
(?)

Bitter Lakes

• Petra

Pyramids of Giza •

Cairo

Ain Musa

SINAI

Elath •

Gulf of Aqaba

Gulf of Suez

Area of detail

LOWER EGYPT

Wadi
Mubara

• Serabit el-Khadim

Arabia
Deser

Western
Desert

• El Amarna

Jebel Musa

Nile River

Valley of the Kings •

• Thebes

Red Sea

The Fertile Crescent

UPPER EGYPT

0 Miles   100   200

0 Kilometers   200

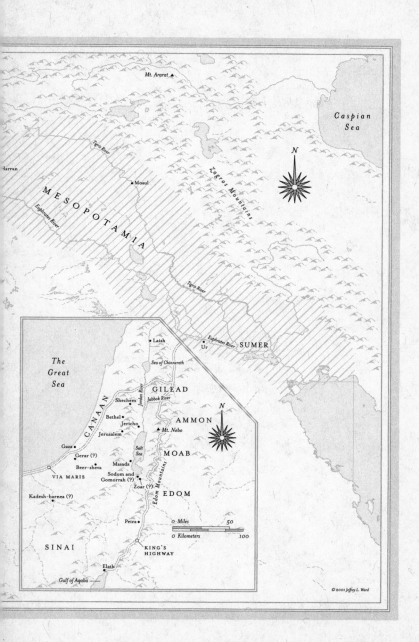

Caspian
Sea

Mt. Ararat ▲

Tigris River

Harran

MESOPOTAMIA

Mosul •

Euphrates River

Zagros Mountains

N

Tigris River

Euphrates River   SUMER

Laish •

Ur •

The
Great
Sea

Sea of Chinnereth

GILEAD

Shechem •

CANAAN

Bethel •

Jordan River

Jabbok River

AMMON

Jericho •

N

Jerusalem •

▲ Mt. Nebo

Gaza •

Gerar (?) •

Salt
Sea

MOAB

Beer-sheva •

Masada •

VIA MARIS

Sodom and
Gomorrah (?) •

Edom Mountains

Zoar (?) •

EDOM

Kadesh-barnea (?) •

0 Miles   50

Petra •

0 Kilometers   100

SINAI

KING'S
HIGHWAY

Elath •

Gulf of Aqaba

© 2001 Jeffrey L. Ward

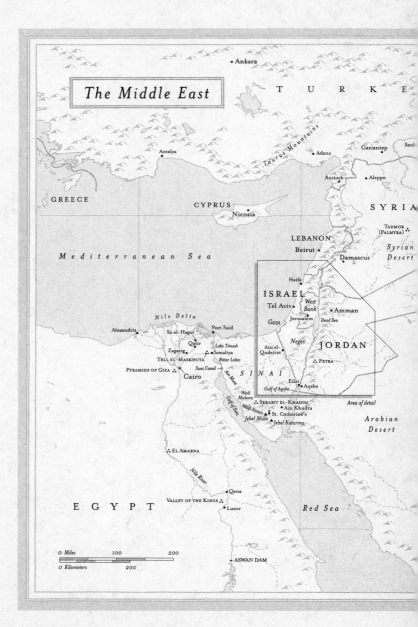

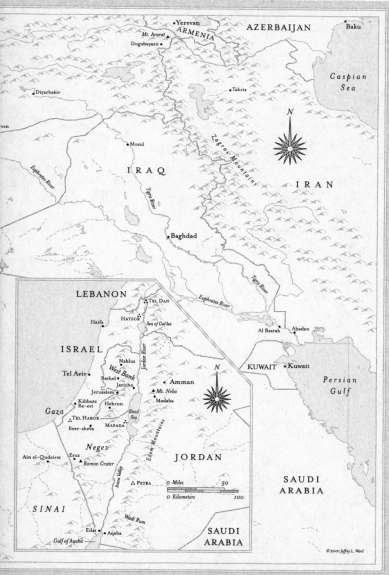

Yerevan
ARMENIA
AZERBAIJAN
Mt. Ararat
Dogubayazit
Baku

Caspian
Sea

Diyarbakir
Tabriz

Mosul

I R A Q
Zagros Mountains
Euphrates River
Tigris River

I R A N

N

Baghdad

Tigris River

Euphrates River

LEBANON
TEL DAN
Haifa
HATZOR
Sea of Galilee
Al Basrah
Abadan

ISRAEL
Nablus
West Bank
Jordan River
Tel Aviv
Bethel
Jericho
Jerusalem
Kibbutz
Be-eri
Hebron
Amman
Mt. Nebo
Madaba
KUWAIT
Kuwait

Persian
Gulf

N

Gaza
TEL HAROR
Dead
Sea
Beer-sheva
MASADA

Ain el-Qudeirat
Ezuz
Ramon Crater
Negev
Edom Mountains
JORDAN

SAUDI
ARABIA

Arava Valley
PETRA
0 Miles   50
0 Kilometers   100

SINAI
Wadi Rum

Eilat
Aqaba
Gulf of Aqaba

SAUDI
ARABIA

© 2001 Jeffrey L. Ward

Contents

Book IV

THE LAND THAT DEVOURS
ITS PEOPLE

Book V

TOWARD THE PROMISED LAND

Preface
The Journey Home

The stones are warm and worn with time: a welcome mat to the past. Place your hand here and you feel instantly at home. It's late afternoon on a warm weeknight in September, and I'm standing at the base of the Western Wall in the heart of Jerusalem's Old City. To my left, a group of white-haired men in black fedoras and wizardly beards wrap themselves in prayer cloths and rock back and forth. To my right, women in dark sweaters and thick wigs nod into tiny prayer books. Everything here feels devoid of time.

Until, out of nowhere, two men in their early twenties come strolling up to the stones. They're dressed like Brooklyn hipsters, with trendy stubble, plaid shirts, skinny jeans. They even pause to take a selfie. And yet, here they are, drawn to the epicenter of Western sacredness.

I strike up a conversation. They're cousins, from the United States, and they've come to seek more meaning in their lives.

"A lot of people think spirituality is for the old," I say. "Young people are too caught up in their digital technology. They don't care about something as abstract and untouchable as God."

"I was the same way," says Lazer Mangel, the younger of the two. "But eventually you find yourself living a kind of empty life, and you find yourself looking for something greater, somewhere to ground yourself. Whatever it is you're looking for, this is the best place to find it."

Fifteen years earlier, I was Lazer. Though I was certainly never hip (and I was older when I first arrived), I too was looking for something I couldn't quite define. My first morning, a friend took me to a hilltop overlooking this spot, and I had the idea of retracing the stories of the Bible through the desert. At the time I was single, a wandering writer surrounded by references to ancient stories I could hardly remember and had no idea could be placed on a map.

My idea was to fill those gaps by taking the adventure of a lifetime. I would travel across the route of the Bible and read the stories along the way. In effect, I would do a topographical midrash—on those stories and, as it turns out, on myself.

When this book was first published, I quickly discovered that many others harbored the same questions. I heard from people in nearly every corner of the world and every walk of life. People shared stories of similar journeys, of using this account in their book groups and Bible studies, of reading certain chapters to their children, and of how my journey finally allowed their spouses to understand why they loved the Bible. After I filmed a three-hour television series based on this book for PBS, people told me about their viewing parties. Nothing could have prepared me for the breadth and depth of hearing from so many people.

But two things happened in subsequent years that brought this original journey into new light. First, 9/11. In the wake of the attack, understanding the Middle East and the roots of religion took on new urgency. Suddenly many of the places I had traveled to were engulfed in conflict, and many of the stories I had written about were appearing in the headlines. I returned to the region and wrote a book about Abraham and his role as the shared ancestor of Jews, Christians, and Muslims.

The second thing that happened was a change in my personal life. I got married and became the father of identical twin girls—Eden, for the Garden of Eden, and Tybee, for an island off the coast of Georgia where I grew up. And three years later, I was diagnosed with a rare, aggressive form of bone cancer in my left femur. Suddenly I was the "walking guy" who might never walk again. As I went through treatment, including a year and a half on crutches, I thought a lot about walking and how this elemental act has always been deeply connected to our spirituality. For as long as people have walked, they've walked to get closer to their gods.

Five years had passed since my original diagnosis when I arrived on this visit to Jerusalem. I was cancer-free and walked with a slight limp. I had reached the end of a yearlong experience visiting pilgrimage sites around the world for a new series on PBS called *Sacred Journeys with Bruce Feiler.* My destinations included India, France, Japan, Nigeria, and Saudi Arabia. What inspired this trip was a paradox: At a time when organized religion is more fluid than ever, pilgrimage is more popular than ever. Two hundred million people go on a spiritual journey each year.

What united all the pilgrims I met is the same thing that inspired me when I set out to retrace the books of the Bible: a desire to understand the roots of these stories. Instead of just accepting a tradition that's been handed down from others, a traveler is forced to engage, to consider, to decide. But above all, the sacred journey is a chance to experience. In a world in which more and more things are virtual and ephemeral, a trip like the one described in these pages makes you feel something real.

I look forward to hearing how it affected you.

Bruce Feiler
Jerusalem, 2014
www.brucefeiler.com

Introduction

AND
GOD
SAID

Go Forth

The call to prayer sounded just after 3 P.M. It came from a minaret, echoed off the storefronts, and stopped me, briefly, in the middle of the street. All around, people halted their hurrying and turned their attention, momentarily, to God. A few old men pulled cloaks around their shoulders and slipped into the back of a shop. Two boys rushed across the road and disappeared behind a stone wall. A woman picked up her basket of radishes and tiptoed out of sight. Part of me felt odd to be starting a journey into the roots of the Bible in a place so spiritually removed from my own. But continuing toward the center of town, I realized my unease might be a reminder of a truth tucked away in the early verses of Genesis: Abraham was not originally the man he became. He was not an Israelite, he was not a Jew. He was not even a believer in God—at least initially. He was a traveler, called by some voice not entirely clear that said: Go, head to this land, walk along this route, and trust what you will find.

Within minutes, the afternoon prayers were complete and people returned to the streets. Dogubayazit, in extreme eastern Turkey, was thuddingly bleak, with two asphalt roads intersecting in a neglected town of thirty thousand. Just outside of town, hundreds of empty oil tankers were parked in a double-file line waiting to cross the border into Iran. The trucks, the town, as well as most of the surrounding country-side, were completely overshadowed by a looming triangular peak with a pristine cap of snow.

Mount Ararat is a perfect volcanic pyramid 16,984 feet high, with a junior volcano, Little Ararat, attached to its hip. The highest peak in the Middle East (and the second highest in Europe), Big Ararat is holy to everyone around it. The Turks call it Agri Dagi, the Mountain of Pain. The Kurds call it the Mountain of Fire. Armenians also worship the mountain, which was in their homeland until a brutal war in 1915. I later met an Armenian in Jerusalem who took me into his home, where he had at least 150 representations of the mountain, including rugs, cups, coats of arms, bottles of cognac, and stained-glass windows. Mount Ararat is the first thing he thinks of every morning, he said, and the first thing his children drew when they were young.

I had come for a different reason. Genesis, chapter 8, says that Noah's ark, after seven months on the floodwaters, came to rest on "the mountains of Ararat." Mount Ararat is the first place mentioned in the Bible that can be located with any degree of certainty, and it seemed like a fitting place to begin my effort to reacquaint myself with the biblical stories by retracing the first five books through the desert. The topography of this part of Turkey, which includes the headwaters of the Tigris and Euphrates, permeates the early chapters of Genesis. Chaos, Creation, Eden, and Eve are all drawn from the fertile union of Mesopotamia, "the land between the rivers" and the birthplace of the Bible.

In recent years, however, this region has been one of the most volatile—and bloody—in the Middle East. Over forty thousand people have died in a largely overlooked war in which indigenous Kurds have tried to gain autonomy from Iraq, Syria, and Turkey. In every travel book I read about the region the author was at least briefly detained. The *Rough Guide* I brought actually superimposed a blank area over the region, saying it was too unsafe for its correspondent. "In our opinion, travel is emphatically not recommended." In some cases, it said, security forces respond to the rebellion by "placing local towns under formal curfew or even shooting up the main streets at random."

Though Dogubayazit was calm today, the underlying tension was still apparent. Approaching the center of town, I had barely made it past a string of cheap jewelry stores when a man approached me, eagerly.

"Hello," he said, in English. We shook hands. "You just drove into town in that brown car, didn't you? You're staying in the hotel, in room 104."

The secret police are working overtime, I thought.

"What are you doing here?" he asked.

"Um, I'm here to find out about Noah's ark," I said.

"Noah's ark!" he repeated. "Well, if you want to learn about the ark you have to go to the green building at the end of this street. Go inside and up the stairs until you get to a dark room. Inside there's another set of stairs. Go up those and you'll find another dark room. In there you'll find the man who knows everything about Noah's ark."

At first I thought he was joking, or laying a trap. I thanked him and continued strolling. I had heard enough horror stories—and seen enough tanks on the road into town—to ignore directions like these. I walked around for a few minutes, bought some plums in the market, and was heading back to the hotel when I stopped myself: Why exactly had I come here anyway?

Inside the green building I found the sagging staircase and proceeded to the second floor. The room was dark and smelled of discarded cigarettes. I hesitated for a minute, took a step forward, then reconsidered. I was just turning back when I heard a noise from above, then steps. Seconds later a figure appeared. It was a man in his early forties, lean, with black hair and an enormous bushy mustache that cascaded over his lips. His eyes were concealed by the gloom. He appraised me for a second, before saying, in perfect Oxonian English, "May I help you?"

"I was told you know about Noah's ark," I said.

He considered my answer. "But you were supposed to go up the second set of stairs."

I agreed.

"Maybe you don't really want to know."

He retreated as quietly as he had appeared and left me standing in the dark. This time I didn't hesitate.

Upstairs, the man was just settling onto a low chair covered with carpets. He gestured for me to sit next to him. Between us was a table covered with books and a handful of photographs. He poured me a glass

of tea and we exchanged niceties. He was a native of Dogubayazit, a
Kurd. Ten years ago he had served time in prison for his role as an insur-
gent. He refused to talk about the war and when I asked his name, he
gestured toward his mustache: "Everyone calls me Parachute." He was
wearing a blue and white horizontal-striped T-shirt that, along with his
dark hair, made him look like a Venetian gondolier. After a while I asked
if it was possible to climb the mountain.

"It is forbidden," he said. "Since 1991, nobody has been to the top."

"Is there anything to see?"

"If you believe something, you can see. If you don't believe, you
cannot see."

"What do you believe?"

"We believe. When we are children, we hear things. They tell us that
this is Noah's countryside. Even today, when something happens, the
people say that it's the luck of Noah."

"Do you have the luck of Noah?" I asked.

"We know that something is there. We find something there."

"I'm confused. You're saying that you know something that everybody else does not know?"

"Yes." His eyes were big, with deep bags under them. He didn't
move at all when he spoke. "I know it's there. I find something there."

"What is it that you found?"

"Ah."

"You won't tell me."

"Hmm."

"When will we hear?"

"One day you'll hear."

"And you'll be famous around the world?"

He crossed his arms in front of his chest in a sly, self-satisfied way.

As Parachute well knew, almost since the Bible first appeared, stories
of sightings of Noah's ark have been a staple of Near Eastern lore, making it, in effect, the world's first UFO. Josephus, the first-century historian, wrote of legends that the ark landed "on a mountain in Armenia."
In 678 C.E., Saint Jacob, after asking God to show him the ark, fell asleep
on the mountain and awoke to find a piece of wood in his arms. By the

nineteenth century the sightings grew more elaborate. In 1887, two Persian princes wrote that they saw the ark while on top of the mountain, which is covered in snow year-round. "The bow and stern were clearly in view, but the center was buried in snow. The wood was peculiar, dark reddish in color, almost iron-colored in fact, and seemed very thick. I am very positive that we saw the real ark, though it is over 4,000 years old."

In 1916, two Russian pilots claimed they saw the ark from the air, and the following year Czar Nicholas II sent two expeditions with over 150 personnel to photograph it. Because of the Bolshevik revolution, the photographs never reached him, though his daughter Anastasia is said to have worn a cross made of ark wood. Most photographs of the ark have similarly disappeared, including dozens allegedly taken by pilots during World War II and more taken by the CIA using U-2 spy planes in the 1950s. Even Air Force One is said to have spied the ark. During a flight to Tehran on December 31, 1977, while Jimmy Carter was traveling to a New Year's party given by the shah, passengers on board claimed they saw "a large dark boat." Said UPI photographer Ronald Bennett, who was on the plane: "It's my opinion that the president probably had Air Force One routed over Mt. Ararat and most likely saw the ark too."

Since that time, technology has only heightened interest. Dozens of books have explored the subject, and more than fifty websites track the ongoing chase. In 1988, a stockbroker from San Diego flew a helicopter along the east slope taking photographs. The following year a pilot from Chicago aired footage of an "arklike object" on CNN. Charles Willis, who was once Charles Manson's psychiatrist, ran four expeditions, and astronaut James Irwin, who once took a Turkish flag to the moon in an attempt to butter up the Ankara government, made five. None has found the prize. As my companion and guide, the Israeli archaeologist Avner Goren, had warned, "Archaeologists won't even take into consideration that there are any remains. This story, like Creation, is crystallized from many traditions." But that won't stop the pursuit. When I asked Avner if any of the recent expeditions interested him, he said, "As a scientist, no. But as an adventurer, yes."

Which is exactly what Parachute was banking on. With prodding he explained that during a trip up the north side of the mountain in 1990, with a colleague from England, he found a piece of black wood one hundred feet long. It was located at twelve thousand feet.

"But it could be a hundred years old," I said.

"We tested it."

"And how old is it?"

"When we find out everything, you'll know."

"But why wait? How much money would it take for you to bring me to it?"

He thought for a moment. "It's not the money. It belongs to us. We found the ark. If you give me a million dollars I won't bring you to it. If you wanted the pictures I wouldn't give them to you."

"You have pictures?"

"Yes."

At this point I decided to go back to the hotel and get Avner, who had been napping. Avner had been to the top of the mountain in 1982 on a climbing expedition (no ark sightings, but lots of pure, clean snow). For the rest of the afternoon the three of us sat in Parachute's den. I asked Parachute what explained the ark's appeal.

"The ark is not so interesting to people," he said, "but Noah has meaning, like Mohammed or Jesus."

"You're suggesting that Noah is as important as Jesus?"

"If we can prove that any of these stories happened, then people will believe in God."

"What about you?" I asked. "What did you think when you found it?"

"I was happy. I was walking along—it was a particularly warm year—when suddenly I fell into this cavern covered by snow and ice. And there it was."

"I would like to believe your story," I said. "But I find it impossible to believe that in four thousand years you're the first person to go into this hole."

"Around here there are only five guides licensed to go up the mountain," Parachute said. "Two are in jail, one is ill, one won't go. That leaves me."

"Will you show me the pictures?"

He refused.

"What if I tell you that you're being selfish, that there are several billion people in the world who would like to know if Noah's ark exists?"

He didn't react.

"What if I tell you that you could be the savior of the Kurdish people by bringing millions of tourists to this area?"

He didn't move.

"What if I tell you that my mother is dying"—a lie—"and that she could die in peace if she knew that Noah was real?"

Nothing.

I was stunned. "Not even for my mother!?" I said. "Do you understand what you have here? More people believe in this book, more people have died because of this book, more people are influenced by this book. . . . You could change the world!"

Parachute was silent for a moment and unfolded his arms for the first time in hours. "You can tell your mother that she can be happy, that in the world there is one person who has seen Noah's ark. The Bible is true."

"So if she sees your ark, will she believe in God?"

"She'll have to," he said. "And you will, too. God is real. I have seen the proof."

Outside, darkness had fallen, and I was a bit unnerved by our conversation. I suggested we take a Turkish bath to decompress. As we walked, I asked Avner what he thought about Parachute's claim. "I suspect he uncovered something," Avner said, "though I don't believe it was the ark." If nothing else, he noted, the chances of finding remains from a five-thousand-year-old wooden boat seemed remote. And yet, now that we were here, the truth seemed far less important. What was important, I realized, was the ongoing hunt, the often-eccentric never-ending quest to verify the biblical story, which itself masked one of the oldest human desires: the need to make contact with God.

Back at the hotel, we picked up some supplies and wandered a few blocks to a run-down, concrete building. Inside we paid a small fee and were ushered into dressing rooms. I stripped off my clothes and wrapped a faded brown dishtowel around my waist. The attendant pointed through several doors, where the musty atmosphere gave way to an empty gray marble sanctuary filled with perfume and steam. The attendant took a bucket of hot water and splashed it over an octagonal platform. I lay down and closed my eyes.

The idea of writing about the Bible had sneaked up on me. Like many of my contemporaries, after leaving home at the end of high school, I lost touch with the religious community I had known as a child. I slowly disengaged from the sticky attachment that comes from a regular cycle of readings, prayers, and services. I separated myself from the texts as well. And ultimately I woke up one morning and realized I had no connection to the Bible. It was a book to me now, one that sat on the shelf above my TV, gathering dust on its gilded pages. The Bible was part of the past—an old way of learning, a crutch. I wanted to be part of the future. Over more than a decade of living and working abroad I found that ideas and places became more real to me when I experienced them firsthand. It was the opportunity—and curse—of being alive in the age of discount airfare.

But even as I traveled, I found that certain feelings from my past kept resurfacing. I sensed there was a conversation going on in the world around me that I wasn't participating in. References would pop up in books or movies that I vaguely understood yet couldn't fully comprehend. I would read entire newspaper articles about wars I couldn't explain. At weddings and funerals the words I heard and recited were just that—words. They had no meaning to me. No context. They were not part of me in any way. And yet I wanted them to be. Suddenly, almost overnight as I recall, I wanted these words to have meaning again. I wanted to understand them.

No sooner had I made this realization than I discovered how daunting it seemed. For starters, the idea of reading the Bible from cover to cover seemed undoable. The text was too long; its structure too convoluted; its language too remote. I went to the bookstore seeking help, but found instead fifty different translations, with assorted concordances, interpretations, and daily inspirationals. Other options seemed equally unappealing. Though there are shelves of books on every aspect of the Bible—from spelling to sex—none seemed to offer what I craved. Were these stories real or made up? When did they take place, and where? Looking further didn't help either. None of the classes I considered tackled these questions. I was left with the book, which sat by my bed for months on end, suffering from renewed neglect. After several years I was no closer to reconnecting to the Bible than I had been at the start.

Then I went to Jerusalem. I had just completed a long project and decided to reward myself with a trip to the Middle East. On my first day in the country I joined an old friend, Fred, who was giving a tour to some high school students. We stopped for lunch on a promenade over-looking the city. "Over there," said Fred, "is Har Homa," a controversial new settlement. "And over *there,*" he said, pointing to the Dome of the Rock, "is the cliff where Abraham went to sacrifice Isaac." Real or not, that piece of information hit me like a bolt of Cecil B. DeMille light-ning. It had never occurred to me that that story—so timeless, so abstract—might have happened in a place that was identifiable, no less one I could visit. It had never occurred to me that the story was so con-crete, so connected to the ground. To here. To now.

In subsequent weeks I had the same experience in a variety of places—the Dead Sea, Petra, the Pyramids. In the Middle East, I real-ized, the Bible is not some abstraction, nor some book gathering dust. It's a living, breathing entity unencumbered by the sterilization of time. If anything, it's an ongoing narrative: stories that begin in the sand, get entrenched in stone, pass down through families, and play themselves out in the lives of residents and visitors who traverse its lines nearly five thousand years after they were first etched into memory. That was the Bible I wanted to know, and almost immediately I realized that the only way to find it was to walk along those lines myself. I would take this ancient book, the embodiment of old-fashioned knowledge, and approach it with contemporary methods of learning—traveling, talking, experiencing. In other words, I would enter the Bible as if it were any other world and seek to become a part of it. Once inside, I would walk in its footsteps, live in its canyons, meet its characters, and ask its questions in an effort to understand why its stories had become so timeless and, despite years of neglect, once again so vitally important to me.

At first, few people thought this was a good idea. I returned home and tried to put it out of my mind, but couldn't. A few months later I traveled back to Jerusalem, and on my first day went to visit Avraham Biran, the dean of biblical archaeologists and the colleague of a friend. Professor Biran listened attentively to my ramblings. He squinted at me from behind clouds of cigarette smoke. And when I finished, he leaned across his desk and told me politely that I was out of my mind. There were few confirmed sites. Most sites that did exist were in war zones. And most were supervised by archaeologists who were far too busy to explain them to me. "It really would be an imposition," he said. I sat back, deflated.

But even as he discouraged me, Professor Biran could not resist reaching out his hand. Over the next two hours, he plucked photographs from his desk, pulled books off his shelf, and eventually took me to the maws of his laboratory to show me some shards of pottery. That night he called me at home. "What you need is someone to go with you," he said, "someone who has a sense of poetry. Somebody like Avner Goren." Several days later, in the Negev, I ran into two young Israeli guides and discussed my plan with them. "What you need is someone like Avner Goren," they said.

Two days later I telephoned Avner at his home in Jerusalem. He agreed to pick me up the following morning and arrived at dawn in a rickety blue Subaru. In his fifties, with a body that reminded me of Winnie the Pooh's, he had squinty blue eyes, bulbous cheeks, a boyish grin, and curly hair. Though he was dressed in standard Israeli fare— blue jeans, T-shirt, and sandals—that morning his most dashing feature was a long white scarf, Lawrence on his way to Arabia but still clinging to Oxford. After greeting me warmly, he drove around the corner to a coffee shop in the fashionable German Colony where we chatted over herbal tea and croissants—instant neighbors in the global bistro.

A charming, charismatic figure, Avner was a romantic, a child of the desert. For the fifteen years that Israel controlled the Sinai—1967 to 1982—he was the region's chief archaeologist and preserver of antiquities. But soon after, he abandoned the academy to become a popularizer of biblical history, one of Israel's most eloquent spokesmen on life in the ancient world. He tutored prospective Israeli and Palestinian guides, gave lectures on ancient history around the world (for the State of Israel, the UN, and others), and was a charter member of a pioneering group of Israeli, Jordanian, and Palestinian educators who were using archaeology to open the fabled Nabatean Spice Trail to cross-border traffic. Indiana Jones, meet Dag Hammarskjöld.

As we talked, a sort of implicit teacher-pupil relationship developed. "I was thinking about which route in the Sinai to take," I said. Avner didn't flinch. "I prefer the southern route," he said. "It offers the best experience." "I'm concerned that I won't be able to get to certain sites in Egypt," I said. "Fear not," Avner said, rubbing his fingers together in the international expression for an exchange of money. Finally, after tiptoeing through this logistical minefield, I told him about my conversation with Professor Biran. "Half the people I meet tell me I'm out of my mind," I said. "They tell me it can't be done." As I finished a smile slowly crept across his face. "I don't think you're crazy at all," he said. "I think it sounds exciting."

I sat back, relieved and exhilarated. "Somehow I knew you would," I said. "By the way, would you come along?"

A year passed between that meeting in Jerusalem and our first foray into the field, in Turkey. During that time I returned to the United States and set about preparing myself for the trip. First I read the Bible, chapter by chapter, verse by verse. It took me almost a month, and I was amazed by how little I remembered. Abraham went to Egypt? Moses committed murder? What were all those rebellions in the desert? I began making a chart linking places in the text to places on the ground. Was Abraham born in Iraq or Turkey? Where was Mount Sinai? Was there really a place called Sodom? This process led me to read about what those places would have been like at the time the stories were written. I started with books on history, archaeology, geography. These were rational subjects, consistent with my past as an undergraduate history major, as a master's student in international relations. Keep it real, keep it concrete, keep it safely removed from spirituality. "This is a literary quest," I kept telling myself. "This is about me and the Bible. This is not about me and God."

As I bounced from topic to topic I realized how little I knew about the ancient world. Books about history led to ones about religion; religion books led to language books; language to culture. In time, the topics became more obscure. I found myself scouring used bookstores for volumes on desert botany, pyramid construction, Babylonian creation stories. I even bought a book called *The Bible and Flying Saucers: The Miraculous Truth,* which included the cover line "The messengers are here!"

The homework itself became part of the adventure. My chart became more and more complex. One bookshelf filled up, and I bought another. My friends wondered about this new obsession. Why was I sprinkling conversations with references to African quail migration or the biological roots of manna? Why did I want a six-volume, 7,035-page reference book for my birthday? "Not to worry," I assured them. "I'm not becoming a nut." And I believed it, too. This was about history, I assured myself, this was about grounding the text in reality. "I'm giving myself a master's degree in the history of the Bible," I said. What could be more fun, or more rational?

For all of my reading, however, the moment I met Avner at the Tel Aviv airport for our trip to Turkey, I realized that my education hadn't even begun. I was dressed in a neatly pressed shirt from Banana Republic with a bag full of books and a new pair of hiking boots. Avner, meanwhile, was nearly spilling out of his T-shirt, beltless baggy trousers made by some bedouin in Sinai, and fifteen-year-old scruffy sandals. The message was clear: My learning was all in my head; Avner's was all in his feet. I had never met a man who knew so much who carried his knowledge so lightly. He knew all the languages of the biblical route—Hebrew, Arabic, Turkish—as well as a few others—English, Greek, and hieroglyphics. He had not only several bookcases full of Bible books but *several rooms.* Yet he was unassuming to the point of being bashful. At times this frustrated me—why didn't he speak up when we ran into a pontificator? But eventually I realized that Avner, in his way, was like the place he idolized. From afar the desert might seem distant and reserved; draw closer and it has a great story to tell.

Avner was like the desert in another way: He seemed completely removed from the modern world. For all his clarity of mind, he was conspicuously disorganized, with more twisted pieces of paper, bent paper clips, and stale pieces of chocolate spilling from his pockets than anyone I ever met. His car was like an archaeological site, with layer upon layer of his life piled up in the backseat. He rarely returned messages. He often forgot where he was going. And he never met me for a trip having not stayed up overnight to pack. Even then, we usually had to go back for his passport. His appearance, which rarely varied from that morning at the airport, reflects this personality. He owns only one tie, which he keeps knotted under his bed. He once addressed a UNESCO conference in Paris wearing hiking boots. And when, late in our journey, his daughter, Smadar, got married, Avner had to buy his first pair of dress shoes.

There was another way in which Avner was a paradox. For all his learning, for all his stature and international acclaim, he had never bothered to finish graduate school. He was too drawn by the opportunity to give a speech, to join a crusade—to go on a trip with someone like me. Remarkably, this blemish did little to stunt his success. If anything it was a testament to his talent that he continued to rise in intellectual circles despite not having the one credential that would seem to be necessary. He was a fellow at the prestigious Albright Institute of Archaeological Research in Israel. He was recruited for prominent digs. He counseled prime ministers. And he knew everyone within a thousand-mile radius of Jerusalem. I never produced a name of someone I wanted to meet— an artist, a scientist, a bedouin, a scholar—whom Avner couldn't deliver within twenty-four hours. And I never attended a meeting with one of those individuals in which the other person, regardless of stature, didn't defer to Avner. As a friend of his told me, "Avner Goren is like Moses. He's a prophet. He has no boundaries, no borders, he's actually part of the land. And the best thing is, he doesn't even realize it."

This set up the unusual equation at the heart of our experience. I wasn't looking for a father any more than Avner was looking for a son (he has one). I wasn't looking for a prophet any more than he was looking for a disciple. And yet, we both were looking for the Bible, which, at the moment, had brought us together at the start of a journey that was still hardly defined.

It was just after 5:30 on our first morning in Turkey when I joined Avner outside our hotel in Gaziantep. The street lamps, at this hour, were still flickering orange. The smells of dawn—cinnamon, cardamom, a whiff of burnt sugar—were just starting to emerge. We had decided to begin our trip by trying to catch sunrise on the Euphrates, before proceeding eastward to the Tigris and the two-day trek through the Turkish highlands to Dogubayazit. We nodded our good mornings with Sait, our driver, and buckled in for the ride. Since meeting him the previous day, Sait's unflappable personality (along with the occasional pack of cigarettes) had helped ease our way through the numerous checkpoints where authorities prodded our passports, our luggage, our bodies, or all three.

Once we were out of town, the air grew agitated, until suddenly a crack of lightning careened across the sky. The flash was followed by another, and the two jolts ignited a series of awakenings. First the sky began to lighten, revealing a clog of slate gray clouds. Then the ground emerged, exposing a flat landscape of pale, spent grass. Gradually other life-forms appeared—groves of young pistachio trees, a stretch of tufting cotton bushes. A turtle crossed the road.

Minutes later we sped past an open floodgate, parked, and ambled down the rocky bank. Large boulders huddled at river's edge, with pebbles trickling into water the color of mint. A woman in a black bedouin dress tiptoed down the embankment carrying a teakettle. The current was swift in the middle of the river, but the edges were smooth like gelatin. From here, the river picks up strength as it passes through Syria and into Iraq, before merging with the Tigris near the Persian Gulf.

By the time we slipped our toes into the water, the sky was light but the sun was still hidden. For a few moments we watched it try to burn through the clouds. Occasionally a ray would peek through, only to be blotted out again. The struggle continued for half an hour, with the sun angling to penetrate the shield, reaching, stretching, and giving off the most storybook sunburst, which was all the more remarkable, since its source was veiled. Finally, at a few minutes past seven, the sun prevailed. Because of its ordeal, it had lost any romantic qualities by the time it slid free. It wasn't orange or red or even yellow, like most morning suns. It wasn't tender at all. It was clear, round, and white.

It was day.

The ride east from the Euphrates started out painless. Compared to the European part of Turkey, with its soaring pines and castles, the Asian part is flat and dusty. In late summer, the fields were blotted with green, but cautiously, as if the crops might sag back into the sand. The main reason was the fickle supply of water, which is ferried across the fields by a ramshackle network of gutters and concrete entrails. At one point we stopped by a roadside gathering, where a boy playing on one of those aqueducts had just been swept to his death. The previous week, a woman said, there had been no water at all.

As we drove we began to discuss the importance of water in the ancient world. In the history of humanity, civilization came relatively late. During most of their time on earth, humans roamed in migrant bands that hunted and foraged for food. This period, the Old Stone Age, began around three million years ago and continued until approximately 15,000 B.C.E. A Middle Stone Age, with communal living, continued for roughly another five thousand years. The bigger change, what Avner called "the most important revolution in history," occurred around 9000 B.C.E. with the advent of agriculture. That change was centered in Mesopotamia, in the area of present-day Turkey and Iraq, where local populations began experimenting with cultivating wheat and barley. As cultivation proved successful, farmers began looking for ways to expand production in order to feed more people. To do that, they needed reliable irrigation, which led them to tap their greatest resource: the Tigris and Euphrates.

What the rivers provided was a regular supply of water and, more important, an annual inundation that covered the desert with arable soil.

The floods of Mesopotamia and Egypt were so unusual in an otherwise arid region that, coupled with the rain-fed mountains in today's Syria and Israel, they formed the incubator of civilization, the Fertile Crescent, a cradle of productivity in a sea of sand. In particular, rivers gave people the incentive to stay in one place and organize themselves—to dig canals, bake bricks, build plows. "Just imagine you have a canal in your area," Avner said. "You have to clean it; you have to maintain it; but you never enjoy the water. It flows to a place that's twenty days away on a donkey. So you take care of the water for people you'll never meet; and somebody else takes care of yours."

With thousands of canals serving tens of thousands of people, the only way to maintain this growing network was to develop an equally elaborate system of laws, schools, trade. Civilization. "Soon enough, individual civilizations started fighting," Avner said. "To survive, the victorious states started annexing their neighbors." Empires were born. The first such empire—Sumer, in lower Mesopotamia—was quickly shadowed by ones in Akkad and Assyria, also in Mesopotamia, and ultimately one in Egypt. The inevitable clash of these titans created a combustion that would make the Fertile Crescent an unprecedented engine of creativity, giving birth to the world's first epic poetry, legal code, religious proverbs, and written word. In time, it also gave birth to a written document that would prove to be an even greater generator of culture.

By late afternoon, we had crossed the floodplain and begun our descent to the Kurdish stronghold of Diyarbakir. One of the oldest cities on earth, Diyarbakir dates back five thousand years and was controlled at times by the Assyrians, Persians, and Alexander the Great of Greece. The Romans built a huge city wall of basalt, which in turn was rebuilt by the Byzantines, who nicknamed the place "The Black." Residents boast that the circular five-mile wall, along with the Great Wall of China, is one of two man-made objects visible from space.

For all its past greatness, the town is chokingly grim today, a mix of concrete buildings around a dilapidated town core. With half a million residents, Diyarbakir boasts a handful of impressive mosques and a market selling carpets, spices, and Medusa-like shags of cheap belts. On this day, the heat baked the bananas and garlicky meat, mixing them with diesel exhaust into a noxious perfume. The one source of delight, and good aroma, was the hundreds of plump watermelons spilled from every flat surface. Sprung from the Tigris and fertilized by pigeon droppings, the fruit is the town's trademark. This week a watermelon festival was under way. Driving into town, we passed a fifty-foot obelisk with a giant, papier-mâché watermelon impaled on top; it reminded me of a Claes Oldenburg sculpture of an olive on a toothpick.

We dropped our bags at our hotel and headed down to the river. The Tigris was narrower here than the Euphrates, and murkier. The muddy banks were lined with reeds. Underneath a stone bridge, a group of adolescent boys splashed in their underwear while an older boy watered a cluster of cows. Nearing six o'clock, there was almost no light on the river; the sky was the color of sludge. Nearby a man tossed a net into the current and pulled it out with a bamboo pole, spilling mullet onto the mud. We sat on a boulder for a few minutes until Avner reached in his knapsack and pulled out a book with a royal blue cover. "Shall we?" he said.

As he flipped to the page I grabbed for my copy, the same one that had sat by my bed for years. I was nervous. This was our first chance to test one of the central ideas behind our trip. In addition to retracing the first five books of the Bible, also called the Five Books of Moses, we planned to read the stories in the locations where they took place. Still a newcomer to the text, I hoped this effort might deepen my appreciation of the stories by freeing them from their covers and replanting them in the ground. For Avner, it would be an attempt to revisit the stories in light of a lifetime of learning. But the truth was, neither of us quite knew what to expect.

"Listen to the words closely," he said. "Listen for the sound of the rivers: 'When God began to create the heaven and the earth, the earth was unformed and void.' " These words suggest a vast emptiness, Avner noted, but the next line is more evocative: "And darkness was upon the face of the deep." "In Hebrew," he said, "the word for deep is *tehom*, which means chaos. In Mesopotamia, chaos was represented by a sea monster, Tiamat. Tiamat is the root for *tehom*. We're only in the second line of Genesis, and already we have a direct link to the cult of water in Mesopotamia."

We continued reading. For the next chapter and a half, the Bible tells the story of how God created the world. On the first day God creates light and dark. On the second day he generates an amorphous mass, "an expanse in the midst of the water," and also forms the sky. On the third day he divides this expanse into the earth and seas and brings forth vegetation. On the fourth day he creates the sun and the stars; on the fifth, birds and sea creatures; on the sixth, cattle and animals that creep. Also, on the sixth day God, using the plural, announces, "Let us make man in our image, after our likeness," and creates an unnamed male and female. Finally, on the seventh day, having "finished" his work, God declares the day holy and rests.

In many ways, this story, which appears without preamble at the beginning of Genesis, seems completely removed from time and place. But in other ways, the story is deeply rooted in a particular time— the second and third millennia B.C.E.—and in a particular place, Mesopotamia. Specifically, Genesis draws on the Mesopotamian obsession with water. Considering the importance of rivers, it was inevitable that water would play a vital role in ancient creation stories. The unanimity across cultures, though, is striking. The earliest stories date from the third millennium B.C.E. and come from Sumer, in today's southern Iraq. Living in an area the size of New Hampshire, the Sumerians generated a vast literary outpouring: Over forty thousand lines of Sumerian script have been found, compared with twenty-three thousand lines of biblical script. The root of the Sumerian worldview was a primeval sea, which split into a vaulted heaven and a flat earth, an idea almost identical to that of Genesis. The Sumerian universe was controlled by humanlike gods, the most important of whom was Enki, the god of water, who created light, plants, animals, and humans.

The Babylonian creation story, also from Mesopotamia, is even closer to Genesis. In the story, the world is presented as a watery chaos, represented by the monster Tiamat. During a rebellion, another god,

Marduk, slays Tiamat and slices her carcass in two, creating heaven and earth. After his triumph, Marduk proceeds to create, in succession, light, the firmament, dry land, heavenly lights, animals, and man. Afterward he rests and celebrates.

"So you see," Avner said, "in both stories, water precedes everything, a struggle ensues, and everything else emerges from that."

"But when Westerners imagine God creating the world," I said, "they don't imagine a struggle."

"Yes, but the struggle is still there," he said. "The Bible states very clearly, 'And God says, "Let there be light." And there was light. And God saw the light: that it was good.' Here you have the start of good things and bad things. On the third day God says twice that something is good. There is clearly an echo of struggle here, getting rid of evil."

"So how did that echo get there?" I asked. "The biblical story was written down in the first millennium B.C.E. These stories come from the third millennium."

"Ah. That's the story of the Bible. Though it was written down later, large parts of it consist of oral traditions that were passed down for hundreds of years, many with the same words. The Bible, like *The Iliad*, combines large amounts of ancient texts."

In the story of Adam and Eve, for example, ideas like the tree of life, the snake, and man being made from clay were well known in Mesopotamia. The name Eve is derived from a Sumerian pun on the word for rib. Even the Garden of Eden has ancient roots. In one prototype, the god Enki summons water from the ground to create a garden, which the mother-goddess fills with plants. When Enki eats these plants without permission he is ostracized and cursed to die. In the story, the garden is located "east of Sumer."

Genesis also places its garden "eastward, in Eden" and begins with a watering: "There went up a mist from the earth and watered the whole face of the ground." The Bible seems to place Eden near Sumer specifically, saying the garden is located at the junction of four rivers. One of those rivers is the Euphrates, another the Tigris. Though we are only in the second chapter, and clearly in the realm of allegory, already the Bible is rooting itself firmly in the ground, in actual places, in geography. The stories seem to be reaching out, saying: These are not mere tales—this is not recreation—these words are as indispensable to you as the landscape, the soil, even water itself. Stories, like rivers, give life.

"All of which raises a question," I suggested. The light was mostly gone by now and a green haze had settled over the bank. The cows had wandered away, leaving only a stir of mosquitoes. "If these stories draw so heavily from Mesopotamia, how are they different?"

Avner removed his glasses and smiled, as if he had been waiting for this. "The difference is God," he said. "He's much more abstract. There's no biography, no mythology. He just appears and begins to create the world, using only words as tools. Yet from the beginning, he's solely in control—at least of nature. His ability to control man is much less complete."

The next morning we headed out early for a two-day drive into the highlands. Quickly the terrain began to change. The congestion of Diyarbakir faded, giving way to pastoral surroundings that seemed to grow more antiquated as we climbed higher. The roads deteriorated and mud houses appeared, with sheaths of tan-colored sesame on the roof. Turkeys scurried in the yards, where men on stools played backgammon. Women with black veils, balancing baskets of zucchini on their heads, dotted the roadside.

Eventually our conversation turned as well. With so much focus on rivers, it was only natural that ancient storytellers fixate on one notable side effect: floods. The Bible gets to this almost immediately, in the sixth chapter of Genesis. After telling the story of the Garden of Eden, the text outlines the successive generations that lead from Adam and Eve to all humanity. Eight generations into this line, Lamech gives birth to a son, Noah, who in turn gives birth to three sons of his own. Around this time, God sees how wicked and lawless mankind has become and announces, "I will blot out from the earth the men whom I created," for "I regret that I made them." But Noah finds favor with God, because he is a "righteous man."

God tells Noah to build an ark out of gopherwood, lined with pitch and divided into three separate decks, which he should fill with seven pairs of "clean" animals, presumably kosher animals like chickens, cows, and fish, and one pair of every other animal. He also takes along his own family. In the six-hundredth year of Noah's life, the fountains of the deep burst apart, the floodgates of the sky break open, and it rains for forty days and nights, until the highest mountains everywhere are covered in water and "all the flesh on earth" is killed.

After seven months on the water, the ark comes to rest on "the mountains of Ararat," where it sits for another three months until the tops of the mountains become visible. Another month passes and Noah sends out a raven, which flies around until the waters have dried from the earth. Then Noah sends a dove, which is unable to find a resting spot, suggesting that water still covers the ground. Noah sends the dove again seven days later, and it returns with an olive branch, a sure sign of life. A month later, Noah removes the covering of the ark, goes ashore with his family, and sets the animals free.

As with Creation, the story of Noah fits into an extensive tradition. Flood stories appear in 217 cultures around the world, according to authors Charles Sellier and David Balsiger. Ninety-five percent of these stories talk about a global flood, Sellier and Balsiger note, 73 percent say animals and a boat were involved, and 35 percent claim a bird was sent out at the end. Babylonian flood stories seem directly connected. In the story of Gilgamesh, Enki warns the hero, Utnapishtim, about a flood sent to destroy humanity and orders him to build a cubical ship. After a seven-day flood, the ship comes to rest atop a mountain and a bird is set free. The Babylonian stories also share a thematic parallel with the Bible. Both stories represent a shift away from mythology and toward history, with names, dates, and biological ages. As Avner noted, Noah is the father of a new generation and the Flood is another example of land emerging from a watery chaos, a second creation.

Beyond its literary roots, the story of Noah's ark begins another, more fascinating side of exploring the Bible today: namely, the race to prove that it happened. Some explorers have claimed they found the "real" Garden of Eden, but even the most credulous Bible enthusiasts believe those efforts are probably fantastical. With Noah, though, and the introduction of historical details, these efforts begin to gain credibility. They reach the point of hysteria with attempts to authenticate later passages like the ten plagues, the splitting of the Red Sea, and Moses' receiving of the Ten Commandments on Mount Sinai. Almost every day of our journey we would encounter another of these enthusiasts, and in time I came to marvel that in addition to creating communities of believers, the Bible had created equally passionate communities devoted to the arcane, quasi-scientific analysis of, say, whether the zebras would have been on the second deck of Noah's ark next to the lions, or on the third deck next to the koala bears. I marveled even more when I got caught up in the same questions.

The story of the Flood has provided a mother lode for such speculation. In the summer of 1929, the English archaeologist Leonard Woolley was digging in the Sumerian capital of Ur when his workers came across a provocative find: a deep stratum of Euphrates silt poised between two layers of civilization. Titillated, Woolley, a former intelligence officer with a flair for the dramatic, lowered himself thirty feet into the ground and that afternoon issued a telegram: "We have found the Flood!" The news electrified the press and intrigued scientists. "We all agree that your theory is mad," one colleague said. "The problem which divides us is this: Is it sufficiently crazy to be right?" Within days even Woolley had to concede that it wasn't, as excavations proved that it was a localized flood. "It was not a universal deluge," he wrote.

But the bait had been laid, and generations of scholars have been unable to resist lowering themselves in after it. One question: Where did all the water come from? Some have said underwater volcanoes, others melting glaciers. Because the text says the forty days of water came from above and below, a few hydrologists have suggested a vapor canopy may have enveloped the earth. (One side benefit of the vapor: It would have blocked ultraviolet rays, thereby helping Noah live six hundred years.) Many have tried to date the Flood. Two oceanographers recently suggested the Mediterranean may have flooded around 5600 B.C.E. Woolley himself placed the event around 2800 B.C.E. But Gene Faulstich, founder of something called the Chronology Research Institute in

Iowa, puts them to shame. Using astronomical dating, he says the Flood occurred on May 14, 2345 B.C.E. It was, he says, a Sunday.

If the Flood has been grounds for speculation, the ark has been ripe for obsession. The Bible says the ark should be three hundred cubits long, fifty wide, and thirty high. A cubit is the length of a forearm from the elbow to the tip of the middle finger. Using eighteen inches as a standard, the ark would have been roughly the size of a soccer field, four stories high. That would make the ark, built without metal, five times longer than the *Mayflower* and, notably, half as long as the *Titanic*. Though most scholars, including Avner, consider the numbers in the Bible to be idealized, such thinking has not deterred enthusiasts. One problem has been that since the world has over one million species of animals today, how could they fit onto one boat? In *The Genesis Flood,* John Witcomb, a theologian, suggests that with common ancestry Noah would have needed no more than 3,700 mammals, 8,600 birds, and 6,300 reptiles, which would have been fine considering volumetric analysis shows the ark could have held up to 100,000 sheep.

But could one family of eight possibly have tended all these animals? That, too, is no problem, says Ken Cumming, a biologist: Many of the animals would have responded to the lack of light by going into hibernation. Even if the animals could have fit and been cared for, could they have been housed in a food-chain-proof way? Easily, says Eddie Atkinson, a reverend and amateur ark-builder: Birds and rodents would have been on the top deck; lions and tigers on one end of the second deck, hippos and rhinos on the other, elephants and giraffes in between. The bottom deck, analysts assert, must have been empty, because according to zoologists at the San Diego Zoo, during their year aboard the ark the animals would have generated eight hundred tons of manure.

By our second day the drive had become downright eerie. All through Turkey the scenery had been pastoral, but hardly otherworldly. Now, six thousand feet above sea level, with an almost complete absence of agriculture, we were entering a palette ripe for mythology—and conflict. Tanks were parked every mile along the highway, with soldiers sitting in front on white plastic lawn chairs. A giant billboard said, in Turkish and English, HOMELAND ABOVE ALL, and in the road signs that show people crossing the road, the people were dressed in traditional costumes.

Most unnerving was the topography itself. The hillside plateaus were covered for miles in basalt coated in pale green fungus that looked like mold growing on charcoal. The basalt, while cooling from a volcanic eruption, had splintered into hundreds of fists, which in turn had splintered into jagged fingers that reached to the sky for relief. Altogether, the formations reminded me of those pictures of bodies frozen, gasping, in the aftermath of an atomic bomb.

As we drove, Avner had been playing with a toy that some friends had given him, a portable Global Positioning System, or GPS, device that tracked our route using military satellites. For several hours he had squirreled himself away in the back, frantically pressing buttons, trying to figure out how to program it. Just before noon he leaned forward, tapped me on the shoulder, and pointed out the window. "Look!" Sait jerked to a stop and through a break in the cliffs, fifty miles ahead and thousands of feet higher than anything around it, was the pure triangular crest of a mountain, like Mount Fuji with its solemn mien. And at that moment I had the first chilling intimation of what walking the Bible might bring. Genesis does not give details about where the ark lands. The Bible may not want us to know. But if a flood did cover the earth, if an ark survived that flood, and if that ark settled on a spot where land first appeared, there was little doubt in my mind that it would have landed here. And for me it was stunning confirmation that the Bible may or may not be true, it may or may not be historical, but it is undoubtedly still alive.

The following morning, after our meeting with Parachute, we turned south for the final portion of this trip. Our first destination was Sanliurfa, a Turkish town not far from the border with Syria that for thousands of years has been associated with the great patriarch of monotheism. Considering his importance, Abraham seems to appear out of nowhere in the Bible. After the Flood, Genesis recites the generations that follow Noah, then relates another story with Near Eastern roots, the tower of Babel.

The story begins by asserting the unity of the world: "All the earth had the same language and the same words." The descendants of Noah then begin to settle in the "land of Shinar," the biblical name for Sumer. In an echo of the agricultural revolution, the men decide to make bricks for themselves, then to build a communal monument. "Come, let us build us a city," they say, "and a tower with its top in the sky, to make a name for ourselves; else we shall be scattered all over the world."

God sees the city and decides to frustrate their plans, declaring, "Let us, then, go down and confound their speech there, so that they shall not understand one another's speech." God then scatters the builders "over the face of the whole earth." The doomed tower came to be called Babel, the Bible says, from the Hebrew word for "confuse."

Following this story, the text outlines the ten generations that lead directly from Noah to Abram. According to Genesis 11, Abram, which means "the father is exalted" (he would later change it to Abraham, "father of a multitude"), was born in Ur of the Chaldeans where he took a wife, Sarai, before leaving for Canaan. The term Chaldeans is believed to refer to a later settlement, around 1100 B.C.E., and was probably added to the story when it was written down. The term Ur, by contrast, has tantalizing ancient parallels and suggests biblical storytellers wanted their bloodlines placed deeply in Mesopotamia. The city of Ur was the capital of Sumer and one of the grandest cities of antiquity. Built around a stepped temple, or ziggurat, believed to have inspired the Tower of Babel, the city squeezed two hundred thousand citizens into labyrinthine quarters.

Like most Babylonian cities, Ur was surrounded by satellite settlements of farmers or shepherds. At times the two groups clashed, as when farmers wanted to grow crops in the marshland and shepherds wanted to graze sheep. The Bible echoes this struggle when it makes Adam and Eve's first child, Cain, a farmer, and their second, Abel, a shepherd. When God expresses favor for Abel, Cain murders his sheep-herding brother. Abraham was probably a shepherd, too. He likely would have lived outside of Ur, but later moved during a period of drought, tension, or economic change. He and his clan would have gone to another city, perhaps stayed five or ten years, then moved again, most likely in a northwesterly direction, until they arrived in Harran, a well-known ancient crossroads.

This type of migration happened throughout the third millennium B.C.E., except for a period of economic collapse around 2000 B.C.E. According to scholars, Abraham was likely born near the end of that downturn, around 1900 B.C.E. To be sure, no evidence exists that Abraham—or any other central character in the Five Books—lived during this period. By contrast, much evidence suggests that Abraham is a compendium—a crystallization, to use Avner's word—of many oral traditions. But one thing is clear: The story is uncannily realistic to the history of the area. As Avner said, "It *could* be true."

This air of authenticity is one reason the story has persevered. All through our drive to Sanliurfa, we saw living details—sheep, shepherds, dust, robes. It became like a game of "I Spy." There's a donkey: "Abraham's transportation!" After a while we became so preoccupied that we didn't even notice when Sait went speeding through a roundabout and suddenly got motioned over by the police. Instantly, our worst fears returned. An officer in a crisp blue uniform came to the window and asked Sait to step outside. As he did, Avner and I hid our equipment and placed a sign from the tourist authority on the dashboard. The officer was joined by another. A green army jeep sped up, followed by a motorcycle. We got out of the car. Suddenly there were five different officials, each wearing a different uniform, prodding our car, our passports, our GPS device. The men seemed like unshaven boys playing grown-up in a quiet war. "It's almost a police state," Avner whispered.

Finally a car pulled up and a plainclothes officer in a black suit spoke to the men in the reverse order in which they had arrived. He examined the situation, the car, us. He spoke with Sait. And then, just as quickly as the tension had mounted, he defused it. He shook our hands and gestured for us to proceed. Before we did, Sait began clearing the backseat of our bags and maps and in plopped a teenage boy. Our penance was to give him a ride. "Probably the son of the cop," Avner mused.

But he turned out to be more than that. Yusuf, eighteen, was studying to be an English teacher. Though he was dressed in ratty jeans and a scruffy T-shirt, his hair was neatly combed over his ears. He offered to take us on a tour—part of the scam?—but insisted he didn't want to be paid. He directed us toward the center of town.

Sanliurfa, like many frontier towns, has an eclectic history. In the Byzantine era it was the center of the cult of Nestorius, a bishop who questioned the divinity of Christ. As late as 578 a local governor was caught performing a sacrifice to Zeus. In recent years it's been a hotbed of Muslim fundamentalism. For us it had a different meaning. While the Bible says Abraham was born in Ur, Islamic legend suggests he was born here.

Leaving our car, Yusuf led us to a park at the base of the twelfth-century citadel that dominates the crowded city. It was early evening by the time we arrived, and dozens of strollers were enjoying a respite from the heat. We approached a door carved into the limestone mountain. Above the door was a sign: "This is the cave where Prophet Abraham was born. Please take your shoes off and go straight to the carpet." We ducked inside where the lime green carpet filled a space about the size of a large elevator. Next door was another room for women. We stared down at the cavern, which was filled with water and a few tossed coins. "People come here from all over the country to collect holy water for their hometowns," Yusuf said.

Outside we continued to a nearby pond, which was lined on one side by a mosque, and on the other by a graceful colonnade. We began to discuss Abraham. Since the Bible is completely silent on his early life, scores of legends popped up over the centuries. According to Jewish lore, on the night Abraham was born, a great star passed through the sky, devouring four smaller stars. Advisers told King Nimrod that the sign meant the newly born son of Terah would one day conquer Nimrod's kingdom and change its religion. The king tried to purchase the boy, but Terah substituted the son of a slave and sent Abraham and his mother, Emtelai, into hiding.

According to accounts gathered in Jewish texts from the early first millennium C.E., even as a boy, Abraham was able to divine from the stars that there was only one God. Since the stars came out at night and disappeared during the day, the boy reasoned, they could not have created the world, as tradition held. Instead, there must be an invisible, single God above them. This view put Abraham at odds with his father, who legend held was an idol-maker. When Abraham smashed his father's idols, Terah turned his son over to the king. Abraham appeared before Nimrod in a vast throne room. The boy approached the throne and began shaking it so hard that all the idols in the room came smashing to the ground. Nimrod ordered that the boy be thrown into a fiery furnace. An immense pile was lit. Abraham was stripped naked, bound, and thrown into the fire. His ropes burned, but he did not.

In Jewish tradition, these stories take place in the Tigris–Euphrates basin. Muslims, however, altered the story so that Abraham was not born in Ur, in the southeast of Mesopotamia, but in Sanliurfa, in the northwest, closer to Harran. As Yusuf explained, in the Muslim version, when Nimrod flings Abraham into the fire, God intervenes at the last minute, turning the flames into water and the firewood into carp. The carp swimming in the pond in Sanliurfa today are said to be descendants of the originals and anyone caught eating them will go blind—a fate that supposedly befell two soldiers as recently as 1989.

"So why do you think this happened here?" I asked Yusuf. Some twinkling lights blinked on around the pool, lending it a carousel-like atmosphere.

"Because this was a very important city in the ancient world. Like Babylon, here many roads came together. It was a junction, a holy place."

"Is it still holy today?" I asked.

He thought for a second. "I don't like to talk politics," he said.

The following day was our last in Turkey, and we planned to visit Harran, the setting of the pivotal scene in which God first speaks to Abraham. We drove south out of Sanliurfa into the dustiest part of the country, on a road so straight it seemed to have purpose. Adobe houses spotted the fields. Even the army barracks had roofs of mud. On the horizon a small bank of hills appeared, beyond which the Rift Valley extended to Africa. "Drop some water here, it would probably make its way to the Dead Sea," Avner said.

As we sped along, I began to feel a certain pull from the landscape, and I realized that this trip had begun to affect me some place deep in my body. It wasn't my head, or my heart. It wasn't even my feet. It was someplace so new to me that I couldn't locate it at first, or give it a name. It was a feeling of gravity. A feeling that I wanted to take off all my clothes and lie facedown on the soil. At once I recalled my grandmother's funeral and the gulping ache I felt when they tossed a handful of soil on her coffin: "From ashes to ashes, from dust to dust." Not until this car ride, staring at this soil, did I fully understand what that phrase meant. Adam had been made from dust; his name is derived from the word *adama*, earth. "For dust you are," God says to Adam, "and to dust you shall return." Here was the source of that soil, I realized, and at that moment I had to resist the temptation to leap out and touch it.

So where did this feeling come from? For most of my life, my religious identity was not connected to a particular place, and certainly not to any place in the Bible. As a fifth-generation American Jew from the South, I had a strong attachment to Judaism, but one based on family, community, ethics, public service; not spirituality or mysticism. And not on any deep-seated attachment to the Promised Land. Instead, I was attached to the South, and like many Jewish southerners, I struggled between a religion that gave me a sense of identity and a place that made me feel at home.

I accepted this dichotomy because like many people my age I was not particularly defined by spiritual quests, or the search for higher meaning. I can be moralistic (I used to teach junior high school). I can be earnest (I briefly enrolled in a master's program in peace studies). I have a high tolerance for public displays of devotion—and faith (I like country music). But I have never been particularly devout myself. This attitude was partly generational. I came of age at a time largely devoid of anguish and hardship; I never witnessed a war; few of my friends had suffered from personal tragedy. Instead, the hallmarks of my life were the emblems of America at the peak of its prosperity: opportunity, possibility, reinvention. Mine was the generation that could have it all. Our ethos was built on the belief that we could control everything: our bodies, our minds, our bank accounts. Got a problem? Change channels, switch jobs, take a pill, go to the gym. Our bibles were our Day-Timers. Our god was self-reliance.

For me this sense of boundless freedom was bolstered by a desire to travel. I always believed that I was able to venture so far afield in my life because I had a strong sense of family and a stronger sense of place. I wasn't looking for a new way of life, or a new place to call home. I have a home, which I happily carry around within me, and which inevitably lures me back from afar. I was like one of those bungee cords you pull out from a suitcase that briefly attaches to something else and then, when its task is complete, snaps back into place.

Now, for the first time, the bungee cord seemed to be catching in another place. What happened that afternoon in Turkey was that some ill-defined part of me, some homeless portion of my consciousness that I hadn't even realized was looking for a home, suddenly found a place where it felt comfortable and surged forward to put down anchor. Here was a piece of ancient land—completely alien, yet completely familiar— that seemed to draw me to it in a way I never thought possible outside my hometown. It's as if my internal zip code were being recalibrated, as if my genes were being jiggled and respun.

Once I recognized this feeling I recoiled at the implications: I was not a different person, I said to myself. I was not being remade. I just felt myself loosening a bit—sort of like you do to a pair of shoelaces before climbing a mountain—then tightening up for a better grip with the ground. This feeling triggered a question that would stick with me for the remainder of our travels. Was I imagining this connection because of a lifetime of biblical associations, or was this ground somehow part of me already? Was I reacting to a spirit that existed in the place, or did that spirit exist within me? Was it in my DNA?

We arrived in Harran in midafternoon and were immediately besieged by another teenage boy anxious to give us a tour. We demurred. "But I know the famous archaeologist Abunar," he said.

"I am Abunar!" Avner said, using the Arabic pronunciation of his name. The boy slunk off, embarrassed. "I probably met his father some- time," Avner said.

We proceeded up the hill to one of the ghastliest places I've ever been. A panorama of isolation appeared, with a village and ancient ruins buried underneath a coating of dirt the color of sour milk. One of the world's earliest settled communities, Harran has been mostly abandoned since the Crusades. T. E. Lawrence discovered an eighth-century mosque here, and its broken pillars and tower are still frozen in time, like a shipwreck under water. Even the village itself seems arrested in its development. Half the homes have beehive roofs, circular domes made of mud that serve as a flue to remove heat in the summer. A few satellite dishes did little to lessen the feeling of desolation.

We walked around for a few hours before climbing to the top of the ruin and pulling out our Bibles. After Abraham arrives in Harran, God—unexpected and unannounced—suddenly starts speaking to him, saying, "Go forth from your native land and from your father's house, to the land that I will show you." It's one of the most famous passages in the Bible, and the one I read during my Bar Mitzvah. "I will make of you a great nation," God says, "and I will bless you; I will make your name great."

Though there were no walls around, the words still seemed to echo a bit. It was late afternoon by now. The sun, off to the west in Syria, set the dust on fire, with plumes kicking up behind a herd of goats. "Why are those words so famous?" I asked.

"Because they're the beginning of everything," Avner said. "Of monotheism, of creating the Jewish people. Leaving this place is leaving behind the old faith, the old pattern of life, the fertility—for a new start."

"So why did he do it?"

"The Bible doesn't say. As far as the text is concerned, God says to do it, so Abraham goes. That's it. But Jewish tradition says that Abraham was the first person to recognize that this was the *one* God."

"But he had never heard God before. He didn't know who or what God was. He didn't *see* God. And suddenly, this voice says 'Go,' and he goes."

"The concept in the Bible is that the voice was such a powerful thing that Abraham had no doubts. He had faith."

"So what would have been the biggest change from the world he left to the world where he was going?"

"The biggest difference would be leaving an area that was the core of civilization to a place that was just emerging. It was not the heart of everything."

"But because he went, it became the heart of everything."

"And that's the point," Avner said. "Abraham begins a new cycle." All through the Bible, he noted, the text follows a pattern of creation, followed by destruction, followed by re-creation. First God creates the world, for example; then, unhappy with how humans are behaving, he destroys it and begins again with Noah. Abraham marks the start of a new cycle, one that will continue throughout the Five Books of Moses. Even more important, God's decree to Abraham to leave Harran and go to the Promised Land, which overlapped much of Canaan, marks an end to the phase of Genesis that takes place in Mesopotamia. As a result, it also brings to a close the part of the story that was dominated by Mesopotamian imagery, specifically water as the chief source of creation.

"Do you want to know the real difference between here and the Promised Land?" Avner asked, not waiting for a reply. "There are no rivers. There are no floods. Canaan was settled. It had some rain. But the water wasn't predictable, or plentiful. In saying *lech l'cha*"—go forth— "God changed the history of the world. He gave Abraham the power of fertility, the power to create a great nation, which up to now had belonged only to the rivers: the Tigris, the Euphrates, the Nile. From now on, people—not water—would control the world. People who believed in God."

We sat silently for a few moments and watched the sun slide out of sight, leaving a pink glaze on the horizon. The herd of goats had disappeared. The dust had completely settled. For the first time since we started, I felt a sense of contentment—and peace. No matter the difficulty of what we were trying to do—regardless of my internal doubts about why I had come—I felt a certain equilibrium, like a child on a bike who starts out wobbly but slowly gains stability. And with that feeling I returned to the paradox at the heart of the injunction "go forth." For all the rational explanations I used to account for choices in my life, for all the intellectual reasons I used to justify this particular endeavor, I now realized it was possible—maybe even likely—that I had been motivated by some internal longing that I hadn't even identified. Some journeys we choose to go on, I realized; some journeys choose us. No journey better illustrates that than the one at the heart of the Five Books of Moses.

A few minutes later, as we stood up to go, Avner looked at his watch and realized it was Friday evening. *"Shabbat shalom,"* he said. "Good Sabbath."

Book I

GOD OF OUR FATHERS

1. In the Land of Canaan

The guard eyed me squarely as we approached his post, moving one hand from his belt to his walkie-talkie. His other arm rested on a rifle. He had gel in his hair and three stripes on his sleeve. "Yes?" he said, arching his eyebrows.

It was 9:35 on a late-autumn morning when Avner and I strode toward the security checkpoint at the Damia Bridge, an Israeli-Jordanian border crossing about thirty miles north of Jericho. We had driven up from Jerusalem that morning to start the next phase of our journey, visiting sites in the Promised Land associated with Abraham, his son Isaac, and his son Jacob. Together they form the holy triumvirate of biblical forefathers, the patriarchs, from the Greek words *patria,* meaning family or clan, and *arche,* meaning ruler. The Five Books describe several forefathers who preceded these men, notably Adam and Noah, as well as many who follow. But the three patriarchs receive special distinction because it's to them—of all humanity—whom God grants his sacred covenant of territory, and through them that the relationship between the people of Israel and the Promised Land is forged.

The story of the patriarchs takes up the final thirty-nine chapters of Genesis and covers the entire geographical spectrum of the ancient Near East, from Mesopotamia to Egypt, and back again, all within several verses. For Avner and me, this scope posed a challenge. Soon after our return from Turkey, we huddled in the living room of his home in Jerusalem and set about devising an itinerary. It was a sunny, comfortable

room, with whitewashed walls, bedouin rugs from the Sinai, and pictures of his two children, as well as the two daughters of his second
wife, Edie, a Canadian who served as office manager for the Jerusalem
bureau of the *New York Times*. Avner sat at the table with his computer,
online Bible, countless topographical maps, dozens of archaeological
texts, and the handheld GPS device, while I paced the floor.

Our most immediate problem was that with no archaeological evidence to relate *any* of the events in the Five Books to specific places, we
were left to the often-contradictory claims of history, myth, legend,
archaeobiology, paleozoology, and faith. There are nearly two dozen
candidates for Mount Sinai, for example, and nearly half a dozen for the
Red Sea. There are countless theories about which path the Israelites
took through the Sinai. In addition, we faced the competing constraints
of religious wars, political wars, terrorism, climate, budget, and health, as
well as the desire to have fun.

Ultimately we settled on a guiding principle: Our goal was to place
the biblical stories in the historical and cultural context of the ancient
Near East. Time and again, rather than focus on *every* story in the text,
or even every *interesting* story in the text, we decided to concentrate on
stories that could be enhanced by *being in the places themselves*. The story
of Jacob and his brother Esau wrestling in Rebekah's womb, for example, while fascinating on many levels, struck us as not likely to be
enriched by traveling to a specific location. The stories of Sodom and
Gomorrah, by contrast, and the crossing of the Red Sea might easily
take on new meanings by visiting their settings. In Judaism, the traditional process of analyzing scripture is called midrash, from the Hebrew
term meaning search out or investigate; in Christianity, this process is
referred to as exegesis, from the Latin word meaning the same thing. In
effect, what Avner and I undertook was topographical midrash, a geographical exegesis of the Bible.

In that spirit, we decided to begin our travels in Israel with a bit of
a long shot. Our destination this morning was Shechem, the first place
Abraham stops in Canaan and the next place the Bible mentions after
Harran. The text makes no mention of what route Abraham, his wife,

Sarah (she's actually called Sarai at the moment, as he is still called Abram), and his nephew Lot took to Canaan. Based on road patterns in the ancient world, one of the most logical places for him to cross into the Promised Land would have been a natural ford in the Jordan River just south of the Sea of Galilee, where the Damia Bridge is located today. Though we were already *in* the Promised Land, we decided to ask if the Israeli Army would let us walk across the bridge to the Jordanian side, then walk back, seeing what Abraham might have seen. Avner explained this idea to the sergeant, who remained at attention. After hearing the explanation, the officer removed his walkie-talkie and relayed our request.

The border post was astir that morning. It was a small crossing—the Jordan here is narrow enough for a horse to jump—but tidy, decorated with cacti, olive trees, and oleanders. The gate was blue and white. Every few minutes a Palestinian truck would approach, ferrying oranges, honeydew, or polished limestone. The driver would dismount and hand over his papers, which the guards would stamp and return. Then the guards would roll open the gate, the truck would pass, and the whole process would start again. We were just becoming lulled by the routine, when suddenly we heard static on the walkie-talkie. The sergeant removed it and held it for us to hear: "I don't care if they write a book about the Bible," the voice said. "I don't care if they rewrite the Bible itself. But they're not going to do it in a military zone, and they're *not* going to do it on my bridge."

The sergeant replaced his walkie-talkie and shrugged. "Sorry," he said, "only Palestinians."

We returned to the highway and turned west toward the mountains. Shechem is located at the northern edge of the central spine of mountains that traverse much of Israel and the West Bank. Our goal today was to travel down this spine, visiting first Shechem and then Bethel, the first two places Abraham stops. The following day we would travel farther south, to the Negev, Israel's desert region and the setting of Sodom and

Gomorrah. Avner suggested we use this time to discuss the historical background of the patriarchs' encounters in Canaan.

As we left the Damia, the road began to climb almost immediately, from six hundred feet below sea level along the Jordan River to two thousand feet above in less than twenty miles. The terrain changed just as quickly, from bleak desert crumbs to garden-fresh greenery. Vendors began to appear, hawking tomatoes, cauliflower, and radishes bunched like roses. My ears began to pop. Deviations like this are commonplace in Israel, a country one-quarter the size of Scotland with as much geographic diversity as the British Empire at its peak. That diversity—and the strategic challenges it poses—may also be a central factor in why Abraham came here in the first place.

For much of history, the narrow strip of land between the Jordan and the Mediterranean has been a curiosity, the foyer to the world, a place to pass through but not to stay. The Egyptians called it "Kharu," the Greeks and Romans "Palestina." The Syrians called it "Canaan." Whatever they called it, everyone coveted it, though none could control it. From its inception, the Fertile Crescent was structured like a modern American shopping mall, with two anchor stores on either end linked by a string of smaller, more vulnerable stores that were completely dependent on their larger neighbors for their economic well-being. In this case, Egypt and Mesopotamia were the anchors, and as they went so went Canaan.

One reason for this dependency is that even though Canaan contained some of the world's biggest cities, these cities were never able to organize themselves into a coherent political body. Instead they were clients of the great powers, divided and conquered by their own crippling mix of mountains, valleys, coastline, and desert, as well as their lack of water. As Avner pointed out, "The Egyptians used to joke that Canaan was 'that poor country dependent on rain.' " This reality sets up one of the crueler ironies in the history of the Bible. Geography prevented the development of a great empire in Canaan, but it was that lack of an empire that may have allowed God to promise the land to Abraham. In other words, the Promised Land, a place that for three thousand years has proven notoriously difficult to control, became the Promised Land in large measure because in the preceding three thousand years no one had been able to control it either.

Besides being true to ancient geographic conditions, the biblical story is also remarkably true to current ones. The State of Israel can be roughly divided into three sections—the head and shoulders of the Galilee; the torso, made up of the central hills, Jerusalem, and Tel Aviv; and the legs and feet of the Negev. The 1937 British plan to partition Palestine gave Jews only the head and shoulders, with a bit of coast. The UN mandate of 1948 added the legs and feet. The central hills, excluding Jerusalem, were originally given to the Arabs and have been fought over ever since. Jews have based their claim to the land largely on the Bible. The central spine of the country was home to most of the major episodes in the Five Books, also called the Pentateuch, from the Greek word meaning five-book work. These sites include Shechem, Bethel, Hebron, and Beer-sheba. The Palestinian claim was based largely on the fact that they were living in these areas before Jews began immigrating in large numbers in the nineteenth century. In recent years, some Palestinians have shifted their claim, saying they were also on the land before the patriarchs arrived in the nineteenth century B.C.E. Palestinians, they now say, are direct descendants of the Canaanites.

About an hour after we left the Damia we arrived at the checkpoint outside Nablus, the Arab name for Shechem, which was handed over to the Palestinians in the mid-1990s. As one of the first cities in the nascent state, Nablus has been a constant site of tension and, after canceling two trips to the area over safety concerns, we decided to rent a car from a Palestinian company in East Jerusalem to save ourselves from being stoned. Our car had Palestinian license plates—white instead of yellow—and several stickers with Arabic writing. They seemed to work. The Palestinian border guide was much friendlier than the Israeli had been and sat on our hood and smoked a cigarette while Avner telephoned our escort. "The Palestinians are just so appreciative that an Israeli came to visit," Avner said.

In a few moments we were joined by Suher, an official at the local tourist authority who was one of the Palestinian tour guides Avner had trained in Jewish history. She was demure, and a little nervous. She had been sent to town seven months earlier. "I don't consider living in Nablus living," she confessed. "It's very different from Jerusalem. Gossip here is at a very high level." She drove into town, which was crowded with white concrete slab buildings bedecked with rugs hanging out to air. Fruit trees dotted the central square, which was bustling and well manicured, though the telephone boxes had no telephones. Across the street was a large institutional building that had been the British headquarters, then the Israeli headquarters, and was now the Palestinian headquarters. An enormous portrait of Yasser Arafat hung from the roof, giving the town the feel of a place poised between democracy and dictatorship.

After a few minutes we arrived at the site of ancient Shechem. Compared with other archaeological sites, this one was fairly run-down, with grass growing over untended mounds of dirt and a graveyard of old auto parts encroaching on the city wall. Excavations show that Shechem was a thriving community as early as the fifth millennium B.C.E., but wasn't fully developed until the nineteenth century B.C.E., reaching prosperity a few hundred years later. The lack of significant remains from the time of Abraham has led some to speculate that Shechem might have been added by later editors of the Bible.

Either way, Shechem's prominence for biblical writers is clear. After arriving in Canaan, Abraham passes through the land "as far as the site of Shechem," which is located alongside the "terebinth of Moreh," a term usually interpreted to mean "wise oak tree." God once again appears to Abraham and renews his promise: "I will give this land to your offspring." Abraham expresses his appreciation by building an altar on the site.

We walked around for a few minutes, and Avner pointed out the city gate and a number of storehouses, as well as a temple and altar from the early second millennium B.C.E., the time of the patriarchs. The Canaanite altars were in town, he noted, while the mention of the oak in Genesis suggests Abraham camped outside the walls, a position consistent with his status as a migrant. The existence of several altars inside the city walls suggests that seminomadic clans might have been welcome inside the city, the two communities—Canaanites and proto-Israelites—living side by side. For Suher, this was welcome news, archaeology that could be used to mend, not divide. But even she couldn't avoid drawing political conclusions.

"We believe this is a very important place, a Canaanite place," she said. "We believe that Canaanites, they are Arabs. That supports our rights on this land."

"So you believe the Arabs were here before the Israelites," I said.

"We believe that, very strongly."

"How do you make the connection?"

"The Canaanites are Arabs, from Saudi Arabia, from Hejaz. I know that we, the Palestinians, are also from the Arabs."

Though historians don't necessarily agree on this point—most say Canaanites were drawn from all over the Near East, not just Arabia—I asked her if this idea would have an impact on the future.

"I don't know if we can make real peace," she said. "I don't know if we will ever settle who was here before the other. But we can live together. We are human. The land is for those who build it. For those who live on it. The Romans were here, but it's not their land. They went back to their country. If we leave the land, we don't deserve it."

"In other words, the Israelites left, so it should be your land."

"Yes. But the Jews are much more clever than we are. They believe in this land more than we do. I don't know why. They, their children: they are very serious about this place."

"So what's your dream for Shechem?"

"I love this place," she said. "I don't know why. I would love to clean it, to bring more people here. To bring children here. It's a feeling. Maybe because we are raised to love this place, to love our history. It's a history of pain. This place has seen a lot of pain. I hope it will go away."

We said good-bye at our car and turned south toward Bethel, the site of Abraham's next layover. We were passing through one of the poorest pockets of the West Bank, a rocky, agricultural no-man's-land. Small trucks and taxis choked the road, which was dotted with mosques and coffeehouses that blocked the view of ageless olive groves. The taxis came in a variety of shades—Mello Yello, mango, Tang—everything around, but not quite, New York City yellow-cab yellow. The road signs were all in Arabic—no Hebrew, no English, no neon. Drenched in sun and dust, the landscape looked like paper, toasted, its edges singed by fire.

In time the hills became more rolling and the olive green a bit more plentiful. We veered around Ramallah on an Israeli bypass road and rolled to the gate of Bethel, a modern Jewish settlement in the midst of Arab domain. Such communities are the tinderbox of the Palestinian-Israeli relationship, an ever-shifting frontier of faith that triggers passions and hatreds that could only be aroused by the potent braiding of faith, family, and text.

We waited for the yellow gate—twice as big as the one on the border with Jordan—and proceeded inside the community. Suddenly we were in Israel again. The buses were red, the signs were in Hebrew, the children wore *kippahs,* or skullcaps, on their heads. Yet the place felt different, tense. The school, the playground, even the bus stops were protected by fences. The entire place was swathed in barbed wire. It was a voluntary ghetto, a Wild West outpost of choice, not force.

We drove up the hill and decided to stop by the director's office, which was in a Quonset hut. The secretary, whose hair was hidden in a net as per Orthodox tradition, looked at us skeptically, as if to say, "Are you for us or against us?" After a brief negotiation, the director agreed to meet us for five minutes. We stepped into his office, which was lined with maps and blueprints. He had a grimace for a face, and a scar across his cheek. I asked him why he was here. "We are here because of the Five Books," he said. "We are living in Bethel, on the road of the patriarchs, and this is our contract." He placed his hand on the Bible, which sat prominently on his desk. Of all the places Abraham visited, why did he stop here, I asked. "I cannot tell," he said. "It's not a high place. It's difficult to defend. If there's a possibility to ask Abraham why, we will ask."

Back in the waiting room, Avner remembered that he knew an

American couple in town. The husband, a guide, was working, but his wife invited us to stop by their home. It was a modest home, barely large enough for the couple, their five children, and several thousand books. "They're my husband's," explained Fern Dobuler, who, like him, grew up in a moderate Jewish household on Long Island. "When we first became religious, I had all these questions. Every time Abby couldn't answer one of them, he went out and bought a book."

Fern was garrulous and gesticulative, in a Catskills-real-estate-broker sort of way. A phys-ed teacher by training, she balanced her athleticism with her religious need for modesty by wearing a long skirt made of sweatpant material and covering her head with a New York Yankees cap. She met her husband in college in New York, where both were active in a pro-Zionist group. One year Yitzhak Rabin, then the Israeli ambassador to the United States, paid a visit. "If you really want to help," he told them, "move to a settlement and be a pioneer." Others delivered similar messages. When Abby's grandmother was dying, she made them promise: "Don't forget you're Jews. Don't forget Israel." A week after she died, Fern gave birth to a daughter and slowly the couple embraced a more traditional brand of Judaism—saying daily prayers, resting on Shabbat. Eventually they came to Israel for a summer.

"We had three children at the time," Fern said. "We rented an apartment in the Old City. It was fabulous. My kids went to the Western Wall by themselves. You could smell history in the air. We came back to New York and every single Friday night Abby would start to cry. 'I wish we could live in Israel. A Jew belongs in Israel.' It was like Chinese water torture. He just wore me down."

The following year they sold their house, their two cars, their real-estate business, and moved back. "At first it was very hard," she said. "We had to learn how to put on gas masks. My oldest son sat in school for a year unable to understand anything. I kept saying, 'What did I do to my kids?' It was hard for me, too. I missed my friends. I missed my house. I missed my central air-conditioning. I lay on my bed at night, saying, 'I can't do this. I can't do this.' My father thought Abby had brainwashed me."

Worse, their money soon ran out and they had to flee the high prices of Jerusalem. "We drew a circle with a half-hour radius," she said, "and started looking at communities. We knew it had to be religious. We wanted something established enough to have teenagers. We wanted a place new enough to have young children. We wanted diversity. This place just fit the bill."

"There's one thing you didn't mention," I said.

"I know," she said. "The Bible is not the reason we came to Bethel, but once we were living here, every time Bethel was mentioned in the weekly Torah portion, only then did I feel part of the community. Part of the extended Jewish people. I remember the first time they read the part where Abraham builds an altar in Bethel, and I thought, That's where I *live*!"

The feeling only grew, she said, once they realized the grave political situation. "Until they had the bypass road, there wasn't a day we would drive without being stoned. It was extremely unpleasant. Once, when my sister-in-law was here, somebody dropped a cinder block on the car. Not a rock, a cinder block. The whole ceiling on the passenger side caved in. I had been sitting in the back with my sister-in-law, who fell to the floor, shaking. If I had been sitting in the passenger seat I'd probably be dead."

I suggested that she seemed remarkably free of anger.

"I don't hold the anger," she said. "You can't live that way. You have to live a normal life. I just don't want to give up any more land. I don't want to give up my home."

"Do you feel living here has brought you closer to God?"

"Yes. Because I see purpose in our living here. If I didn't, it would be very hard. I wonder how anybody who's Israeli and not religious can stand it. If they don't have that connection to God, with all the aggravation and hardship, why stay here?"

"Why *do* you stay here?"

"I stay here because Jews belong in the land of Israel. God *gave* us this land, and it's not up to us to give it back. When we stood at Sinai as a Jewish people and said, 'We accept the Torah,' we didn't just do it for that generation in the desert. We did it for all future generations."

"Tell me about the land. Do you have a different relationship with it?"

"There are many things about living in Israel that are wonderful. One of those is the land. When my kids used to go on field trips in America they went to a museum, to the Empire State Building. Here when you go on a field trip they drop you off in the middle of nowhere and you walk, for hours and hours and hours. A field trip is seeing the land, connecting to the land. You don't have to see a thing. There's an expression, 'To walk in the land of Israel is a holy thing to do.' "

We pulled out our Bibles and began to discuss the sections that take place in Bethel. After Abraham leaves Shechem, he travels south to the hill country "east of Bethel," where he once again builds an altar to the Lord. Later Abraham revisits the place on his return from Egypt. After that, Bethel only grows in importance, becoming, after Jerusalem, the most frequently mentioned place in the Bible. Jacob, during his flight from Beer-sheba to Harran, sleeps there and has his famous nocturnal vision of angels ascending and descending on a ladder. He awakens and erects a pillar to mark the place, calling it Bethel, house of God. Years later, on his way home from Harran with his wife and children, Jacob again stays in the place. Fern began to read this passage, from Genesis 35.

"And God said to Jacob: 'Arise, go up to Bethel and remain there; and build an altar there to God.' " Jacob responds, instructing his family, "Rid yourself of the alien god in your midst, purify yourselves, and change your clothes. Come, let us go up to Bethel, and I will build an altar there to the God who answered me when I was in distress and who has been with me wherever I have gone." Jacob hides the idols under the same terebinth tree in Shechem that his grandfather used. Then he travels to Bethel, where God again invokes the name he earlier gave Jacob: Israel, meaning Striven with God. "And God said to him, 'You whose name is Jacob, you shall be called Jacob no more, but Israel shall be your name.' Thus He named him Israel."

As she was reading, Fern began to choke up. She closed the book. "Maybe it was my destiny that I ended up in Bethel," she said. "There are such special people here." She got up and walked to the one shelf that wasn't covered in books, where she retrieved a large framed photo of a mother and her son. She handed it to me. "They were killed about two years ago now. They were gunned down on the way back to Bethel from a family gathering. When we first came to Bethel they were the first family that had us over. I didn't speak Hebrew. She didn't speak English. But there was such warmth there, and welcome. Just very special people. We went to their funeral. We went to the funeral of a kindergarten teacher. We went to the funeral of a young man in his early twenties. My children go every six months to someone else's funeral. When I lived in America the only funerals I went to were for old people."

"So why do you keep her picture?"

"Because I don't want to forget them. It's part of our life here. We have a cemetery. It's filling up!"

"And that doesn't make you want to stay less?"

"It makes me want to stay more. It strengthens my pride for this place. Not only was Abraham here, and Jacob. But now I've been here, and my children, too. Not only did they make sacrifices. We made sacrifices, too. And we did it for the same reason. We believe in God."

Avner and I were quiet for much of the way home. Once again an impromptu meeting had produced a connection to the Bible so profound—and so personal—that I felt it in my gut. I was struck by how *physical* Fern's experience was: First she felt a longing for her biblical roots, then she came to Israel, then she felt as if she had become a part of the story herself. It's as if the act of going through those steps had taken her closer to God. Was there something inevitable about that process?

For the time being, I was focused on more tangible issues, specifically trying to figure out what Canaan was like when Abraham got there. The Bible is strikingly unhelpful in this regard. Abraham's initial encounters seem almost hurried over in the text. The account of Abraham's travels from Shechem, to Bethel, to the Negev is covered in only four verses. The absence of any details raised a question, which I asked Avner the following day: Is there a connection between what we were seeing and what Abraham would have seen? "Let's take a drive," he said.

We turned south from Jerusalem toward Beer-sheba along the same route Abraham would have taken, the Patriarchs' Road. The original path would have been three or four feet wide, Avner noted, a stone-riddled trail winding around the mountains to avoid steep climbs. The Romans later widened it and paved it. Today it's a four-lane highway, with regulation shoulders, guardrails, light poles, the longest tunnel in Israel, as well as the longest bridge. At a scant two hundred yards, the bridge doesn't even cross a river; it crosses a ravine. "It's a small country," Avner said apologetically.

The road has other Israeli idiosyncrasies. The first is that almost every driver—including Avner—was cradling a mobile phone. Also, every car had at least one bumper sticker, mostly on political topics, like GIVING UP TERRITORY IS DANGEROUS FOR JEWS, some were emotional, like SHALOM HAVER, or "Good-bye Friend," which is what President Bill Clinton said at the funeral for slain Prime Minister Yitzhak Rabin. "We're drawn to written things," Avner said, explaining the stickers. "We're still a people of the Book."

We zigzagged along the mountains for an hour while Avner began to sketch what Abraham would have found in Canaan. Though today the central hills are a mix of coffee-colored ridges, butterscotch boulders, and caramel soil—blended with groves of olive trees—the land wasn't always this parched. In the patriarchs' time, Canaan was a leafier place, covered with sycamores, oaks, and pistachios, as well as fields of wheat and barley. Canaanites built their cities in areas flush with trees, and thus water. Specifically this meant the Mediterranean coast, the Galilee, and the foothills of the central mountains. Abraham may have stopped in these areas, but when it came time to settle more permanently he moved farther south, to the threshold of the desert. "Wandering tribesmen didn't need areas to cultivate," Avner said. "They also didn't want conflict with cities. They wanted to be on the edge of civilization."

After several hours we neared the edge ourselves. The browns and beiges dissolved into a chalky moonscape of ashen hills, cracked mounds, and mesas that jab the air like fists wrapped in gauze. Suddenly

Avner steered the car over, jumped out, and plopped down in the dirt. "You need a geology lesson," he said.

As he started constructing a model in the sand, I pulled out my Bible. After Abraham arrives in the Negev from Bethel, a severe famine strikes the land and he is obliged to seek relief in Egypt. This excursion inaugurates a new, much more detailed part of Genesis, in which Abraham finally emerges a more fully realized character, with feelings for his wife and nephew, and the foundations of a code of conduct centered on right and wrong. As Abraham is about to enter Egypt he says to Sarah, "I know what a beautiful woman you are. If the Egyptians see you, and think, 'She is his wife,' they will kill me and let you live. Please say that you are my sister, that it may go well with me because of you, and that I may remain alive thanks to you." Events transpire as he predicted. The pharaoh takes Sarah into his possession and pays Abraham a rich dowry, including sheep, oxen, asses, and camels, as well as male and female slaves. But God intervenes before the pharaoh has relations with Sarah, and she is released. Abraham and Sarah, now further enriched with gold and silver from the king, return to Canaan.

Once they arrive, tensions arise between Abraham and his nephew, Lot, who also became wealthy in Egypt. "The land could not support them staying together," the text says, "for their possessions were so great." Their herdsmen start to quarrel. Abraham, in a touching act of generosity, tries to assuage the problem, saying to Lot, "Let there be no strife between you and me, between my herdsmen and yours, for we are kinsmen. Is not the whole land before you? Let us separate: if you go north, I will go south; and if you go south, I will go north." Lot surveys the land, noticing how well watered the land of Jordan is, "like the garden of Eden." Lot, naturally, chooses the nicer land, "the whole plain of Jordan," while Abraham is left with the deserts of Canaan. Soon, though, God appears to compensate Abraham for his munificence. "Raise your eyes and look out from where you are," God says, promising to give Abraham all the land he sees, including Jordan. "I will make your offspring as the dust of the earth, so that if one can count the dust of the earth, then your offspring too can be counted."

While Abraham's offspring may be entitled to the entire area in the long term, in the short term Abraham is confined to a narrow, almost uninhabitable patch between the central mountains and the Dead Sea. "That's where we are now," Avner said. While I was reading, he had molded a mound of sand into a strip, like a baguette. "These are the central mountains," he said, pointing to the model. "These mountains were old, worn down over time. Then, about two million years ago"—he gestured toward a ravine he had dug alongside the mound— "the Rift Valley was created." The rift, a giant scar across the face of the earth, extends from Lake Victoria in Central Africa, up through the Sinai and Jordan, all the way to the Euphrates. It reaches bottom at the Dead Sea, 1,300 feet below sea level, the "lowest spot on earth."

Once the rift appeared, the eastern side of the hills dropped off far more dramatically than the west, creating a geological oddity. When rain clouds from the Mediterranean reach this ridge, they suddenly get hit with a thick wall of air. The air is denser here because the Dead Sea is so low. The lower the ground, the more atmosphere there is. The more atmosphere, the more pressure in the air. One consequence of so much pressure is that it sucks the moisture out of the air. "It's like if you press your lips against your sleeve and blow," Avner said, "your sleeve becomes hot. That's how this desert was created. It's the private desert of the Dead Sea. I hate to say it, but it's the smallest desert on earth."

"How many superlatives do you have?" I said.

"Let's see, Jericho is the lowest city on earth. The Sea of Galilee is the lowest freshwater lake on earth. The Dead Sea is the lowest—"

"I get the idea."

"Do you?" he said, smiling. He gestured for me to follow.

We got back in the car and made the steep descent to the Dead Sea, continuing to read. Suddenly at this point in the story, Genesis 14, Abraham gets drawn into a war, indicating, if nothing else, that he is growing in stature: A mere shepherd would not attack a large army. Four kings from Mesopotamia who have come to the Negev, possibly for the copper mines, terrorize the region. Eventually five kings from the city-states of Canaan, specifically the Jordan River region where Lot is living, engage them in battle. The Mesopotamian kings triumph, seizing the wealth of Sodom and Gomorrah, and taking Lot prisoner. When Abraham learns of his nephew's plight, he pursues the kings, defeats them, and rescues Lot. "Your reward shall be very great," God tells Abraham. How can that be, the octogenarian Abraham protests, "seeing that I shall die childless?" Fear not, God says, your offspring shall be as numerous as the stars.

Sarah, seeing her husband's frustration, follows Near Eastern custom from the time and offers him her Egyptian maidservant, Hagar, as a concubine. When Hagar gets pregnant, though, Sarah begins to treat her harshly and Hagar flees. An angel rescues Hagar, who then gives birth to a son, Ishmael. God reappears when Ishmael is thirteen and asks Abraham to follow another Near Eastern custom: circumcise himself and his son. This act is portrayed as a sign of the everlasting covenant between God and man, but for a God torn between acts of creation and destruction, it's also a fitting emblem: forever branding a man's source of creation with a mark of destruction.

One day, when Abraham is sitting at the entrance of his tent, the Lord visits in the guise of three men. Abraham, who doesn't know that the men represent God, follows bedouin tradition and orders that they be given food and water. "My lords, if it please you, do not go on past your servant. Let a little water be brought; bathe your feet and recline under a tree. And let me fetch a morsel of bread." Abraham hastens to Sarah and asks her to prepare a meal of choice cakes and curd. He then slaughters a calf, "tender and choice," and serves it, too.

After eating, the men ask Abraham where his wife, Sarah, is. He tells them, and one of the men announces, "I will return to you when life is due, and your wife Sarah shall have a son!" Sarah, who is then ninety and no longer having "the periods of women," is listening and laughs out loud. She adds, to herself, "Now that I am withered, am I to have enjoyment—with my husband so old?" "Why did Sarah laugh?" God asks Abraham. Sarah grows frightened and denies she laughed, but God repeats, "You did laugh."

At this point, the men suddenly decide to leave and Abraham escorts them out. Along the way, God decides to reveal himself and the purpose of his visit. "Shall I hide from Abraham what I am about to do?" he asks. God then announces that he intends to destroy Sodom and Gomorrah, because "their outrage is so great, and their sin is so grave!" No explicit sin is given. Abraham, in the first instance in which he stands up to God, protests, saying, "Perhaps there are fifty righteous people in the city." The two negotiate the number down to ten—another sign of Abraham's growing stature—and God departs.

In Sodom, Lot also welcomes the visitors warmly, but that night his neighbors demand the right to have sexual relations with the men. Lot resists, but the people of the town insist. "Where are the men who came to you tonight?" they ask Lot. "Bring them to us, that we may be intimate with them." This is a clear reference to homosexuality (and the origin of the word *sodomy*) and God responds by destroying the city, using what the King James Bible calls "brimstone and fire," and what modern translations often call "sulfurous fire." Before this happens, though, God instructs Lot and his family to flee, but not to glance behind them. When Lot's wife does look back, she becomes a pillar of salt.

Avner and I had now reached the bottom of the descent and he pulled to a stop once again. We stepped out of the car at the southern tip of the Dead Sea into a mixture of sulfurous air, oppressive heat, and deceptively inviting turquoise waters. The climate here is like an anti-greenhouse, with all the moisture sucked out of the air. Because of the heat, water evaporates at a faster rate here, meaning the sea contains 25 percent solids and a retching 7 percent salt—six times saltier than the ocean. People are said to be able to float in this brine, but that's not quite true. The one time I went in, I felt like a wonton—not quite floating, not quite sinking, and covered in a fatty soup. There is one benefit to this otherwise deadly place. The thicker atmosphere prevents ultraviolet rays from reaching the ground, which means, Avner said, that the Dead Sea is the "best place to get a suntan in the world." The sun, coupled with minerals from the water, is so effective against psoriasis that German and Austrian health plans actually pay patients to fly to Israel rather than stay at home applying lotions.

In the ancient world, the Dead Sea, which the Bible calls the "Salt Sea," was less of a novelty and more of a frightening marvel. To explain,

Avner led me on a short hike up the cliffs. We scrambled over rocks so brittle they sometimes broke loose in our hands. After a while, we crawled through a narrow opening into a formation called the Cave of Two Chimneys. It was a cylindrical chamber about the size of a spiral staircase with matching two-story knobbly pillars that looked like drumsticks. Only these towers weren't made of wood. They were made of salt.

"*Entirely* of salt?" I asked.

"Lick it," he said.

These columns proved to be the most unexpected sideshow of the lowest place on earth. Because water evaporates so rapidly here, the floor of the Dead Sea is lined with a layer of minerals several miles thick. With so much atmosphere, the air actually pushes down on the water, which in turn pushes down on this layer of minerals, squeezing out the salt, the most malleable of the minerals. The salt is forced deeper into the earth and eventually out toward the shore, at which point it pushes up through the ground into assorted asparagus-like formations. The two chimneys were striking examples, and when we scampered to the top of the hill we saw several more. The process continues to this day. Avner told me that when he came here as a boy there were gas-station pumps near the road. When he returned a few years later, the mountain had expanded so much its outer edge had overtaken the pumps. "It's a living mountain," he said.

Which brought us back to Avner's model in the sand. We were sitting now atop Sodom mountain, overlooking the Dead Sea. There were no cars, or people, for miles.

"Sodom is the first example of biblical storytellers taking an actual place," Avner said, referring to salt flats around the Dead Sea, "and using a story to explain how it developed. With the Flood, or Mount Sinai, the Bible tells the story and we can try to match the place or not. Here we know the place, and the Bible tells us what it means. Every schoolkid today calls these formations Lot's wife."

"But why such a violent story?"

"Because to them, this was a place of death."

He pointed me back to the text. After his wife dies, Lot and his daughters flee first to Zoar, then to a cave in the high country. Avner tapped me on the arm and pointed across the Dead Sea. "That's Zoar," he said. As the Bible describes, it was green, and above it was a range of mountains. "And before you get to the dirty part, let me tell you that in those mountains is a cave, which the Byzantines identified as Lot's." Once settled, Lot's daughters, concerned by the lack of men, get their father drunk and commit incest. The elder daughter has a son, who becomes father of the Moabites; the younger has a son who becomes father of the Ammonites. Both nations settle across the Jordan River, adjacent to the Promised Land. "Do you see those mountains?" Avner said, pointing above Zoar. "That's Moab. Further north is Ammon."

"So the writers knew what they were talking about," I said.

"Oh, they knew, deeply. They also knew that Moab and Ammon would later become rivals of Israel. This is a retroactive justification for why they were the enemy: They were conceived in incest."

"It's almost as if the Bible's a Baedeker," I said. "It's certainly better than my guidebooks."

"It's better because of the story," he said. "It's very literary, yet very obvious. It's good versus evil. Anybody who hears this story can immediately tell you which side is good. That's the reason so many of these stories work: The moral is very clear."

Back in Jerusalem I lay awake that evening, dazed and enthralled by our early experiences. I had no idea that even gentle pushing on the topography of the region would yield such immediate results. I felt as if I'd entered some virtual reality game and reemerged in a parallel world four thousand years ago. In particular I was surprised by how the stories and the places seemed so intimately connected as if each carried the memory of the other deep within it. Bring them together, as we were doing, and both were enhanced.

But for all the added texture, I still felt somewhat removed from the central figure. Who was Abraham? What motivated him? What did he look like? I went back to see Professor Biran, who invited me to accompany him on a trip.

It was 7:00 on a Friday morning when we left Jerusalem on our way to Israel's northern border and Biran's ongoing excavation in the biblical city of Dan. At eighty-eight, Professor Biran sat in the passenger seat while his longtime secretary, Honey, drove. A native of Palestine who grew up along the Nile, Avraham Biran was certainly a pioneer. An archaeologist by training, he was also the first postwar governor of Jerusalem, a consul general to the United States, head of the Israeli Department of Antiquities, and, after retirement, one of the most productive excavators of his era. He was a compact man who favored a mathematician's clothes—short-sleeved shirts and polyester pants—but also managed to be effortlessly urbane. He reminded me of Burgess Meredith as the avuncular trainer in *Rocky*.

"I never liked the name Avraham," he said. "But I like the name Abe even less. I went to Los Angeles and they asked me my name. 'Avraham,' I said. They had to think about it, but after a while they said, 'Oh! *Ab*-raham. We'll just call you 'Abe.' And I said, 'Oh, no you won't.' "

Despite this ambivalence, Professor Biran had a deep affinity with his namesake. Abraham, he noted proudly, was a man of breadth— a shepherd, a warrior, a diplomat, a husband, a father, an uncle, a judge—the world's first Renaissance man. Based on contemporaneous images, he would likely have worn a knee-length pleated wool skirt, probably brown, with a long felt shawl draped over one shoulder. To this he would have added a bronze belt and sandals. His shoulder-length hair was likely parted in the middle, and he probably had a pointed beard and no mustache. As for skills, carpentry was popular, as was minstrel music and storytelling. With Abraham in particular, we know that he was wealthy, with large herds and enough status for pharaohs and kings to negotiate with him. The fact that he came from Ur of the Chaldeans is intriguing. In antiquity, Chaldea was famous for one thing: astronomy. This explains why some suggested Abraham used his knowledge of the stars to divine that there was only one God. Josephus went further, suggesting that Abraham taught astrology to the Egyptians, who then taught it to the Greeks, which would make Abraham the father of not just western religion but also western science.

Abraham was also a frequent traveler, meaning he probably touched countless sites in the Promised Land, including Dan. After more than three hours we neared the site, a sprawling, tree-shrouded mound of about fifty acres within shouting distance of the Lebanese mountains. These sites, called *tels,* are the staple of Near Eastern archaeology, layer cakes of history in which each generation built on top of the previous one. Tels are particularly common in this region, because with no rivers, cities were constructed in the few places with reliable water, in this case a spring. Originally called Laish, this site was later renamed Dan, after one of the twelve tribes, and lent its name to the vivid expression of Israelite unity, "from Dan to Beer-sheba."

Professor Biran explored his excavation for a while, checking to see what his graduate students had recently uncovered, while Honey showed me around the ruins, which mostly date from the first millennium B.C.E. Around noon he met us and announced he had something to show me. We hiked uphill, until the dense canopy of eucalyptus and avocado trees unfolded, revealing a brilliant blue sky. Biran was using a cane, which attracted the attention of a flock of white butterflies.

"Now I have a question for you, my friend," he said. "Who invented the arch?"

I thought for a second, a series of images flickering through my mind: stones, columns, keystones, slaves. "The Egyptians?" I said.

He looked at me, disappointed. "The Romans," he corrected. "You learned in school that it was the Romans. That's why I didn't believe what I saw when I first came here. We were working two thousand years earlier than the Romans—at the time of the patriarchs."

We rounded a corner and from out of the trees a large mound of rubble interrupted the path. Instead of thick underbrush, the area was clear, dominated by piles of dirt and stones.

"One thing about digging for the Bible," Biran said. "You have to put your faith in accidental discoveries." He was particularly interested in how ancient cities protected themselves. In Dan, his team discovered that the southern wall was held together with columns.

"The conclusion would be that they built all ramparts in this manner," he said. "But we weren't satisfied with that answer." They pushed toward the north, where they found walls built on a slope, with no columns. Next they moved west, where they found a third technique, walls supported by buttresses. Finally they pushed east. "And there we didn't find a stone wall at all," he said. "We found packed mud." More important, within the mud construction was the outline of a gate.

As he relived the experience, Biran grew more animated. He began scurrying over the edge of the cliff. With arms, legs, and cane working in impressive tandem, the years seemed to peel from his body. When his team uncovered the gate, which they left attached to the mud bank behind it, Biran insisted his draftsman draw the structure. The draftsman refused. The dig had run past its closing date; he wanted to go home. Biran insisted, and hours later the man came sprinting. "You've got to come look at this," he said. When Biran reached the site, he found the traces of an arch.

"Now this is what people come from all over the world to see," he said. We'd arrived at the base of the structure. The pile of rubble at the top had unfurled into a three-story arch with the outline of a semicircle on top. It looked like an entrance to a coliseum, except that it wasn't made of marble but of crumbling, loaf-sized bricks of mud. It was two thousand years older than any arch known to exist.

"What's remarkable about this," he continued, "is that you can't find a building built years ago of mud brick that's still standing. It's impossible."

He turned to face me. "And this is where Abraham comes in," he said. "This is why I brought you here. In Genesis 14, before Sodom and Gomorrah, you read about Abraham pursuing the kings who took Lot prisoner. And the text says, 'He came as far as Dan.' It was called Laish then, but that doesn't matter. My point is that the king of this place, seeing how Abraham had won a great victory, invited him to walk up these steps. This is as close to the physical steps of Abraham that you will ever get."

He was caught by his own statement and for a moment abandoned his academic distance. As he did, I finally caught the glimmer of humanity in the text I'd been looking for. The chapters of Genesis devoted to Abraham have two prominent themes: how God acts toward the patriarch, and how the patriarch acts toward God. In the beginning, Abraham willingly accepts God's promise of land and descendants. He leaves Harran for Canaan without question. He arrives in Shechem, hears God's promise, and builds an altar. He does the same in Bethel. Even the famine in Canaan, which drives Abraham to Egypt, was a test of his devotion, which Abraham pursues admirably. Eventually, though, he tires of the tests and empty promises. When will he have descendants? he asks God. When will he see a physical manifestation of God's word?

It was through this struggle—so human, so understandable—that I first felt a connection to Abraham. Like him, readers of Abraham's story are expected to accept the words of God as true. Here's what God did; here's what he said. Embracing those words is a matter of faith. For me that task was difficult. Perhaps it was my concrete nature, or my natural obeisance to science, reason, or skepticism. Maybe it was fear of entering a realm that I couldn't control or see. But I found myself wanting more. Before I could consider what the biblical characters feel toward God, I needed to feel a connection to them. I needed something to touch, a physical manifestation of their lives.

And here it was. Here was a way, however abstract, to touch Abraham and through him, to touch his world. Leading me up the short flight of stairs, Professor Biran took my hand and placed it against the wall, which was crumbly like stale bread. "Do you feel that?" he said. He was referring not to the texture, but to the surge of excitement.

"Every time I come here I feel the same thing," he said. "And I say to myself, that's what Abraham must have felt. It's a sense of history."

I withdrew my hand. A dusting of dirt came off on my fingers. "And if people say, 'You've got no evidence of this. You're making this up'?"

"I say, You're right. I have no evidence the Abraham walked here. I would never publish it. But in a lecture, on a tour—to you—I would say it, because people are familiar with Abraham, because it makes his story more real. And because even though I'm a scientist, I can still have faith." He smiled, and for the first time all day there was a touch of mortality in his voice. "And because it's my name as well. So what the hell? I want to feel part of the Bible, too."

2. Take Now Thy Son

They were dancing in the streets on Sunday in one of the holiest enclaves in Israel.

It was two days after my trip to Dan when I awoke to read in the *Jerusalem Post* that a festival was under way in Hebron, the first place Abraham purchases land, the burial site of his family, and home to more bloodshed in recent years than any place on the biblical route. If Shechem was bad, Hebron was worse: Avner suggested we hire a driver, then postponed two trips when shooting erupted. The opportunity to go on festival day seemed prudent (if nothing else, there would be heightened security), and after learning that Avner had other plans, I hurried to the bus station. Even without him, this seemed a good opportunity to plunge into the next section of Genesis, chapters 20 to 26, which contain some of the more memorable passages in the patriarchal narrative, including the birth of Isaac, the death of Sarah, and the gripping scene in which Abraham is asked to sacrifice their son. These chapters also introduce another ongoing theme in the Pentateuch, tension between the patriarchs and their sons.

A police van stood waiting to escort the bus, which had bulletproof glass on the windows and chain-link fencing over the windshield. Inside, every seat was taken, mostly with ultra-Orthodox Jews. As we crossed into the West Bank, the man beside me, in his fifties with a gray beard, handed his prayer book to his wife and walked to the front. There he unfolded a smaller book from a plastic envelope, lifted the micro-

phone, and recited a prayer. When he finished he was joined by a cho-
rus of "Amen's" as he returned to his seat, repackaged his book, and
reclaimed his prayer book from his wife.

"It's the prayer for traveling," the man beside me explained. He had
traveled with his family from Brooklyn to revisit the place where he'd
met his wife. She was sitting nearby, breast-feeding a baby. Her sister sat
next to her with two more children. "Together we have twelve," the
man explained.

As we drove, the man gave a tour to his eight-year-old son, Noah,
pointing out the longest bridge and then the longest tunnel in Israel.
"That's Efrat," the man said, referring to a controversial Jewish settlement.

As we neared Hebron the tension mounted. We stopped to pick up
hitchhiking soldiers, who stood in the aisles with their machine guns.
We pulled to a gate, and several women in front of me craned to watch.
Hebron has been a flashpoint for nearly a century. One of the few spots
to have an almost continuous Jewish presence since 1540, Hebron
enjoyed largely peaceful relations until 1929, when local Arabs rioted,
killed sixty Jews, and wounded fifty more. Banished for decades, Jews
began returning to the nearby town of Kiryat Arba after the Six-Day
War in 1967. Eventually a few brazen settlers moved into the city itself
to be near the Tomb of the Patriarchs, the burial home to Abraham,
Isaac, and Jacob, along with Sarah and Isaac's wife, Rebekah. Rachel,
Jacob's wife, died on her way to Hebron and was buried outside
Jerusalem.

In 1980, a local Jewish high school student was murdered in Hebron,
and later eight more were shot from a building. Jewish settlers swarmed
the neighborhood, seeking retaliation. That began a cycle of murder
and revenge that only worsened after the 1993 Oslo Peace Accords,
which gave the Palestinians control of the city. Twenty percent was
reserved for Jews, an area the size of a few city blocks. The fifty-five
families who occupy the Jewish quarter today are like the core of one of
those stackable Russian dolls: a Jewish enclave surrounded by an Arab
city; an Arab city surrounded by the Occupied West Bank; the West
Bank surrounded by the Jewish State; the Jewish State surrounded by

the Arab World; the Arab World surrounded by the West. Who has the upper hand; who is more vulnerable? It's not that the answer is complicated. There simply is no answer.

We traveled through eight checkpoints in the next ten minutes; the watchtowers grew taller. We were descending through the Arab body of town into the Jewish heart. A boy across from me, no more than thirteen, changed the prayer tape in his Walkman and continued nodding, oblivious to the stress. Outside, at one of the checkpoints, a soldier focused the scope on his sniper's rifle. He was wearing a helmet with a visor that shielded his face from the sun, but he appeared to be not much older than Noah, who continued answering questions from his father.

"And do you know why we're coming here?" the father asked.

"Because Abraham is buried here," the boy said, jubilantly.

"That's right," his father said.

"He's the father of the Jews," Noah added.

"That's right," his father said. "And Isaac's buried here, too. Do you know Isaac?"

The boy acted puzzled for a second. "The uncle of the Jews?"

Even around the bus depot, the streets were clogged. Arab vendors pushed forward hawking raisins, dried apricots, pink velour rugs, and every electronic gadget imaginable, from portable microphones to blenders. Hello? Hello! Shalom! *Bevakahsha!* Up a small hill, an even greater throng lined the plaza. Tens of thousands crammed into the mile or so in front of the tomb, an imposing, four-story limestone building on top of the burial caves that looks like a cross between an Ottoman fortress and a college gymnasium. Even a cannonball could not penetrate these walls.

Out in front, dozens of Orthodox Jewish vendors vied for attention. One foldout table overflowed with books offering guidance from long-bearded rabbis. Another sold jigsaw puzzles with pictures of the Western Wall. Four boys wearing sandals, white shirts, and *talit,* traditional Jewish prayer shawls, danced on the sidewalk, here a do-si-do, there a hora, occasionally clicking their heels like square dancers. The scene looked like the opening number from *Fiddler on the Roof*. There were bumper stickers, blankets, places to wash, and everywhere boys holding plastic canisters, which they shook and asked for contributions for various charities. All around dozens of loudspeakers screamed slogans, prayers, and testimonials of salvation. "Are you Jewish?" someone asked, tugging at my arm. "Are you Jewish?" Another spun me around. In months of traveling around the Middle East, I was never asked that question more than during my trip to Hebron.

"Are you Jewish?" a woman behind a table cried. Her station was scattered with boxes wrapped in aluminum foil and copies of a pamphlet, *L'Chaim,* "The Weekly Publication for Every Jewish Person, Dedicated to the Memory of Rebbitzin Chaya Mushka Schneerson."

When I said yes, she asked me for my favorite Hebrew letter. There are 304,000 characters in the Torah, she said, and the Lubavitch movement was making a Bible with each character assigned to a different person. She also asked for my mother's name. "Is she Jewish?" she said, a not-so-subtle way of discerning whether I was a "true" Jew. I said yes and gave her several more names. "God bless you," she said.

Closer to the cave I stopped by a booth that sold photographs of Rebbe Schneerson. The man behind the table, a Frenchman named Michel, claimed to be the official photographer of the movement. I asked him why there were so many Lubavitchers in Hebron today.

"We come here to celebrate," he said. "We come every year. This is where our relatives are buried."

"How does this compare to the Western Wall?"

"The Western Wall has less meaning for me than this. The Wall is a physical thing. These are actual people. We believe that Abraham, Isaac, and Jacob are not just buried here, we believe they're still alive." He told me the story of someone who had lost a sword, went inside a cave to look for it, and encountered Abraham.

"The patriarchs are still alive," I said, "or their spirit is still alive?"

"They are alive."

"And what will you ask them for?"

"Whatever we need. We ask, and they provide. Somebody wants to get married. Somebody is going to have a child. I will ask for peace. We need peace more than anything."

I walked up another hill and merged with several thousand people squeezed in line behind a bank of metal detectors. We were waiting to enter one of the most sacred spots in Judaism, the first place Abraham purchases a spot in the Promised Land and thus starts to claim his covenant.

In Genesis 23, following the birth of Isaac and Abraham's aborted sacrifice of him, events that Avner and I would come to later, the Bible reports that Sarah, at the age of 127, dies in "Kiryat Arba"—the city of Arba—"now Hebron, in the land of Canaan." Abraham mourns and bewails her. Then he rises from beside his deceased wife and says to the local residents, "I am a resident alien among you; sell me a burial site among you, that I may remove my dead for burial." The locals, whom the Bible identifies as Hittites, another migrant people from Mesopotamia, warmly receive the idea. "Hear us, my lord," they say to Abraham. "You are the elect of God among us. Bury your dead in the choicest of our burial places." Abraham then offers to buy the cave of Machpelah, on the land of Ephron, son of Zohar. Ephron proposes to donate the land, but Abraham insists, ultimately paying four hundred shekels of silver, "the going merchants' rate." He then buries Sarah on the site.

The fortress that I was about to enter is said to exist on the exact spot where Abraham buried Sarah. It was built two thousand years ago, perhaps by Herod the Great. Despite its scale, the building uses no mortar. Inside, it contains a courtyard and two colonnades containing memorials to Abraham, Sarah, and Jacob. The memorials to Isaac and Rebekah are in an adjacent room. The burial caves themselves are hidden beneath a marble floor. After the Six-Day War, Moshe Dayan, the flamboyant military commander and amateur archaeologist, sneaked in one night and lowered a twelve-year-old girl down a narrow hole to look for the caves. She found a long corridor and a blocked entrance. Later, Jews again entered in the middle of the night, removed a Muslim prayer rug, and scouted the caves, finding bones and earthenware from the first millennium B.C.E. These shed little light on the patriarchs, but do indicate that the cave was a holy site as early as three thousand years ago.

Tension surrounding the tombs flared dramatically in 1994 when Baruch Goldstein, an American Jewish settler, entered on the last day of the Muslim holy month of Ramadan and gunned down twenty-nine Palestinians, before being beaten to death. Thirty more Palestinians died in riots that followed. Since then, Jews have been limited to half of the facility—the one including the tombs of Abraham, Sarah, and Jacob. Muslims have the other half. Each side gets unlimited access on ten days a year. Today was one of the Jewish days, which accounted for the thousands waiting by the metal detectors. After the first bank, there was a second, where visitors were asked if they had weapons, video equipment, plastic knives, even compacts for makeup. Compacts? "It could have a mirror," the guard said. "Crack a mirror, it becomes a weapon."

Inside, the crowd was almost overbearing, spilling through a maze of small rooms, larger rooms, spiral staircases, and impromptu prayer circles. The atmosphere was as fervid as a medieval cathedral on pilgrimage day. In the smaller rooms, chairs were huddled and worshipers crowded in casual exchange. The covered courtyard was even more intense. In front of each shrine, men nodded in prayer, swaying in unison, but chanting in isolation. Behind them stood scores of women, hiding their faces in their books and generally swaying in a circle instead of front to back. Well behind the worshipers, and by far the majority, were the families, hundreds of them, sitting on the floor, mothers tending their children, children scampering away. One woman was spooning her young son kernels of corn from a can.

I wandered from shrine to shrine, before arriving in the room dedicated to Isaac and Rebekah. There I saw Michel, the photographer I had met outside. We started talking when suddenly he interrupted himself, "Are you Jewish?" When I told him yes he asked why I wasn't wearing a *kippah*. I explained that I hadn't brought one and that they were out of temporary ones at the door. I continued my question. "But you need a *kippah*!" he exclaimed. I reached in my bag, pulled out a notebook, and ripped out a piece of paper. "How will you keep it on?" he asked. By this point several people were watching. "I'll hold it," I said. I did so and continued our conversation, but my pose was so awkward he quickly dismissed himself and went to pray somewhere else. I removed the piece of paper and walked toward the other side of the room; several more people hissed at me along the way. I returned the paper to my head. I could not remember feeling more naked—or chastened—as I slouched through the crowds toward the door.

Outside I walked the few steps through the crowded Arab market that splits the Jewish Quarter in two. Up above was a sign: THIS MARKET IS BUILT ON LAND STOLEN FROM THE JEWS. The central square of the Jewish Quarter is hardly bigger than a city block, with several limestone apartment buildings crowded around a playground. Overshadowing the quadrangle were three enormous water towers, like booster rockets on the space shuttle, with Israeli flags painted on the side.

"Sixty percent of our water comes from Arafat," a man watching his children explained. He had a salt-and-pepper beard and knitted *kippah*. "We have to check it for poison. Every week we get a backup shipment from Jerusalem."

David Wilder was a resident of Hebron. Born in New Jersey, he moved to Israel in the 1970s, married an Israeli, and came to nearby Kiryat Arba. Six months earlier, he, his wife, and their seven children moved into the disputed neighborhood.

"We had to think about it," he said. "My wife and I had been discussing various options, when one day a terrorist jumped into the bedroom of a sixty-three-year-old rabbi who lived here and killed him. That convinced us to move."

"Why that?"

"Because the whole act of terror is an attempt to push us out. They figure they kill enough people, eventually we'll get up and leave. The only way to counter that is to do the opposite. Actually, the major problem we have is that we don't have enough room. I'm not the only crazy one around here."

"And are you crazy?"

"You tell me. I don't think so. I think we're about as normal as any-body can possibly be."

"But you're choosing to put yourself into a tinderbox."

"We're here as representatives. We have to remember why the Jew-ish people live in the Land of Israel. David Ben-Gurion, Israel's first prime minister, when asked what his claim to the land was, held up the Bible. If we weren't here today, the Bible would have no meaning."

"So when you read the Bible, and you read about Abraham coming to Hebron, do you feel an attachment?"

"When we pray three times a day, we say in the beginning, 'The God of Abraham, the God of Isaac, the God of Jacob.' And when we stand here and realize, this is where they are, this is where they lived, this is where they've been for the last 3,700 years—it does something to a person. You're living in a city, and it's a city. It smells, it's dirty, but it's also very spiritual. And that's what keeps people here. The only way to live here is to have that spiritual pull that gives you energy to put up with what you have to put up with."

"Is that spiritual connection to the place, or the patriarchs?"

He thought for a second. "The connection is to God. He's the one who brought us here. Abraham didn't come here because he wanted to. He came here because God told him to come. And it's not just him. It's a history that runs from Abraham to David, who lived here for seven and a half years. Moses sent the spies, and they came to Hebron. Just the other day I held this jug in my hand. It was four thousand years old. And it was me. There is this chain that goes from four thousand years ago to today. How can you erase it? How can you say it doesn't exist? The fact that we can be here—and are here—means we are preserving it for my children and grandchildren and great-grandchildren. They should have access to it. It shouldn't be a place that once existed. It should be a place that always exists."

I took the bus back to Jerusalem that afternoon and a few days later hooked up with Avner to continue our trip south, to the region where

Abraham first put down roots. Following the destruction of Sodom and Gomorrah (and before Hebron), Abraham travels south to Gerar, where he meets King Abimelech. Echoing the earlier incident in Egypt, Abraham says that Sarah is his sister. Abimelech takes Sarah for himself, but is warned off by God. The king summons Abraham and asks why he told a lie. "I thought surely there is no fear of God in this place," Abraham says, "and they will kill me because of my wife." And besides, he says, she actually *is* his sister, since they have the same father (though different mothers). Abimelech, like the pharaoh, repents by giving Abraham sheep, oxen, and slaves, adding, "Here, my land is before you; settle wherever you please." Abraham prays to God, who rewards Abimelech with children.

God then rewards Sarah with a child as well. In Genesis 21, Isaac, the long-promised next generation, is born. "God has brought me laughter," Sarah says. While joyous, the presence of Isaac, whose name derives from a Near Eastern root meaning laughter and gaiety, actually confuses the issue of the patriarch's succession. Sarah recognizes this and responds with an action that would prove to be one of the most monumental in world history: expelling Hagar and Ishmael from their home. "Cast out that slave woman and her son," Sarah announces, "for the son of that slave shall not share in the inheritance with my son Isaac." Abraham is troubled by Sarah's action, but God comforts him. "Do not be distressed over the boy or your slave; whatever Sarah tells you, do as she says, for it is through Isaac that offspring shall be continued for you." As for Ishmael, God continues, "I will make a nation of him, too, for he is your seed." It's this line that Muslims cite as their claim to be one of God's chosen people, directly descended from Abraham.

The next morning Abraham gives Hagar some bread and water and sends her into the desert. When the water runs out, near Beer-sheba, Hagar leaves the teenage boy under a bush so she doesn't see him die, then bursts into tears. God opens her eyes and reveals a well, which she uses to give water to the boy. God stays with the boy until he grows up and marries.

Around that time, King Abimelech announces to Abraham, "God is with you in everything that you do," and the two sign a pact of peace—

ful relations. For a time this *pax Canaanica* stands, but eventually Abraham complains that Abimelech's men seized his well. Abimelech claims no knowledge of the act. Abraham sets aside seven lambs as an oath that he, in fact, did dig the well. The two make a covenant, calling the place Beer-sheba. *Beer* is the Hebrew word for well; *sheba* means both seven and oath. Abraham plants a tamarisk on the site in honor of the Lord.

By this point certain patterns in the Bible are becoming clear. For one, wells are crucial. In addition, there are repeated examples of tense relations among the patriarchs and local rulers in Canaan. Also, the story constantly has God repeat his promise to Abraham, in what appears to be an escalating manner: "I will give you this land," "I will give this land to you and your descendants," "I will give this land to you and your descendants, who will rule over the rest of the world." To help understand the roots of these patterns, Avner suggested we stop off in Beer-sheba to meet a colleague of his, one of the senior archaeologists in the Middle East.

Eliezer Oren lives in a spacious ranch house in a neighborhood lined with lemon trees and gated homes. He ushered us into his office, stacked with books and pending Ph.D. theses, and festooned with pennants from Harvard, NYU, and Penn. Above his desk was a silhouette, cut out of black paper, showing him as a Sherlock Holmes figure with a meerschaum pipe. With his bushy mustache and formal demeanor, he reminded me of stories I had read about the grand archaeologists of the past—Heinrich Schliemann, Leonard Woolley, Arthur Evans—sitting in the desert being served five-course meals on silver trays with crystal goblets.

"You have made a correct observation," he said when I asked about the importance of wells. "Water is the key to all life here. But more important, water symbolized attachment." Abraham, he explained, was not a pure nomad, one who wanders from place to place. Instead he was a pastoralist, one who wanders but returns regularly to a few places.

"That's why he came to Beer-sheba," Eliezer continued. "It's the edge of the desert, but there's water here. It's the same reason Beer-sheba was picked to be the hub of desert administration—by the King-dom of Israel and much later by the Turks. Modern Israel is doing the same thing. Such an important location is always a place of worship."

I asked him why God promised Abraham such a specific piece of land, and not the entire world.

"In ancient civilization, religion is not international," he said. "It does not cross boundaries. Religion is closely integrated with land. The god of Babylon is not the god of Egypt, the god of Hebron. It's only Judaism and later Christianity and Islam that made God universal."

"Why, then, is the relationship between God and man expressed in a contract?" I asked.

"Now why would this surprise you?" he said.

"It's very anthropomorphic. It's almost putting it in terms of a busi-ness relationship, yet it's the most intangible of relationships. Also, it's not a relationship of equals."

"To start with, from all the records we know, in the ancient Near East the relationship between gods and man is always contractual. Every single one of them: the Hittites, the Mesopotamians, the Assyrians. And a contract is binding. Every partner has its obligation. If man behaves in a certain way, then he assures the prosperity of his family, his tribe. The gods, meanwhile, must make it rain and make the land bear fruit. In this respect, the Bible is beautifully embedded in its surroundings. If the relationship was not codified through a contract, I, myself, would be very worried that the Bible was not part and parcel of the ancient Near East. Finding so many contracts assures me that the Bible, indeed, is an accurate account."

"So would rival groups accept these contracts?"

"Usually not. The contract is between you and your god. Other people have their gods. The struggle between cities is over hegemony. To put it in the terms of children, 'My god is stronger than your god.' That's why a contract is so important. It guarantees that a relationship has a history, continuity. My father had a contract with God, so I have it, too. And you don't just sign it, you read it out loud. You pronounce it. Abraham renews the contract, as does Isaac, Jacob, Joseph, and

Moses. It's like renewing your driver's license. In Mari, up in Syria, we actually found similar contracts written down. We've finally proved it archaeologically."

"So let me ask you," I said. We'd been sitting for close to an hour now and would soon be overstaying our welcome. "Is the archaeological research you're doing enhancing your ability to believe that the stories in the Bible might have happened, or undermining it?"

"I'm going through a certain transformation," Eliezer said. "When I was younger, I was in my rebellious phase. In my lectures, I kept saying that since we don't have evidence, these stories did not take place. That goes for the patriarchs, the Exodus. The older I get, perhaps I get more stupid. But I feel that my archaeological experience only enhances my understanding that even if I cannot relate a certain event, or personality, in the Bible with a specific archaeological stratum, it doesn't matter. At the end of the day, the question is this: Is the Bible unusual for its time and place? And the answer is: It's not. It's part of it. Dating is becoming secondary in my opinion. When I'm digging here, I'm digging with Abraham."

"So what effect has that had on your faith?" I asked.

"Those are different camps," he said. "But I can tell you this: today I treat the Bible with much more respect."

"Can you give it a grade, in terms of archaeological accuracy?"

For the first time all morning he grinned. "A plus plus."

We said good-bye and drove the few minutes to Tel Sheba, the ancient site. Overlooking the Negev, the site had all the ingredients of well-preserved tels in Israel, a guard gate, a green map for tourists, an ice cream stand, and knee-high remains of mud brick and limestone. There is a familiar, almost elusive geography to these places. To be blunt: There's little to see. But in the same way that people who do crossword puzzles learn the keys that unlock those blank squares, the frequent visitor to archaeological sites begins to see through the blank spaces to the thriving story lying just underneath. And what better story than the

great ages of Palestine—the patriarchs, the kingdom of Judah, the conquest by Rome.

Tel Sheba is a small site, around five acres, or one-tenth the size of
Tel Dan. Though the biblical events likely took place a few miles away,
under the modern city, the tel contains buildings from the Iron Age,
beginning in the tenth century B.C.E. According to Avner, who perked
up like a kid returning home as we entered the gates, the city was probably a military headquarters for the kingdom of Judah, starting around
926 B.C.E., with limited civilian population.

The tel's most notable feature is a well, located just outside the city
gate. The water is collected from an underground river, and as we
arrived, one of Avner's former students was demonstrating the process
for a group of visitors. The well poses a curious question. Common
sense would dictate that it be inside the gate for security reasons, but it's
on the outside. Avner's explanation was that even in the early first millennium B.C.E., centuries before the Bible was written down (and a
thousand years after Abraham likely lived), Beer-sheba was already
known as the place of Abraham's well. Pilgrims visiting the site would
have needed protection, which would explain why there was a military
base nearby. If he's correct, Beer-sheba would have been one of the
world's first tourist attractions, a full millennium before people came to
the Holy Land looking for pieces of Jesus' cross. Two thousand years
later, it seems safe to say that the Bible, besides its ability to inspire piety
and devotion, has also prompted more tourism than any other work in
history.

We wandered inside the gate where we caught sight of a small
group of visitors in their forties. Approaching, we saw that one of the
men, in a beard and T-shirt, had a map spread out on one of the ancient
altars. "I had this vision," the man said, in English. "I saw a line. Abraham
entered the country from the north—" He opened a Bible and began
turning pages. "He went to Shechem, then Bethel, then Hebron, then
he came here, to Beer-sheba." Having satisfied the group that they were
in the right place, the man retrieved a shofar, a long, curly ram's horn,
polished smooth. The man reared back and blew the horn with jet-

engine intensity, eliciting a screechy plaint. The others held hands and prayed.

At this point, a thin man with blue Dockers and a blue-and-white-striped button-down shirt stepped into the center of the circle. The leader—a preacher, a rabbi, a guru?—filled a Dannon strawberry yogurt carton with bottled water and held it in his right hand as if he were about to pitch a baseball side-armed. He rested his left hand on the thin man's head, said a quick prayer, and with a swell of force that seemed to draw strength from the three thousand years of history beneath his feet, slammed the carton into the man's abdomen, creating a powerful splash, eliciting deep, mournful moans from the small congregation, and from the man himself, prompting a gasping cry: "Torah! Torah! Hallelujah!! Praise, Jesus. I am found!"

At first tentative, but fascinated, I watched from the narrow walkway. Within minutes, though, one of the women approached me. "I don't know who you are," she said. "But God has sent you." She invited me to join them. I asked what religion this ceremony was. "We're all believers," she said. "He who accepts the Messiah is circumcised in the heart." The man being blessed, John Powell, stepped forward and explained. He was an American, a Gentile, he said. He had found Jesus Christ as his savior when he was eighteen and for years studied the Bible and spread the word of God. In his twenties he found a passage in Second Corinthians, which indicated to him that the Church had become too removed from its Jewish roots and had forgotten the meaning of the seven feasts, the seven pieces of furniture in the Temple, the seven days of Creation. "The Spirit gives life through symbols," he said. He vowed to return to the Old Testament and moved to Kissimmee, Florida, near Disney World, to start a new mission.

As he was preparing to move, a friend in Massachusetts had a vision of him peering into a well. "This well was not being used," he said, "but I put a bucket in and pulled out fresh water, pure water. The people gathered around thought they had seen a miracle." He turned to John 4, where Jesus comes upon Jacob's well near Shechem, and decided to come to Israel. After arriving, he learned that visiting Shechem would be unsafe. "The Lord took me back to Genesis," he said. "To chapter 26, where Isaac builds a well in Beer-sheba. It's the same well that Abraham had dug, though it had been filled in by the Philistines. And I realized: This was the well that was not being used. I saw the connection. I felt the spiritual pull between my work and Beer-sheba." With some friends he met in Jerusalem, he decided to come here and sanctify his vision.

At this point John's wife, Starr, joined him in the center. She was wearing a peach-colored turtleneck. The leader, Luke, began to fill the yogurt cup with water. John was concerned that the cup had become dented and used his finger to unpucker the dent to ensure that his wife had the same amount of water. Once again Luke cocked his arm, summoned the Lord, and slammed the cup into Starr's stomach, lifting her off the ground in the process. Then he flung water onto her face. It was chilly atop the tel, the breeze was blowing. But it didn't matter. Starr was crying now, as was half the group. "From this day forth you will come out of the Land of Israel," Luke said. A woman, Barb, stepped forward with a *talit* made of white silk with blue stripes. Thirteen-year-old boys receive these shawls when they become men, she explained. She wrapped it around John's shoulders and recited the Wayfarer's Prayer, the same one I heard on the bus to Hebron. When she finished she asked John if he owned a *talit*. He shook his head. "Well, you do now," she said. John leapt like a boy. "Wow!" he said. "Glory be! Somebody asked me the other day if I wanted to buy one, and I didn't know which one was right. Thank you. Hallelujah! Praise Jesus."

Barb and several others then proceeded to turn the *talit* into a wedding canopy and invited John and Starr to repeat their vows. The entire episode was astounding not only in its raw emotion, but also in its pandemic religious inclusion—part baptism, part Bar Mitzvah, part wedding, part rebirth. I was struck by the idea that John and I, from different backgrounds, had come to this place for the same reason: It was in the Bible, the patriarchs had passed here, there was meaning in this soil.

After the ceremony, Barb retrieved a tiny vial of margarine-colored oil. She dabbed some on John's forehead, then Starr's. It smelled of lilac. "Father, we come to you in the name of Jesus," Barb said, crying. "You can put some right on my eyelids," John said, but she resisted. "I don't know what's in this, so I better not." "No, I beseech you," he said, and she obeyed. Finally, in her emotion, Barb fell to her knees. John and Starr were wearing sandals, and Barb began reenacting the last moments of Jesus' life, spreading oil on John's toes. A general sobbing ensued, and husband and wife collapsed to the sandy ground in a giant exhale of prayer, now, at last, reconnected to the dust of eternity, which more than water, oil, or the sound of the shofar, had the ability to give them purpose to their lives. "God bless," they muttered. "God bless. God bless."

We left Beer-sheba a few minutes later and turned west for the hour-long drive toward Gerar, our last stop of the day. Heading now along the border of the Negev I began to realize how markedly the light shifts in Israel. In the north, which is hilly, the light is often refracted by a natural filter of trees, lakes, mist, and flowers. In the central mountains, with its mix of settlements, highways, and factories, the sun is brighter. In the south, with its open, sandy plains, the light is despotic. On this day, the sun was so big and relentless it threatened to burn a path right through our skin.

Perhaps because of this change in climate, the cities along the desert edge often feel like outposts, bulwarks against the wilderness. Gerar, in particular, feels this way: Canaan's last stand. Identified with Tel Haror, near Gaza, Gerar has a certain middling stature: It's bigger than Beer-sheba, smaller than Hatzor. Not a major city, but not a minor one, either. One archaeologist I know calls it *Tel Mechukmak,* Hebrew slang for ugly-duckling tel. In antiquity, Gerar was a place for wandering pastoralists to test their strength. For the patriarchs, camping beside Gerar was like opening out of town, a warm-up for the major leagues.

At first glance, the site doesn't help its own cause. For starters, it's difficult to find. There is no public face, no welcome center, no buses filled with schoolkids. Even Avner had to double- and triple-check his map. It's also hillier than many tels, and more relaxed. In the 1950s the Jewish National Fund, not realizing the mound was an ancient site, covered it with eucalyptus trees, giving it the feel of a city park. The lower area is even decked out with playground equipment. We parked and hiked to an abandoned mosque in the upper city, draped in green and white banners. Many Islamic countries use green in their flags, Avner noted—Libya, Iran, Iraq, Saudi Arabia—because to bedouin of the desert, green symbolizes life.

On the lower level we roamed the city's elaborate earthen ramparts, which were designed to make attackers believe the city was stronger than it actually was. The reason for the deception is that around 1800 B.C.E. so many pastoralists were flocking to Gerar that the city was no longer able to contain them and the ramparts were designed to keep them away. It's this background that the patriarchal stories reflect.

Gerar is first mentioned in Genesis 20, when Abraham has his encounter with Abimelech. It pops up later in a similar role with Isaac. Following the death of Sarah, Abraham instructs his servant to travel back to Harran to get a wife for his son. Abraham makes the servant swear not to take a wife for Isaac "from the daughters of the Canaanites." The servant does as instructed, and soon arrives at a well in Harran, where he meets Rebekah, a beautiful maiden and a virgin, who he decides is perfect. The servant returns to Rebekah's house and meets Laban, who consents to his sister's betrothal, saying, "The matter was decreed by the Lord."

Back in the Negev, Rebekah meets Isaac for the first time, and the two marry. "Isaac loved her," the text says, "and thus found comfort after his mother's death." At this point, Abraham, now 175 years old, dies and is buried in the Cave of the Patriarchs. Though he had six children from a subsequent wife, as well as Ishmael, Abraham wills all he owns to Isaac. Most important, Isaac inherits Abraham's most precious possession, the covenant from God that says the family's descendants will someday rule Canaan.

Like his father, though, Isaac is initially unable to conceive an heir. Rebekah is barren. Isaac pleads with the Lord on her behalf, and she conceives twins, Esau and Jacob, who struggle inside her. The issue of lineage, which was already clouded by the split with Ishmael, now seems more dicey than ever. "Two nations are in your womb," God explains, "two separate people shall issue from your body; one people shall be mightier than the other, and the older shall serve the younger." Once again, the younger son, in this case, Jacob, is tapped for posterity. Unlike Isaac, who earns his status by virtue of being born to Abraham's wife, Jacob earns his by force. There's almost something proto-Darwinian in this dictate: The stronger will inherit the land.

This theme of the patriarchs' growing strength is echoed in the story of Isaac in Gerar, which begins in Genesis 26. A famine strikes Canaan, and God tells Isaac not to go to Egypt, as his father had done, but to stay in Gerar. In another echo of Abraham, the men of Gerar ask about Isaac's wife. Isaac, fearing that the beauty of his wife will endanger her, says Rebekah is his sister. Once again, Abimelech realizes the ruse and warns his men not to touch her. Isaac and his family then settle in the area and begin to cultivate. "And the man became great, and grew more and more until he became very great," the text says. "And he had possessions of flocks, and possessions of herds, and a great household; and the Philistines envied him."

Though the use of the Philistines here refers to a later population and is considered an anachronism, everything else is accurate, Avner said. "There are fields," he noted. "Though we're on the edge of the Negev, there is arable land."

What happens next, though, is crucial. Responding to the envy of his people, Abimelech asks Isaac to leave Gerar: "Go away from us, for you have become mightier than we!" Isaac flees to Beer-sheba, and Abimelech eventually sues for peace.

"So let me get this straight," I said. We had sought relief on a shady spot on the embankment and were sitting under a willow tree. "Abraham is not threatening to Abimelech in Genesis 20. He shows up; he's a big leader. He's strong enough for Abimelech to take him seriously."

"Right."

"But Abraham is not a danger."

"Correct."

"Abimelech invites him to live wherever he wants. But by the time Isaac comes, in Genesis 26, something has happened to make him threatening."

"Okay . . ."

"But what happened to make him threatening?" I asked.

"It says Isaac became 'bigger and bigger.'"

"And what about Jacob?"

"He never spent much time in this area. He mostly lived in the north, near Hatzor."

"What's the significance of that?"

"Well, Hatzor was the strongest city," Avner said. "He must have felt pretty strong to go there."

"And maybe that's the point," I said. "There's this whole geopolitical side of the story. This one man, Abraham, is in the process of becoming a people. By putting him peacefully in Gerar, then putting Isaac here as a threat, then moving Jacob to Hatzor. The Bible offers clues about their rise to power."

"But remember, it's still the power of God."

"But the will of God cannot be implemented unless his chosen people are strong enough to implement it, which they won't be until after Moses. That's the whole point of the Exodus, isn't it? The people weren't spiritually ready to conquer Canaan. So it's not just power, it's enlightened power. And that process takes a big leap forward here, in Gerar."

We sat quietly for a few minutes absorbing the exchange. I felt an exhilaration—and a security—I hadn't felt before in our conversations, a feeling that I was more connected to the soil. Minutes later (though it seemed like an hour), Avner touched me on the shoulder. "Shall we go?" Walking back toward the car, I felt the shock of return, as if waking from a daydream. The absence of any people—any development—had made it so easy to disappear into the past that I hadn't even realized it was happening. Was this evidence that I was finding it easier to enter the stories? Sitting at the site, I had no armor of distance to separate me from the text. Even the minor events that take place in Gerar had revealed another layer of meaning. It was as if the places, not just the characters, wanted to speak: "See, we could feel the Israelites growing. We could tell by the size of their flocks, by how much food they ate, how much water they drank. We knew sooner than any person." The land, as I was seeing, has its own story to tell. All you had to do was put your ear to the ground, and listen.

A few days later, Avner and I met at dawn for one encounter I had looked forward to since we began: following the path that Abraham took the morning he went to sacrifice Isaac, an event referred to in Hebrew as akedah, the binding. The sun was barely visible through the haze above the Mount of Olives when we arrived at the Promenade in West Jerusalem overlooking the Old City. It was here, more than a year earlier, that I had first considered retracing the Bible. Since Abraham and Isaac would have passed this spot on their way north from Beer-sheba to Mount Moriah, an event described in Genesis 22, we decided to walk the several miles from here to what sits on Moriah today, the Temple Mount.

The Promenade was almost deserted on this morning, except for a few strollers. Part of no-man's-land between 1948 and 1967, the site is now a popular park, landscaped with ferns, pines, rosemary, and sage. Lovers gather here at night, kite fliers in the afternoon. A few joggers passed us in a blur. "How do they find the time for that?" Avner wondered, rubbing his Buddha belly.

We zipped up our knapsacks and set off down the slope. Jerusalem is a geographic anomaly in the Middle East, a hilly, tree-shrouded city in the central elevations of Palestine that became holy three thousand years ago and remains holy for a third of the world. As a Jewish sage put it in the first century C.E., "The world is like a human eye. The white is the ocean that girds the earth, the iris is the earth upon which we dwell, the pupil is Jerusalem, and the image therein is the Temple of the Lord." Jerusalem today has some of the best traits of other cities—hills like Rome, stone like Athens; some of the worst traits of others—traffic like Bangkok, cramped housing like Tokyo; and light like no other place on earth. In the mornings and evenings Jerusalem is bathed in the most incandescent sunlight, an effusion of gold dust that flirts with the pink highlights of Jerusalem stone, winks off the polished roof of the Dome of the Rock, and seduces anyone within its gaze. If sunlight has rejuvenating qualities, Jerusalemites probably benefit most. Of course, they need it more than most, since the City of David and Solomon is also the place of Mohammed's ascension to heaven and the site of Jesus' resurrection—all of which make one of the world's most beautiful cities also one of its most uptight.

For natives, Jerusalem never loses its embrace. Avner was born into a line stretching back to the early nineteenth century. His mother, Leah, was what Avner called a "Mayflower Israeli," one of the earliest Jewish families. Avner's father, Yair, was born in Tel Aviv and grew up in the Galilee, near Tel Dan. As a sixteen-year-old boy, Yair went to work in the Dead Sea mineral plants and secretly traveled on weekends by bicycle throughout Jordan (then called Transjordan) buying up weapons once used by Lawrence of Arabia for use in the Jewish defense movement. When he later moved to Jerusalem during the War of Independence, he was issued a rifle with a broken handle inscribed with an English name. He recognized it as one of the weapons he had procured. "These were weapons the Arabs used to gain independence from the Turks," he recalled later when I went to visit him in his nursing home. "Now the Jews were using them to gain independence from the Arabs."

Yair was a jolly, voluble man, with a belly considerably larger than his son's and a twinkle just as bright. He had written several volumes of memoirs and favored an expansive, at times commanding, conversational style that may have contributed to his son's considerable learning, but probably encouraged his diffidence as well. Yair left the army in 1954 and began working as an electrical engineer. He and his wife already had two children: Avner, born in 1944, and Noa, born in 1949. Avner was a bright kid, a math and astronomy whiz, who never did his homework and was expelled from the most prestigious school in town. "He didn't finish one book," Yair said. "But he did well on exams!" On weekends, Yair would lead Avner and Noa on biblical tours of the city. "But I didn't need to carry the text," Yair said. "When I wanted to quote something, I knew it by heart. Every single word. I didn't have to look it up, as you do."

For all his love of the Bible, Yair Goren was passionately antireligious. He was the charter member of a group called the League for the Prevention of Religious Coercion, which was designed to preserve the rights of secular Israelis to eat nonkosher meat and drive on Shabbat. Avner, though, had other ideas; he felt drawn to the tradition. "I thought it was a part of me," he said. "I wanted to know more." When Avner announced his desire to have a Bar Mitzvah, Yair tried to dissuade him. On the day of the event, his mother attended proudly; his father stayed at home. "Didn't anyone tell him he should go?" I asked Avner. "Oh, no," he said. "My father's very stubborn. I'm nothing compared to him."

I asked Yair why such an antireligious man felt so attached to the Bible. "When I was about twelve years old, I loved, simply loved, literature," he said. "And I used to read poetry. One day I read a passage from Isaiah, chapter 5." He began quoting from memory. "Now let me sing to my Beloved a song of my Beloved regarding His vineyard: My Beloved has a vineyard on a very fruitful hill. He dug it up and cleared out its stones, and planted it with the choicest vines. . . ." The quote continued for another three verses. "It was wonderful," Yair noted, "simply wonderful! And ever since then, near my bed, was the Bible."

And what about his walks? What did Yair learn from them?

"When you read the Bible in your room, it contains very nice pieces of literature," he said. "But when you do what you're doing now, when you read the Bible in Shechem, in Hebron, you say, 'Here it is!' And you feel connected to a story in a different way. You feel you belong."

"So do you think Avner learned that lesson?"

"Everything Avner learned about the Bible he learned from me!" Yair boasted. "As for other subjects"—he threw up his arms in mock disgust—"I can't be responsible for them."

"But he's my teacher," I said. "Do I have an inferior teacher?"

Suddenly Yair grew serious. "Avner is the best teacher I have known in my life."

"But how can a bad student be a good teacher?"

Now he became bombastic again. "Only bad students make good teachers!"

Avner and I had been hiking for almost an hour when we arrived at the first of three hills we had to surmount, Abu Tour, a stately, tree-lined neighborhood mixed with Arabs and Jews. I asked if the threat of conflict had bothered him as a child. "There was always the mystery of having the division," he said. "Particularly with the Old City in Jordanian hands. There were these grand walls, hiding this great place. I dreamed about the *kotel*"—the Hebrew term for the Western Wall—"and the Temple Mount."

"Did you ever see the *kotel*?"

"My father used to take us to this place not far from the Promenade. He said if we looked real hard we could see it. As a matter of fact, I could never identify it. But I didn't tell him."

We came to a stop on the far side of Abu Tour. Up above us, within the Old City, was the Dormition Abbey, a turreted German church built on the spot where Mary, in lieu of dying, is said to have fallen into eternal sleep. Looking down, I spotted a plaque at the base of an almond tree. "And the Lord said unto Abraham, 'Lift up thine eyes, and look from the place where thou art, northward and southward and eastward and westward.' " I smiled at the coincidence, until Avner pointed out that the passage was not from Genesis 22, when Abraham brings Isaac to Moriah, but Genesis 13, when he's looking at Mount Sodom, one hundred miles to the south. Like father, like son.

Below our feet lay a steep descent into the Hinnom Valley, one of several gorges surrounding Old Jerusalem. In a story often recalled for tourists, in 1948 the Israeli Army secretly erected a cable across the valley to ferry supplies to a small garrison on Mount Zion. The army would lower the cable during the day and raise it at night. The author of the idea was Yair Goren. "He's still upset that few people know he did it," Avner said. In the 1980s, French aerialist Philippe Petit stretched a highwire across the same spot and walked across without a net. Pausing in the middle, he reached into his pocket and released a dove.

We started down the mountain, passing some hollow tombs and a dead horse, before arriving in the Arab village of Silwan. The Ottoman splendor of Abu Tour gave way to tin-roofed poverty and crumbling concrete alleys. A cock crowed. From here the climb was straight up, past the Gihon Spring, to the City of David, the earliest boundaries of

Jerusalem. In time our knees began to strain and we stopped to buy some orange juice and Arab bread. To the east was the Valley of Kidron, where the Bible says judgment will be rendered on resurrection day. Muslims believe that on that day, Mohammed will sit under the Dome of the Rock, Jesus will sit on the Mount of Olives, and a wire will be stretched from one to the other. All humankind will walk across the wire; the righteous will reach the other side; the rest will drop into the valley and perish. No matter what religion, it seems, the tightrope is the route to eternity.

By nine o'clock we neared the base of the Temple, about a hundred yards higher than the City of David. The solemn white walls were visible now, with caper bushes poking out of the cracks like green icing dripping from between layers of a cake. A few palm trees waved at the sky. Our pace quickened. I could see Avner's body come alive with a sense of direction, and purpose.

Considering his childhood of biblical walks, it might have seemed inevitable that Avner would embrace archaeology after finishing high school. But he was more interested in math and philosophy. What changed his mind was a rare moment of peace in Israel in the early 1960s during which time the country rallied around archaeology as a way to link contemporary Jews with their forebears. While serving in the army, Avner was assigned to a tank brigade in the Negev and spent his weekend volunteering on one of the most storied digs of the century, Yigal Yadin's excavation at Masada. "It was a wonderful time," Avner remembered. "People came from all over the world. It was the first excavation that evoked strong patriotic feelings about Israel." At the end of his service, a week before enrolling at Hebrew University, he changed his registration from mathematics to archaeology. Three years later he enrolled in graduate school.

The connection between archaeology and patriotism reached its zenith around this time. In June 1967, Avner, along with millions, listened on the radio as Moshe Dayan led the first Israeli troops into the Old City, finally bringing the monuments of Jewish history into the State of Israel. Two days later Avner made the trip himself, walking from the Jaffa Gate through the scarred streets, and finally arriving at the sacred site his father had always wanted him to see.

"At first I cried a lot," he said. "Then I went up and touched it. I knew everything about it, from years and years of studying. But now, at last, I could feel it."

A few months later, Avraham Biran, then the head of the Israeli Department of Antiquities, came to see Avner and asked if he would become chief archaeologist of the Sinai, which Israel had also just seized. "It took me a few seconds to catch my breath," Avner said. "Then I told him, 'Yes!' "

It was late morning by the time we passed through the Dung Gate and joined the line of visitors waiting to climb up to the Temple Mount. Down below, at the Western Wall, worshipers genuflected in black-hatted piety, their shoulders wrapped in *talit*. As we neared the metal detectors, Avner began rifling through his knapsack, nodding for me to look away as he slipped something into his coat pocket. At the security station, the guard patted my bag. "Bible?" he asked gruffly. Suddenly I realized what Avner had been doing. My throat caught. Would the guard notice a translation? "No, sir," I said. He waved me through.

"What was *that* about?" I said to Avner.

"It's illegal to bring Bibles to the Temple Mount. They're worried about fanatics."

"Seems awfully ironic," I said. "This place is here because of Abraham. But if he showed up with a copy of his own story they wouldn't let him in."

"Welcome to the Middle East."

We stepped through the archway and into the stone piazza. More than thirty-five acres, the park was calm this morning, with visitors wandering among trees, washing in spigots, and kneeling in shoeless prayer. Children scampered everywhere. The Temple Mount is perhaps the world's most notorious shrine to the tension between faith and family. In Genesis 22, soon after Abraham's encounter with Abimelech in

Gerar, God suddenly decides to put Abraham "to the test." "Take your
son," God says, "your favored one, Isaac, whom you love, and go to the
land of Moriah, and offer him there as a burnt offering on one of the
heights which I will point out to you." The following morning, Abraham splits wood for the offering, takes his son and two servants, and sets
out. On the third day he looks up and sees the place from afar. The spot
from which he views his destination is believed to correspond to the
Promenade. From there, Abraham sets out alone with the boy.

The exact location where they visit, "the land of Moriah," is not
known. When David arrived in Jerusalem in the tenth century B.C.E.,
almost a full millennium after Abraham would have been there, he purchased the rock atop the highest hill in the city, claiming it was Moriah.
It was David's son Solomon who built the first temple in 970 B.C.E.
After Nebuchadnezzar destroyed it in 586, a second temple was erected
between 525 and 515. "It was so much smaller," Avner said, "that when
people who had known the First Temple saw it they burst into tears."
Herod enlarged the facility in the first century B.C.E., but the Romans
burned the entire compound to the ground in 70 C.E.

The site remained in ruins until Arab caliph Omar Ibn-Khatib conquered Jerusalem in 638. According to the Koran, Arabs also trace their
roots to Abraham, through Ishmael, but the two books differ, with the
Koran implying Abraham went to sacrifice Ishmael, not Isaac, and did so
in Mecca. In the seventh century, Islam was still a young religion, anxious to portray itself as the heir to Judaism and Christianity. Omar asked
an aide, a converted Jew, where he should build a shrine to Mohammed.
The aide recommended a spot on the northern side of the mount, so
that Muslims praying south toward Mecca would include the site of the
Temple in their obeisance. Later, tradition arose that the shrine was built
over the spot where Mohammed ascended to heaven.

On our way toward the Dome of the Rock, we ran into a friend of
Avner's, a Muslim guide. "The main reason this building is here is
Prophet Mohammed," he said. "But Muslims believe that Jesus, Moses,
Solomon, even Abraham were all prophets of Allah. So there is a con-
tinuation. This is a spot where people come to meet God." He excused
himself and we went inside the mosque.

The Dome of the Rock is the jewel of Islamic architecture, "one of the most fantastic buildings on earth," as Avner put it. The mosque's eight-sided base is covered in blue Persian tiles the color of sapphires; its round top is coated in 24-karat gold. Inside, carpets line the floor, where worshipers kneel in prayer; at the center is a giant rock, the peak of the mountain. Tradition holds that when Mohammed rose from this spot, the rock tried to follow. It failed, but created an underground cave. Today the cave is lined with Plexiglas to prevent pilgrims from chipping off a piece of history.

Outside we walked to the edge of the plaza, where two women in orange Eisenegger windbreakers asked me to take their picture. Rosemarie and Sandy, both in their forties, were visiting from Norfolk, England, volunteering at an orphanage. This was their fifth trip in fifteen months. "We just come when the Lord tells us to come," Rosemarie said.

"And why come to the Temple Mount?"

"This belongs to Jesus," she said. "And they've got this abomination standing here. We came to claim this back for the Lord."

Rosemarie began pointing out all the spots where Jesus walked during his last days on earth, including the garden of Gethsemane, where he prayed; a spot on the Temple Mount where he met Pontius Pilate; and the Mount of Olives, where he ascended to heaven.

"So what's it like to visit these places?"

"Ooooh, it's wonderful," she said. "You know, it's my Jesus! It's not the sites, it's the spiritual dimension. It's like reading Scripture. You can read the same Bible twenty thousand times and every time the spirit will come talk to you and give you something new."

"So you think others should come."

"Absolutely. We come to visit the dead stones—the tombs, the shrines. They're wonderful, and God will speak to you through those, but it's the living stones that matter, the people. We're all living stones. We worship a living God. If you come here and say, 'Lord, what do you want me to see?' he'll show you. You can see it from his eyes. And if we have him in us, then he never dies."

We said good-bye, and Avner and I made our way to a partially hidden bench and pulled out our Bibles. When Abraham and Isaac set out for the site, the boy carries the wood, while Abraham carries the knife and the fire. "It was so difficult to make fire," Avner explained, "that they carried a charcoal ember." Bedouin do it even now, he said. "They have a special plant, like cane. They put the charcoal inside the husk, wrap it in cotton, and it burns slowly all day. At night they break the cane, blow on the charcoal, and start the fire."

While Abraham and Isaac are walking, the boy turns to his father and says, "Father! Here are the fire and the wood; but where is the sheep for the burnt offering?" Abraham replies, "God will see to the sheep for His burnt offering, my son." Once they arrive, Abraham binds his son to the wood and raises a knife to slay him. At that moment God interrupts, crying, "Abraham! Abraham! Do not raise your hand against the boy, or do anything to him. For now I know that you fear God, since you have not withheld your son, your favored one, from Me." Abraham spots a lamb, which he burns instead, naming the spot *adonai yireh,* "the Lord will see."

Because of this story's drama and its potential chilling consequences for history, the *akedah* has been one of the most discussed chapters of the Bible. Some Jewish thinkers said God tested Abraham precisely because he knew that Abraham would pass the test. Some Christian thinkers see in the event a prefiguration of the sacrifice of Jesus: Just as Abraham did not withhold his son Isaac, so God did not withhold his son, Jesus. Søren Kierkegaard, the nineteenth-century philosopher, said Abraham agreed to sacrifice his son because God required proof of his faith. "Therefore," Kierkegaard wrote, "though Abraham arouses my admiration, he at the same time appalls me. He who has explained this riddle has explained my life."

Given our recent travels, one meaning intrigued me. The *akedah* comes at the midpoint of the patriarchal narratives, in the midst of a stretch of chapters that clearly indicate a struggle over the issue of succession. First come the barrenness of Sarah, the birth of Ishmael, the arrival of Isaac, and the banishing of Ishmael. These events are followed by the marriage of Isaac, the barrenness of Rebekah, and the struggle between Jacob and Esau in the womb. If nothing else, God, who puts so much emphasis on Abraham and his descendants inheriting the Promised Land, seems to want that process of inheritance to involve testing and perseverance. God insists on testing the patriarchs, but he requires something akin to total devotion in return.

In that way, the binding of Isaac is the perfect paradigm for God's ideal of a father-son relationship. Just as God is the father figure who requires the total submission of his favored son Abraham, so Abraham is the father figure who requires the same from *his* favored son Isaac. In the end, of course, God intervenes and saves Abraham from the ultimate submission, which in turn saves Isaac as well. The biblical story thus becomes a perfect looking glass: Look at it from Isaac's point of view, and one soon sees Abraham's point of view, for both are children in the story. Look at it from Abraham's point of view, and one soon sees God's point of view, for both are fathers in the story. This may be the story's greatest gift. Abraham, by binding his son on God's orders, binds *himself* forever to God. Both are creators who almost destroy.

But as I sat on the Temple Mount, I realized that the *akedah* also accomplishes something else. It's the first time that God explicitly challenges Abraham, or anyone else in the Bible. Up to now, God has created the world; he has formed the Garden of Eden, then banished Adam and Eve; he has flooded the world, then salvaged Noah; he has commanded Abraham to "go forth." But here he openly tests Abraham's faith, and, by extension, the faith of the readers. The *akedah* is the first truly interactive moment in the Bible, the first time the reader is forced to ask: "What would I do in this situation?"

In asking that question, I realized how removed I had been keeping myself from the text, how distant I still was from the human emotion at the heart of the stories. I also realized, in forcing myself to consider an answer, that the places, the atmosphere, even the archaeology of our trip—however impersonal at times—had been getting to me. Before starting this journey, I probably would have doubted Abraham's resolve. I would have questioned whether he truly would have killed his son on orders from an invisible god. Now, at a minimum, I believe he might have done it. In the context of his life (God, after all, had allowed his wife to give birth to Isaac after she stopped menstruating)—and his time—I believe he might have done it. As for me, I doubt whether I

would have shown such resolve. I doubt—in the context of my life—
whether I could have taken the horrifically real step of sacrificing a
child in deference to an order I couldn't verify was real, from a source I
couldn't prove existed. Still, far more significant to me at the moment
was how seriously I was prepared to consider the question. If anything,
part of me *wanted* such resolve, craved such faith.

As for Avner, a father of two? I turned to him. We were sitting on a
stone bench overlooking the Mount of Olives. The sun was directly
overhead now. The tree above us provided little shade. "So would you
have done it?"

He thought for a second. "Many times I have imagined how awful
it would be to be a father in this situation. But I don't know. I don't
know if Abraham would have done it either. That's one of the myster-
ies of the story."

It's the same with the mountain, he said. "We don't know where it
happened. But I don't think it matters. I think there's an attempt here,
like with Mount Sinai, not to point to the actual place, not to create a
place that people can worship. The point is to create the message of
being devoted so deeply to God."

"And it works," I said. "This is one of the great stories in the Bible."

"It's like a crystal. You can look through it and see a hundred different angles, but none is more beautiful than the stone itself."

3. A Pillow of Stones

We were lost. It was several days after our trip to the Temple Mount and Avner was driving his clankety blue Subaru through the labyrinthine streets of Rehavia, Jerusalem's toniest neighborhood. Compared with the Escher-like madness of the Old City, the more elegant sections of "New" Jerusalem are posh with citrus trees and bougainvilleas, stately 1930s stone apartment buildings, and arched mansions with vine-covered walls housing foreign consulates. Rehavia, in particular, contains the prime minister's residence, the president's residence, and many of the city's intellectuals—the Bloomsbury of Zion. "Martin Buber lived in that house," Avner said. "Einstein stayed around the corner." It's also a place where the roads are rarely contiguous and even an experienced desert tracker like Avner can easily get lost. "Excuse me, could you tell me where the other road with this name is?"

We eventually found the apartment building and rang the front bell. The garden brimmed with gardenias, honeysuckle, and cherry-red geraniums. "Are you looking for Professor Malamat?" the woman said. "He's around back." "Are you looking for Monsieur Malamat?" a man in back instructed. "He's just up the side." Eventually we found the door. "Ah, now I remember," Avner said. "I haven't been here in twenty years." He pressed the buzzer.

Soon we would be leaving for the more pioneering part of our journey—traveling down the Nile in search of Joseph, who was sold into slavery by his brothers; then retracing the Exodus through the Sinai. But first we had to examine the stories of Jacob. Since most of the places Jacob went were places his father and grandfather had already been (and thus we had already visited), we decided to step off the road for a few days and explore some of the questions we had been delaying: namely, What is the Bible? Who wrote it? And how do we know whether it's true? To help, Avner suggested I meet a few of his colleagues. The first was Avraham Malamat, a historian, the patriarch of biblical scholars, and Avner's teacher.

His wife greeted us warmly and led us into the den, a sunny room lined with cushioned benches where students had been gathering for decades in a lively salon. On the coffee table were three bowls filled with chocolate-covered almonds, chocolate cookies, and chocolate bonbons. Professor Malamat had a smudge of chocolate on his lips, which his wife wiped off when we arrived. He had been unwell in recent months, and his pale hair was drawn over his pink forehead in wisps, his face plump like a mango. He had a cane, which only served to accentuate his authority when he pounded it on the ground after each of his proclamations. I had yet to meet a timid Bible scholar.

"Welcome to my home," he said, gesturing grandly and noting that he had 10,500 books in his personal library. "How many about the Bible?" I asked. He seemed surprised by the question. "Ten thousand five hundred." It was the largest private collection in Israel, he said. Avraham Malamat had come to Jerusalem in the 1930s and spoke Hebrew, German, French, Arabic, English, and assorted Mesopotamian dialects. He had studied at Oxford, lived in America, and traveled around the world. "I'm from Vienna," he said. "Do you know where that is?" Feeling a bit disparaged, I was eager to prove I knew a bit about the world, too. "So, did you know Freud?" I said, cockily.

"Dr. Freud!" he said, pounding his cane. "He was my neighbor! He lived at 19 Berggasse. We lived at Number 12. I used to see him every day. When he came back from the country on weekends, his little white poodle would run down the stairs and leap into his arms."

I was flabbergasted, but at this point committed. "So," I said. "Did he ever ask you about your *mother*?"

"Just the opposite," Professor Malamat said. "Whenever my mother would walk me by his house she'd say, 'If you don't behave, Dr. Freud will put you on his couch.' " He paused. "I don't even think she knew what a couch was."

He tossed a bonbon onto his tongue.

Sufficiently in his grasp now, I moved on to the topic at hand. One thing that fascinated me about the Bible was how it came into being. There are thirty-nine books in the Hebrew Bible. The books are divided into three categories: the Law (*torah*), the Prophets (*nevi'im*), and the Writings (*ketuvim*). The Hebrew term for the Bible, *tanakh,* is an acronym for these groups. For Jews, the first group, containing the Five Books of Moses, is the most sacred. According to the Bible, these books were written by God and revealed to Moses at Mount Sinai. They contain about half narrative, half religious instruction. In Hebrew, the first words of each book serve as its name, thus Genesis is *bereshit,* or "At the beginning," and Exodus is *we'eleh shmoth,* "Now these are the names," and so on. In English the names come from early translations into Greek.

Genesis, from the Greek word *geneseosis,* or origins, tells the stories of Creation, Noah, and the patriarchs. Exodus, from the Greek word *exodos,* or departure, relates the escape of the Israelites from slavery. Leviticus, from the Greek word meaning priestly, and Numbers, a reference to the numerous censuses in the book, intersperse stories of the Israelites' sojourn in the desert with more than six hundred *mitzvot,* or laws. Deuteronomy, from the Greek term for repeated law, focuses on Moses' farewell address to the Israelites on the brink of the Promised Land. These books were later coupled with the other thirty-four to make the Hebrew Scriptures. Early followers of Jesus added five narratives, twenty-one letters, and a book of visions. Originally these were viewed as addenda to the Hebrew Scriptures, but as they gained in importance, Christians began calling the earlier books the "Old Testament" and the supplement the "New Testament."

One lesson I quickly learned was that one's view of the Bible often depends on which Bible one reads. Christian Bibles, for instance, arrange later books in the Hebrew Scriptures in a different order than Jewish Bibles. Catholic Bibles, in both their translations and their content, differ from Protestant Bibles, which differ from Anglican Bibles, which differ from Greek Orthodox Bibles. This discord began in antiquity. The term *bible* is derived from the Greek *biblia,* meaning "books," which in turn comes from the word *byblos,* or papyrus, a plant from the Nile that produced early paper. The oldest complete version of the Hebrew Bible is the Septuagint, a series of Greek translations from the third century B.C.E. that differed slightly from the original Hebrew, mostly by including the books known as the Apocrypha. The term *septuagint,* which means seventy, comes from a legend that seventy-two elders did the translating. The Septuagint is the best source of information on the pre-Christian Bible and is the Bible quoted in the New Testament. The definitive Hebrew version of the text dates much later—to around the first century C.E.—and is known as the Masoretic, or Traditional, Text.

While seemingly insignificant, these translations have had enormous impact on how we view the Bible. For example, the original Hebrew text had no vowels, since Semitic languages originally had none. Also, the text had no chapters, which were added in thirteenth-century England, and no verses, which were added in sixteenth-century Geneva. It wasn't even on paper, but on papyrus, parchment, even leather. When I asked Professor Malamat how he viewed the text, for example, he said, "The picture in my head is scrolls."

What I most wanted to know from him was how to view the content of these scrolls. As William Dever, the American archaeologist, has written, "We must constantly keep in mind the fact that the Bible is a garment of a very ancient literature in a dead language, until the discoveries of modern archaeology, the sole relic of a long-lost culture, and the product of an ancient world totally foreign to most of us."

For my purposes, this raised a question: How reliable is the Bible as history? I began by asking Professor Malamat how much we now know about the period the Pentateuch describes.

"We know very much about certain pockets," he said. "For example, about the eighteenth century B.C.E. we know *very* much. More than the Middle Ages. At Mari, we found thirty thousand documents that describe what people bought, what they sold, what they ate. I was having dinner in Oxford once and I sat next to a woman who studied medieval Europe. She envied me. I said we had ten thousand Assyrian menus. She said, 'The entire continent of Europe doesn't have ten thousand menus from that time.' "

"But only pockets," I said.

"Right. We know a lot about Mesopotamia. We know a lot about Egypt. But we have less material for here. The one question I cannot answer is, 'Why didn't Palestine yield as much material?' "

"So why didn't Palestine yield as much material?"

He smiled. "I think because it was written on papyri, and papyri deteriorate. Or maybe it's because you have so much oral tradition. Maybe there's a law that if you don't have much written tradition you have an oral tradition."

I asked him how long oral traditions could survive without being written down.

"*Very* long," he said. "We fool ourselves. They could survive for two thousand years, easily. You must have heard of the Niebelungs, the German story of Siegfried. The oldest kernel is from 800 C.E., but it has survived another twelve hundred years and was only written down for part of that. Also, everyone, including Hitler, tried to put in his own stuff."

I suggested we look at one story, Jacob, and see how accurate it is. From a narrative point of view, the story of Jacob marks a significant increase in psychological complexity. Unlike Abraham, Isaac appears infrequently in Genesis and is mostly seen as a transitional figure, with little distinctive personality of his own. His twins, however, seem to make up for his lack of charisma; both are born with specific personalities. "The first one emerged red," the text says, "like a hairy mantle all over, so they called his name Esau," which means Rough One. "Then his brother emerged, holding on to the heel of Esau; so they called him Jacob," which means Heel Holder. These initial characterizations are clue enough to their characters, but the text goes even further. "When the boys grew up, Esau became a skillful hunter, a man of the outdoors," while Jacob was a plain man who stayed in camp. "Isaac favored Esau because he had a taste for game; but Rebekah favored Jacob."

One day Jacob is cooking lentil stew when Esau returns from hunting. Esau says to Jacob, "Give me some of that red stuff to gulp down, for I am famished." The text says this exchange is why Esau later gives birth to the land of Edom, across the Jordan river, implying a connection between Edom and *adom,* the Hebrew word for red. But Jacob insists that Esau first sell his birthright as the elder son, which entitles Esau to succeed Isaac as the head of the family. Esau responds, "I am at the point of death, so of what use is my birthright to me?" But Jacob insists, "Swear to me first," and Esau does. "Thus did Esau spurn the birthright," the text says, implying that he was not entirely tricked. My first question for Professor Malamat was did such birthrights exist?

"Absolutely," he said. "They go back to Mesopotamia. First sons were considered sacred, the key to the family line. They received double inheritance and were given a seat of honor over their brothers. Also, in this case, they received the special covenant with God."

"So could these rights be transferred?"

"Yes. We have a Nuzi document in which a son actually buys the right from his brother."

In a second story of manipulation, Rebekah helps Jacob finagle a greater birthright from his father. One day when Isaac is old and "too dim to see," he summons Esau and says, "I do not know how soon I may die. Take your gear, your quiver and bow, and go out into the open and hunt me some game. Then prepare a dish for me such as I like, and bring it to me to eat, so that I may give you my innermost blessing before I die." Rebekah overhears her husband and instructs Jacob, her favored son, to fetch two choice kids so she can prepare Isaac's favorite dish and he can receive his father's blessing. "But my brother Esau is a hairy man," Jacob protests, "and I am smooth-skinned. If my father touches me, I shall appear to him as a trickster and bring upon myself a curse, not a blessing." "Just do as I say," Rebekah insists, and he does.

Rebekah dresses Jacob in Esau's clothes, covers his hands and neck with the skins of the kids, and gives him the dish. Jacob goes to visit

Isaac, who asks, "Which of my sons are you?" "I am Esau," Jacob says, "your first-born; I have done as you told me." Skeptical, Isaac asks, "How did you succeed so quickly?" Jacob responds, "Because the Lord your God granted me good fortune." Isaac bids Jacob to come closer so he may feel the boy's arms. "The voice is the voice of Jacob, yet the hands are the hands of Esau." He smells the boy and announces, "Ah, the smell of my son is like the smell of the fields that the Lord has blessed." Finally Isaac relents and gives his innermost blessing to his second son.

> May God give you / Of the dew of heaven and the fat of the earth,
> Abundance of new grain and wine. / Let peoples serve you, / And
>   nations bow to you;
> Be master over your brothers, / And let your mother's sons bow to you.
> Cursed be they who curse you, / Blessed be they who bless you.

No sooner does Jacob leave than Esau returns and does as he has been instructed. When he and Isaac uncover the ruse, Isaac is seized with "very violent trembling" and Esau bursts into "wild and bitter sobbing." "First he took away my birthright," Esau wails, "and now he has taken away my blessing." Finally he threatens, "I will kill my brother Jacob." When Rebekah hears this, she instructs Jacob to flee at once for Harran, to visit her brother Laban. Before Jacob leaves, Rebekah tells Isaac that if Jacob takes a bride "from among the native women," she will be distraught, so Isaac instructs Jacob, "You shall not take a wife from among the Canaanite women." Jacob promptly sets off for Mesopotamia. Would someone in the ancient Near East undertake such a grueling trip just to meet a wife?

"Of course," Professor Malamat said. "Jacob goes back to his clan. He doesn't go to a foreign people. The Bible says that God hurt people if they married foreigners. There is a bias against Canaanites. We try to make it nicer these days, but it's not nice. The biblical storytellers *hated* the Canaanites, because the Canaanites didn't believe in God."

Jacob arrives in Harran and promptly meets Rachel, the daughter of his uncle Laban. Jacob tries to impress her by rolling the stone covering off the mouth of the well, and, in an episode repeated nowhere else in the Bible, he kisses Rachel and breaks into tears. Jacob then explains that he is Rachel's kinsman and they go to meet her father, who offers Jacob a job. Jacob responds, "I will serve you seven years for your younger daughter Rachel." Besides being the younger of Laban's two daughters (and thus parallel to Jacob), Rachel is described as being "shapely and beautiful," while Leah is described only as having "weak eyes." Laban agrees, and the seven years pass, though they seem like just days to Jacob, "because of his love" for Rachel.

At the end of his service, Jacob demands his reward and is given a bride, with whom he has marital relations. The following morning he discovers that Laban, in what appears to be an unwitting but poetic retribution for Jacob's deception of Isaac, has substituted Leah for Rachel. "Why did you deceive me?" Jacob asks, to which Laban responds, "It is not the practice in our place to marry off the younger before the older." Laban offers to let Jacob marry Rachel if he works another seven years, which Jacob agrees to do. Another seven years pass, and Jacob marries Rachel. But God, seeing how Jacob prefers Rachel, makes her barren. Leah, by contrast, gives Jacob four sons. Rachel's servant gives him another two sons. Leah's servant adds two more. Leah then contributes two more sons and a daughter, Dinah. Finally God remembers Rachel, and she bears him a son, Joseph.

My question to Professor Malamat was, would such switching of brides truly have happened?

"It was common to marry the firstborn daughter first," he said. "If Jacob wants the more beautiful daughter, he has to work another seven years. You have to understand, the most important thing in a marriage was not love. It was not romance. It was children."

"So all in all," I said, "how would you evaluate the story in terms of its historical accuracy?"

"I believe in the historical background of the story," he said. "There might have been a man like Jacob. It's quite possible. Of course, there are many anachronisms in the story. Edom did not exist at the time of the patriarchs; that detail was probably added later. But I say, 'Good show!' I like anachronisms. I always quote Shakespeare's *Julius Caesar*. There's a part where someone says, 'And the clock strikes three.' That's a good line, but in Rome there were no churches during that period—Christianity wasn't even invented—and no clocks. So that's an anachronism."

"So who introduced the anachronisms?"

"The writers. Those who, at the end, edited the Bible we have now." Which is where the real controversy begins.

In 1800 the Bible was regarded by much of the world to be true, the unchallenged word of God. The Pentateuch, in particular, was written by Moses; the stories were historically accurate, the contents divine. In the course of the nineteenth century, this view came under relentless scrutiny. In one of the momentous intellectual revolutions of the last two centuries, a series of European and American scholars, working in the novice fields of literary criticism and archaeology, removed the Bible from its untouchable heights and planted it firmly in history.

The first area for exploration was authorship. Studious readers had long observed contradictions in the text. Events are reported in one order, then repeated in a different order. The Moabites are said to have done something; then the Midianites are said to have done the same thing. Moses gets the Ten Commandments at Mount Sinai, then at Mount Horeb. Also, events are described that Moses couldn't possibly have known, like his own death. Over time, the rabbis had tried to explain these seeming contradictions, but some commentators refused to go along. Their views were hurriedly squelched. One eleventh-century critic was dubbed "Isaac the Blunderer." A sixteenth-century scholar had his book banned; a seventeenth-century scholar was imprisoned. By the nineteenth century, an enlightened consensus emerged that certain tensions in the text could no longer be avoided: foremost among them, that God has different names. Genesis, for example, tells two different versions of Creation; in one the protagonist is Elohim, in the other it's Yahweh.

By century's end, German scholar Julius Wellhausen compiled a number of these budding ideas into a unified theory, the Documentary Hypothesis, easily the most destabilizing doctrine in the history of the Bible. Using linguistic analysis, word frequency, even syllable count,

Wellhausen concluded that the Bible has four separate sources. The oldest he termed "J," for the German word for Yahweh, which was responsible for many of the narrative sections. The second source was "E," for sections mentioning Elohim. The largest source comprised the legal sections and was termed "P," for the priests. A later source, found only in Deuteronomy, was called "D."

This thesis has dominated scholarship ever since, with critics scrambling to unmask the ghostwriters. The "J" source must have lived in the kingdom of Judah, the reasoning goes, since Abraham buys land in Hebron, which is in Judah. The "E" source must have lived in the kingdom of Israel, since Abraham stops first in Shechem. Later scholars grew even bolder. Harold Bloom, the Yale literary critic, wrote a best-selling book in which he proposes that "J," because of its style and sensitivity, was written by a woman. Richard Elliot Friedman of the University of California has gone further. In *Who Wrote the Bible?* he says that "D" can be dated to 622 B.C.E. and attributed to Baruch, a scribe in the court of Jeremiah. The redactor, he says, a fifth person who combined the various sources, was named Ezra and lived in the time of the Second Temple.

Recently, the Documentary Hypothesis has come under increased criticism, with scholars complaining that the identifications are weak, convoluted, or just plain unhelpful. One German scholar declared Wellhausen's theory "dead." For a newcomer, trying to make sense of the alphabet soup was far more daunting than enlightening, and just the hint of the subject from Professor Malamat had me nearly jumping, like one of Dr. Freud's patients, on his couch.

"Basically there are good things in it," he said. "But times have changed. It's been one hundred years. Many people, good writers, say they can take a page of Goethe and find four sources. He was in a bad mood two hours after he wrote the first two lines. Let me show you a book you haven't seen." He sent me into his office and up a ladder, to the top shelf, where I removed a frail volume, *The Book of Genesis,* by C. J. Hall. "No other teacher has this book," he said.

I opened the book from the back, where the Hebrew text of Genesis was divided into four fluorescent colors, each assigned to a source.

With its intersecting blocks of varying lengths it looked like a Mondrian painting. "You see!" he cried. "Can you read just the blue? Can you read just the yellow, the orange. Can you read it?!? Now you see how impossible it is."

"So you're saying I should forget the sources."

"If you can."

"How can I forget them, once I know them."

"Look, it's a game," he said. "In my class I call it phantom. These are phantom sources. There are certainly different styles to the stories: Sometimes there is poetry, sometimes prose, sometimes long lists of laws. Probably these stories were written down by different people. But you will never meet these people, you cannot shake hands with them. Therefore I don't deal with it. You should take the story as a whole. You shouldn't divide it into sections and say this came from the fifth century, this from the eighth. You read it like Goethe, like literature."

"You're telling me that as a historian you read it as literature."

"It is literature," he said. "In Oxford once I bought this book that said that from the Bible to Shakespeare there was no great literature. To hell with Shakespeare! The Bible is better than Shakespeare. From the Bible to eternity there will be no greater literature."

"So it's the best thing ever written."

"I think so."

"And the best thing that ever *will be* written?"

He banged his cane on the floor approvingly.

If literary criticism was destabilizing to the Bible, archaeology was downright revolutionary.

The day after meeting Professor Malamat, I took a bus to a house just south of the Promenade. When I knocked on the door, a gentle man appeared, with a trimmed beard, a slight shuffle, and an averted glance. He fussed with a cigarette and poured me a Sprite. Like many archaeologists, Gabriel Barkay seemed uncomfortable with the details of modern life. Archaeologists, I had observed, seem to exist in a complex, multidimensional notion of time. Walk onto a site and they make instant connections: This piece of pottery from Mesopotamia is similar to that piece of art from Egypt, which from the eighteenth century B.C.E. to the fourteenth century B.C.E. completely dominated Canaan, which was later attacked by the Phoenicians, who wrote something in the ninth century B.C.E. that is uncommonly similar to something the Israelites wrote in Genesis, while they were in Mesopotamia, dreaming of Egypt. Got it? Now document it.

As a boy I used to like going with my father, a builder, to construction sites. While he would go inside to check the workmanship, I would stay outside in the piles of white sand and construct imaginary communities. I was reminded of this on occasion when Avner would lurch to the side of the road and plunge to the ground. No matter where we went, he always came back dirtier than me. Ultimately that's the image I carry of archaeologists: grown-ups playing in the sand. They're adult versions of sandbox architects, taking materials they find in the ground, arranging them in a certain coherent order, and sprinkling in their own imaginations to create a thriving reality where the rest of us would see nothing, or worse, pave it over and build a mall. They're squabblers at times; absentminded often. But, at their best, they're sort of inverted prophets. If prophets foretell the future, warning of what might come, archaeologists foretell the past, warning of what already happened.

And, best of all, they're not modish. As Agatha Christie, whose second husband, Max Mallowan, was a prominent Assyriologist, wrote: "The great thing about being married to an archaeologist is the older you get, the more he loves you."

Gabi Barkay was not particularly old, but he was a veteran of Israel's academic wars and a student of the relationship between the Bible and archaeology. I had come to discuss this relationship, which in two hundred years has altered both the world of science and the world of religion. Archaeology, or the "study of beginnings," was invented in Europe in the nineteenth century largely for two reasons: to dig up The Iliad and The Odyssey, and to dig up the Bible. European Christians believed that they, not the Jews, were the rightful heirs to Palestine and needed to safeguard it. This had been the motivation behind the Crusades and now inspired a multinational scavenger hunt. As historian Moshe Pearlman wrote: "It was the greatest hunt in history, mounted on the largest scale, at the most lavish cost, pursued over the longest period over the broadest area by the most remarkable assembly of hunters ever committed to a search for buried treasure."

The idea of locating biblical sites began as early as the fourth century, when Constantine's mother, Empress Helena, traipsed across the region and, using divine inspiration, identified the location of the Nativity, Calvary, and the Holy Sepulcher, the tomb where Jesus was buried. By the time Napoleon conquered Egypt in 1798, he brought scholars who carted off objects, among them a slab of basalt found in Rosetta with writing in Greek, demotic script, and hieroglyphics. Translated by Jean-François Champollion, the Rosetta Stone first allowed scholars to read ancient Egyptian.

Other explorers were more eccentric. Lady Hester Stanhope, the niece of Prime Minister William Pitt, was born into London society in 1776. Ostracized for her outlandish behavior, she sailed for the Middle East, where she dressed as a man and started digging up biblical venues looking for gold. She found none and eventually retired to Lebanon, though her exploits made her famous as the godmother of biblical archaeology. The godfather was American clergyman Edward Robinson. Traveling from Alexandria to Jerusalem in 1837, Robinson, a self-styled Connecticut Yankee in King David's court, used his knowledge of Hebrew and the Bible to map over two hundred sites.

The defining moment of archaeology as an academic discipline occurred half a century later with yet another eccentric Englishman. "The founding father, without a doubt," Gabi said, "is William Matthew Flinders Petrie. He's *the* great mind that started it all." An Egyptologist who dug in Palestine, Petrie (1853–1942) discovered how pots can tell time. Because pottery often breaks, each generation makes its own, with defining characteristics. Each style of pot is found in only one stratum of a tel. By linking each pottery style with a specific period, archaeologists could understand when each stratum was developed. This simple observation unlocked the ancient world. Before, scholars had difficulty distinguishing remains from different millennia. Now, pots could date places more closely.

Petrie's discoveries set the stage for the golden age of biblical archaeology, led by William Foxwell Albright. "Albright was a giant," Gabi said. "The scope of his knowledge was awesome. He was good in Hebrew, good in Akkadian, good in hieroglyphics, good in pottery, good in historical texts. He is described by his biographer as a twentieth-century genius, and it is correct—even with the criticism."

Albright (1891–1971) was a contradictory figure. On the one hand, working from Johns Hopkins University in Baltimore (where Avraham Biran was his first doctoral student) and the American School of Oriental Research in Jerusalem (where Avner was a fellow), he established biblical archaeology as a formal discipline. On the other hand, as the child of Methodist missionaries, Albright had something of an agenda. He was one of a series of scholars—G. E. Wright, a minister; Nelson Glueck, a rabbi—who carried a pick in one hand and a Bible in the other and set out, more or less, to prove the Bible. Their effort was a direct response to Wellhausen, who had caused a crisis particularly in Protestant denominations, which rely heavily on the divine word of Scripture.

"I think his religious background was an obstacle," Gabi said. "The fact is, in America there was a tendency to dismiss the Bible as being a religious truth, not a historical one. Albright was very affected by people having a tendency to ignore the Bible. He wanted to resurrect it."

"How does proving the Bible help faith?" I said.

"I'm a local Jew," he said. "I don't care whether this or that detail is incorrect in the Bible. It doesn't change my attitude toward the Bible, toward religion, toward God. Or toward myself. But in America there was an idea that the Bible is a kind of machine; if you prove that two of the screws really existed, then the whole machine existed, and if you take *out* two of the screws, the whole thing collapses. But the Bible is not a machine. It doesn't have screws."

The race to shore up the Bible proved so successful that for decades a sort of golden triangle existed among scholars, funders, and the press. Religious institutions would fund elaborate excavations, scholars would rush to sensational conclusions ("I have found the Flood!"), and the press would run breathless stories. This magical stew of romance, adventure, and faith proved irresistible to the public, who scooped up books and magazines on the Bible's great comeback. Werner Keller, a German journalist, crystallized this trend in 1956 with his book *The Bible as History,* which sold ten million copies. Few readers know that the real title in German can be roughly translated as *See, the Bible Was Right After All.* Objectivity was not the point; boosterism was.

Inevitably, a backlash followed. By the 1960s, a new generation of archaeologists introduced more scientific techniques unencumbered by faith. As a result, archaeology, which had begun as a way to support the Bible, slowly started to undermine it. Jericho couldn't have burnt down when the Bible says, revisionists claimed; there are no remains of a burnt city at that time. William Dever, who trained as both a minister and an archaeologist, led the way. "The sooner we abandon the term biblical archaeology the better," he wrote. By the 1990s the schism had become so great that one group, called the "minimalists," claimed that since no concrete evidence of the patriarchs exists, the entire Pentateuch must have been made up at a later date. Less than a century after Petrie, biblical archaeology seemed to be dead. "I wish to regard the Bible as an artifact," Dever wrote. The text, in other words, had become just another piece of pottery.

But then, as it has so many times before, the Bible fought back.

"Look," Gabi said. "Serious people know that some parts of the Bible go well with archaeology, others do not. So what? I'm not going to find in archaeology, ever, a business card that says 'Abraham, son of Terah.' But it doesn't matter. It's not a book of history. It's a book of faith."

Others seem to share this view. Dever himself converted to Judaism and started criticizing the minimalists.

"So in the end, biblical archaeology isn't dead," I said.

"Perhaps there's even a rejuvenation," he said. "What I'm doing is biblical archaeology. I am dealing with Jerusalem in the First Temple Period and I cannot ignore such an important text. I wish all archaeologists had such a gold mine. I have information about daily life, burial customs, the landscape. Indian archaeology in Arizona doesn't have that."

He began to tell a story. In 1979, Gabi was excavating burial caves on the slope of the Hinnom Valley in Jerusalem, just paces from where

Avner and I had been during our walk to the Temple Mount. One day he was hosting a group of children from an archaeology club. A twelve-year-old boy was constantly tugging at his shirt, asking silly questions. At the time the team was digging in a first-millennium cave. "I thought to myself, This is a place to put little Nathan. So I said to him, 'Don't leave this place until it's cleaner than your mother's kitchen, and don't touch anything you find.' Five minutes later I felt my shirt being pulled from behind. I turned around and saw this terrible little creature with two large pieces of pottery in his hands. I thought I was going to shoot him."

"Where did you get those pots from?" Gabi asked.

"Under the stones," Nathan replied.

"What stones?"

He returned to the site and immediately realized what had happened. Nathan, ever zealous, was not content merely to clean the kitchen; he wanted to remodel. He took a hammer, smashed the floor, and underneath found the pottery. "Of course, if the pottery was under the floor," Gabi said, "it wasn't a floor. It was a ceiling that had fallen during an earthquake and buried the contents of the chamber. As a result, looters must have thought what I did. I realized that little Nathan had just made the discovery of my life."

Gabi sent the children home and began digging with more experienced students. Inside they found a repository with more than one thousand objects. Near the bottom of the chamber Gabi discovered what *Biblical Archaeology Review* later named one of the ten biggest finds of the century: two pieces of rolled silver the size of cigarette butts.

"It took us three years to unroll them," he said. "And three more years to read them."

For the first time he was leaning forward in his chair. I could see his academic crust melting away. Once again he was that boy in the sand.

The process of unrolling proved especially taxing. First they softened a piece, using saline solution and formic acid. It cracked and broke. Then they heated it, first to 250°C, then 600°C. That also didn't work. Finally, looking to harden it, they coated the piece with Plextol B-500, an acrylic glue, then picked it apart with a dentist's tool. This time it worked.

"Immediately I tried to read it," Gabi said. "It was in ancient Hebrew. And the first thing I saw were the four letters, YHWH. Yahweh. The first time in Jerusalem."

The inscription, it turns out, was from the Bible.

"I have the priestly benediction from the Book of Numbers, chapter 6, written on pieces of silver that date back 2,600 years. And these are the very same words which my father used to bless me when I came back from synagogue. Besides the archaeological importance, it has a personal impact as well."

"Which is what?"

"I'm close to these words. I'm close to the biblical text. The very fact that it was written by people who lived here, and I live here myself. It speaks to me. 'May the Lord bless you and keep you. May the Lord shine his face upon you and favor you. May the Lord lift up his face toward you and grant you peace.' "

"Is this the most satisfying thing you've ever found?"

"It's the most important thing. These are the earliest biblical verses ever found—three hundred years earlier than the Dead Sea Scrolls. And it has an impact on what we were discussing earlier, Wellhausen and the dating. Already in the seventh century B.C.E., as proven by these pieces, the text existed. It was not made up by some people in the Hellenistic period."

"So did you ever call Nathan and tell him what he found?" I said.

"No, but I gave a lecture ten years later. I told the story to a group of professional archaeologists. I realized while speaking that somebody was standing to the side of the hall. A very tall soldier. He was making me nervous. When I finished I went over and asked him why he was standing there. Was he interested in archaeology? He said, 'I'm Nathan.' I was so shocked I forgot to ask him his last name. And to this day I don't know who he is." Gabi lifted his hand to his eyes. He was uncomfortable expressing emotion. "By now, he should be a father," he said. "Maybe he's reading the priestly blessing to his children, like my father did to me."

A few days later Avner and I left Jerusalem for our final trip to the Galilee and the epic tel of Hatzor, which the Bible describes as "the head of all those kingdoms." Located just north of the Sea of Galilee, Hatzor is the biggest tel in the country and was one of the largest cities in the ancient world. At its peak in the second millennium B.C.E., the city had a population of twenty thousand.

Hatzor played a pivotal role in modern history as well. In 1955, Yigal Yadin, the former chief of staff for the Israeli Army, led an excavation that proved vital to the Jewish state. For Yadin, archaeology was more than a science, it was a way to justify Israel's existence. Gabi called him a "secular fundamentalist." Unlike Albright, he didn't care about bolstering faith. But if he could prove that Joshua conquered Hatzor, he could boost the country. Yadin was a "prophet of national rebirth," wrote his biographer, Neil Silberman. "Rising to the lectern with the confidence of a master, he would look out over audiences of eager listeners, charm them with his wit and erudition, and inspire them to see in the modern State of Israel a poetic culmination of all Jewish history." For him, archaeology was a "profoundly patriotic activity."

Today Hatzor sprawls across two hundred acres in Upper Galilee like a giant, bottle-shaped mesa. On a sunny afternoon, a few tourists wandered the remains. They struggled to link the stubby walls with the grand account of Joshua. They weren't alone. During Yadin's tenure, the composer Leonard Bernstein visited Hatzor. He was viewing some Canaanite ruins uncovered by Avner's mentor, Trude Dhotan, when a call came from the upper tel, "We've found Solomon's Gate!" Bernstein was thrilled. "This is magnificent!" he announced. "I'll write an oratorio, I'll write a symphony, I'll write an opera." He hopped in a jeep and went hurrying to the spot. Five minutes later he returned, dejected. What he had imagined was a soaring gate, no doubt adorned with trumpets and flags, turned out to be little more than a few stones in the ground. "He was devastated," Trude recalled. "He never wrote an oratorio, a symphony, or an opera."

Avner and I explored the site, as he pointed out features typical of Canaanite cities—the small homes with courtyards, the giant palace with plaster walls. Eventually we arrived at Solomon's Gate, which on the surface was not so impressive, until Avner noted that the design was the same as one in Megiddo. According to the book of Kings, which follows the Pentateuch, Solomon built such walls in Jerusalem, Gezer, Megiddo, and Hatzor. "What we have here is a clear piece of archaeological evidence that supports the text," Avner said. "But you have to be able to read the stones."

"Everybody in Israel seems to be able to read them," I said.

"That's true. A kid here will know what a tel is, that stones mean people."

"And that's the point: Stones mean people. Few around the world understand that connection."

We hiked down to the lower tel, which was unexcavated and covered in grass. On top of a small hill we retrieved our Bibles. A grasshopper leapt onto my lap. Though the text never says Jacob was in Hatzor, it does suggest he came close. On his way to Harran, after hearing of his brother's threat, Jacob comes upon a "certain place." The place was probably on the Patriarchs' Road and thus near Hatzor. Taking one of the stones of the place, he puts it under his head and lies down to sleep. He has a dream in which he sees a ladder, with "angels of God" going up and down on it. God appears and renews his covenant, promising to give Jacob the land promised to his father and grandfather.

Later, on his way back from Harran with Leah, Rachel, and their children, Jacob again settles near here. He flees Harran under tense conditions with his father-in-law, Laban. Jacob believes Laban has cheated him, so he decides to leave without saying good-bye; Rachel, in retaliation, steals her father's idols. Laban pursues them, but he and Jacob reconcile. Jacob then faces an even greater threat: his brother, who is coming to meet him with four hundred men. Jacob sends his servants with extravagant gifts for Esau, including two hundred she-goats and twenty he-goats, two hundred ewes and twenty rams, forty cows and ten bulls, twenty she-asses and ten he-asses.

That night he sends his family across the Jabbok River in what is today Jordan, and remains alone on the other side. A man wrestles with him overnight, and when the man sees that he has not won, he "wrenches Jacob's hip at its socket, so that the socket of his hip was strained." The two become entangled again, and the man says, "Let me go, for dawn is breaking," to which Jacob replies, "I will not let you go, unless you bless me." "What is your name?" the man asks, and Jacob tells him. The man then announces, "Your name shall no longer be Jacob, but Israel, for you have striven with beings divine and human and have prevailed." The man departs, and Jacob names the place "Peniel," which literally means "face of God," but which the text says means, "I have seen a divine being face to face, yet my life has been preserved." The text then adds, "The children of Israel to this day do not eat the thigh muscle that is on the socket of the hip, since Jacob's hip socket was wrenched at the thigh muscle." No animal is given for this dictum.

Looking up, Jacob sees Esau approaching. Jacob bows seven times before his brother, who then comes running to greet him. The two embrace and weep. Jacob introduces his family and Esau asks why they are bowing down. "To gain my lord's favor," Jacob says. But "I have enough," Esau says. "Let what you have remain yours." But Jacob insists, "for to see your face is like seeing the face of God," and Esau accepts a small present. Esau then returns to Edom and Jacob travels to Shechem, just south of Hatzor, and settles with his family.

So why stop here and not farther south, like Beer-sheba or Gerar? I asked Avner.

"Why not?" he said. "It's better land, more room for grazing. The text says Jacob is a 'people' now, no longer a family."

Once in Shechem, what follows is the final contact between the patriarchs and the Canaanites, a last chance for the "people" to test its strength. Dinah, Jacob's daughter with Leah, is raped by a local dignitary named Shechem, the son of the city's chief (and no apparent relation to the town). Shechem wants to marry Dinah and offers her family rights to settle the land. "Intermarry with us," Shechem's father proposes to Jacob's sons. "Give your daughters to us, and take our daughters for yourselves. You will dwell among us, and the land will be open before you." This is a mark of the family's status, and Jacob's sons pretend to agree, but only if the residents agree to be circumcised, to "become like us." The residents concur, but two of Jacob's sons—Simeon and Levi—

change their mind and plunder the town, abducting the women, children, and wealth. Jacob is furious. "You have brought trouble on me," he tells his sons, "making me odious among the inhabitants of the land." Fearing retaliation, he leads the family away.

"But why run away?" I said. "The patriarchs' clan is clearly the strongest it's been. The Canaanites are so respectful they want to intermarry. They even agree to be circumcised. Why not go ahead and fulfill the covenant?"

"Because there's something missing," Avner said. "The brothers are not the ones to bestow circumcision. Circumcision is a covenant between man and God. Jacob's sons are trying to circumvent that."

"So they're not ready."

"They may be stronger than ever. They can stand up to the biggest cities in Canaan now. They may even be more clever than the Canaanites. But they haven't yet received the laws—the Ten Commandments and others—that will make them servants of God. The conquest must wait. They've got to go into bondage."

We left Hatzor and drove a few miles south to Vered Ha-Galil, our final stop in Israel. Vered Ha-Galil is a legendary ranch overlooking the Sea of Galilee started in 1961 by Yehuda Avni, a Chicago transplant whose original name was Edward Schneider. We had run into Yehuda on our way to Hatzor during a pancake breakfast (his wife knew Avner's mother), and he invited us to return for an afternoon horseback ride.

Yehuda greeted us at the door and led us to the porch with a pitcher of lemonade. He was a weather-worn man with a longshoreman's hands, and when he said his uncle had been a milkman on the West Side of Chicago it seemed fitting. He developed his love of horses by helping his uncle deliver bottled milk from a horse-drawn wagon. As a boy, he would sit in religious school pretending to read the Talmud, with a copy of a Zane Grey novel tucked inside. "Every now and then the rebbe would catch me and give me a few whacks," he said.

After a while, Avner opted to make some phone calls and Yehuda and I walked to the stables. Vered Ha-Galil is a rarity, a private farm not associated with a kibbutz. In addition to the horses and a few cabins for tourists, Yehuda and his family grow oranges, olives, and litchis. A leafy informality prevails, with haystacks on the road and Dolly Parton on the stereo. Once we mounted our horses and stepped onto the trail, the panorama of history opened before us. Up above was a Crusader fortress. Down below the Mount of Beatitudes, where Jesus delivered the Sermon on the Mount. Directly in front was the highway. "When Abraham chased the kings to Dan," Yehuda said. "He came on that road. Every great power in history passed through here."

We started down a hill and up another. Our horses' hooves clicked on the limestone and lava. A hawk swirled overhead. Yehuda, then still known as Edward, left Chicago in 1943 to join the 82nd Airborne in France. Two years later his company liberated a Nazi concentration camp in Germany. "Those still alive were like skeletons," he said. "I spoke Yiddish, and I asked somebody his name. He was afraid. 'Are you Jewish?' he asked. Then he touched me, and touched my rifle. He called his people. 'Look, there's a Jew standing here, and he has a gun!' The whole group crowded around me, just touching me. They were crying. I was crying. It was an unforgettable moment."

After the war, Yehuda moved to Geneva, enrolled in the university, and lived with an Italian girlfriend. One day she announced she was going to a meeting of the Zionist movement. "I wasn't the least bit interested in the meeting," he said, "but of course I was interested in her." At the meeting a Swiss officer described his experience in the Israeli War of Independence and declared the need for volunteers. Yehuda, seeking an adventure, volunteered, and a month later boarded a boat for Haifa. The day before he landed, the war ended. Yehuda decided that he would stay two weeks and return.

"I got off the boat and started walking down the main street, Har Herzl. I walked down the south side of the street, then the north side, and I had this strange feeling. It's not a matter of a revelation, but I said to myself, 'Look, here you are in a country where you don't know a soul, you have no friends or relatives, and yet you feel completely at home, like you've never felt anyplace else.' That walk, from one side of the street to the other, was decisive. I had made up my mind that this was the country where I was going to live."

"So what was the feeling?" I said.

"Later I was told that Theodor Herzl, the founder of Zionism, wrote that deep inside, somewhere, someplace, every Jew has a niche in which he knows that Israel is his land. It just felt self-obvious, like it was in my DNA."

"Your DNA!?" I was shocked—and fascinated—to hear a reference that reminded me of the feeling I had in Turkey.

"We Jews are divided into three categories," he said. "The Cohanim, who are the priests; the Levites, the servants of the Temple; and the masses. Scientists recently did DNA tests on the Cohanim. They found that for generations the Cohanim have passed down the same Y-chromosome from father to son. The chain goes back three thousand years. Now that says something. As a tribe we Jews have various characteristics. The fact that I'm a farmer and ride horses, the same way my forefathers were farmers and rode donkeys, makes sense."

"So who's the father of this strand?"

"It goes back to the Bible, Abraham, Isaac, and Jacob. There are many things we can't be proud of as a people. But the fact is, we're closely identified with this piece of land. And as far as I'm concerned, just being here, being able to play some part, is again helping this land come to flower. When I came here this was rock and thistle. Over the years I've helped transform it."

A few minutes later we arrived at our destination, a fourteenth-century way station built by Mamluk warlords from Egypt, and Yehuda dismounted. We tied our horses to an oak tree and stepped inside the two-story caravansary—a motel for passing caravans—built around a courtyard. It reminded me of a hotel where Avner and I ate dinner in Diyarbakir, right down to the alternating layers of white limestone and black basalt. Yehuda had a dream to turn the facility, abandoned in 1900, into a hotel. "All I need is $750,000," he said.

He'd done it before. After that day in Haifa, Yehuda helped set up a kibbutz in the Negev, got married, then started a rose farm in another planned community. Eventually he decided to break away from organized settlements and set out on a six-month walking tour looking for land. "It was just like the early Israelites," he said. "The fertile areas were already occupied and the only open spaces were the rocky ones. One day I was walking with a surveyor and we came upon a hill. We waded through thistles up to our waists. We both looked out; there were no trees or anything. I said, 'This is it.' He said, 'This is it.' And that was it." He called the ranch "The Rose of Galilee."

I asked him if archaeology had played a role in fostering the connection between people like him and the land.

"I can answer you very easily," he said. "Follow me." He led the way back through the courtyard and up a short, steep hill. A few speckled horses from a kibbutz were grazing on top. A monarch butterfly alighted on a cow's skull. On top of the hill was a well, covered by a stone dome. "Instead of the word 'archaeology,' use the term 'family history,' " Yehuda said. "I used to bring my children here. This is Joseph's well. It's a place of pilgrimage. Muslims believe this is where Joseph was thrown into a well by his brothers. Contemporary scholars don't agree; they say it happened further south. But everyone agrees that Joseph was here, and therefore Jacob." He tossed a rock into the well, which was about fifty feet deep.

"Over there," he continued, pointing to his house, "we found a farm from 200 B.C.E. The man who lived there had a winepress, which we excavated. He probably made wine for the community of Chorazin. Later the winepress was verified by Yigal Yadin."

"Yadin?" I said. "Who called him?"

"He used to stop by the ranch. We got to know each other, and afterward I used to help in Hatzor. He was very passionate, intense. In order to be a successful archaeologist you have to be more than an excavator; you have to be able to promote. He was really good at that."

"It sounds like you're an amateur archaeologist."

"I'm an amateur historian," he said. "Back in the early sixties I had a worker, Sait. We used to sit on the press and have our lunch, and we would muse, 'Who was this man who lived here? How many wives did he have? How many children?' After a few days Sait came back and said,

'Yehuda, your problem is solved. I talked to the elders of the village. They said to do this: If you want to know who the original owner was, you have to come up here and sleep overnight, using as a pillow one of the stones from his house. And at that point the original owner will come to you in a dream and identify himself.' " Yehuda smiled at the similarity with Jacob. "But don't ask me, I haven't done it yet."

"What? You haven't done it yet?!?"

"Yet. But I believe in subliminal consciousness. You pick up shreds here, shreds there. Then all the shreds come together and you have a picture."

"So do you feel connected to that man?"

"Sure. I'm a continuation. He was here then and I'm here now. And my children and grandchildren are connected also. I assume that in another couple hundred years there'll also be some sort of relations of mine here. It's a happy situation."

As he was speaking he had turned away from me and was looking out over the horizon, where the white sun was dipping into an orange film. And I realized for the first time why we had really come on this ride. I realized without even asking what Yehuda Avni had in common with Avraham Biran, what he shared with Gabi Barkay and Avraham Malamat, what connected him to Fern Dobuler and David Wilder. They were all pioneers. They were founders. They were taking a land that once was hostile—partly occupied and partly abandoned—and slowly making it their own. And they were doing so for completely different reasons that all had one thing in common: a voice inside them told them this land was home. For some the voice was God. For others it was history. For all it was the Bible. And this, I realized, was the legacy of Genesis: this place, the land of Abraham, Isaac, and Jacob, the home of David, Solomon, and Jesus, would forever be associated with beginnings, with making fresh starts. With Creation.

And perhaps, even more, with legacy.

Before coming to Israel, I thought of the place in terms of its twentieth-century achievement—carving a country out of the desert, making a home in a hostile world. I knew, of course, that Jesus had walked in the Promised Land. I knew that David and Solomon had built in Jerusalem. I knew, abstractly, that the patriarchs had passed here. But I don't think I had ever fully imagined the place as the foundry out of which the Bible was forged, as a literary landscape as rich and bountiful as Shakespeare's England, Flaubert's France, or Joyce's Ireland. If anything, what I discovered was that the wars of the past one hundred years, the tensions of the last one thousand years, were made more bearable—and more meaningful—by the events of four thousand years ago. And what I also discovered is that those events are arguably *more* alive today than at any time since their first telling. The past not only enriches the present here; it *is* the present.

One reason, curiously, is academia. All of the scholarly research about the Bible I dabbled in at the beginning of this process—the history, the archaeology, the literary analysis—far from deadening the stories, as I briefly feared, had actually helped make them more alive. It did this by giving the stories more context, more color, and, oddly, more credibility, first by attacking them, then by allowing them to revive. The fact that I met so many scholars who not only confirmed the accuracy of the Bible but also reinforced its beauty—its sheer power to bring these professional skeptics to unexpected emotional depths—freed me to shuck off my own intellectual misgivings and follow a similar route. Not only could I walk in Abraham's footsteps, I could walk in Avraham Biran's, as well. I could follow Gabi Barkay's lead, and Avner Goren's, too. I could find, for myself, a new, more personal way into the text— my own re-creation, as it were—which, I now realized, is exactly what I'd been doing all along.

And what Yehuda Avni had been doing for years. "So," I said to Yehuda after a while, waking him from his reverie. "Are you a patriarch?"

"Everyone's a patriarch," he said. "I have the same respect for somebody who lives in the middle of Haifa and has a shop, or is a carpenter or a craftsman. He came to work as an immigrant from Poland or Russia or Morocco, and established himself, raised a family. Israel is full of people like me, who started with nothing and have created something."

"But that's the story: going forth, leaving your clan, going out and taking a rocky land, and making it home—"

"And never finishing," he said, completing my sentence. "Right now I have a list of two, three pages of items that need to be done. I'm like Erskine Caldwell, *God's Little Acre*. This is my little acre. My mission is to make it as beautiful as possible." He clasped his hands together in a ball. "Israel is like an onion," he said. "You can start unpeeling. You begin with the battles that were fought here in 1948. Peel back another layer, you have the Crusader era, the Byzantine era, the Talmudic era, the Roman era. You have the Israelites, the Canaanites. You're not just looking at rock and stone, you're looking at flesh and blood."

"So what's at the heart of the onion?" I said.

"It's people, living on the land, creating, dying. Being. Life is very banal when all is said and done."

"Why is that banal? Why isn't that beautiful?"

"Banal can also be beautiful. You're born, you grow up, you marry, raise children, have a family, love. You die, they continue. And along that line you live. I get up every morning and enjoy looking at the Sea of Galilee. I enjoy talking to people. I enjoy my work. Perhaps that's not banal after all. That's God's little dream."

Book II

A
COAT
OF MANY
COLORS

1. On the Banks of the Nile

El Al Flight 443 touched down in Cairo after dark. The plane taxied to a stop on the tarmac and the door opened onto a slab of thick black air. Stepping onto the stairs, I felt the familiar slap of desert, like staring into a hair dryer. But unlike Jerusalem, here the air contained something else. Here, there was the smell of water.

The distance between Jerusalem and Cairo is almost impossible to measure. By foot it should take about a month, by camel two weeks, by bus a day. But for most of history, such conventional means rarely worked. Abraham made it fairly easily, as did Mary and Joseph when they fled Bethlehem with the baby Jesus to escape the wrath of Herod. But Moses, going the other way, took forty years, and still fell short. Napoleon got bogged down in the dunes, as did the English army a century later. During the first thirty years of the Israeli state, the 250 miles from one city to the other was wider than any desert, and more impenetrable.

Even the advent of air travel, which has reduced the trip to an hour, has done little to reduce the distance. The first time I arrived, a year earlier, the flight landed on the other side of midnight and I disembarked into a huddle of dark-bearded men and gun-toting soldiers. Generations of anxiety instantly came bubbling up in my throat like bile. Inside the terminal I faced a dizzying clamor of dim red lights and out-stretched hands. I went to change money for a visa, but when I signed the traveler's check the clerk insisted it wasn't valid. "But you just approved it," I said. "Sorry," he said. I started to raise my voice, and he reluctantly slid over the money.

Outside the airport that night, hordes of leather-coated taxi drivers came surging. Bartering with one produced catcalls from the others, and later poundings on his hood when they thought I had prevailed in the negotiations. An hour later, after twenty minutes spent driving around Giza looking for my hotel, I was ready to pound the hood myself. My frustration only grew when I arrived in my room, with its stained red carpet, dripping faucet, and avocado glow from the fluorescent lamp. I felt helpless, an emotion that worsened in the days to come when something I ate quietly gutted my stomach and left me intimate with Cairo's tradition of seatless toilets. It was as if some childhood prejudice against Egypt had spread to my body, Tutankhamen's revenge.

But something else happened on that trip. After gulping down my disorientation, I ventured into the lobby to inquire about guides and the attendant spent fifteen minutes unfolding tattered pieces of paper until he found the name of a guide who spoke English. I went outside for a walk, initially ignoring some teenagers who were heckling me, until I realized that they were merely offering a smoke and trying to ask me a question, "Do you know Michael Jordan?" And by the following night I felt so comfortable that I said good-bye to my guide and boarded a public Volkswagen minibus in the direction of Giza. When I asked for the right stop, the fifteen people in the van joined in the conversation and eventually persuaded the driver to change his course. Half of the riders disembarked early to walk me to my destination. "The biggest surprise about the Middle East," I declared to friends, "is how friendly the Arabs are." Tutankhamen's allure.

That allure lingered so long that for the Egyptian leg of our trip I welcomed Avner's suggestion that I contact a friend of his who runs excursions down the Nile and go ahead for a few days. One shadow hanging over this trip was the issue of how easy it would be to travel around the country following several attacks on tourists by Muslim extremists anxious to destabilize the government by driving away foreign currency. An intelligence officer in Israel had warned, "Don't go to

Luxor." I was going to Luxor, as well as to Aswan, both of them in the Nile Valley. At the moment the only way to visit these places was with police protection, which meant going in groups, which meant being met at the Cairo airport by a man with my name on a sign. I felt somewhat guilty for arriving in Egypt to investigate the enslavement of the Israelites with such conspicuous modern amenities. But given my previous arrival experience, and considering my relief at finding two working lights and a bottle of water in my hotel, I felt liberated, even though I was still several steps away from that storied part of the Bible.

Waking up in Egypt reminded me quickly that I was back in the Third World: You can't drink the water, but you still must eat. The Egyptian breakfast is not quite as plentiful as the Israeli, but it has a similar feel. Plates of white and yellow cheeses, bowls of steamed plums, and lots of creamy things with spices that look like crawly insects sprawled on top. Arabs like their spices still on the stem—oregano, coriander, fennel, cumin. I practically had to chew through a crown of thorns to find my way to a broiled tomato: Take that, English imperialism.

Traveling from Lower Egypt, which is the north of the country, to Upper Egypt, which is the south, was once as forbidding as traveling from Egypt to Palestine. The two lands were bitter enemies, with Upper Egypt typically symbolized by the vulture goddess and Lower Egypt by the cobra. The first time the two were unified, around 3100 B.C.E., is considered the beginning of Egyptian history. Thomas Mann, in his reimagining of the Joseph tale, had Joseph dragged by caravan for a month to Lower Egypt, then another nine days by barge to Upper. "The empty boat was characteristic of the country," Mann wrote, "for it was the clumsiest freighter to be found anywhere in Memphis; with a belly hold built for cargo space, latticed wooden weather-boards, a cabin consisting only of a mat-covered shelter, and a tiny but very heavy rudder fastened perpendicular to a pole at the stern." In the nineteenth century one could go by railcar, in the twentieth century by automobile. What modern technology rendered painless, though, terrorism rendered void. Since the uprisings, Middle Egypt has been off-limits to foreigners and Upper

Egypt accessible only by plane, which I planned to take at 6:15 A.M., not four hours after I fell asleep.

The flight itself spanned pillows of arid desert, interrupted by plunging multicolored canyons. The soil, in the early morning light, seemed like giant chunks of raw chocolate. But then, suddenly, the terrain shifted. The soil began to blacken. A vivid green grass sprouted up like hair on one of those Chia pets. Palm trees leapt from the ground, an army of squirming artichokes. The vision of this ribbon of green from a landscape of brown was jolting, sort of like seeing dill weed sprinkled on a candy bar. But then the mind begins to kick in. This is the mother of life, the father of civilization. This is metaphor itself.

The Nile.

Another man with a sign met me at the Luxor airport and we drove to our first stop, the temple of Dendera, where I would meet up with the group. Though part of me wondered whether visiting Upper Egypt, which doesn't appear by name in the Bible, would help my search, Avner assured me it would. "Egyptian history is even more important to the Bible than Mesopotamian," he said. "Plus, these are the greatest monuments of the ancient world! You can't understand the Bible without understanding them." The scenery was lush, like some leafy vision of a rain forest. The vegetation covered every inch of the ground, like a salad bar, with date palms, sugarcane, onions, and clover. But the green wasn't everywhere. Up above, lording over the strip, were the eastern hills of the Sahara, burnt as toast. And down below, like the world's biggest gutter, was the river itself, black, brown, olive. Life.

The Nile is to rivers what the Bible is to books. Covering one-sixth of the earth's circumference, the river flows 4,180 miles, almost twice as long as the Mississippi, and longer than the Tigris, the Euphrates, and the Colorado Rivers combined. The river has two branches. The White Nile, the longer, begins in central Africa, feeds into Lake Victoria, then steams north through the Sudan. The Blue Nile begins in the Ethiopian highlands and joins the White in Khartoum, where together they roll 1,600 miles to the Mediterranean, which ancient Egyptians called the

"Great Green." The river, naturally, inspires awe in everyone who sees it. Herodotus called Egypt the "gift of the Nile." Napoleon said Egypt contained, "in the Nile, the spirit of the good, and in the desert, the spirit of evil." But for purple grandeur, no one beats the English historian Emil Ludwig, who wrote in his 1936 epic, *The Nile*:

> *Its basin contains the biggest lake of the eastern hemisphere, the highest mountains, the biggest city of its continent. Its banks are peopled by the richest bird life of the northern hemisphere, by nearly every animal species known to Paradise, by vegetation ranging from Alpine flora and the tropical forest, through swamp, steppe, and desert to the richest arable land on earth. It feeds hundreds of different races, men of the mountain and men of the marsh, Arabs, Christians, and cannibals, pygmies and giants. The struggles of these men for power and wealth, for faith and custom, for the supremacy of colour, can be traced farther back here than anywhere else in the history of mankind—for six thousand years.*

As with the Tigris and Euphrates, the key to the river's power was its floods. For nine months a year, 20 percent of the river's volume comes from the White Nile, 80 percent from the Blue. From August to November, though, monsoon rains in the Ethiopian highlands cause the Blue Nile to swell and provide 95 percent of the waters of the annual inundation. Ancient priests said that Isis, mourning every summer for her brother Osiris, shed tears into the river, making it flood. Later, Muslim tradition held that the flood began with a divine drop every June 17. Though the inundation was regular (until the Aswan High Dam tamed the river in 1968), it varied in height from year to year. As a result, the pharaohs developed their own version of Groundhog Day. On the first day of the flood the priests would open a Nilometer, a marble well that measured the height of the water and was decorated with two copper eagles, one male, one female. If the female eagle "screamed" first, a minor flood was predicted. If the male eagle screamed first, a great flood was predicted, and the pharaoh immediately raised the price of corn.

The extraordinary virility of the flood comes from its silt, a black alluvial deposit so rich in nutrients that as recently as the 1960s, before the dam trapped most of the silt, the land could yield *two* crops in a single year. Ancient Egyptians called the flooded territory Black Land, as opposed to the Red Land of the desert, and never built temples in the ribbon of fertility. The silt's potency comes from its wide menu of ingredients. The Blue Nile brings volcanic ash and residue from bush fires; the White Nile adds vegetable and plant debris from its swamps. Nile silt has magnetic powers, from its high degree of iron oxide, and even contains gold, though not enough to be profitably panned. Altogether, the silt's fertilizing power has been calculated at $85.36 an acre. (By way of comparison, it costs an average of $5.43 today to fertilize an acre of soybeans.) Like manna, Nile silt is all things to all people.

Perhaps the best expression of this universality came when I arrived on the river that afternoon and started speaking with some of the local workers on board the ship. I asked what they thought of the Nile. One said it was a trunk, another an arm, another a backbone. Mohammed, a shopkeeper, said it was "the only thing we have."

"What about your girlfriend," I asked, "or your mother?"

"I think it's bigger than those," he said. "I only see my mother once every four months."

"You're saying the Nile's more important than your mother?"

"The river doesn't ask for money."

Our first stop after leaving the airport that morning was the city of Qena and the temple compound of Dendera. Situated at the top of a congested stretch of the Nile Valley, fifty miles north of Luxor, Qena has long been something of a frontier. In the nineteenth century it was home to vice, as Cairo strongman Mohammed Ali exiled prostitutes and belly dancers here. Recently it's been home to fundamentalism. In 1992, Qena was the site of the first attack on tourists, when militants ambushed a tour bus, killing, among others, a fourteen-year-old boy. The government responded by razing a nearby village.

Security was tight as we approached, and reminded me of Hebron. Dendera is one of dozens of temples dangled along this serpentine span of the river like charms on a bracelet. The thousands of tombs and scores of pharaonic monuments make the Nile Valley the largest open-air museum in the world. As such, it continues to attract tourists, despite the terror. The group I was meeting was composed largely of retirees from Manchester, England. Their guide was a well-dressed twenty-six-year-old Cairene named Basem, who had a master's degree in Egyptology, spoke the Queen's English, and, had it been cooler, probably would have worn a tweed blazer with elbow patches. As it was, he was the only person wearing long sleeves. "I feel it's a great duty to teach people about the history of Egypt," he said. "I love to say good things about my country. Generally speaking, about the Middle East, the world has very bad images."

He led the group inside the gates and stopped in the open plaza. Compared to the flat, matzohlike ruins of Israel, the monuments of Egypt are remarkably intact. They're plump, multilayered biscuits of antiquity, full of flavor. One reason is sand. When archaeologists started searching the Nile Valley in the nineteenth century, the temples were largely underground, covered by centuries of Saharan sand blown from the west. When they removed the dunes, not only the buildings were preserved but also the hieroglyphics, and sometimes even the paint.

Dendera is a sterling example of preservation, mostly because it was built late, around 125 B.C.E. It's a reconstruction of an earlier temple dedicated to Hathor, the cow goddess known for her milk-giving fertility, and was designed to emulate its predecessors in an attempt to legitimize Egypt's then-foreign rulers. The building's trademark is a relief of the most famous of those carpetbaggers, Cleopatra, the last pharaoh from the line of Greek-born Ptolemys. Her chubby-cheeked face is far removed from what she really looked like, Basem noted—beak nose, high cheekbones, prominent chin—but far closer to the image created by Elizabeth Taylor.

Because they're so well preserved, Egyptian temples are virtual textbooks of ancient religion, three-dimensional scrolls. Each temple was built in the image of the cosmos. Egyptian creation stories show similarities to Mesopotamian stories, and thus to Genesis. In the beginning were the Great Waters, full of serpents and frogs, and the Great Egg. The Egg split into two, out of which arose Amen-Re, the god of light, who in turn created a pantheon of gods who controlled the sun, moon, land, plants, animals, and humans. Each temple was constructed as a reverse expression of this story, a moving from the human world to the divine. First one passes through a doorway showing the pharaoh making offerings to the gods. Next comes an outer hall, or hypostyle hall, whose forest of columns was designed to evoke a papyrus thicket. In Dendera, these columns require three sets of arms to encircle them. Beyond this room lie a series of vestibules and ultimately the sanctuary, with images of the deity. The sanctuary was said to rest on the original hill of creation. In deference, floors got higher and ceilings got lower the closer they got to the holy of holies. As Basem pointed out, this gradual elevation meant that each temple was like a pyramid on its side.

After exploring the site for a while, I ventured up a set of stairs to the rooftop sanctuary, where every New Year's Eve Hathor's statue was carried to await dawn. Touched by the rays of her father, the sun god Amen-Re, Hathor's soul would be revitalized for the coming year. While I was admiring the view of the Nile, Basem walked up next to me. I asked him what interested him most about ancient Egypt. Was it the river, the religion, the buildings?

"The people," he said. "The people are the ones who made these things. Certainly the river made civilization possible, but it was the people who tamed the river and utilized its resources. Personally speaking, when I take groups to the temples, I usually talk about the pharaoh, I talk about the gods, because the people want to know that. But in my own private reading I prefer to read about how the people were living. How a farmer used to wake up, go to the fields, go to the temple once a year for the festival."

"So do you think they're like you?" I said.

"This country has been invaded many times," he said. "The Persians came here in 336 B.C.E. Then the Greeks arrived, and the Romans. The Romans left, the Arabs came. Then we got the French, the Turks, the English. We're all a mixture. Part of me is from Saudi Arabia and another part from Turkey."

"Does that mean you can't relate to ancient Egyptians?"

"Physically I do. I was brought up in this country. I drank its waters,

I saw its fields. But I don't relate to the ancient people in their way of thinking, because my religion is totally different. They used to worship many gods. They worshiped the sun, because it's powerful. They worshiped the water, because it gave them irrigation. They worshiped the crocodile, because it was strong. They looked at nature and took their religious views from it. Now we don't do that. We're Christian or Muslim, and in neither do we take our religious views from nature."

"So where do you take them from?"

"We have the Bible and the Koran," he said. "We take guidance from God."

After the tour we boarded a bus and headed to the boat for lunch. Ever since the advent of leisure travel in the nineteenth century, the Nile has been a popular destination. Baedeker published its first guidebook to Egypt in 1878. Its eighth edition, published in 1929, touted the salutary effects of the dry winter climate. "Phthisis (if not too far advanced), asthma, chronic bronchitis, rheumatoid arthritis, gout, Bright's disease, and other diseases of the kidneys are some of the most important ailments that are at least alleviated by a visit to Egypt. Invalids should remember that a stay of a few weeks only is not sufficient and should remain from the beginning of November to the middle of April."

Today almost three hundred cruise ships are licensed to take tourists along the 150-mile stretch between Luxor and Aswan, the Champs-Élysées of the ancient world. Since these vessels don't need to be seaworthy, they're not exactly enormous cruise liners à la *The Love Boat.* Instead they're closer to luxury barges with several floors of cabins, ornate rooms for dining and dancing, and a deck for indulging the antipsoriatic qualities of the sun. Our boat, the *Royal Rhapsody,* had a particularly impressive array of charms, including chandeliers that swayed as we ate, an in-house video system that favored Disney's *101 Dalmatians,* and towels folded every night on the beds in the shape of mountains, rivers, even crocodiles.

But for all the luxury, there was something surreal about the experience. Just going ashore was something of an enterprise. The crew lowered a touring boat onto the water, lowered a gangplank onto that, then lowered a ladder to the start of the plank. A dozen or so passengers would wobble down to their places, followed by a half-dozen guards dressed in *galabiyah* robes carrying AK-47s, several supervisors dressed in coat and tie, and a porter wearing a tuxedo and balancing a silver tray with tiny glasses of lemonade covered in plastic wrap. The atmosphere was somewhere between Agatha Christie and Mad Max.

Later, when I ventured south of the Aswan Dam and joined an even larger boat, designed to replicate a Mississippi River paddleboat, that had only eight people on board, the experience was even more post-apocalyptic. If the world ends, this is how it will happen: six nationalities dressed in vermilion and white-lace Egyptian robes and assorted unflattering headgear—cardboard fezzes, red-and-white-checked kaffiyeh—eating London broil, French onion soup, and baked Alaska, followed by dancing in a blue-and-orange flashing disco as the bartender, naked except for a grass skirt and African mask, gyrates with drunk passengers to tomba chants, French chansons, and, how could it be otherwise, Celine Dion singing "My Heart Will Go On," the theme song from *Titanic*. If Burton and Livingstone had expected this when they uncovered the source of the Nile in the late nineteenth century they might have decided to stay at home and read a good book. As one Londoner on board said: "There is no end to the humiliation of tourists on holiday."

Given this atmosphere, the most delightful part of the trip upriver was sitting on the deck, watching the banks of the Nile. The absence of development was striking, especially compared to Cairo. Ninety-five percent of Egyptians live on only 5 percent of the land, and most of those live in Lower Egypt. Upper Egypt, by contrast, which earned its name because it's "up river," is an agricultural backwater. In the course of several days, I could count on one hand the number of buildings I saw higher than one story. The number of crops was greater: corn, sugar-cane, sesame, dates, figs, pomegranates, pistachios, bananas, mangoes, garlic, and onions. The proximity of Egypt to the Promised Land was most evident in the vegetation, including the acacia tree, which the Bible says was used to make the ark; the *Ziziphus Spina Christi,* which was used to make Christ's crown of thorns; and the carob, also called St. John's bread.

I was sitting on the deck at the end of the first day when Basem appeared and asked if he could sit down next to me. Though he was fasting during daylight hours in honor of the Muslim holy month of Ramadan, he didn't seem to lose energy as the day went along. If anything, he seemed to welcome the opportunity, even at this late hour, to engage in an impromptu tutorial.

What was even more remarkable about Basem was his knowledge of the ancient Near East. He was like a younger Egyptian version of Avner, only neater and in linen pants. I mentioned that I could detect echoes of Canaan, and more of Mesopotamia, in what we had already seen, and asked how much contact ancient Egypt had with its neighbors. "It depends on which millennium you're talking about," he said.

Though settlements existed in the Nile Valley as early as the Neolithic Age, around 6000 B.C.E., Egyptian history is said to begin around 3100 B.C.E., when the quasi-historical ruler Menes first unified Upper and Lower Egypt and began the dynastic tradition that dominated the country for the next three thousand years. Under the pharaonic code, the king was not merely the political leader, he was the embodiment of the gods; to rebel against him was to reject divine order. During the Old Kingdom, which began around 2686 B.C.E., the pharaohs leveraged their power, along with that of the Nile, to create unprecedented technological advances and perhaps the most unified culture in the Fertile Crescent, with myths, religious practices, and elaborate monuments. It was during this period that the pyramids of Giza redefined the relationship between the earth and sky. Unlike the Tower of Babel, here some men, at least, could climb to heaven.

During this period, there was little struggle between Egypt and its counterparts in Mesopotamia, since both civilizations were still being established. "Egyptians were lucky," Basem noted. "The Nile gave them easy communication and helped unify them." By contrast, the Tigris and Euphrates were harder to control. Since they're not surrounded by desert, the two rivers could support more people, which meant cities developed at a faster rate. Eventually those cities started to fight one another. "They were older than we were, but we lasted longer," he said. "Why? Because they clashed more than us. They had the Sumerians, the Akkadians, the Assyrians, and each one wanted control. Here, Upper or Lower Egypt always dominated the other; it was never a prolonged struggle."

Though some early pharaohs traded with Canaan, it was not until the Middle Kingdom (2050–1786 B.C.E.) that Egypt began exerting a stronger hand in these areas. During this period, which corresponds to the time of the patriarchs, Assyria, to the north, was still the greater influence in Canaan. Egypt, though, because of its regular floods, would have been an easy place to escape to during a drought, as both Abraham and Jacob do. A more intriguing period in Egyptian history followed, a sort of Dark Ages, during which the country was overtaken by a mysterious sect of outsiders called the Hyksos. Many believe this time corresponded to the period when Joseph and his brothers came to Egypt. The Hyksos, who were probably Canaanites fleeing hardship, controlled the country for about 150 years beginning in the eighteenth century B.C.E. and, if nothing else, awakened the giant within Egypt. Once the foreigners had been expelled, the newly emboldened pharaohs of the New Kingdom (1570–1070 B.C.E.) began an aggressive military surge into Canaan and Assyria, all the way to the banks of the Euphrates.

"First the pharaohs built fortresses in the Sinai," Basem said. "Then, for the first time, they conscripted people into the army. Finally they went out to see if any other people were stronger than they were. From that day, every Egyptian king for six hundred years was leaving the country, exploiting other people, trying to conquer them. In the beginning it was for safety, then it was for wealth. Ultimately it was for power. That's when the struggle with Mesopotamia began."

That rivalry, of course—the cold war of antiquity—provided the backdrop for the Pentateuch. And I was beginning to realize that if I hoped to understand the Bible I had to take what I learned about Mesopotamia and balance it with similar information about Egypt. Genesis: the gift of the Tigris, the Euphrates, *and* the Nile.

. . .

After Basem left I sat for a while and watched the sun set over the river. It was a vivid scene, made even more poignant by our gradual drift upstream. First the sun was yellow, then orange, then red. The sky turned deeper shades of lavender. At the outset the air was brilliantly clear, a significant break from the haze of midday. Feluccas, narrow fishing boats with crisp, white triangular sails, dotted the water. Boys stood inside them fishing for Nile perch, a process that involved taking a broom and beating the water in back of the boat, then scurrying to the front, where the frightened fish flee, and dropping a net into their path. Bait and switch never seemed so cruelly effective.

On the shore, meanwhile, smoke billowed up from a brush fire. A few bushes lined the edge of the water, followed by a grassy plain and a strip of date palms tilting like pinwheels on a stick, first green, then gold, depending on the light. The call to prayer came, but without visible buildings or minarets, it seemed as if the mud itself was making the cry. As we continued our steady glide upriver, the boat began to feel as if it might be floating back in time: Kurtz, Lord Jim, Livingstone. Not just temples, maybe the river, too, was a pyramid to the past.

After a while I began to realize that, compared to the Tigris and Euphrates, the Nile was having a much more visceral effect on me. It's as if the current was dragging me through a series of mental images, like frames in a filmstrip. On the one hand, each image took me further back in history, from Burton, to Napoleon, to Cleopatra, to Rameses. On the other hand, each memory took me further back into my own imagination, into some shifting realm of fantasies about the unknown, and anxieties about strangers and strangeness.

For me, being on the Nile was a bit like being in a bad night of sleep, with my mind ricocheting through a series of associations before it landed, inevitably, on some truth I didn't want to face: as much as I romanticized this place, I also feared it. Part of this feeling was self-induced drama, brought on by a combination of little sleep and a few yellowed paperbacks I brought along about the exotic, if deadly, Nile expeditions of the nineteenth century. Part of it, though, was the water. As safe and anchored as I felt on the land I'd been seeing across the Middle East, I felt uncomfortable on the water. Sand can be touched, laid on, held; water can only be grasped at, passed through. As a matter of pure geography, I prefer the land. I'm clearly not alone in this feeling. If anything, I suspect it's one reason so many Near Eastern origin stories, including the one in Genesis, begin with land emerging out of watery chaos. Water is turbulent and alien in these formulations; land is safe and secure.

This hints at a deeper reason behind my anxiety: an aversion to the Nile itself. This feeling, I was beginning to see, like many I unknowingly carried around within me, stems largely from the Bible, and the deep cultural prejudices I inherited from it as a child. The Nile may have given rise to the greatest civilization of antiquity, but that civilization, in turn, almost annihilated the Israelites. In my mind, Egypt was the adversary, the aggressor, the other. And before I could embrace—or even appreciate—this part of the Bible, I first had to overcome any latent hostility to Egypt.

After a while the sun slid behind the trees. As richly as the sky had been illuminated, suddenly it began to fade. A breeze appeared, like a warning. The pastels dimmed and saddened a bit. A cottony beard of fog sprouted on the water. It was as if the Nile was cocooning for the night, protecting itself. When your god is the sun, you are bathed in godliness for half of every day. When it goes away, you're left with emptiness and dread.

The next day we traveled a few miles inland to visit the Valley of the Kings, which, after the pyramids, is probably the most famous cemetery in the world. Located in the hills on the west bank of the Nile so that buried pharaohs would have first dibs on the rising sun, the necropolis is an underground network of dozens of tombs housing the kings and their families. The area is shaped like a human hand, with fingers reaching away from the Nile into the Theban hills. Thebes was the capital of unified Egypt for much of the New Kingdom, and thus the place most pharaohs wanted to be buried. As a result, tombs were dug so closely together that builders of one crypt would often stumble upon another and have to reroute their corridor, like ants in a colony.

One reason for this congestion was the strict mythology that surrounded death. After the pharaohs died, their souls were believed to survive in order to commune with Amen-Re, the sun god, and Osiris, the god of the underworld. The deceased's soul passed into a hall of truth, where Osiris held court, judging the king's life. To pass into the afterlife, the deceased's body also needed to exist, which inspired the most famous preservation technique in history, mummification. According to one estimate, Egyptians mummified more than one hundred million people. The technique involved removing the brain through the nostrils, extracting the organs, then filling the cavity with burnished myrrh. The cadaver was then soaked in salt—seventy days for the pharaoh, forty days for noblemen—painted, and wrapped in linen. According to Herodotus, the wives of men of rank, as well as "any of the more beautiful women," were not embalmed immediately. "This is done to prevent indignities from being done to them. It is said that once a case of this kind occurred."

Entering the tombs today is like entering someone else's death wish. Each of the corridors, a narrower, creepier version of an airport jetway, is decorated over every inch of every wall and ceiling with elaborate paintings describing the pharaoh's journey through the underworld. Every night, Amen-Re boards a barque, descends into the underground, and voyages through the hours of the night, before rising again at dawn. The deceased pharaoh follows a similar path. He passes twelve gates, each guarded by a god, before having his heart weighed against the Feather of Truth. If deemed guilty, the pharaoh's heart is consumed by a crocodile-headed god; if deemed innocent, the pharaoh is resurrected, like Amen-Re. The collective versions of this story are called *The Book of the Dead*.

"As you see, it's the perfect book," Basem said inside the tomb of Seti I. "On one wall is the text, on the other the pictures. It even begins with a cover photo, an oversized picture of the pharaoh."

Actually it's more like a scroll, and after hours wandering from tomb to tomb, looking at painting after painting in a Freudian display of nocturnal intrigue, I began to realize that nighttime was perhaps even more important than daytime in the Egyptian imagination. This would help explain the fascination with prophecy, magic, and life after death. This would help explain the importance of dreams. And most of all, this would help explain the story of Joseph.

By all accounts, the tale of Joseph, which picks up after the rape of Dinah and occupies the last thirteen chapters of Genesis, is the most unified story in the Hebrew Bible, a novella of perfect proportions. As scholar Nahum Sarna has written: "There is an unparalleled continuity of narrative set forth with the consummate skill of a master story-teller who employs to the full the novelistic techniques of character delineation, psychological treatment, the play upon the emotions and the cultivation of suspense." By equal consensus, the story owes a clear debt to the darker dimensions of Egyptian life.

Joseph is the eleventh of Jacob's twelve sons, and the first by his favorite wife, Rachel. At seventeen, Joseph tends flocks in central Canaan with his brothers, and brings bad reports of them to his father. Because Joseph is the child of his father's old age, the text says, Jacob favors Joseph and gives him what some translations call an "ornamented tunic," and others a "coat of many colors" (the exact meaning is unclear). This gesture infuriates his brothers. Joseph then riles them further by relating two dreams in which his brothers, represented first by wheat, then by stars, bow down to him. "Do you mean to reign over us?" they ask. In retaliation, the brothers decide to slay him.

One day Joseph follows his brothers to the town of Dothan, north of Shechem in the Galilee, and they announce, "Here comes that dreamer! Come now, let us kill him and throw him into one of the pits, and we can say, 'A savage beast devoured him.' We shall see what comes of his dreams." At the last minute, Reuben, Leah's oldest son, intervenes. "Shed no blood!" Reuben declares. "Cast Joseph into the pit out in the wilderness, but do not touch him yourselves."

At that moment a caravan of Ishmaelites, or Midianites, a people from across the Jordan descended from the brothers' great-uncle Ishmael, pass by bearing goods for Egypt. Judah, another of Leah's sons, announces: "What do we gain by killing our brother and covering up his blood? Come, let us sell him to the Ishmaelites." After all, Joseph is our brother, Judah says, "our own flesh." The brothers agree, and they sell Joseph to the tribe for twenty shekels, an amount consistent with contemporaneous accounts of foreigners being sold into Egypt. The brothers then take Joseph's coat, dip it into blood from a slaughtered kid, and have it carried to their father. "Please examine this," they say. Jacob recognizes the coat and wails, "My son's tunic! A savage beast devoured him!" He rends his clothes, puts sackcloth on his loins, and mourns for many days. His children try to comfort him, but Jacob refuses.

Joseph, meanwhile, arrives in Egypt and is sold as a servant to the house of Potiphor, a courtier of the pharaoh and his chief steward. God stays with Joseph during this time, the text says, and Joseph rises to become head of the household. Described as being "well built and handsome," Joseph rejects repeated advances from Potiphor's wife. One day she grabs him by the coat and says, "Lie with me!" But in an echo of the story of his brothers, he leaves his coat behind and flees. She takes the coat and says to her husband, "The Hebrew slave whom you brought into our house came to dally with me; but when I screamed at the top of my voice, he left his coat with me and fled outside."

Potiphor promptly throws Joseph into prison, but God stays with Joseph, the text says, and assures that the chief jailer is kind to him. While in prison, Joseph hears that two of his fellow prisoners, a cupbearer and a baker, have had dreams that they cannot interpret. "Surely God can interpret!" Joseph says. "Pray tell me your dreams." The cupbearer's dream involves three branches that bud into grapes, which then get pressed into the pharaoh's cup. Joseph says the dream means that in three days the cupbearer will be pardoned. The baker's dream involves three open baskets of food, which birds pick clean. Joseph says the dream means that in three days pharaoh will behead the baker and birds will pick his body clean. In three days, the pharaoh's birthday, both dreams come true.

Two years later, the pharaoh has a dream that out of the Nile emerge seven cows, handsome and sturdy, that graze on the land. They are followed by seven more cows, ugly and gaunt, that eat the earlier set of cows. He has another dream in which seven ears of grain, solid and healthy, grow on a single stalk. They are followed by seven ears, thin and scorched, which swallow up the seven solid ears. None of the pharaoh's messengers can interpret his dreams, so the cupbearer recommends Joseph, who's still in prison. The pharaoh sends for Joseph and asks him to interpret the dreams. "Not I!" Joseph says. "God will see to Pharaoh's welfare." The dreams are one and the same, Joseph declares. "Immediately ahead are seven years of great abundance in all the land of Egypt. After them will come seven years of famine, and all the abundance in the land of Egypt will be forgotten." As for why the pharaoh has the dream twice, "It means that the matter has been determined by God."

Joseph further recommends that the pharaoh take steps to preserve food from the seven fat years to use during the seven lean years. The plan pleases the pharaoh, and he asks Joseph to organize the effort. "You shall be in charge of my court," the pharaoh says. "Only with respect to the throne will I be superior to you." Removing the signet from his hand, the pharaoh puts it on Joseph's hand, and dresses him in linen robes, yet another important coat in Joseph's life.

According to scholars, foreigners did, on occasion, become prime minister of Egypt. Also, the swearing-in ceremony, during which Joseph receives the ring and robes, is well known from art during the New Kingdom. As for interpreting dreams, it was a highly coveted skill, usually performed by priests. As Basem explained, "They might have been magicians; we don't know. What we do know is they used books of interpretations. If you looked into a mirror, this meant you'd have a second wife. If you looked out a window, this meant you'd prosper in the afterlife. If you went to a certain city, this meant you were going to die." In a further sign of accuracy, the word the Bible uses for interpreters is Egyptian in origin, as are other details, like the use of cows, which were not common in Palestine. Ultimately, these uncannily accurate details of daily life—perhaps unknowable to later scribes—suggest that the story of Joseph, like those of his forefathers, began as an oral tradition, with deep roots in the Nile.

As if to reinforce that connection, the story soon brings Jacob's brothers into Egypt. The famine that Joseph predicted forces ten of his brothers to seek relief in Egypt, where they unknowingly appear before their brother. Joseph recognizes them and, in a gesture that seems part a retaliation and part a test, accuses them of being spies. He insists they leave one brother behind and return with Jacob's missing eleventh brother, Benjamin, whose mother is also Rachel. They do so and Joseph appears to honor them with a banquet, at which point he falsely accuses Benjamin of stealing a goblet. Judah begins to apologize until Joseph cuts him off, reveals himself at last to his brothers, and forgives them. "Do not be distressed or reproach yourselves because you sold me hither," Joseph says. "It was to save life that God sent me ahead of you." The brothers then bring their father, Jacob, to Egypt and the pharaoh invites them to live on his best land, in Goshen, part of the fertile Nile Delta north of Cairo. As further proof of the good relations the Israelites enjoy with Egypt, Jacob is mummified when he dies. The task takes forty days, as it would for a nobleman, but he is mourned for seventy days, as if he were a king.

"So what do you think?" I said to Basem. We had been in half a dozen tombs by now and seen countless images that could have illustrated Genesis itself. "Do you think the story is true?"

"Do you want me to speak from the point of view of religion, or the point of view of history?" he said.

"Neither. I want you to speak from the point of view of yourself."

"Myself? I think religion is more powerful than history. I think Joseph existed."

For several more days we traveled at a similar pace, seeing temples during the day, enjoying the river in the afternoons, eating five-course meals at night. Compared with seeing holy places in Israel, most of which have few tangible remains, visiting sacred sites in Egypt is a much more physical—even carnal—experience and hints at what places of worship must have felt like across the ancient world. With their large, blocky walls and soaring columns the temples seem to carve out sacred spaces like brackets dropped from the sky. Enter here and escape the onrush of time; enter here and contemplate eternity.

Because Egyptian temples were built so early in the course of human history, they often seem closer to the natural world than to other man-made structures. One reason is they are unencumbered by architectural precedent; they refer to nature, not to other buildings. Early temples, for example, used actual bound papyrus, like thatch, for columns. When these were replicated in stone, architects copied everything, including the flower at the top and the bulge in the middle. These columns are bulkier than their European counterparts—linebackers, not halfbacks—and are bunched like reeds.

The more striking feature of the temples is their decoration. In Kom Ombo, just north of Aswan, where we arrived on the third day, the temple is a hulking tribute to schizophrenia. One side is devoted to Horus, the falcon-headed god of medicine; the other side to Sobek, the crocodile god of fertility. Wandering around the compound, I was struck by the juxtaposition of the grand, almost torsolike shape of the columns with the graceful finery of the hieroglyphs, tattoos on the body of the gods. It was as if the mere act of storytelling was so powerful that it could no longer contain itself and needed to be splashed onto every surface. This is storytelling of the most public kind, the gradual transference of local myths into the permanence of history. And what stories they were—full of love, jealousy, rivalry among the gods, vicious wars, and tender truces.

Today, five thousand years after this process started, the monuments of the Nile Valley are a testament to the sheer awe that educated and lay Egyptians alike felt at the impact of their own stories. The walls are not merely sprinkled with writing, they are *covered* with it. Every inch of available space is lined with falcons, ibises, crocodiles, cats, rams, egrets, owls, and beetles. There are houseware hieroglyphs—saws, scissors, knives, jars. Agricultural ones—moons, stalks, flowers, seeds. And gastronomic ones—wines, grains, fruits, nuts. There's even a Noah-like menagerie—vultures, ducks, salamanders, baboons. These hieroglyphs climb the walls, ring the columns, and line the lintels until one is so numbed by their presence that it's easy to forget the profundity of it all.

As I stared into the script, like being swallowed in a three-story dictionary, I tried to think of other buildings with so much writing on them. Not Greek temples. Not Gothic cathedrals. Not Japanese shrines or Muslim mosques. The only thing one can conclude is that language was such a novelty, such a profound revision of how people viewed the world, that builders wanted to inundate visitors with the force of language in the same way that the river inundated people with the force of life. And perhaps that's the point. The volume of words on the public monuments of ancient Egypt is comparable to that other magnum force of Egypt, the flood. If language is going to triumph over nature, it first must become nature—the pictograms themselves; then divert attention from nature—use those pictograms to tell stories; then dominate it—erect tall buildings that show the triumph of stories over nature. Egyptians may or may not have been the first to do this, but they were the most effective, at least in the Near East. And in so doing, they may have laid the foundation for the greatest written document to come out of antiquity.

As scholar Nahum Sarna observed, generations of readers have known that Joseph offers one of the most compelling narratives of the Five Books of Moses. From Thomas Mann to Andrew Lloyd Webber, Joseph has inspired more popular retellings than any of his forefathers. Even a lay reader, upon arriving at the Joseph story, perks up. There's a thematic explanation for this attachment: In his descent from chosen son to indentured servant, and in his subsequent rise from captivity to freedom, Joseph's life mirrors the larger story of the Five Books of Moses. But there's another reason: In its abundance of details and its stirring, Hollywood-style plot twists, the story of Joseph is just plain fun to read.

Wandering around Kom Ombo, I felt for the first time that I understood why. With Joseph the Israelites have their deepest interaction with Egyptians and their prodigious gifts of narrative. One can almost feel the imagination and narrative techniques of the patriarchs progressing as they wandered from Mesopotamia, through Canaan, into Egypt, and from each imbibing clues to the importance of stories. The Bible may be the beginning of Western religion, but it's also the culmination of a profoundly Near Eastern sense of how to build a people through storytelling. Egyptians, in particular, were interested in the components that make for good yarns: sex, revenge, power, devotion, despair, and reconciliation. The world's first pulp novels were carved on the walls of Egypt's temples. And these pulp novels may have inspired the Israelites to rachet up the importance of drama in their own national history. From now on, these stories would have to be public, not only retold for all to hear, but inscribed for all to see. From now on, the written word was king.

Two days later, on my last night in Upper Egypt, I went to see the sound and light show at Karnak Temple. A futuristic presentation with lasers and classical music, narrated with melodramatic commentary, the show is part of a global trend—castles in France, monuments in Israel, battleships in the United States—to lure visitors to abandoned sites at night. "I know it sounds corny," a friend advised. "But don't miss it."

We gathered outside a line of parallel sphinxes and a voice—British, deep, stentorian—began. *"May the evening soothe and welcome you, oh Traveler through the night. You will travel no further, because you are come. Here, you are at the beginning of time."*

The voice led us through the largest compound on the Nile. Built over 1,300 years, Karnak is a monstrosity that at its peak in the early second millennium B.C.E. boasted assets including 65 villages, 433 gardens, 421,662 head of cattle, and 81,322 workers. The temple itself, dedicated to Amen-Re, could contain ten Notre Dames or eighteen Parthenons. One Egyptologist called it "an archaeological department store containing something for everyone."

"The solemn threshold you have just crossed was forbidden to mortals. The City of God was a fortress where a garrison of mystic votaries watched over the divine scheme of things."

With each step one could sense the accumulation of power: Thutmose III built this, Seti I added that. The greatest builder was Rameses II, who stuffed 134 columns into the Hypostyle hall and carved images of himself as a triumphant imperialist. One wall shows Rameses crushing the Hittites in Mesopotamia, though records show the contest a draw. Even pharaohs, it seems, had spin doctors.

"Do not be overwhelmed by the sheer size of these ruins. The citadel that arose here was not designed on the scale of man, but on the grand scale of God."

Eventually I decided that while the nighttime setting was spectacular, the commentary was a bit much, so I ducked away from the group. I tiptoed into the darkness, as green shadows from the lasers ricocheted off the columns. A grit filled the air. The voice continued. *"Don't try to count the columns, the colossi, the sphinxes, the obelisks. Try rather with every step you take to hear the whispered response of the ever-present god."* Out in the open, the sky slowly came into view and I was struck by how every object I could see—the moon, a palm tree, a bird with one leg—was grist for a hieroglyph. And it was while noticing this sense of inclusion, while walking around this abandoned temple where every object was poured into the brew of religion, that I began to realize the extent of the changes I had been experiencing on this trip.

Before setting out on this journey, reading the Bible for me had been largely an act of imagination, of trust—that these characters saw these things, said these things, did these things. The characters were almost completely disembodied from time and space. But now, reading the Bible from the inside, as it were, from the places themselves, I could feel myself moving closer to the stories. The Bible was no longer metaphor to me. It was no longer the story of some other people in some faraway places. The places, at least, were familiar now. And for someone from a distinctive place, whose favorite books were always ones with rich, almost overpowering settings—Faulkner's South, Tolstoy's Russia, Updike's New England—that sense of immersion was the first step to the most satisfying feeling I ever have while reading: a feeling that I actually inhabit the story. I climb through the pages, slip through the scenery, and enter some parallel place full of swamps, or canyons, or castles, or dales. And not until I cross that divide—not until I walk in that world—can I fully enter the minds of the characters, and feel their desires as my own.

Three verses from the end of Genesis, Joseph, on his deathbed, tells his brothers: "I am about to die; but God will remember you, and bring you up out of this land to the land which he swore to Abraham, Isaac, and Jacob." It was his greatest prediction, and with it Joseph seems to draw a distinction between himself and his forefathers. He's not a patri-arch, he's a prophet. And for me, standing now in the capital of ancient Egypt, perhaps in the very place that Joseph stood, at the farthest point of the Fertile Crescent from where his great-grandfather was born, and realizing that Joseph *predicted* the Exodus, which meant that he knew his descendants would be enslaved by the pharaoh and then freed by God, was the most powerful expression of optimism—and faith—I had ever encountered.

It was also, at that moment, an overpowering challenge that I sensed I could no longer continue to avoid. Would I place such credence in a generations-old promise I never actually heard? Could I meet this stan-dard of commitment—to *anything*? Would I have such faith? Here, at the end of Genesis, was a stirring new prototype of dedication. Even among all the pantheon of Egyptian gods—tactile, visual, with suns for bodies and crocodiles for heads—Joseph continued to believe in his own god: invisible, untouchable, unknowable.

Yet undeniably real.

2. And They Made Their Lives Bitter

This is what it takes to cross the street in Cairo: First you have to determine which cars are moving and which are not. This is not as easy as it might seem. Streets have no particular distinction between where cars should be driven and where they should be parked. Step onto a thoroughfare at, say, 9:00 on a Tuesday morning in early winter, as I did with Avner from our hotel, and one is overwhelmed by the sheer volume of cars. Cars in the left lane going in one direction, cars in the right lane going in the same direction. Cars on the sidewalk going in the opposite direction. Cars in the middle parked. Often the only way to tell which cars are operating is to feel the hood. A warm hood means the engine is running and it's best to stand back. A cold hood means the car is stalled and the driver has stepped away—for a few days.

"Making this walk reminds me of what a friend of mine said of Tehran," Avner said. "Wake up on one side of the street, stay there until tomorrow."

If Egypt is the gift of the Nile, Cairo is the cleanup job left after all the boxes have been opened and all the guests have gone home. Named Al Kahira, the "Conqueror," by tenth-century Arabs, Cairo has been the largest city in Africa and the Middle East for almost a millennium. Today, with a population nearing twenty million, the "Mother of the World" has more vehicles than the Nile has fish. As a result, it has more congestion than almost any place on earth and a daily derby of pedestrian crossing.

The biggest hazard is the blue-and-white buses, which careen around the city like boxes of SweetTarts being kicked around crowded movie theaters, threatening to spew their contents. The next gravest threat is the public vans, like the ones I used on my first trip, which constantly speed up and slow down as the barker hanging out the passenger window reaches down to scoop up a veiled lady and her basket of cabbage and deposit them in the backseat. Taxis are the most ubiquitous. Black with white splotches over their front and back bumpers, they look like holstein cows being herded down the street. Unlike real cows, though, these taxis have horns that work. As Avner put it, "The only reason these cars have steering wheels is so they have a place to put their horns."

Even Cairenes are overwhelmed by the traffic. When we finally arrived at our destination, the Egyptian Museum, I asked the director of public relations, a friend of Avner's, if she had any advice for how to cross the street. She took the question as a matter of life or death. "Look left, look right, look ahead of you, look behind you, then stare at the driver and make yourself appear strong. Then they'll let you in." She added, "Above all, take nothing for granted."

Inside the museum we left our bags and proceeded into the atrium. More like a warehouse than an archive, the Egyptian Museum feels like a giant pharaonic pawn shop, where four-thousand-year-old sarcophagi are stacked on top of three-thousand-year-old cartouches on top of five-thousand-year-old mummies. And everything needs dusting. Founded in 1858, the museum outgrew its current facility within months and has never quite recovered. Allowing one minute for each object, it would take nearly nine months to view its 136,000 artifacts. Forty thousand more objects lie crated in the basement, where many have sunk into the ground, requiring excavations. Egypt: where even the museums are archaeological sites.

We began to stroll through the corridors. Now several months into our travels, Avner and I were growing more comfortable with the haphazard, make-it-up-as-you-go rhythm of our trip—and more comfortable with each other. From the minute we met up in Egypt, Avner

exuded a boyish glee that I hadn't fully seen since Turkey. I realized that
in Israel, he felt torn between his natural affinity to the tels, the Temple
Mount, and other portals to the past, and his obligations to the modern
world: balancing his checkbook, finding a clean shirt to wear. Here, out
of reach of his cellular phone and never late for a meeting, he could
fully indulge his obsessions with the minutiae of ancient life, with the
subtle, ever-shifting puzzle of what event along the Nile might have
prompted some cultural shift in Canaan, or what religious upheaval in
Egypt might have triggered some biblical plot twist. This was archaeology as literary sleuthing (no wonder Agatha Christie felt so at home in
this world) and we never played at it more than at the Egyptian Museum.

Specifically, we were looking into one enticing possibility, long irresistible to historians, that the monotheism of the Bible may have had a
connection to ancient Egypt. Might the Israelites have learned to worship one god by following the lead of some maverick pharaoh? Or
might the Egyptians have learned the same thing by taking an idea from
the patriarchs?

We arrived at the Amarna Gallery, a well-lit room at the back of the
ground floor that offers a possible answer to that question. Amenhotep
IV, who ruled Egypt from 1377 to 1360 B.C.E., was the second son of
Amenhotep III and his wife, Tiy. At the time, Egypt was continuing its
aggressive empire building, which brought unprecedented riches to the
priests and bureaucrats. The young pharaoh believed these courtiers had
too much power and in the sixth year of his rule abruptly moved the
capital 250 miles north to the desert frontier of El Amarna. Once there,
he radically changed the state religion, demoting Amen-Re, the sun god,
and elevating the marginal god Aten, who represents the sun at midday
only, to sole god. In effect, Amenhotep was the world's first monotheist.
To prove his devotion, he changed his name to Akhenaten, "Agreeable to
Aten," and renamed the capital Akhetaten, "the Horizon of Aten." He
also closed all the temples of Egypt, erased the name Amen from all
monuments, and even changed the plural *gods* to *god*. Donald Redford,
the Egyptologist, has likened this gesture to throwing aside Christ, the
Trinity, and all the saints, and declaring that the cross was not just the
symbol of salvation but the one true God itself.

Akhenaten honored the new god by taking another radical step, ordering his artists to be more expressive. As a result, they created a pro-toplasmic style where everything was soft and flowing. In the gallery, several towering statues of the king featured captivating, almost grotesque, imagery—pursed lips, elongated fingers, distended belly—that makes him look like a cross between Dennis Rodman and Grace Jones. Judging by these images, some modern scholars say the king was black. Some say he was deformed or suffered from a debilitating disease, like hydrocephalus, a disorder of the brain that results in enlarged skulls, or Froehlich's syndrome, a disorder of the pituitary gland that results in infertility, a lack of sex drive, and feminine fat distribution. Others say he was a hermaphrodite. Everyone agrees he was unique, as Egyptologist James Henry Breasted put it, "the first individual in history."

"You have to realize how remarkable this was," Avner said. "Egyptian art was not realistic, it was stylized. If you lined up all the statues of the pharaohs before Akhenaten, they look like the same person. Egypt hated change. The secret of life was continuity. The flood came at the same time every year; the water rose in the same way. Everyone prayed that the world would stay as it is. It's quite a strange concept for us, but it's very Egyptian. To change even slightly the art style was a great revolution."

This breakthrough, especially in the realm of religion, was so unex-pected that it raises the tantalizing possibility that it came from outside Egypt. Perhaps some foreigner penetrated the highest corridors of the pharaonic court and planted in the mind of the young king the idea that there was a single god. One man fits this description perfectly. In Genesis 41, when Joseph is called before the pharaoh to interpret his dream, Joseph says, "Not I! God will see to Pharaoh's welfare." Accord-ing to traditional dating, which places Abraham around 1900 B.C.E., Joseph would likely have lived long before Akhenaten, during the time of the Hyksos, around 1700 B.C.E. The Hyksos were foreigners, and thus likely more sympathetic to an outsider like Joseph; also they intro-duced horses, which would be consistent with the biblical description of Joseph using chariots during his tenure as prime minister.

Recently, several maverick scholars have tried to advance the theory of Joseph's influence on Akhenaten by more closely aligning the dates of the two figures. In his book *Stranger in the Valley of the Kings,* historian Ahmed Osman says Joseph was actually Akhenaten's grandfather Yuya. Something of a mystery to scholars, Yuya was not a member of the royal court but eventually rose to second in command under Thutmose IV, the same title Joseph has in the Bible. Even more remarkable for an outsider, Yuya's daughter, Tiy, married Akhenaten's father. Perhaps Tiy whispered the tenets of monotheism to her son.

Most scholars continue to dispute this connection. First, they say, Akhenaten's monotheism was not particularly similar to the one described in the Bible. Instead of being a populist creed, Akhenaten's religion was more of a declaration regarding the king's relationship with his divine father. Second, unlike Yahweh, Aten did not represent all the qualities of nature; he was merely the sun disk. Also, Aten did not display the emotional qualities of the Israelite God—revenge, violence, compassion, devotion. In the end, Yahweh is the God of a people; Aten is the god of the pharaoh. As Donald Redford put it, "Hebrew religion is essentially indigenous to a particular ethnic group, and underwent a natural evolution over centuries of prehistory. Akhenaten's program is a self-conscious modification of an existing system, undertaken at a known point in time, based in the highest circles of the realm and involving a contretemps with a coterie of high officials."

If Akhenaten's system was so imposed, how did the people react?

"We don't know," said Avner. "We have no records whatsoever. It would seem that it wasn't very popular because it was easy to turn back to the old style."

"And how long did that take?"

He pointed up the corridor. "Let's go upstairs and see."

We walked up a broad staircase to the second floor, where the chaos of the ground floor gave way to a dozen carefully preserved, perfectly clean rooms housing one of the most famous archaeological discoveries of the twentieth century, and one of the purest ways to view pharaonic power.

Akhenaten and his wife, Nefertiti, had only daughters. Late in his reign, the "heretic king," as Akhenaten was called, actually shared the throne with a mysterious figure who may have been his son-in-law, or possibly his wife. When Akhenaten finally died, he was succeeded by another son-in-law, a nine-year-old boy named Tutankhaten. For three years the boy king remained in Akhetaten, following his father-in-law's religion, until the ousted priests of Amen-Re reasserted themselves and executed a palace coup. The king moved back to Thebes, changed his name to Tutankhamen, and allowed polytheism to be restored. Any chance that Egypt may have developed an overarching monotheism like the Bible's died with this gesture.

Tutankhamen was basically an insignificant figure, the Zachary Taylor of pharaohs, who died when he was eighteen. His death was so sudden that royal gravediggers hadn't even finished his tomb and placed him instead in an abandoned noble grave. Much smaller than his forebears', Tutankhamen's tomb was remarkable only because it's the only gravesite from the New Kingdom that eluded robbers, thereby setting the stage for one of the great ironies of Egyptian history. Akhenaten may have been the world's first individual, but Tutankhamen became a greater celebrity—more famous in death than in life.

The reason for that fame was an unusual partnership between an eccentric aristocrat and a shy archaeologist. George Edward Stanhope Molyneux Herbert, the fifth earl of Carnarvon and a distant relative of adventuress Hester Stanhope, spent eighteen years and a quarter of a million dollars at the beginning of the twentieth century on a fruitless hunt for a lost tomb in the Valley of the Kings. All the graves had been found, experts said. Anything that wasn't found had already been looted. Robbery was so endemic that often the priests who were preparing the mummy for burial were secretly plotting to plunder the grave. By 1922, Lord Carnarvon had decided to give up his pursuit, until his excavator, Howard Carter, persuaded him to fund one final year.

On November 4, after foraging for months under another tomb, Carter came upon a closed wooden door, sealed with a jackal, the symbol of the priests. In an act of Herculean self-control ("I would have gone crazy," Avner said), Carter refilled the tunnel, hired Sudanese guards to protect it, and sent a telegram to Carnarvon in England: "AT LAST HAVE MADE A WONDERFUL DISCOVERY. RE-COVERED SAME

FOR YOUR ARRIVAL." It took the earl two weeks to arrive, and on November 26, Carter and Carnarvon officially broke through the second door and inserted a lighted candle, which didn't burn out, meaning there was oxygen inside. Carter inserted his head. "A long silence followed," Carnarvon recalled in his memoirs, "until I said, I fear in somewhat trembling tones, 'Well, what is it?' " "Wonderful things," Carter said, adding later, "As my eyes grew accustomed to the light, details of the room within emerged slowly from the mist, strange animals, statues, and gold—everywhere the glint of gold."

That dusting of gold has helped make the contents of King Tut's burial site one of the best-known works of art in the world. Despite everything I knew about Tutankhamen—I had a poster of him above my bed as a boy—I was still unprepared for the sheer volume, the pure beauty, of the contents of his tomb. Arranged in the museum in the order that Carter and Carnarvon discovered them, the 2,300 objects offer a macabre tour of Egyptian necrology, a pop-up *Book of the Dead*. First come the objects designed to ease the soul through the afterlife: two life-sized guards, three gilded couches, four dismantled chariots, several model boats. Then come objects for his daily use while he awaits resurrection: containers for food, game boards for entertainment, trumpets, axes, and canes—all covered in gold. In addition, there are clothes chests inlaid with images of the king fighting ostriches and antelope. There are miniature coffins containing gold figurines of the king and a lock of hair from his grandmother, Tiy. And there was a shrine, protected by four carved goddesses, and containing four gold jars in the shape of the pharaoh, holding his vital organs.

The highlight of the collection is his personal effects, which were stored in an elaborate nest of a sarcophagus, on top of a coffin, on top of a mask, on top of the mummy. The innermost coffin, in the shape of the king, was made of three hundred pounds of solid gold—worth $1.5 million at current prices. In addition, over seventy-five miles of gold thread were used in the jewelry. "Still, it's not the gold," Avner said. "It's the artwork." The closer to the mummy, the more elaborate the ornaments. The body was decorated with bracelets, pectorals, rings, earrings, collars, and belts. These, in turn, were made of turquoise, amethyst, onyx, and jasper. And they were arrayed in a rainbow—aqua, vermilion, black, and gold—that seemed much closer to African batiks of today than anything out of Europe. The mask itself, a glimmering figurehead, was made of twenty-six pounds of gold, inlaid with quartz, obsidian, and stripes of lapis lazuli the color of the Mediterranean. Not until I stared into its black eyes, lorded over by the cobra and the vulture, did I fully understand how Egypt, a place renowned for its culture, could also be feared for its power. Even an eighteen-year-old boy like Tutankhamen, when draped in the vestments of authority, could be a terrifying sight. Perhaps this duality—beauty and terror—could explain the dual image that Egypt holds in the Bible: A land that welcomes Joseph's family at the end of Genesis becomes, by the beginning of Exodus, a place that wants his descendants dead.

"Remember, it's not just a single man who's buried here," Avner said. "It's Egypt that's buried here. The decorations are the whole country. On the one hand you think, what a waste. On the other hand, you think about the greatness of the nation. This is the finest art, the finest philosophy, the finest design, coming together in service to the king."

"So when you see this, what makes you most excited?" I said. "The mask, the tomb—"

"The human touch," he said. "This was designed by people, it was built by people."

I told him about my conversation with Basem, in which he said he felt distant from ancient Egyptians because they had different beliefs.

"I believe that if I were to come back at that time," Avner said, "I would be able to bridge the gap. I feel they were people like us, despite their beliefs. It's like coming to Egypt today. People in Israel think Egyptians are different from them. Still, it was fun to talk to the driver on the way from the airport. He was very curious about Tel Aviv. He had heard it was a great city. What is the cost of living there? How are the people there? In spite of the gaps, which are big, we're much closer than people think."

"But what makes you think that?" I said. "In Exodus, Egypt is the enemy."

"Not so fast," he said. "Egypt is not a bad place in the Bible. It's the pharaoh, he's a bad man."

"But I thought you said those were the same thing."

He smiled. "The pharaoh of Joseph was not a bad man. Remember, he saved Joseph from prison and invited his family to live in Goshen. It was a different pharaoh, four hundred years later, who put the Israelites into bondage. That's when the Bible changes its mind. That's when Egypt becomes the enemy."

The issue of Egypt as enemy was on our minds the following morning when, after having dinner with some friends of Avner's, we made the daylong taxi trek to Giza and began to confront two of the more confounding—and abiding—questions of biblical history: Were the Israelites actually enslaved in Egypt? And if so, did they build the pyramids?

Our first stop was fifteen miles south of Giza at the funerary complex of Saqqara. Here, in the twenty-seventh century B.C.E., King Zoser erected the first pyramid, a four-stepped stone monument, covered with white limestone, that looks something like an oversized wedding cake, only square and without the flowers. Over 150 feet tall, it was, at the time, the largest structure ever built of stone and, according to one historian, the "beginning of architecture." Before then, pharaohs had been buried in subterranean tombs covered by mastabas, mud-brick structures about the size of a modern minivan that looked like loaves of bread. Pyramids, from the Greek word *pyramis,* or wheaten cake, allowed the soul of the deceased pharaoh to ascend closer to the sun god. Indeed the shape of the structure is thought to be a three-dimensional re-creation of a sun ray, a physical embodiment of the divine. In all, ninety-seven pyramids remain standing.

The three jewels in this series are grouped together like collectibles on a coffee table, just west of downtown Cairo, on a sandy plateau above the Nile. It was late morning when we arrived, and walking up the hill, through the clog of souvenir shops and camel rides ("Special price for you!"), we decided to say hello to the chief archaeologist. The previous day, the dean of the Department of Tourism at Helwan University, in downtown Cairo, had given us the man's name and suggested we inquire about his recent discoveries. We approached the office, which was shaded by palm trees and crawling with cats. "Do you have an appointment?" the guard asked. "No, we have an introduction." He led us to a waiting room. "Do you have an appointment?" another man asked. "No, we have an introduction." He asked us to sit down. "Do you have an appointment?" a woman asked. "No, we have an introduction." She disappeared for a few seconds and invited us into the director's office. "You don't have an appointment," he said, not getting up, not stopping work, and, for the first time I had ever seen in the Arab world, not offering us a drink. "I'm a very busy man," he said.

I explained the nature of our project and why his friend thought he might be able to guide us during our visit. "Have you read my writings on this subject?" he asked. I mentioned that I had seen his article in the EgyptAir *Inflight Magazine*. "Well, I also have a chapter in the book called *Ancient Egypt* and an article in *Archaeology Magazine*. I write for *National Geographic* and—" Avner mentioned that he was familiar with some of his writings. "I think you should go read all of my writings," he said, "then call back and get an appointment." He nodded to indicate that our meeting was over. Chastened, we mumbled our apologies. He handed us a card that read Dr. Zahi Hawass, Director of the Pyramids, Cairo, Egypt. It was embossed in gold. We left his office and spent the next three hours wandering around the complex. Everywhere we were asked for admission tickets, I flashed the golden card. It saved us well over $100.

The pyramids are the only surviving object of the Seven Wonders of the Ancient World and would probably still make a list of the seven most wondrous objects in the world. Stop a hundred people anywhere on the planet and ask them where the pyramids are and it's hard to imagine a score below 100. The oldest and largest of the pyramids, built to house the Fourth Dynasty pharaoh Khufu, or Cheops, around 2650 B.C.E., is 480 feet high and covers an area of 13.6 acres, equivalent to seven square blocks in midtown Manhattan, or twice the size of Times

Square. The building uses 2,300,000 limestone blocks, each one about the size of a large refrigerator-freezer and weighing an average of three tons, with a few reaching fifteen tons. Lined end to end, these stones would pave a single-lane road from San Francisco to New York.

While the Great Pyramid alone could provide enough questions for a special boxed set of Trivial Pursuit, its dimensions have been grist for elaborate theories, which attempt to prove it has New Age, or maybe that's Old Age, power. The pyramid, for example, is said to be located at the exact center of the earth's landmass. Each of its bases measures 9,131 inches long, for a total perimeter of 36,524 inches. Though that number may appear insignificant, move the decimal point two places and you get 365.24, the exact length of the solar year. Also, the average height of all land on earth above sea level is said to be 5,759 inches. The Great Pyramid, naturally, is precisely that high. While these calculations may seem amusing, to many they are deadly serious, even spiritual. Basem was leading a tour the following week of women from America who had applied for special permission to meditate inside the pyramid. They were apparently bringing apples, convinced that if they placed them in the exact center of the structure the fruit would never spoil.

Such calculations, inevitably, have been applied to the Bible in an attempt to link the pyramids with the prophetic traditions of Judaism and Christianity. To some, the pyramids are a divine revelation and foretell the future. The Great Pyramid, for example, was covered with 144,000 casing stones. The Bible says the number of people who will save the world on Judgment Day will be 12,000 from each of the twelve tribes, or 144,000. The Great Pyramid was built with ascending and descending passages to allow the king to be buried and his soul to escape. The point where the passages meet is 1,170 inches aboveground. If you subtract this figure from the starting date of construction, the resulting figure is said to predict the start of the Israelites' Exodus from Egypt, the death of Christ, and the assassination of Archduke Ferdinand. Further, if you draw a line from the center of the pyramid through the east-west axis you will apparently hit the exact spot where the Israelites crossed the Red Sea, and later where they crossed the Jordan. According to Art Bell, an American pyramidologist, this line "also passes directly through the town of Bethlehem, the birthplace of Christ. As incredibly precise as this may seem, the Pyramid actually pinpoints Christ's birthplace." As if that's not enough, one website I saw insisted that NASA images show three pyramids and a sphinx on the surface of Mars and that both complexes were built by God, in the shape of Orion's Belt, in such a way that they are communicating with each other in a plot to destroy the world. Photos were provided.

One reason for all this hysteria is a deeply serious question: Do the pyramids have any relation to the stories in the Bible? The idea that they do has been around since the first millennium C.E., when, unable to read hieroglyphics, few knew why the pyramids were built. Sir John Mandeville, an English pilgrim of the fourteenth century who wrote a travel book widely read across Europe, said the pyramids were "granaries of Joseph," built to store grain after he interpreted the pharaoh's dreams. "Some men say that they are sepulchers of great lords that were formerly; but this is not true." The wishful idea of the pyramids as Judeo-Christian creations was given credence in the nineteenth century when British scholars Piazzi Smith and David Davidson called the pyramids the "Bible in stone" and said they were built by the Israelites as a resting place for God. Even as late as the 1970s, when Israeli Prime Minister Menachem Begin paid a state visit to Egypt, he stood with Anwar Sadat at the pyramids and boasted, "Our forefathers built these." Sadat, dumbfounded, replied, "I don't see this." Aides came scurrying, but Begin brushed them away. "Begin was a very formal guy," Avner said. "It was hard to whisper in his ear."

What the aides were pointing out, no doubt, was a simple case of mathematics. The first of the Giza pyramids was begun around 2600 B.C.E. Abraham was likely born around 1900 B.C.E. Even outmoded thinking from earlier this century dated Abraham to no earlier than 2200 B.C.E., which in any case wouldn't place Joseph in Egypt until 150 years later, which in turn wouldn't have produced a sizable enough population of Israelites until several hundred years after that. The Bible says, in Exodus 1, that the Israelites were forced into bondage by the pharaoh, who feared their size. Egyptian documents confirm that there was a significant Central Asian population, like the Israelites, in Egypt during the New Kingdom, in the middle of the second millennium B.C.E. But that was over a thousand years from when the pharaohs built in Giza. The bottom line is clear: It was as long from the pyramids to Moses, as it is from Emperor Constantine to us. We didn't build Constantinople; the Israelites didn't build the pyramids.

So who *did* build the pyramids?

"Actually, it's not that complicated," Avner said. We had wandered around the site for a while and settled on a corner of the middle structure, built for Khafre, Khufu's son. Over the years, people have devised hundreds of theories on how the Egyptians built the pyramids: using slaves, cranes, catapults, slingshots, lasers, crocodiles, bulls, aliens—or some combination thereof. In fact, they used people, Avner said, as many as one hundred thousand, hired by the state and organized into teams of ten. Most of the stone was quarried near Cairo, floated across the river on barges during the flood, then dragged up the plateau using levers and rollers. When each layer was complete, the crews built a ramp of sand and brick to drag the blocks to the next level. Moreover, these people were not slaves like those found in the American South— individuals owned by other individuals—they were usually peasants recruited by the state to serve the pharaoh and were housed, clothed, and fed. Even foreigners wouldn't have resisted. As one historian put it, "Better to live a well-fed factor in Egypt than die a starving 'free man' on the steppes of Asia. Whether emigrating voluntarily, or sold by their village headman, or captured in battle, it is doubtful whether any of the Asiatics regretted their fate." In the end, the pyramids are less a feat of construction and more one of organization.

Avner gave an example to prove this point. "The first project I organized when I worked in the Sinai as chief archaeologist was the restoration of an Egyptian temple," he said. "We had to move blocks that were three and a half tons. But the place was on top of a mountain, and there was no way to bring in machinery, or cranes. So we brought ropes, winches, and about thirty bedouin. At first we couldn't do it. We put all the Israelis on one side, and the bedouin on the other. We said,

'Hey, hup, pull,' but the bedouin were just leaning on the rope and they fell down like dominoes. Eventually we devised a system and were able to do it. It taught us that all you need is the right organization, and you can achieve quite a lot."

"If that's the case, why all the crackpot theories?" I said.

"We've just lost the appreciation for manual work, because we don't do it anymore. Also, most of the people coming up with these theories know nothing about ancient Egyptians. If you get to know them, it's easy to understand how they could invest so much labor. There was a very deep motivation of faith. They took part in a very important process that blessed them, their children, and their country."

"What about the symbolism? Why so many theories about that?"

"It's the times. People are in a deep search for meaning. Mystery plays a very big role, as do cults. There's a huge crisis of belonging. The pyramids are the most visible religious structures on earth. It's natural that they inspire such beliefs."

And inspire they do. No matter how many times you see them, they still make you happy. This is their secret, I believe: a perennial ability to inspire awe and speculation in each generation. In this way, Smith and Davidson were right. The pyramids are to Egypt what the Bible is to Israel: the great blank slate onto which each age imposes a meaning and takes a set of lessons unique to its time and place. In some ways it doesn't matter what the builders of the pyramids, like the authors of the Bible, had in mind. The genius of their creations is that their meaning is subtle enough to change over time. As one proverb oft quoted around Giza says: "Things dread time; Time dreads the pyramids."

Late that afternoon we decided to descend the narrow passage to the heart of Khafre's pyramid. We flashed Dr. Hawass's card at the entrance and started down the shaft, which was no more than four and a half feet high. Claustrophobia quickly engulfed us. It was the first time I felt like Indiana Jones, just hoping one of those giant stone balls didn't trap us inside. The deeper we got, the lower the roof, until we were bending over like baboons, dragging our arms on the ground. "No one who has not crawled along the galleries beneath a pyramid," wrote Egyptian archaeologist Zakharia Gnomein in 1956, "and experienced the silence and darkness, can fully appreciate the feeling which at times overwhelms one. It may sound fantastic, but I felt that the pyramid had a personality, and that this personality was that of the king for whom it was built and which still lingered within it, possibly the soul."

Every now and then the path would level out for a few moments and we could stand up, then it would fall again, and we'd have to bend over. I heard one man say earlier in the week that after making this trip he had "pyramid legs" and couldn't walk for a week. As it was, even in early winter, one could feel the air being sucked from the corridor and sweat accumulating at a rapid rate. Every visitor to the pyramids leaves behind twenty grams of water, I had read, just by breathing and perspiring, which in turn creates corrosive salts. The mere act of entering the pyramid, it turns out, slowly diminishes it.

Twenty minutes later we reached the bottom of the corridor, where a man stood at the entrance to the tomb, asking for baksheesh, a small bribe. We demurred and stepped into the chamber, about the size of a subway car, which at the time of burial in the twenty-sixth century B.C.E. would have contained the mummy, the viscera, and an idol with what one observer called "fierce and sparkling eyes" bent on slaying intruders. Ancient writers believed the tomb had no entrance, but in 1818 Giovanni Battista Belzoni, a former circus sideman from Italy, dynamited the sealed portal and discovered the tomb. As a mark, he scrawled his name in black paint on the wall, which is still visible. With no decoration, and no contents other than the empty sarcophagus, the room was creepy, an echo chamber where the echoes bounce five thousand years.

"Think of Tutankhamen, and how much more important Khafre was than him," Avner said. "Then you can imagine what was in this room. My personal theory is that he died before the pyramid was completed, which is why this chamber was not higher. It's a sign of the reverence they must have felt toward him that they continued building even after he was dead."

"So let me ask you," I said. "If you could have witnessed one moment in the construction, which would it be?"

"I always imagine the moment when they remove the last stone that was blocking the passageway until the pharaoh's coffin was lowered into place and all the stones came tumbling down to fill up the passageway."

"And if you could've asked one question?"

"For me the question is not 'how?' " he said, "but 'why?' "

We walked back to the entrance of the compound and took a cab back to the city. Though it may seem ungrateful, the only thing more disconcerting than Cairo with all the cars is Cairo without them. At 5 P.M. the streets were totally empty, as Muslims broke their daylight fast for Ramadan. The only people visible were the scores of police eating tin bowls of rice and chicken and coming back to life with the rush of food. This daily Ramadan ritual, break-fast, is so important that two days earlier, the guard operating the metal detector at the Luxor airport waved passengers through his checkpoint so he could eat. Such determination, though, doesn't get in the way of courtesy. At least half the people I encountered eating their first meal of the day offered me a bite. In Luxor I was sitting by myself in the airport lounge when an elderly man who had been mopping the floor sat down across from me and pulled out a paper bag. He looked in his bag, looked at me, then came and sat down next to me. Without saying a word, he put the entire contents of his meal in one hand: three dried dates. Despite my protest, we ate his meal together that evening.

This evening our destination was Helwan University, where Ali Omar, of the Department of Tourism, had invited us to break the fast with his staff and meet the former head of the Egyptian government's department of antiquities. Upstairs a banquet was under way, with a dozen tables arranged in a square and brimming with chicken, meatballs, rice, moussaka, pita, tomatoes, cucumbers, and mango juice. When the distinguished archaeologist took time to write on a calling card "Professor Dr. Abd el Halim Nurel Din, Professor of Egyptology, Head of the Department of Egypt, Cairo University, Giza," I feared we had another case of inflated formality. I could not have been more wrong. Professor Nurel Din, pushing seventy, and dressed to Third World professorial perfection in a brown tweed suit, brown leather vest, mustard shirt, and brown tie, was a charming man with an easy laugh and an avuncular insistence that we eat dessert—sweet cakes topped with honey and pistachio chunks—before talking about ancient Egypt.

The first thing I wanted to know was why there was such confusion about who built the pyramids.

"I can't answer that," he said. "Everybody is trying to take credit. When Qaddafi came here, he said the pyramids were built by the Libyans. The black Americans say, 'These are our pyramids.' It's nonsense. I have hundreds of reasons to say these pyramids are Egyptian, they were built by Egyptians, with Egyptian mentality, on an Egyptian plateau. And if you take the Jews, or the Libyans, or the Americans, if they're so smart, why didn't they build the pyramids in their country? They were kind enough to come here and build them for us? It's all very funny."

"But there are two thousand theories," I said, "involving aliens, lasers, slaves."

"It's just a pyramid," he said. "It's the result of four hundred years of experimentation to achieve that shape. People wanted to be connected to the rays of the sun. Also, Egyptians believed the earth came out of the water in a pyramid. They wanted to be buried in a monument with the same shape. It has nothing to do with astronomy or astrology. But once you're impressed with something, you can't get it out of your mind. I'm sorry to say, that's why we have Egyptmania. That's why we have Pyramidiots."

I asked him about the Bible, and about how closely he thought it reflected Egyptian history.

"First of all, as an Egyptologist, as a person acquainted with the ancient Near East, I do not believe very much in trying to have a link between the biblical prophets and certain periods, or certain people, in Egypt. I never try to discuss that, simply because we don't have any evidence that the Israelites were in Egypt. We don't have any evidence that they left Egypt. We don't have any evidence of Joseph or Moses. When we don't have evidence, it's just too hard.

"But I'm a good Muslim," he continued, "and good Muslims should be respectful of other religions. Also, it's hard to imagine why the Israelites would invent a past in slavery if they didn't experience it. That's not evidence, but it is interesting. I think it's safe to say that they were here, and that they learned a lot."

So what did they learn?

"Egypt was a pioneer in many things," he said. "It was one of the strongest countries in the ancient Near East. But above all, Egyptians had a feeling of dignity, of grandeur. They believed they were special. They believed they were blessed. Maybe that's what the Israelites learned: a sense of destiny."

And where might the Egyptians have gotten that feeling?

"They had a chance, because they were living in a place that was safe. The borders were secure. The weather was good. It was easy to reach other countries. Plus, they had the Nile. Ancient Egyptians found themselves in a situation that facilitated their having great achievements. Once you leave, the world becomes much less friendly. In any direction, you get desert."

I thanked him extensively and sneaked one last piece of cake. As we were heading out, I mentioned that we were leaving the following morning for the land of Goshen, where Moses was born, and for the Red Sea. Did he have any advice?

He looked a bit concerned. "Be sure and keep your passports with you," he said. "And unlike Moses, I hope you come back."

3. A Wall of Water

Our final wake-up call in Cairo came at 4 A.M. The predawn fog, mixed with the pollution, created a double veil over the city. The Cairo Tower, a 617-foot, latticed, concrete minaret in the shape of a lotus flower, was not even visible from our hotel window, just across the river.

Downstairs our driver and guide were already waiting. At the urging of several friends, we had hired not only a jeep but also a police escort for our day in the Delta, an area regarded as too unstable for foreign visitors. Our driver, however, a former policeman himself, had purposefully evaded the escort on his way to the hotel and suggested we go alone. He was backed by Yasser, our guide, a burly man in his twenties who was wearing black combat boots and a black uniform, and carrying a black walking stick, all of which gave him the slightly menacing appearance of an army commandant or, worse, an officer in the S.S. Under the circumstances, we had little choice. We were in their care for our most ambitious day so far, as we set out to re-create one of the monumental passages of the Hebrew Bible, the Israelites' flight to freedom across the Red Sea. Instead of just visiting this site, we hoped, in a bit of romantic folly (and an indication of how committed we were becoming to our effort) to cross the water ourselves. Along the way, we also hoped to tackle some of the most heated debates about the historicity of the Bible. What caused the plagues? Who was the pharaoh of the Exodus? Where was the Red Sea? And, of course, could it have been parted?

The streets were as empty at 5 A.M. as they had been at 5 P.M. the previous day. The deserted overpasses, underpasses, and tunnels made crossing the city like being in a giant race-car video game, especially when our driver, Ahmed, a mustachioed man with an iron gaze, took the occasion to accelerate over ninety miles per hour, even while we were still downtown. Most people would have had their morning meal at 4 A.M., Yasser said, then elected for "a bit of a lie-in" this Thursday, ahead of the weekly day of rest on Friday. "It's Ramadan," he said. "People are lazy. By six o'clock tonight it will be busy." As a result, the streets remained empty even beyond the airport, and a drive that had taken well over an hour during my first visit took less than twenty minutes.

The northeastern quadrant of Cairo is the city's plushest, with casinos, nightclubs, art deco houses, a soccer stadium, and palaces built for successive kings, sultans, caliphs, emirs, pashas, strongmen, dictators, consul generals, military generals, and, now, presidents for life. Unlike their counterparts in ancient Egypt, contemporary leaders not only live on the east side of the Nile, they're buried here as well. Nasser's grave is in the area, as is the tomb of the unknown soldier. The shah of Iran died here during his last years in exile. It's also home to a memorial to the 1973 war, called the Tenth Ramadan War in Arabic and the Yom Kippur War in Hebrew, in which Sadat regained, then relost some of the Sinai. Eight years later Islamic radicals infiltrated a parade in honor of the war and assassinated Sadat, who was subsequently buried in the area. One reason so many palaces are here is that it's closer to the Sinai, so leaders could flee in times of peril. It's also closer to the airport, for the same reason. "Life is nicer here," Yasser said, "and more expensive." He estimated the cost of a two-bedroom apartment at half a million Egyptian pounds, around $175,000.

Yasser was an affable, talkative man who had graduated with Basem from Helwan University and was studying for a master's degree in the history of mummification. He had an encyclopedic knowledge of hieroglyphics and near flawless use of Egyptologist English—polaris, natron salts, spinal cord marrow—but almost no knowledge of where we were going. "Most tourists have no interest in these places," he pleaded. He did, however, have a great nose for character. When we mentioned we had met the director of the pyramids the previous day, he needed no prompting to announce, "I don't like him much. He doesn't deserve the tributes he seeks." He added, "He's not like Professor Nurel Din, who advanced rapidly from professor to head of antiquities for all of Egypt. He's a great man." We were off to a promising start.

The farther we got from downtown, the more the scenery shifted from crumbling apartment blocks to dusty intersections to mud-brick villages to dilapidated farmhouses. The Delta has always been Egypt's breadbasket, a fan-shaped web of estuaries and canals that sprouted from the Nile like tines on a rake. During the *Gemini IV* space mission in 1965, American astronaut James McDivitt stared down 115 miles and saw what he thought was a giant flow of lava, a triangle of muddy brown pouring into a vast blue sea. The triangle was the Nile Delta and the sea it ran into, the Mediterranean.

Today, despite diminished water because of the dam, the Delta is still the leafiest region of Egypt, the one area outside of the narrow riverbanks where nature seems to sprout uncontrollably. Feluccas sail through fields of cotton, rice, and corn. Water buffalo stomp through marshes filled with herons, storks, and loons. In ancient times, wealthy Egyptians hunted ducks through the swamps, using throwing sticks as weapons and hunting cats for retrieval. There were hippopotamuses here until 1805, when the last one was shot, perhaps by Napoleon's soldiers, who are said to have shot the nose off the Sphinx.

In addition to the area's greenery, what was most remarkable about the Delta was how untouched it seemed by time. We fell back into the game we had played on our way to Harran. I spy a worker pulling mud from the river: a slave? I spy a basket made of bulrushes: a baby? I spy some girls doing laundry on the banks: one of them a pharaoh's daughter? We had stumbled upon another primeval tableau, a land emerging out of watery chaos. We had reached another beginning in the Bible.

One of the more striking features of the story of Moses is how humbly it starts, yet how epic it feels. It clearly aims to mix mythical elements—a body drawn from water, a slave raised by a king—with historical ones—a pharaoh building cities, a people working in servitude—to create a sort of metahero who incorporates many of the qualities of previous biblical elders, yet ultimately supersedes them. Genesis includes four major characters—Abraham, Isaac, Jacob, Joseph—as well as Adam, Eve, Cain, Abel, and Noah. Moses alone fills the next four books, Exodus, Leviticus, Numbers, and Deuteronomy. He is the central character of the entire Hebrew Bible, yet one of the most human heroes ever painted, plagued by self-doubt. As biographer Jonathan Kirsch has written: "He is a shepherd, mild and meek, but also a ruthless warrior who is capable of blood-shaking acts of violence, a gentle teacher who is also a magician and a wonder-worker, a lawgiver whose code of justice is merciful except when it comes to purging and punishing those who disagree with him, an emancipator who rules his people with unforgiving authority." Above all, he is "God's one and only friend, and yet he is doomed to a tragic death by God himself."

Exodus begins with the advent of a new king over Egypt, "who knew not Joseph." While the old pharaoh encouraged Joseph's family to settle in Goshen, the new pharaoh fears their descendants are becoming too numerous and orders that all newborn Israelite boys be drowned in the Nile. During this time a Levite family bears a son, but the mother is able to hide him. After three months she takes a wicker basket, caulks it with bitumen and pitch, and sets her son afloat on the river. The baby's sister is sent to watch. The daughter of the pharaoh discovers the basket and takes pity on the boy inside. "This must be a Hebrew child," she says. The pharaoh's daughter asks the girl who is watching to bring her a Hebrew wet-nurse. The girl, naturally, brings her mother. It's the pharaoh's daughter, however, who gives the baby his name, Moses, because, she says, "I drew him out of the water."

As with other biblical accounts, the story of Moses' birth has many ancient parallels. Hercules also survived efforts to kill him as a baby; Oedipus was left exposed on a mountain; Romulus and Remus were put in a chest and cast into the Tiber. Perhaps more relevant (because it predates the Bible), Sargon, founder of the Mesopotamian empire of Akkadia in the third millennium B.C.E., was born to obscure origins, cast in a wicker basket lined with bitumen, and drawn out of the river by a god. But as Avner pointed out, the differences between Sargon and Moses outweigh the similarities. Sargon was abandoned because of an illicit relationship, not a genocidal dictate. Also, Sargon's finder did not know the boy's origin, as the pharaoh's daughter does. "In many ways, Moses is closer to Jesus," Avner said. "He's born in humble origins, passes through the highest courts, flees to the desert, then returns with a new set of beliefs."

Since the Bible is mostly silent on Moses' youth, commentators invented various stories. In one, Moses is sitting on the lap of the princess when he knocks off the pharaoh's crown and tramples it. This was considered a bad omen, and the pharaoh was advised to kill the boy. The pharaoh proposes a test instead. Aides put two bowls before the boy, one filled with gold, the other with red-hot coals. A usurper would presumably grab the jewels, but Moses grabs a coal and places it on his lips, thus saving his life and, the reasoning goes, causing him to stutter— a trait alluded to later in the text.

As for the Bible, it picks up the story when Moses, as an adult, witnesses an Egyptian beating a Hebrew, "one of his kinsmen." Moses looks around to make sure there are no witnesses, then murders the Egyptian and buries him in the sand. The next day Moses sees two Hebrews fighting. He asks the offender, "Why do you strike your fellow?" The Hebrew responds, "Who made you chief and ruler over us? Do you mean to kill me as you killed the Egyptian?" Moses realizes his crime has been discovered and becomes frightened. When the pharaoh learns of the murder, he tries to kill Moses, who flees to the desert. He eventually arrives in the land of Midian, an ancient territory believed to be near southern Jordan today. There, like so many others in the Bible, he meets his future wife by a well. He comes upon the seven daughters of a Midianite named Jethro, who are being threatened by shepherds. Moses rises to the girls' defense. In gratitude, Jethro invites Moses to marry his daughter Zipporah.

Back in Egypt, the pharaoh dies, and the Israelites continue to "groan" under their bondage. Their cries reach God, the text says, who recalls his covenant with the patriarchs and decides to act. One day, while Moses is tending Jethro's flock, he comes upon Horeb, "the mountain of God," which later would serve as the place where the Ten Commandments were revealed. An angel appears in a blazing fire from a bush. The bush is "all aflame," yet not consumed. God begins to speak from the bush: "Moses! Moses!" "Here I am," Moses says, using the same response Abraham gives to God in Harran. "Do not come closer," God says. "Remove your sandals from your feet, for the place on which you stand is holy ground."

God then introduces himself and invokes the names of Abraham, Isaac, and Jacob. Moses promptly hides his face, for he is "afraid to look at God." The Lord continues, announcing that he is mindful of the suffering of the Israelites and intends to liberate them from Egypt and deliver them to a land of milk and honey. Moses will be the liberator, God announces. "Come, therefore, I will send you to the Pharaoh, and you shall free My people." But Moses objects, saying he's not a great man. But "I will be with you," God says. Moses continues to demur, saying that when the Israelites ask who sent him, "What do I say?" God's answer is one of the most famous and elliptic in the entire Bible, and is rendered in Hebrew as *ehyeh asher ehyeh*. Translators interpret the response as meaning "I am who I am," "I shall always be what I have always been," or "I will be there however I will be there." God elaborates by saying, "This shall be My name forever. This My appellation for all eternity."

Moses, however, remains unpersuaded. In an effort to convince him, God turns Moses' staff into a snake, then turns it back into a staff. He then teaches Moses to use his staff to turn the Nile into blood. Moses is still unconvinced, claiming he's not a man of words. "I am slow of speech and slow of tongue," he says, giving birth to the idea that he stutters. This time God gets angry and says that Aaron, Moses' brother, can speak for him. Aaron is setting out from Egypt already to meet Moses, God says. Finally the reluctant savior agrees and sets out for Goshen.

The unusual circumstances of this story—the fact that Moses gets his name from an Egyptian and is raised in the pharaonic court, the fact that he claims not to speak well—have led many to speculate that Moses wasn't an Israelite at all. Sigmund Freud, in his influential book *Moses and Monotheism,* says that Moses was an Egyptian who learned monotheism from Akhenaten and was inspired to lead a revolt of foreign slaves out of a desire to overthrow his symbolic father. Freud says Moses gave the slaves the idea that they were a chosen people, which in turn led to anti-Semitism. "It was one man, the man Moses, who created the Jews. To him this people owes its tenacity in supporting life; to him, however, it also owes much of the hostility which it has met and is meeting still."

Leaving aside Freud's psychological interpretation, many scholars agree with his underlying thesis, that Moses might have been an Egyptian. One reason is his name. In Exodus 2, the pharaoh's daughter says she names the boy Moses, or Moshe in Hebrew, because "I drew him out of the water." This linkage, however, is believed to have been added by later editors who were thinking of the Hebrew word *mashah,* which means to draw out. By contrast, since the pharaoh's daughter is unlikely to have known Hebrew, her choice for the boy's name probably comes from the Egyptian word *moses,* which means child, and is the same name at the root of Thutmose and Ramoses, later Rameses.

Also, in trying to explain Moses' religious beliefs, many observers suggest that disgruntled priests of Akhenaten could have formed their own cult and that Moses might have picked up ideas from them. Finally, Moses might have stuttered because he didn't speak Hebrew, in which case he would have needed Aaron as his translator. "This doesn't make the Bible less true," Lucy Plitman, a professor at Tel Aviv University and an advocate of this theory, told me. "If anything this makes it more plausible. I want to use skepticism to get at the truth."

Traditional commentators reject these views. To them, Moses enjoyed his extraordinary background because he was an extraordinary person. Citing a line in which the Lord says to Moses "I make you a God to pharaoh," Philo, the Jewish writer from the first century C.E., wrote, "Did not Moses enjoy an even greater partnership with the Creator of all things, having been found worthy of being called by the same form of address?" Moses, he deduces, was "the greatest and most perfect man who ever lived."

By 8 A.M. a warm light had settled over the Delta and the morning's activities were well under way. A cluster of workers stood in a parking lot waiting for a lift to the fields. A group of boys were piled into the back of a vegetable truck, on their way to school. There were no private cars, only buses, trucks, and vans. The telephone poles that lined the road were barnacled with the kind of ceramic telephone conductors that I hadn't seen since I was a child. The only sign of modern life was a few streetlights with solar panels for power.

Our first stopover was the town of Zagazig, known in antiquity as Bubastis, the House of Bastet, after the goddess of the cat. Pilgrims used to sail here from all over the region for an annual festival of drinking and lewdness. In the fifth century B.C.E., Herodotus claimed that seven hundred thousand people consumed more wine in one day than during the rest of the year put together. The town was also known as a feline free-for-all. As Joseph says, in Thomas Mann's novel, "the city smelt so strong of catnip that it almost turned a stranger's stomach."

Today, the site of the ancient city is overgrown and nearly abandoned, with a few stone cartouches overturned on the ground and a sagging barbed-wire fence around an ancient animal cemetery, where mummified pets were buried. A small residential area contains remains of mud-brick houses like the ones the Israelites were said to be building in Exodus. We walked around for a few minutes, then decided to stop in the small museum. It was closed, not open until 9:00, the guard said. It was 8:40.

"But we are—"

"Sorry," he said.

"But we only want—"

"Sorry," he repeated.

"But maybe—"

"No chance."

Baksheesh?

"Come right in."

Before spending time in the Middle East I had heard countless tales of baksheesh and always wondered how one knew when to wield such a tool. As it turns out, one needn't wonder. Egyptians, at least, make their desires quite clear. One still has to learn the proper amount, but as

Yasser said, "Any amount is enough; any amount is not enough. No matter what you do, they complain."

Moments later, after touring the mostly empty museum, we piled back into the jeep and turned north. Before reaching the eastern perimeter of the Delta and the likely site of the biblical Red Sea, we hoped to see the ancient garrison towns of Pithom and Rameses, which Exodus says the Israelites built for the pharaoh during their bondage. To do that, we needed to leave the main road and navigate a web of dirt roads to Sa el-Hagar, one of several candidates for the city of Rameses.

Almost immediately we got lost. If no tourists go to Zagazig, no people at all come to Sa el-Hagar. Any hint of development quickly disappeared and we were in a borderless, unchanging never-never land of cabbage carts and rice paddies, wooden wheelbarrows and cattails. The arterylike canals close to Cairo multiplied into hundreds of capillaries that carried water to the spongy ground. Alongside the narrow waterways, wooden pumps were set up to distribute the water for irrigation. In lieu of electricity, the pistons were tied to donkeys, who walked in a circle, ladling water as they went. The region seemed more overgrown than Eastern Turkey, but less developed. The tallest objects were palm trees, silhouetted against the haze, which had now replaced the fog.

We stopped for directions. Then stopped again. We stopped a third time, and a fourth. Whoever popularized the theory that men don't ask for directions has never visited the Egyptian Delta. But the directions were often contradictory: left past the third mound of dirt, right at the fork in the canal; left at the tractor, right at the burning manure. Eventually at a gas station we got directions that sounded right—"Stay on this road, not left or right"—if only because they sounded as if they came right out of the Bible. Within seconds, Avner produced a passage, Joshua 1:7, with the same instructions: "Turn not to the right hand or to the left, that you may prosper wherever you go." It's no wonder it took the Israelites forty years to cross the desert; they spent half that time just getting out of town.

In the meantime, while Ahmed was getting increasingly frustrated, the rest of us occupied ourselves with the bottomless brainteaser of ancient Egypt, the Rubik's Cube of the Bible: Who was the pharaoh of Exodus?

By the time Moses arrives back in Goshen, in the Nile Delta, the stage is set for the signature showdown of the Pentateuch, the battle between the God of the Hebrews and the god-king of the Egyptians. Exodus is more than an event, it's the seminal demonstration of how God involves himself in the daily lives of the Israelites, exercises control over other nations, and ultimately changes the course of history. Exodus is also living history, referred to over 120 times in the Hebrew Bible, reenacted every year by Jews at Passover, and recalled every year by Christians at Easter. It's also living metaphor, as leaders from Mahatma Gandhi to Martin Luther King Jr. have invoked the plight of the Israelites and the plea of Moses, "Let my people go!"

Considering this transcendence, it's surprising—even troubling— that the story of the Israelites' flight to freedom appears nowhere outside the Bible. This makes dating the event almost impossible. The only evidence even remotely related is a reference in an Egyptian victory stela from the fifth year of Merenptah, circa 1209 B.C.E., that mentions four entities recently subdued in Canaan: Ascalon, Gezer, Yenoam, and Israel. This would seem to put the Exodus no later than 1250 B.C.E., since it took the Israelites forty years just to get to Canaan.

Even the Bible does little to advance the matter of dating. The most concrete reference, found in 1 Kings, says that Solomon built the Temple in Jerusalem in the fourth year of his reign, which was 480 years after the Exodus. Considering that Solomon took office around 970 B.C.E., that would place the Exodus around 1450 B.C.E. The text, however, also says that the Israelites were in Egypt for 430 years, which would place Joseph's arrival around 1900 B.C.E. and Abraham's birth around 2200 B.C.E., about three hundred years earlier than scholars believe. Meanwhile, the text says that Moses is the great-grandson of Levi, one of Joseph's brothers, which would mean the span from grandfather to great-grandson lasted 430 years, another improbability. A more likely explanation is that these dates, like others in the Bible, are allegorical. The figure 480, for example, is equal to 12 x 40, the two most prophetic numbers in the Bible.

With no dates to go on, the conversation relies instead on a few scraps of detail from the text and a large helping of historical conjecture. Exodus 1:11 says that the Israelites built the garrison cities of Pithom and Rameses. According to archaeologists, these were built during the reign of Rameses II, roughly 1279 to 1214 B.C.E. (Egyptian dating is notoriously unsure). In addition, Rameses II also invaded Canaan in the early years of his reign, which suggests that the region could have been vulnerable to conquering by the Israelites. Largely for these reasons, Rameses II has been the consensual pharaoh of the Exodus for several generations. He was the stiff-hearted king in the films *The Ten Commandments* and *The Prince of Egypt*.

Many scholars resist this connection. As Professor Nurel Din explained, "Why do people try to connect it to Rameses II? Simply because he was a great man. He was a great military man, he was a man of peace, he was the greatest builder in ancient Egypt, he had the biggest statue, he was the husband of a well-known lady, he had more children than any king of Egypt, he lived longer than any king of Egypt. Even nowadays he has the best preserved mummy. His mummy was sent to Paris, just to be preserved, and it was received as a king." Moreover, he said, "the biggest square in Egypt is called Rameses, the biggest street in Egypt is called Rameses, whenever you send statues of Rameses anywhere in the world, people line up to buy tickets. In ancient, and modern, times, there is no doubt that Rameses II is great. And once you are great, people try to connect you with great events. But it's just not true."

He suggested Thutmose III, who ruled from 1479 to 1425. Besides being compatible with the Solomonic figures, Thutmose III was the son of a concubine, who took over as king after Thutmose II was unable to have a son by his wife/half-sister Hatshepsut. Within a year, though, Thutmose III was joined in a coregency by Hatshepsut, leaving open the possibility that he was humiliated by a mass exodus of slaves. Because he was short and stocky, and known for being militaristic, Thutmose III has been called "Egypt's Napoleon." Was the Red Sea his Waterloo? Unlikely, Avner noted. From the fifteenth century until the early thirteenth century B.C.E., Egypt exercised hegemonic control over Canaan, making an Israelite conquest of the area forty years after the Exodus all but impossible.

Yasser, for his part, also shied away from traditional choices. He based his decision on his knowledge of mummies. "Rameses II was an old man when he died, not like in the movies," he said. "He would have been unable to ride a horse into the Red Sea. He died of old-man diseases." As for Merenptah, Rameses II's son, who is also considered an option: "His mummy had lots of salt, more than most kings. It's possible he died in the water, but more likely that he just stayed longer in the natron salts." Yasser was equivocating. "Give us your vote," I prodded. "Get off the fence," Avner joked. "I would look for a strong king," Yasser said. "One who trampled his enemies. I would think Seti I, the father of Rameses II. He attacked the Libyans. He built forts in the Sinai. And Seti means death, the god of death. If you're called Seti, you are called evil."

Avner disagreed with Yasser, preferring the more traditional view, but for nontraditional reasons. As an archaeologist, he tended to reject the notion of a single, mass exodus of hundreds of thousands of slaves. Instead, he preferred the idea of waves of smaller flights—*exodi,* if you will—that took place over many years, perhaps decades. These likely took place in the thirteenth century, he said, because the entire region was undergoing dramatic change. "The year 1200 B.C.E. was a landmark in ancient history," he said. "It's not only that the Israelites got to the Holy Land. The Sea Peoples, a mixed population from Greece, started moving into the Near East. And Egypt, which had been the prime power for over a millennium, lost its power and never regained it." Why? "We don't know," he said. "It's like the Soviet Union—who can say why it collapsed? There was no victory that defined the change, but when it was over, one hundred years later, the region was no longer dominated by either the Egyptians or the Hittites. The world was divided into many states—Amorite, Edomite, Israelite—which allowed David and Solomon to build their empire." Since this change began under Rameses II, Avner said, he is the most likely candidate.

"So, now it's your turn," he said.

"Okay, I'm off the fence," I said.

Since we don't have much historical evidence, I suggested, and since we don't have references from Egypt, the most logical place to turn for clues is the Bible. Exodus 1 says the Israelites were building Pithom and Rameses, which would seem to date their enslavement to sometime in the thirteenth century. The text says it was this pharaoh who ordered that all Israelite boys be murdered, whose daughter took in Moses, and who later threatened to kill his surrogate grandson after he murdered an Egyptian. But Exodus 2 says this pharaoh subsequently died, meaning his *son* would have been pharaoh by the time Moses returned from the desert. The son who took over from Rameses II was Merenptah, a decrepit man (his father had ruled for sixty-six years) who was bald and overweight. In the fifth year of his reign, a group of Libyan tribes who had long threatened Egypt swept into the Delta, imperiling the authority of the king. Even more than under Thutmose III, this chaotic situation would have been an ideal opportunity for some slaves to escape while the pharaoh was busy fighting a war in their midst. "I'm going with Merenptah," I said.

"But what about the victory stela?" Avner said. "Already by that time, Merenptah claims to have defeated Israel in Canaan."

"It could be an exaggeration," I said. "Pharaohs were famous for that. Or, if you use your theory of a rolling exodus, it could be that some Israelites had already escaped and were on their way to Canaan. Either way, the fact that he mentions the Israelites at all indicates that he was afraid of them. They were no longer just slaves, they had become a threat. Why else would he chase after them?"

"Fair enough," Avner said.

"Still, why not tell us who the pharaoh was?" I said. "Why doesn't the Bible use his name?"

"The names meant nothing," he said. "Nobody in Israel knew that there was a Rameses or a Thutmose or a Merenptah. They didn't care."

"Should *we* care?"

"Maybe. We should certainly understand Egypt. We should understand that the Israelites lived here, that they were part of this culture, but that they left here, hoping to find a better life. Maybe that's the reason the Bible doesn't give us the pharaoh's name. It wants us to have this conversation. It wants us to relive the Exodus."

After almost two hours of driving around the Delta, we still seemed no closer to Sa el-Hagar. We were traveling on roads without any signs, without any pavement, without any other cars. The only people to give us conflicting directions were farmers who happened to be plowing near the canal, and they were becoming increasingly rare. "The distances have been getting longer the closer we've gotten to the place," Avner said. Finally we emerged into a small clearing—a town?—huddled with houses with grass roofs. A man rolled by on his bicycle. Ahmed lowered his window. "We are looking for Sa el-Hagar," he said, in the one Arabic expression I now knew by heart. "This is Sa el-Hagar!" the man exclaimed. It was 10:50 A.M.

We drove a few miles to the tel, which was closed. Ahmed climbed over the fence and walked to the small guard building. He returned with several men, who unlocked the gate and invited us into the compound. I reached for my wallet but was told to wait: Some baksheesh is given at the beginning of a service, it turns out, some at the end. One needs a Ph.D.

We walked up a small hill and began to catch glimpses of the tel, an enormous empty mound of slightly reddish dirt that rose out of the surrounding countryside, which was still covered with trees and fields. With almost no visible remains, the tel seemed like it belonged on the face of Mars. As the size of the site began to become apparent, Avner started sprinting to the top of the highest hill. "I've never seen such a huge tel!" he said, giggling with delight. "Just look: This is one big city! I visited a tel once on the other side of the Delta. It took an hour to walk from one side to the other. But it was nothing compared to this. This is bigger than the Old City of Jerusalem!"

We hurried down the hill, sand flying in every direction, and came to the one area of the tel that had been excavated, a giant temple to Amen that had been shattered, as if by a hammer flung by the gods. Cracked pillars and splintered lintels littered the ground. The randomness, and the rawness, reminded me of the feeling I had in Harran of being inside a terra-cotta jug that had been flung to the ground and broken into a thousand shards. Only here, because the structure was Egyptian, the shards were covered in hieroglyphs. Avner jumped on one fallen pillar that was wider than I am tall and pointed out the name of a daughter of Rameses II. "We came all this way and found the signature of the woman who found Moses," I said. "Not bad!"

"But remember, Rameses II had ninety-five children," Avner said. "Fifty-five boys and forty girls."

"No wonder he didn't mind having another grandkid around," I said.

"No wonder he built such a big house."

As it turns out, this probably wasn't his house at all. Sa el-Hagar, otherwise known as Tanis, was once thought to be the site of the biblical city of Rameses, or what Egyptians called Pi-Rameses, the Delta residence of the pharaohs. Petrie raised money to excavate the tel by promising insights into the plight of the Israelites. His dig seemed to confirm the biblical connection when he found ruins with visible marks from Rameses II. But later excavations proved that these monuments were moved here from another site, Qantir, which is more likely the town of Pi-Rameses that the Bible describes. Qantir, about twenty minutes away, is smaller than Sa el-Hagar, but still large by Egyptian standards. A third site, Tell el-Maskhuta (the Arabic spelling of tel has two *l*s), is probably the site that the Bible refers to as Pithom. Though once excavated, it was now covered in undulating mounds.

What was clear from visiting these sites was how vital the Delta was in the late second millennium B.C.E. These were not frontier towns, forgotten by the central authority; they were bustling cities whose intake from international commerce was central to the strength of the country. Indeed, the volume of trade coming from Palestine, coupled with the Delta's enormous food-generating powers, produced multiple thriving cities within a very small area, much more congested than anything in Canaan. The Land of Goshen was the Northeast Corridor of ancient Egypt, with all the benefits—and drawbacks—of a concentrated zone. This might explain the large gathering of immigrant labor; it also might explain how if conditions worsened, and word spread quickly, a relatively rapid emigration would be possible. Think of the Irish decamping after the potato famine, or Americans fleeing the Dust Bowl, and one gets a sense of the possible undercurrents of the Exodus. As with other stories in the Bible, economic revolutions join with geographic realities and spiritual objectives to create a story that serves both the mythological needs of the nation as well as the glory of God.

By the time we finished exploring the tels it was almost 2:00 and we'd lost track of time. We still hoped to cross the Red Sea by sunset. We rejoined the paved, two-lane road and began sprinting east toward the Suez Canal. We passed through a few small communities, each with what appeared to be a designated purpose: one for fixing lorries, another for making furniture. The only consistent curiosity was dozens of dovecotes that hung from many buildings and trees. Dovecotes, also known as pigeon farms, are wooden bird shelters with large bottom trays designed to gather droppings, which are then used as fertilizer. As Avner explained, once Nasser built the dam and trapped the silt in Aswan, alternative means of fertilizing became necessary. Egypt: the gift of the pigeons.

About twenty-five minutes into our drive we burst through a border of palm trees and suddenly found ourselves in open desert. The transition was abrupt, and unnerving, the inverse of what I had seen on my flight to Luxor. The ground was slightly higher here, and thus out of reach of the many canals from the river. We were in a land bridge between the Delta and the Sinai, a dead zone between the Nile and the Red Sea. It was tempting to visualize the hordes of Israelites racing to an unknown fate at water's edge. It was even more tempting to imagine this landscape as the setting for one of the bleakest countdowns in history, the world's first Top Ten List: the plagues.

After Moses returns from the wilderness, his first act is to ask the pharaoh directly, in the name of God, to let the Israelites depart from Egypt. The pharaoh dismisses the request and redoubles his tormenting of the Israelites, insisting that they start gathering their own straw for making bricks. Moses makes a second appeal to the pharaoh, who asks for proof of Moses' god. Aaron tosses a rod onto the ground, which becomes a serpent. Unimpressed, the pharaoh has his magicians turn the same trick with their rods. Aaron's serpent promptly devours the others. The pharaoh's heart "stiffens," and he denies Moses' request.

God then initiates a series of "signs and wonders" designed to persuade the pharaoh to release the Israelites. In the first act, Aaron spreads his rod over all the waters of Egypt and turns them to blood. Egyptian magicians duplicate this act, too, and the pharaoh walks away, unpersuaded. God then overruns the country with frogs, which enter the palace, the pharaoh's bedchamber, even his bed. This time the pharaoh feigns acceptance, but when God withdraws the frogs, the king rescinds his offer. God responds by covering the land with lice, and the magicians, unable to duplicate this act, announce, "This is the finger of God." Pharaoh's heart remains stiff.

Six more plagues quickly follow. The land is overrun with insects, pestilence strikes the livestock, humans and animals are overcome with boils. Hail lashes the landscape, locusts swarm the territory, and darkness covers the country. Each time, the pharaoh refuses to back down. Several times he pretends to, but God now stiffens his heart. God wants to display *all* his signs, he tells Moses, and make a mockery of the Egyptians. Finally God tells Moses, "I will bring but one more plague upon Pharaoh and upon Egypt; after that he shall let you go from here." Moses passes the warning on to the pharaoh, saying that at midnight God will kill every first-born in the land of Egypt, "from the first-born of Pharaoh who sits on his throne, to the first-born of the slave girl who is behind the millstone; and all the first-born of the cattle." A loud cry shall be heard in the land of Egypt, Moses warns.

The pharaoh remains stiff-hearted. The confrontation is set.

Almost since these stories were recorded, commentators have tried to find natural explanations for each of the ten plagues. Philo said that God-given elements of the universe—earth, water, air, and fire—all conspired in a state of hostility against the impious country. Another theory held that a comet passed too closely to earth, showering debris that was mistaken for hail and trailing dust that darkened the sky. More recently, a number of commentators have tried to find a single explanation for all ten plagues. Greta Hort, a biblical ecologist, has suggested that the plagues could be traced to an unusually high flood triggered by heavy rainfall in the Ethiopian Highlands. The amount of tropical red soil in one of the Blue Nile tributaries would have been uncommonly high, creating the illusion of blood. In addition, a higher-than-normal number of flagellates drawn from the highlands would have killed many fish, which in turn would have caused the frogs to seek refuge on the land, where they would have died from anthrax, which had also been spawned by the dead fish. The virus, *Bacillus anthracis,* later killed the livestock and caused the boils, Hort suggested. The excessive amount of water, meanwhile, would have generated an excessive amount of mosquitoes (an alternative translation of lice), as well as the insects. All this destruction, inevitably, left the land decimated, so that by the time the khamsin, or strong easterly wind from the Sahara, arrived in March, it kicked up all the dust and left the air black as night.

While Hort leaves out the bloody final plague, a more cataclysmic theory that includes the death of the firstborn sons has been gaining currency in recent years. In 1985, the British journalist Ian Wilson published a book called *Exodus: The True Story,* which elaborated on the theory that a volcanic eruption on the Mediterranean island of Thera around 1450 B.C.E. caused the plagues, as well as a tidal wave that parted the Red Sea. According to this view, giant clouds of volcanic ash covered the entire Eastern Mediterranean, triggering not only the darkness but also unusual behavior among frogs and insects. Theran ash, he suggests, contained iron oxide, which was mistaken for blood, and rained down in pellets, which were mistaken for hail. The dust also caused the boils, he notes, citing examples from Vesuvius and Mount Saint Helens. He even goes so far as to suggest that the volcano triggered plague ten, which he says was mass ritual murder. "Faced with an unprecedented series of natural disasters, whose origins they would have had no way of understanding, what would be the Egyptians' natural reaction? Inevitably to interpret the events as anger on the part of the gods. How could the gods be propitiated? For the ancients there was only one obvious way: by sacrifice."

Such elaborate explanations for the plagues, while engrossing, seem to beg a common question. Proponents of these theories, like promoters of other theories about biblical events, seem to espouse them in an effort to prove that the Bible happened, that it's real, that it's a matter of science. This is what Gabi Barkay was referring to when he said some observers view the Bible as a kind of machine: If you can prove that two of its screws existed, you can prove the whole machine must have existed. But after examining many of these theories, I came to believe that far from enhancing the Bible, they often undermine it. The reason is simple: If the biblical stories can be explained entirely by natural causes, what does that do to the supernatural? In other words, if a volcano caused the plagues, where does that leave God?

In many ways I could relate to the thinking behind these theories. It's certainly easier to look for naturalistic explanations for seemingly inexplicable phenomena, especially considering the alternative, which would be to attribute them to divine intervention. When I first started reading the Bible closely I, too, wanted—maybe even needed—to hide behind the screen of history, topography, science. I was interested in the setting of the story, I said. I was interested in the historical context. I was interested in the *characters,* by which I meant the patriarchs, their wives, Moses, the Israelites. But in doing so, I was strenuously—at times acrobatically—avoiding showing interest in the *central character of the entire book.* I did this, I was coming to see, because I deeply wanted to avoid *thinking* about that character, about what that character meant to the story, and about what that character might mean to me. But in doing so, I was shielding myself from a principal storyline of the Bible: the relationship between humans and the divine.

Not until I reached Exodus did I finally begin to recognize the futility of this exercise in self-delusion. As it happens, the text itself reveals precisely what caused the ten plagues. God caused them. To miss that point is to miss the essence of the tale, the battle between the god of the Israelites and the gods of the Egyptians, the battle that Eliezer Oren referred to as "My god is stronger than your god." Biblical storytellers clearly understood this struggle, because the plagues expressly attack the things that Egyptians held most sacred: the sun, the animals, the river. As the Bible says, summing up the experience, "The Lord executed judgment on their gods."

With that judgment the Bible makes a significant break—and with it, I, at least, made a break as well. Up to now, the Israelites have been wandering, from Mesopotamia, through Canaan, to Egypt, and absorbing elements from all these places. They are now ready to break away and begin forming their own culture, their own empire. They must now become active participants in their own story: actors, not just reactors. God makes the meaning of this transition clear. "This month shall mark for you the beginning of the months," he says. All Israelites shall sacrifice a lamb, he exhorts, and put its blood on their doorposts. This lamb shall be roasted, eaten, and the leftovers burned.

Also, in the first instance in which God seems to address the *readers* of the Bible, not just the participants, he says the Israelites should mark this passage forever in the ritual holiday of Passover, by eating unleavened bread for seven days as a sign of how they left Egypt in haste. In other words, each of us should mark this moment in time and relive it every year. We should enter the story ourselves, reimagine ourselves in bondage, and reconsider the feelings of awe, fear, apprehension, and expectation we have upon being released by a god we're just seeing—and feeling—for the first time. Put more directly, as I was just understanding, we should embrace our ignorance of God, and our own reluctance to recognize the need we inherently have for him, until he, on his own accord, reaches out and frees us. We should, in eating that meal, in painting that blood, in reliving that transformation, open ourselves, ultimately, to him. Because while the Israelites are having the first Passover feast that evening, the Lord sets forth, striking down all the firstborn in Egypt. It's this act, at last, that breaks the pharaoh, and he summons Moses and Aaron. "Up, depart from among my people," he says. "Go, worship the Lord as you said! Take also your flocks and your herds, as you said, and begone! And may you bring a blessing upon me also!" At last the Israelites are free. At last we are free—or at least seem to be.

Half an hour after emerging from the trees we began to descend the sloping sand toward an odd sight, a perfectly linear horizon in an otherwise undulating landscape. The road began to straighten, like a runway. Suddenly from this unusual terrain came an even stranger vision: an enormous oil tanker, sitting on the horizon like a beached whale. For a second I was startled—was this an antimirage?—until I realized: This was the mother of modern Egypt, the gateway of the modern Middle East, the Suez Canal.

As we approached the banks, the strangeness of this waterway became more apparent. Unlike the Nile, the Suez Canal doesn't flood, so it doesn't bear silt and therefore isn't lined with green. Instead, the three-hundred-foot-wide canal slices through the desert bringing no apparent benefit to the sand on either bank. One reason for this unfriendliness is the canal's unusual cocktail of fresh- and saltwater. The canal connects the Mediterranean with the Gulf of Suez, both of which are saltwater. In between, however, it joins with the Bitter Lakes and Lake Timsah, which are freshwater. The canal has other distinctive features. At one hundred miles, it's the longest man-made waterway in the Eastern Hemisphere, twice as long as the Panama Canal, though only a twentieth as long as the Saint Lawrence Seaway. It's also perhaps the world's leading canal with roots dating back to the ancient world.

The first attempts to link the Red Sea and the Mediterranean were made by Pharaoh Necho II, who lived around 600 B.C.E. Herodotus claimed that 120,000 workers had died before an oracle predicted the canal would only benefit Egypt's enemies, and the project was abandoned. The Persian emperor Darius completed the first leg around 500 B.C.E., linking the Red Sea with the Great Bitter Lake. From there, ships could pass into a smaller canal built by Rameses II that linked the lake with the cat city of Bubastis, and from there to the Mediterranean. In other words, assuming the Exodus wasn't caused by the Thera volcano, the Israelites *could have built the first Suez Canal*! Menachem Begin would have been proud.

Napoleon considered extending the canal from the Bitter Lakes, but his idea was vetoed by his engineers, who said there was a thirty-three-foot height difference between the Mediterranean and the Gulf of Suez. In fact there is none. The discovery of this error in 1840 prompted French consul Ferdinand de Lesseps to propose the project to

Egyptian Mohammed Said Pasha. The British objected, claiming it would lead to war, but Said proceeded anyway, using French and Turkish money. The effort, which began in 1859, employed twenty thousand Egyptians and took ten years, ultimately bankrupting Said's successor and nephew, Ismail, who was forced to sell his 40 percent to Britain, effectively making the canal the property of the crown. As Prime Minister Disraeli reported to Queen Victoria: "You have it, Madam."

The canal was significant because it cut the time needed to travel from Western Europe to India and the Far East by half, and this importance was apparent on November 17, 1869, when six thousand dignitaries from around the world gathered for the gala opening. Ismail had built an opera house in Cairo and commissioned Verdi to write *Aïda;* a platoon of five hundred cooks and one thousand servants were brought from France and Italy; and the pyramids were illuminated with magnesium light, the precursor to the sound and light shows of today. Predictably, the event almost turned into a disaster. The fireworks dump blew up, nearly destroying the new town built for the occasion. A ship ran aground, blocking the canal. And not until de Lesseps had the ship blown up could the armada of seventy vessels, led by the emperor of Austria dressed in a white tunic, scarlet pantaloons, and a cocked hat with a green feather, sail between the grandstands, declaring Africa an island. Perhaps the most intriguing moment of the canal's opening went unnoticed by the public. Several months earlier, the Prince and Princess of Wales were on hand when the sluices were first opened and great quantities of salt water from the Mediterranean came pouring into the Bitter Lakes, instantly killing all the freshwater fish.

As the ancient omen predicted, the canal has been a continual source of tension between Egypt and its enemies. In 1956, Nasser, needing resources, nationalized the canal. Britain and France were outraged and recruited Israel to advance into the Sinai, a pretext that allowed them to "safeguard" the canal by occupying it. At this point, the Soviet Union threatened to get involved on the side of the Egyptians, and the UN was brought in to evacuate the British, French, and Israeli troops. By the time the fracas ended, Nasser had emerged victorious and the canal was almost destroyed. The battered region had barely recovered when the war of 1967 caused further damage, leaving the waterway blocked by sunken vessels. Though it reopened in 1975, the canal remained surrounded by Egyptian and Israeli troops until 1982, by which time many supertankers were too large to pass through the three-hundred-foot width and chose to sail around Africa instead.

Today the area is eerily quiet, a boulevard of postindustrial arks in an otherwise flood zone of sand. When we stopped and walked to its edge, I was amazed by the haphazard dunes that seemed almost man-made, as if the canal were dug only recently. A burnt-out bridge lay discarded nearby; and it struck me that the damage could have been caused in any of a half-dozen wars. I was also fascinated by the color of the water, a vivid turquoise. Altogether, it seemed the perfect setting for a biblical/sci-fi film, *Raiders of the Lost Ark* meets *Star Wars*.

For all its apocalyptic atmospherics, the canal was also deeply emotional, a living tribute to a timeless dream. "There's a lot of emotion in this place," I said to Avner. "You can feel it."

"Absolutely," he said. "There's the canal, the water where Moses might have crossed. But for me there are also a lot of bad memories—of the wars, and the fronts. I was here under heavy shelling many times. In the 1973 war one of the worst mortar fights was not far from here. It's called the Chinese Farm, where the Israelis crossed and met an Egyptian brigade. There was horrendous shelling for days, and I lost many friends. It's still hard for me to come here."

"So where *did* Moses cross?" I asked.

We sat down and pulled out our Bibles. In Exodus 12, with permission from the pharaoh now in hand, Moses rallies the Israelites—a total of "600,000 men, aside from children"—and sets out for the Promised Land. Instead of leading them by the "way of the Philistines," which probably means the northern border where they would have encountered fortresses, God sends them via what the Hebrew calls *yam suf*, and what English Bibles call the Red Sea. They stop at several towns—Succoth and Etham, whose locations are unknown today—before changing direction and camping in Baal-zephon, near the sea. At this point the pharaoh changes his mind, summons six hundred chariots, and leads his army after the slaves. When the Israelites spot the Egyptians they realize they are trapped. "Was it for want of graves in Egypt that you brought us to die in the wilderness?" they cry to Moses.

God, who has been leading the Israelites in the form of a pillar of smoke during the day and a pillar of fire at night, moves the pillar of smoke behind the Israelites to protect them from the advancing Egyptians. Moses then holds out his arms over the sea and God drives back the waters with a strong eastern wind, forming a "wall of water" to the right and left. The Israelites cross on this boulevard of dry ground. The Egyptians, freed from the smoke, start to follow. But as soon as the Israelites reach the other side, Moses holds up his arms and the sea returns to normal. The Egyptian army is swallowed alive. The fate of the pharaoh is not mentioned.

Inevitably, efforts to decipher where this event took place have preoccupied biblical readers for centuries. One nagging problem is the confusing nature of the name the Bible gives to this body of water, *yam suf*. *Yam* is the Hebrew word for sea; *suf* is the Hebrew word for reed. No body of water with this name is known from antiquity. Even more confusing for many Western readers is how this term has been translated. By all accounts it was the Greek Septuagint, translated by Jews in Alexandria in the third century B.C.E., that introduced the most famous mistranslation in history, "Erythra Thalassa," Red Sea, for what should have been Sea of Reeds. This mistake was picked up by the Latin Vulgate and embedded into English with the King James Bible in 1611.

Straightening out the name does help the identification somewhat, but not conclusively. There are five major candidates for the Sea of Reeds: (1) the Mediterranean, specifically a bay north of the Delta; (2) the marshy area just south of the Mediterranean; (3) Lake Timsah, or Crocodile Lake, a large lake halfway between the Mediterranean and the Red Sea; (4) the Bitter Lakes, a series of lakes just to the south of Timsah; and (5) the Red Sea itself, specifically the Gulf of Suez.

Again, the name does provide clues. The Hebrew word *suf* is generally considered to be a borrowing from the Egyptian word *tuf,* or papyrus. Papyrus grows only in fresh water, which would seem to rule out the Mediterranean and the Red Sea (though in Numbers 21, while the Israelites are on their way to Edom, the Bible apparently uses *yam suf* for the Gulf of Aqaba). Also, since the ancient marsh north of the Timsah is now covered by the Suez Canal, and therefore unknowable, it has few proponents. Instead, informed speculation centers on Lake Timsah and the Bitter Lakes. It is possible these were part of a continual stream of lakes, all of which are referred to as *yam suf*. But differences do exist among them. The Bitter Lakes are bigger and deeper. Timsah, by contrast, is relatively shallow, often no more than three feet deep. It's tempting to imagine the Israelites, on a windy day, wading across this body of water, while the Egyptians mindlessly followed and got their chariots stuck in the mud.

As for me, now that I was nearing the area, the matter of finding the *actual* spot where the Israelites crossed was beginning to seem less important. This feeling was a mark of exactly how much change I'd been undergoing. When I first came up with the idea of retracing the Bible, I was fascinated by questions of archaeology and identification: the precise place where Abraham went to sacrifice Isaac, the specific valley where Jacob had his dream; the exact mountain where Moses met God. Now, more than a year later, I was shifting my objectives. I still found these questions fascinating, but more in an academic, recreational sort of way. Instead, the questions that were drawing me more were those of symbolism, character, metaphor. I was reading the text less as a Baedeker now and more as a Bible. I was reading it for meaning.

That change, which first began in Israel, became more fully realized in Egypt, as I discovered the powerful emotions that ancient sites are still able to evoke. They are testaments to the ability of places to mark holy spaces where humans come into contact with their god. And what better example of that contact than the parting of the Red Sea. In dividing the waters, God shows his mastery not only over nature but also over humanity. He uses wind, smoke, and water both to save the Israelites and to destroy the Egyptians. In this sense, it doesn't matter where the event happened, or whether it happened. As Martin Buber, the Jewish philosopher, said, "What is vital is only that what happened was experienced, while it happened, as the act of God."

What's also important is that, in recording the event, the writers show their mastery of storytelling. As Avner said, "I remember as a child imagining the wall of water on both sides of my bed." Reading it as an

adult, one can see even more. The dramatic events surrounding the crossing of the sea harken back unavoidably to the opening verses of Genesis:
the dividing of the Red Sea recalls the splitting of the watery world into
two; the destroying of the Egyptian army evokes the slaying of the forces
of chaos. In this passage, the Bible serves up yet another creation story.
And this time the product is not the world; it's the nation of Israel. As
Avner said, "*Now* the people are free. Now the real work begins."

Back at the car it was past 3:00 and Ahmed and Yasser were getting
antsy. None of us had eaten since 4 A.M. Delirium—and exhaustion—
were starting to weigh heavily. Also, the sun was about to set. Still, we
had yet to attend to the main purpose of our journey. I may have been
less interested in the precise location where the Israelites crossed, but we
were still interested in experiencing what they might have gone through
during their flight. But where to do that?

We turned south toward Ismailia, a garden city erected during the
construction of the canal and named after Ismail, which sits at the
northern cusp of Lake Timsah. The city was largely deserted by the time
we arrived, as most people had gone home early on Thursday afternoon
in advance of the Muslim sabbath. The once grand avenues seemed like
emblems of a ghost town, with baronial mansions turned into tenement
houses for workers in the run-down resorts around the lake. We drove
through the streets for twenty minutes, trying to suss out the best way to
get afloat. We stopped and asked a local policeman, who gave us directions to a hotel on the lake.

There were few cars in the parking lot of the Mercury Hotel, and no
one in the lobby. Clouds had started to form overhead and the sense of
vacancy was now accented by a stormy gloom in our car. Ahmed and
Yasser stayed in the jeep as Avner and I went to the front desk and asked
if we could rent a boat. The woman looked at us quizzically, then glanced
at her watch. "We have a boat leaving ten o'clock tomorrow," she said.
"But we need it this afternoon," we pleaded. "Impossible," she said. I
reached for my wallet. "No, no," she said, waving my hand away. "It can't
be done. You need permission from the police, from the army, from Cairo.

It takes two weeks." "But we're going home tonight," I said. She dropped her head. "Sorry. Maybe you should try the boats in the park."

Back in the jeep Ahmed and Yasser were half asleep and were not interested in trying the park on the northern shore of the lake. "Can't you just take a picture?" Yasser said. I shook my head. "Let's try the park," I said. Ten minutes later we found the chain-linked entrance to Mallhala Park; it was padlocked. I shook the gate for a second and a man emerged. Avner explained what we wanted and the man went inside and used the telephone. A few minutes later a car appeared, and a well-dressed man stepped out. Seeing that we were foreigners, he berated the guard for not letting us in and opened the gate. We paid the small entrance fee and drove inside.

The park was set up for summertime recreation, with a few steel umbrellas over picnic tables, a grassy area for soccer, a mosque, and a narrow beach about the width of two towels. The complex was entirely vacant, and a bit eerie. One reason is the unusual nature of the lake. Close to where we were standing, Timsah, which covers an area about seven square miles, looks like any lake in Minnesota. But the center of the lake has been completely taken over by the canal, as if a superhighway were plopped down in the middle of a duck pond. When we arrived, two enormous tankers were passing in front of the beach, close enough to hit with a Frisbee.

Feeling desperate now, I sprinted quickly from one side of the park to the other until I spotted a small cabin with a handful of rowboats chained together in front. My heart leapt. I knocked on the cabin, nobody answered. I knocked a little louder, still nobody answered. I screamed. No reply. I even went to the boats themselves and tried to dislodge one. I couldn't. Either way, I didn't see any oars. However romantic it might seem, the idea of paddling across the Suez Canal with a palm branch, dodging oil tankers, hardly seemed prudent.

It started to rain. I slumped back to the pavilion, where Avner was speaking with the man who had let us in. "It's winter," the man said. "It's Ramadan. It's raining. Are you sure you need to do this?" I thanked him and turned back toward the car. Of course I didn't need to cross the Red Sea, no more than I needed to climb Mount Moriah or lick Mount

Sodom. I didn't *need* to be here at all, yet here I was, nearly halfway through my travels, called by some unhearable voice, following some unfollowable path. And where had it gotten me? For the moment, standing in the rain at the Suez Canal, staring at the desert in front of me, feeling the pull of civilization behind me, having dragged a small carload on this quixotic quest, and having landed, trapped, in the most predictable of dead ends: an uncrossable body of water.

Back at the car I explained the situation to Yasser and Ahmed. They did little to disguise their displeasure. It was almost time to break the fast, they said, and they wanted to return to Cairo. By the time Avner arrived they were openly sulking. Cheerily I announced a desire to give it one more try. We could drive south along the waterfront of Lake Timsah, I said, and if we reached the end without finding a boat, we could give up and go home. We went around the car in an informal vote. Ahmed stared ahead; he was apparently voting no. Yasser was more vocal; he wanted out. I turned toward Avner. He looked at the others, then at me. And as he did, I realized how long we'd been traveling together, how much we'd seen already, and how lucky I was to have found him. As much as he knew about the Bible, he seemed to know more about the nature of travel, about how to go to places, leave a bit of yourself behind, take a bit of the place with you, and in the process emerge with something bigger—an experience, a connection, a story. Maybe that's one reason the Bible has such enduring power: At its heart, it's a great adventure tale.

"I think we should give it a try," he said.

Along the waterfront the choices were not promising. The farther south we drove, the more industrial the lake became. We saw several container ships docked in a shipyard, but I figured the chances of their taking a $10 offer of baksheesh to ferry us across the lake were small. We spotted some tugboats, but even they seemed unlikely. Also, there were few people around anyway. The quays were totally abandoned. The sense of misery in the jeep was now palpable. The sense of righteousness worse. It looked like Ahmed and Yasser were right. You couldn't cross the Red Sea at dusk during Ramadan. Our flight of fancy had come up short. I felt disappointed, and a bit silly. The romantic folly behind our journey never seemed more palpable. What was I expecting? A crack of lightning, a raised staff, a miraculous parting of the tankers?

In time we emerged from the commercial zone into the last residential stretch and I was preparing to concede defeat, when all of a sudden we rounded a bend and I spotted to our right a small fishing enclave, with dozens of newly painted, bright white rowboats. "That's it!" I shouted, flinging open the door. Ahmed screeched to a halt and I leapt from my seat. Avner followed and we went sprinting to the narrow beach. All the boats were empty, except one, which was just pulling into the shore. An older man jumped off and began dumping fish into a barrel.

When the man finished, Avner spoke to him for a second, asking if he might take us for a ride. The man seemed agreeable, chuckled a bit, and after consulting with the teenager who was manning the oars, invited us aboard: me, Avner, Ahmed, Yasser. If the police escort had come, he couldn't have fit. There were now six of us struggling to find seats in a boat the size of a bathtub. I sat in the stern, closest to the oarsman. Mohammed was sixteen, with maroon pants and a black turtleneck with CAT imprinted on the collar. A wet blanket covered his knees. His boat was made of eucalyptus, he said, and the turquoise paint on the seats was a week old. "Does the boat have a name?" I asked. "*Number Fifty*," he said.

He steered us carefully through the bay, which was crowded with anchored rowboats. This part of the lake was similar to the northern tip, with turquoise water lapping against a few yards of beach. The dredged area where the canal intersects the lake was several miles away. With no tankers passing, we had a clear view of the sandy shore of the Sinai. All around us, the water was shallow, and you could see the vegetation on the bottom. The farther we got from the fishing boats, the more the lake began to take on a natural, pristine feel. Huge sprouts of marsh grass blossomed from the banks, with cattails swaying like candle flames. The image of Moses in the basket was unavoidable. Regardless of its relevance to the biblical story, Timsah, at least, is a lake with reeds. A fish jumped out of the water and squiggled back in place. It stopped raining.

"So what kinds of fish do you catch?" I asked Mohammed.

"Mostly gray mullet," he said. "Sometimes perch, or Moses fish."

"*Moses* fish?" I repeated.

"It's good to eat," Mohammed said.

"I think it's a kind of flounder," Avner added.

As we were speaking the sun slowly broke through the clouds. Quickly the entire feel of the scene changed, as the light filtered through the yellowy grass and filled the air with a saffron glow that when it reflected off the sheen of the water—turquoise and gold—reminded me of Tutankhamen's mask. Instantly I recalled the sense of power—and fear—I felt upon seeing the mask in the museum. And in so doing I began to see the Exodus in a different light. No matter how oppressive the pharaoh must have seemed to residents of Goshen, for the Israelites, crossing this (or any other) body of water would have been a profoundly frightening experience, akin to what religious refugees must have felt like boarding boats in Europe in the 1600s and sailing for the New World. No matter how full of hope they were, they were still leaving the most civilized place on earth for the most barren. In the case of the Israelites, this meant leaving Egypt behind for the desert. They were "going forth" from a world they knew to a world that didn't yet exist based solely on the word of a god they'd never actually seen. Perhaps no one since Abraham could understand the depth of faith that required.

And in sensing the mix of anxiety and awe, I felt an emotion I hadn't experienced since my earliest days in Turkey. It was the feeling of the land reaching up to touch me, elbowing aside my preconceived views of the Bible as a sterile collection of stories set in places I couldn't see, involving characters I couldn't relate to, experiencing desires I didn't have. What emerged instead was a vibrant view of the Bible as a collection of living tableaux, set in actual places, involving genuine people, experiencing the most basic of human desires: the longing to live in a place, with their own beliefs and their own aspirations.

Before coming to Egypt, I had been somewhat apologetic about this leg of our trip. I would travel down the Nile in search of Joseph; I would visit the pyramids and the land of Goshen; but I didn't expect to find much directly related to the Bible. Now I realized more than ever that you can't understand the Bible without understanding Egypt. The text itself seems to hint at this connection. Joseph could simply have lived in Egypt. Instead he rose to prime minister. Moses could have been raised in any household. Instead he grew up in the pharaoh's. From the use of dreams with Joseph, to the importance of the Nile to Moses, Egyptian motifs fill the Pentateuch and lend a geographic—and cultural—balance to the Mesopotamian themes that dominate the early chapters of Genesis. Even the story of the parting of the Red Sea has an Egyptian antecedent. During the reign of Snefru, the father of the king who built the Great Pyramid, the pharaoh one day convened a rowing party. A young woman dropped a brooch into the Nile and became inconsolable, so the pharaoh summoned a magician who separated the waters, reached to the dry ground, and retrieved the brooch. The waters soon returned to normal.

Like many, I suspect, I'd always thought of Egypt in the Bible as being the adversary, the wicked tyrant of the west. Now I'd come to see that that view was too narrow. Egypt, like Mesopotamia, was a powerful empire that the Israelites first had to understand and cohabitate with; later they could draw ideas from it; later still they could supplant it. In effect, the Israelites were taking the best elements of each belief system they encountered along their journey and combining them with their own notion of a universal God to create a new pan–Near Eastern religion that could therefore become the dominant creed of the Fertile Crescent.

And maybe it was appreciation at having made that discovery; maybe it was the sense that I had touched the two outer wings of the biblical narrative and was now on my way to the desert core, the place where the people finally receive their blessing; or maybe it was relief at having persevered through a trying day (and the antagonism of Ahmed and Yasser), but as I sat on the water that afternoon, listening to the gulls, smelling the salt, I felt something inside of me suddenly open up that I didn't even know was closed. I felt a quiet snap of release, like a door clicking open in the middle of the night, beckoning me to a place I'd always been afraid to go. So when Mohammed mentioned that he rowed to this spot every day trawling for *Moses* fish, I felt myself giving in to the emotion.

"So what do you know about Moses?" I said.

"He was a prophet, wasn't he?" the boy said.

"Yes, he's the one who split the sea," I said. "Do you think you can do that for us?"

Mohammed smiled and tugged a little harder. "Sorry," he said, "that's a miracle."

And for the first time since I started the trip, I felt myself start to cry.

Book III

THE GREAT
AND
TERRIBLE
WILDERNESS

1. A Land of Fiery
Snakes and Scorpions

Light. The first thing you notice about the desert is the light. It's a white light, bleached across the horizon, that bounces off the blue helmet of sky, picks up the glint of quartz in the sand, and washes out everything in its sight. The desert may be defined by the absence of rain, but a watercolor painting of the place would have far more water than color.

The second thing you notice about the desert is the space. The panorama is almost overwhelming, with sand blowing across the ground, bushes bent against the wind, and everywhere rocks, mesas, dunes, and mountains. Montana may be Big Sky country, but the Sinai is Big Land country. One almost needs wide-angle vision to take it all in, and even that's not enough. Stand facing the Sinai from the Suez Canal, as I did with Avner in early spring, having returned to begin the next leg of our trip, retracing the Exodus through what the Bible calls "that great and terrible wilderness," and two eyes are not enough to take in the scene; two arms are not enough to embrace it. The Sinai would diminish any crowd.

The last thing you notice about the desert is the noise. In preparing for this part of our journey, I steeled myself for the silence. The desert would surely feel isolated, an island of seclusion. But once I stepped into the open terrain I was amazed by the din—the wind whining through the mountains, the sand tinkling against your face, the rocks crunching beneath your feet. As Jim Crace wrote in *Quarantine,* a retelling of Jesus' stay in the desert, no wild land is ever truly silent. "Earth collapses with the engineering of the ants; lizards smack the pebbles with their tails; the sun fires seeds in salvos from their pods; pigeons misconnect with dry branches; and stones, left loosely to their own devices, can find the muscle to descend the hill."

The desert may be empty, but it's the least quiet place I've ever been.

And the most alluring.

From the moment I crossed the Suez and set foot in the Sinai I felt a sense of exhilaration. It was partly the openness of the place, partly its inhospitality. It was partly the feeling of anticipation after the changes I marked in Egypt. But mostly it was the feeling of being drawn to the land. Having passed, at least in spirit, through the congested histories of Mesopotamia, Canaan, and Egypt, I understood even more the importance of the Sinai to the Bible, to the need of the Israelites to shed the skins of other cultures and start growing one of their own. The desert destroys affectation; it demands authenticity. The Sinai, in particular, poised between Africa and Asia, compels a certain clarity. Come with a vague sense of identity; leave with a deeper sense of self. If God knew this, as the Bible suggests, he may, indeed, have known everything.

The importance of discovery hits one almost immediately in the Sinai, if for no other reason than it's impossibly easy to get lost, even for a onetime resident like Avner, who from 1967 to 1982 was the chief archaeologist of the Sinai. As we started our trip, accompanied by a new driver, Yusuf, a reed-thin Nubian from Aswan with Dagwood hair and a constant smile, we were disoriented at once. We were heading south on a two-lane, coastal highway from Lake Timsah, looking for Ain Musa, the Spring of Moses, believed to be the Israelites' first stop in the desert. The narrow strip of blacktop was mostly barren, with a few budding resorts popping out of the sand: Queen Beach, Banana Beach, Mykonos. The resorts were just road signs and empty shells at the moment, part of Egypt's nascent effort to turn the Sinai, one of the most desolate peninsulas in the Middle East, into a Club Med–style paradise. We drove into a few of the abandoned complexes and even skirted the shore, in a vain attempt to find someone to ask for directions. Finally we were ready to give up and turn south, when we spotted a few palm trees on the horizon, a cartoon vision of a mirage.

The Spring of Moses is one of about four hundred oases in the Sinai. A compact area about the size of a baseball diamond, the oasis is little more than a cluster of trees—mostly palms, with a few eucalyptuses and tamarisks—huddled around a spring. The landscape seems random, as if the palms had been dropped from the sky. They protrude from odd angles, jut, swoop, lean, and prod. Some are dense with fronds, like one of those sponge brushes used to clean drinking glasses. Others look like tired feather dusters. Many are barren, with their tops decapitated in one of the Sinai's recent wars. An Israeli battery stationed at the oasis bombed the Suez Canal during the War of Attrition between 1967 and 1970. Even the palm trees here have a past.

We got out of the jeep with our Bibles and sat on the stump of a tamarisk tree facing the Suez Canal. After they cross the Sea of Reeds, an event described in Exodus 14, the Israelites briefly celebrate by chanting the Song of Miriam, widely regarded as one of the oldest pieces of text in the Bible. "I will sing to the Lord, for He has triumphed gloriously; / Horse and driver He has hurled into the sea. / The Lord is my strength and might; / He is become my salvation." Then the Israelites set out into the "wilderness of Shur." After three days they arrive at a place called Marah, where the water is too bitter to drink. When the people complain, God points Moses toward a piece of wood, which he tosses into the water, making it sweet. Having performed this miracle, God promises the Israelites that if they obey him, he will protect them from the desert. He then leads them to Elim, where there are twelve springs of water and seventy palm trees. Tradition holds that Ain Musa is one of these two sites, an identification helped by the fact that the water here is strongly malodorous and works as a laxative—bitter by any definition. "There certainly are seventy palm trees," I said, to which Avner replied, "Would you care to count?"

As with many places in the Sinai, the absence of evidence hardly matters, as modern visitors have decided these sites *are* the ones mentioned in the text. As we were sitting, a tour bus rolled up and fifty

South Koreans disembarked, said a quick prayer by the spring, and prepared to re-embark. "This is the site of Marah," the minister explained, when I asked him why he had come. Moments later a van full of American college students appeared and repeated the ritual. Their professor was less confident. "I don't worry about assigning places," he said. "In the end it doesn't matter whether they took the northern route, the central route, or the southern route. What matters is that they were here." Minutes later, a carload of Frenchwomen arrived. "Who cares if the Israelites were actually here?" one woman said. "We're here because it's biblical!"

We piled back in the jeep and headed south. Outside its few resort towns, the Sinai is essentially empty, sixty thousand bedouin in an area the size of Ireland. As a result, there are only a handful of paved roads, and those are vulnerable to flash floods. One shifts instead among two-lane highways, dirt causeways, dried riverbeds, and open terrain. Because of this variety, each all-terrain vehicle must be a veritable Pullman-style sleeper, capable of surviving for days on end with the help of pillows, cushions, cans of tuna fish and okra, raw onions, extra water tanks, and garishly colored blankets that looked like beach towels from Atlantic City. In our case, the only thing we didn't have in ample supply was cassette tapes. Yusuf had only one: a Bob Marley collection called *Exodus*. For months afterward if anyone mentioned the word *Sinai* in conversation, I would instinctively repeat the reggae lyric, "Movement of the people!"

The Sinai has actually been defined by its absence of people. Often referred to as "24,000 square miles of nothing," the peninsula is a giant isosceles triangle wedged between Africa and Asia that has always served as something of a spillover zone for people who wanted to pass through it in order to get to someplace else. About fifty invading armies have crossed its plains since the Early Bronze Age, but few have tarried: never the prize, always the prizemaid. The name Sinai, which is thought to be derived from the Mesopotamian god of the moon, Sin, may have been transferred to the area from the Euphrates Valley by one of those armies or by a wandering Semitic tribe, not unlike Abraham's.

Because of its proximity to places of belief—and conflict—the Sinai has also been an escape ward, a refugee park for persecuted prophets. In addition to Moses, Elijah came here, as did Mary and Joseph. Christian extremists fled here in the early years of the Church, and Empress Helena later built them a chapel, which eventually gave rise to Saint Catherine's monastery. More recently, the Sinai has held tantalizing possibilities for persecuted Jews. In the nineteenth century, when Theodor Herzl first resurrected the idea of a Jewish homeland and ran into concern among the Turks, who controlled Palestine, he suggested the northern Sinai. Jews could make the desert bloom, Herzl suggested, with garden cities along the Mediterranean. The British liked the idea and sent an expedition in 1903. But when surveyors realized the difficulty of finding enough water—the average rainfall is forty millimeters a year, about an inch and a half—the British soured on the idea. Later Zionists tried to encourage Egypt to issue its own "Balfour Declaration" and invite Jews to settle in the area, but the plan never ignited. Had the idea worked, many of Judaism's most hallowed rituals—from the veneration of Jerusalem to the Passover seder—might have taken on a slightly different meaning. The desert would no longer have been a necessary evil; it would have been home.

The fact that Herzl recommended the northern Sinai is not accidental. The Sinai is divided into three distinct regions, each more inhospitable than the last. The northern tier is the most classically desert, with silken dunes, breezy oases, and marshy flats. But it's also the most temperate. Most of the bedouin population lives in this area. The vast middle, full of sandy hills and colored canyons, is known as the "Wandering Plateau," from the biblical story of forty years in the desert. This stretch is so scarred with mines and jeep tracks that it has been likened to a canvas by Jackson Pollock. The southern zone is the most dramatic. This jagged region is an irregular tableland, with hills slowly tilting upward, erupting in a startling array of craggy red granite mountains created from the fault line of Africa's Great Rift. As the fifteenth-century monk Felix Fabri wrote, commenting on these geographic differences: "Every day, indeed every hour, you come into a new country, of a different nature, with different conditions of atmosphere and soil, with hills of a different build and color, so that you are amazed at what you see and long for what you will see next."

This unusual menu of terrain has provided endless grist for one of the most heated battles surrounding the Bible: What route did the Israelites take through the Sinai? Inevitably, this question presupposes two things that are unprovable—that the Israelites were enslaved in Egypt at all and that there was an Exodus—but such disputes have done little to squelch debate. Generally speaking, there are three proposed paths: northern, central, and southern. The shortest and most direct route would be along the north, on the main artery of the ancient world, the Via Maris. This road was used by Egyptian kings in their military endeavors with Asia and was likely the one used by Abraham and Joseph when they came *from* the Promised Land. Because this road was so popular, however, Egyptians had fortified it with outposts, which would have meant dangers for fleeing slaves. Also, there are few mountains on this road, and thus no logical place to receive the Ten Commandments. Finally, the text says specifically, "God did not lead them through the land of the Philistines, although it was nearer." Though the use of the term *Philistines* is an anachronism, this passage clearly refers to the coastal plain. "The northern route can be easily discounted," Avner said.

The central route would be the next most reasonable. If Moses first saw Mount Sinai on his way to Midian, as early passages of Exodus suggest, and if he later met Aaron on the same road on his way back from Midian, logic would suggest that the Mountain of God be somewhere in between Midian and Egypt. Since Midian was likely located in the Arabian Desert just east of present-day Eilat, the most likely location of the mountain would be on the central route. This path would also make the most sense if the Sea of Reeds was either Lake Timsah or the Bitter Lakes. But the central theory also has problems. First, the middle of the Sinai is by far the least hospitable part of the peninsula. Second, the mountains are hardly grand. Third, it's hard to imagine it taking a month to get from the Sea of Reeds to any mountain on this road (which is what the text says it takes), considering that the distance is no greater than several hundred miles.

For sheer drama, the southern route is by far the most obvious. There are a series of oases along the Gulf of Suez, where the Israelites could have stopped on their way south, then the mountains, which present a perfect backdrop for the earthshaking events surrounding the Ten Commandments. Also, there's more water in the south, which would make it easier to support a large population. It is colder, though, which would make it more difficult to survive. And perhaps more crippling, the southern Sinai is completely out of the way—from Midian, from the Promised Land, from everyplace but certain death.

All in all, there is no good answer. As Avner said, when I asked him where the event most likely took place, "As an archaeologist, I don't have a scientific solution. As a man of the area, I don't see how a campaign in the Sinai could go on for forty years. There's no place that's a great place." Faced with this conundrum, we chose what's considered the traditional route, the southern one, if for no other reason than since Empress Helena's visit in the fourth century C.E., pilgrims have been coming to the area for *1,500* years, believing it to be the one. Since our objective was less to prove the Bible and more to witness its atmosphere and lingering appeal, we turned south toward the mountains with few second thoughts.

The last stop of our first day, down the western coast from the canal, was a series of turquoise mines. We pulled off a main road and made our way down the rocky basin of Wadi Megara, one of several dozen dried riverbeds that trickle largely north to south in the Sinai like raindrops down a foggy window. Already the area was hillier than the north, with mounds of chipped stone and flint that looked like spices from Goliath's cabinet—cinnamon, salt, nutmeg, garlic. The only color other than beige came from the acacia trees, which lined the narrowest parts of the wadi like spinach soufflés on stilts. It occurred to me that Goliath, on his way home to cook, might never have to touch the ground; he could walk from one side of the Sinai to the other stepping only on the tops of acacias, the lily pads of the desert.

The Sinai has long been prized for its natural resources. As early as the third millennium B.C.E., even before the pyramids were built, mineral-crazed Egyptian pharaohs sent expeditions to the Sinai to mine for copper, malachite, and turquoise. Many of these stones made their way into the pharaohs' funerary stashes—from the ground to the ground without ever being worn in public. Because of their royal connection, artists carved depictions of the pharaohs into the entrance of the mines, often as high as one hundred feet above the ground. William Flinders Petrie discovered many of these depictions and carted them off to the Cairo Museum in the early 1900s. In the early 1970s, Avner was leading an expedition in the area when one of his guides, not realizing the inscriptions had supposedly been removed, blithely pointed out an image of the pharaoh on a narrow precipice above the valley. "I almost fell down because I stopped breathing," Avner said. "There was a complete Egyptian relief that was still there, that Petrie never discovered. It may be the earliest relief ever found."

We climbed up a small cliff to get a better view. The relief was actually incomplete, suggesting the Egyptians had left suddenly. "So why in our story do we have to come here?" he asked. The answer, he said, not waiting for a reply, is that it provides clues as to how history is written in the desert, a matter of seminal importance in the story of the Exodus.

Even more than the matter of where the Israelites went, the question of how many Israelites went on the Exodus has been a nagging source of curiosity. The text says clearly that the number was six hundred thousand men on foot, aside from women and children. In addition, it notes, a "mixed multitude" went with them, presumably a variety of non-Israelites who took advantage of the chaos to join the flight to freedom. Later, the text notes that a census after the first year revealed 603,550 able-bodied men, excluding Levites. A second census, forty years later, put the number at 601,730.

These numbers are clearly not accidental. But are they real? The first, perhaps most obvious problem is how the seventy people who came to Egypt with Jacob could have produced six hundred thousand men in just 430 years. According to one study, each Israelite family for four centuries would have to have eight children in order to come close to the figure of six hundred thousand, which would make the statement in Exodus 1 that the Israelites "were fruitful and increased abundantly" the understatement of the second millennium B.C.E. Even more troubling is how this male population of six hundred thousand, which with women and children would easily have reached two million, could have existed in Egypt in the first place. Based on the best guess of historians, two million people would represent at least 20 percent of Egypt, which would make their enslavement tentative at best, and the fact that they could escape without being mentioned in any official document unimaginable. This would be like having the entire population of the American South decamp for Mexico before the Civil War, and have nobody in Latin America, the United States, or Europe *ever write it down*.

One explanation is that the Hebrew word for thousand, *elef,* can also be translated as clan, which would mean that the Israelites would have taken six hundred contingents, or around six thousand men. This view has problems, too. Numbers 3 clearly says that the number of firstborn sons of the Israelites was 22,273, a tricky figure to achieve for six thousand women, even if they were "fruitful and abundant" Israelite women. Another common explanation is that the figure six hundred thousand is meant to represent the population of the united monarchy of Israel *after* it arrived in Canaan, in the mid–first millennium B.C.E., around the time the story was written down. This would make the figures relevant to the end of the Exodus, not the beginning. Either way, it seems safe to assume that six hundred thousand is not a historically accurate figure.

"The point is," Avner said, "that the Israelites had a different sense of history than we do. They weren't trying to record facts objectively. They were trying to tell a story, and let the facts support the story." The point could be made most clearly, he said, with the mines where we were now standing. The Egyptians faced a serious threat from the local pastorals of the region. "We know this because nearby the Egyptians built a defensive wall, which they wouldn't have needed unless they feared being taken over," he said. "Also, at the head of each cave was a big relief of the pharaoh smashing the heads of the local people. But we have no traces from those people themselves."

"But you know they were here?"

"Yes, because the Egyptians told us. And the moral is that people could live in the desert without leaving any remains that archaeologists today can discover. Desert people don't build permanent buildings, they have no time or reason to carve reliefs in caves, and all their personal goods—tents, baskets, rugs—get destroyed by the sand. The Israelites could easily have been here, even though we haven't found any evidence of them."

"Even six hundred thousand?"

He raised his eyebrows. "Whatever God will allow."

We drove around the corner and found a windblown niche to set up camp for the night. We parked the jeep at the entrance and laid our sleeping bags around a fire. Avner pointed out that the hills were young by Sinai standards, "only four hundred million years old." The molded sandstone appeared almost grotesque, as if someone had clenched his hands around moistened clay and squeezed out fingers of peach-colored stone. The surface was equally varied—puckered, dimpled, torn—and reminded me of weathered skin, pink with tenderness, spotted with age.

As we unpacked our belongings and began settling in for the evening, I was struck by how Avner seemed to know exactly how to act: how to shield his head from the sand; how to set up a candle in a nook to prevent it from blowing out; how to keep his exertions to a minimum. He was like a piece of furniture you continually move around a room until you put it in the one spot—there!—where it suddenly seems most at home.

As comfortable as Avner seemed in this environment, I felt uncomfortable. I certainly felt drawn to the place; I felt that tug of earth I first experienced in Turkey. And now I no longer resisted the feeling. I knew it was part of some larger realigning of my sense of place that was happening inside me. But on a more immediate level, I didn't know how to act: where to sit, where to lie down, where to put my bags. Take my jeans off because it's getting hot; put my sweatshirt on because it's getting chilly. I was shocked to discover on that first evening, for example, that the biggest problem in the desert is not heat, which I naively expected, but cold. "That's why desert goats are black," Avner explained, "and bedouin tents, even beetles. Black absorbs heat. You can escape the sun; all you need is shade. But you can't escape the cold." I may have felt attached to the desert, but I was still far from feeling at home.

As the sun set, Yusuf heated up some flat bread, the bedouin precursor to matzoh, by laying it directly on the white broom logs. We tore off pieces of bread, stiff as bark, and scooped up servings of tuna, canned okra, and foil-wrapped triangles of processed cheese. Soon the wind picked up and began blowing sand against the walls, like rain sprinkling against a windowpane. Occasionally the wind would die down, leaving only the cliffs, quiet and patient. The setting seemed devoid of time, like being in the deepest stacks of a library. And the resulting sensation—part excitement, part stagnation—reminded me of an old joke I heard about what Moses said to the Egyptians as he left: "Don't do anything until I get back."

If possible, the allure of the place only grew as evening fell. What had been a stark white sheet of light during the day, which flattened every scene into two dimensions, slowly became a soft amber smile that rounded edges and blushed out the hills. It was at night, finally, that the third dimension appeared, when the stars filled the sky in a perfect bowl. "I once led a group from Chicago," Avner said. "There was a thirty-year-old English teacher who looked up at the sky on her first night in the Sinai and said, 'Wow, it's like a planetarium!' "

As funny as that was, as I lay down to sleep, I realized she may have had a point. The stars were so bright, the constellations so clear, that it's hard to imagine anyone lying here at night and not realizing that the sky, at least, was round. Maybe the sages were right. Maybe Abraham did look up at the sky and realize that it contained—in its beauty and power—the divine.

We awoke in the morning to clear blue skies above and, for the first time I could remember in the outdoors, no dew. The absence of water is not a tease here; it's stark reality.

We ate breakfast—bread, cheese, tuna, honey—and started out for the day. Our first stop was a freestanding sandstone formation, about the size of a large jungle gym, that was covered with tiny etchings. As we got out of the jeep, Avner pointed out some artemisia growing along the ground, a white wormwood plant with leaves the color of sage and tiny yellow flowers like Venus flytraps. I liked the smell and held a sprig under my nose. By the time I stood up Avner sneezed, sneezed, and sneezed again. I suddenly realized that one consequence of the Israelites beginning the Exodus in spring is that their allergies would have been acting up. No wonder they complained.

The etchings were of ancient writing, as well as stick-figure animals—horses, camels, ostriches—that once roamed in this area. "At one time, semischolars identified these inscriptions with the Israelites and concluded they must have come this way," Avner said, referring to the southern route. "Now we know the writing was from much later, Nabatean, Byzantine, Greek. And in any case, that's not the way to do scholarship: begin with what you hope happened and work backward to try and prove it."

"But these inscriptions still seem pretty old," I said. "How did they survive in the open air?"

"Because they're only 1,800 years old," he said. "And for these rocks, that's pretty young."

The more important point, he said, was the numerous pockets and openings that peeped through the rock like eyes on a potato. These windows, called *tafuni,* were caused by faint traces of humidity in the air many millennia ago that got trapped inside the rock and dissolved the stone from the inside, like a cancerous speck of water that, when it was exposed to wind, revealed an open cavity. Considering that Exodus echoes with stories in which Moses draws water from a stone, I wondered if the Israelites might have known of this phenomenon.

"The only way we know it is from using very fine instruments," Avner said.

"But it's not improbable that God would know that water was inside," I said.

He looked at me, as if I were speaking in a foreign tongue. "So you're believing in God now?" he said, half teasing.

"Isn't that the point of coming here?"

We drove a few miles and parked the jeep for our main trek of the day, a several-hour hike up a narrow trail to the rock-hewn temple of Serabit el-Khadim, which means "Heights of the Slave." Built in the early second millennium B.C.E., Serabit el-Khadim represents an attempt by the pharaohs to inspire and dominate the bedouin who worked in the local mines. Because of the heat and scarcity of water, the mines operated only six months a year, which seems an apt enough expression for the control the pharaohs were able to maintain over the local culture. In one corner of the ruined temple an inscription shows a Semitic worker on a donkey. (The term *Semite,* which applies to the descendants of Shem, one of Noah's sons, broadly refers to groups of people from Mesopotamia or South Asia.) Since Egyptians didn't ride donkeys, the carving is considered a clear sign that foreigners were well known in the area—either coming from Asia, or going back.

A few minutes' walk away, along a spine with a breathtaking view of the Sinai's central plain, Avner led us to the mouth of a small cave, where we removed our knapsacks, water bottles, and hats and slid on our backs down a red clay chute into a cramped cavern about the size of the space underneath a pickup truck. He pulled out a flashlight and shined the beam on a small verse of script, etched in pale white on the terra-cotta stone. The letters were much simpler than hieroglyphics, but still animal-like or anthropoid: ox, fish, eye, house. There was space between them and a clear system at work in their styling. But which system? When Petrie first found these inscriptions in 1906 he couldn't decipher them. Not until Albright arrived in the 1940s did he realize that these weren't Egyptian, but the initial forms of a Semitic alphabet, the precursor to our alphabet, and all alphabets. The snake would later become the N; the fish, the D; the head, the R; the hand with bent fingers, the K. These letters, now called the protosinaitic inscriptions, are believed to be the oldest letters ever found—perhaps an eye chart, perhaps a poem, perhaps some laws or commandments. "We don't know," Avner said.

But it was that last possibility that became even more intriguing as we descended the mountain, hiking over a dried waterfall. As Avner explained, the Semitic alphabet was developed in the ancient Near East in the middle of the second millennium B.C.E., once again out of the combustion of cultures in the Fertile Crescent. Previous forms of writing—cuneiform along the Tigris and Euphrates, hieroglyphics along the Nile—were complex systems involving hundreds of signs that were decipherable only to a rarefied, priestly class. "The great achievement of the Semitic alphabet," he said, "was that each sound was represented by one symbol and each symbol represented one sound." In Egypt, by contrast, there were five hundred hieroglyphs, and words were written using a mix of ideograms, which represented things, and phonograms, which represented sounds. "You often had to know in advance what the word was in order to read it," Avner said.

More striking, for me, was the realization that this alphabet was just coming into being during the time the Israelites themselves would have just been coming into being, and in the same region. This added a new dimension to the importance of writing in the Israelite worldview, and, in particular, in the Bible. Based on historical realities, it would have been unrealistic even for a great leader like Abraham, at the start of the second millennium B.C.E., to have been able to read a contract with God. In fact, in Genesis, Abraham's covenant with God is not written down, nor is Isaac's, Jacob's, or Joseph's. These covenants were delivered orally, renewed with words, and occasionally commemorated by raising stones.

By the time of Moses, however, just five hundred years later, this reality would have changed. Not only would a great leader probably have been able to read, but the time was approaching when even some laypeople would have been able to understand the written word. This brings the Ten Commandments into a new light. The commandments, delivered in the Sinai and described in the Book of Exodus, are the first things of any importance that the text says are actually *written down*. This reinforces the idea that the commandments are a bond not just between God and the priestly class, or even between God and Moses, but between God and the entire people. The traditional explanation of why the Ten Commandments were written is that writing had become a significant cultural tool by the mid–first millennium B.C.E., when the Bible itself was written down from oral sources. But seeing the inscriptions made me question that view. If writing was so important to later biblical scribes, why didn't they have Abraham write down his original covenant with God, or have *anything else* in the entire book of Genesis inscribed into stone?

A more intriguing, and perhaps more likely, explanation is that by the time of the Exodus, the ideas of literacy and writing were building in the ancient Near East, at the very time the Israelites were forming their nation. The inscriptions near Serabit el-Khadim suggest these notions were certainly alive in the Sinai at the time the Israelites would have been leaving Egypt. As I speculated during our walk, this remarkable convergence cannot be mere coincidence. It suggests, instead, that the story of Exodus—and in particular the story of the Ten Commandments—almost surely has roots that date back to the second millennium, when the Semitic alphabet first came into existence. This doesn't mean these stories are true. But it does mean that the Israelites' knowledge of such a momentous historical change—the development of writing—indicates remarkable foresight of how this simple act would revolutionize the world. The written word would change not only each person's relationship with other people but each person's relationship with God. Not least because it opened the way for the people of the covenant to eventually become the people of the Book.

By the time we got down the mountain it was midafternoon, we hadn't eaten much, and we were depleted by the sun. Even compared to the incessant heat of the Dead Sea and the Nile, the heat of the Sinai was severe—especially when contrasted with the chill of the evening. The local bedouin call this phenomenon the "four seasons of the day."

We got back in the jeep and drove inland now, toward the south-central mountains, along Wadi Feiran, one of the largest dried riverbeds in the Sinai. It runs toward the Gulf of Suez from the base of Jebel Musa, or Mount Moses, the mountain that Byzantine travelers identified as Mount Sinai. The wadi passes just to the south of an east-west belt of mountains that divides the Sinai roughly in half. We were on a craggy, barren tableland, about 1,200 feet above sea level, much higher than the Delta, but considerably lower than the mountains to come. Also, compared to the brown sands of the north, the terrain was grayer here, and rockier. The hills looked like armadillos, with narrow black dikes of basalt that run along the spines in dramatic fashion, making them appear fiercer. The ground was the color of squirrels.

After about an hour the valley narrowed, and a few trees began to peak through the rocks. The road had become more winding, until around one corner we were greeted by a burst of green, a dense forest of date palms, hundreds of them clustered together and stretching for miles. This was an oasis on steroids, muscled with fronds so dense and plentiful they actually blocked out the sun. We slowed to take in the spectacle, and several kids and dogs began running after our jeep. We pulled over to take a break and in no time were surrounded by several dozen toddlers, teenagers, young women and men, the unquestioning embrace of bedouin hospitality. An old woman came out of one of the dozen or so shacks and greeted Avner with a kiss on either cheek. She recognized him from the fifteen years he lived in the Sinai and employed many bedouin in his role as chief excavator and caretaker of ancient sites. "It's like you're a gift from heaven," she said.

She gestured to the group and within moments the assembled horde was busily transforming a patch of sand beneath some trees into a makeshift lounge, where our break would become a meal, would become a campsite, would become our home for the rest of the night: time slowing before our eyes, forcing us to adapt to the more leisurely pace of the place. One person brought plastic mats, another cushions, still a third pulled down some blankets from an overturned palm tree that served as a clothesline. Nearby, some girls played with toy cars. A fourteen-year-old boy was smoking unfiltered cigarettes. Several old men were squatting on the ground playing a checkerslike game, using stones as light pieces and donkey dung as dark pieces. Everyone seemed to be moving simultaneously, but not going anywhere in particular. Goats wandered around, needing to be shorn. Babies squealed like plastic squeeze toys. A mother was breast-feeding her daughter behind a tree.

Once the carpets and cushions had been arranged, the commotion seemed to collapse on itself, as everyone gravitated toward the small campfire (started, even in the heat, for boiling water) and the makeshift living room on the valley floor. The scene reminded me of a traditional Japanese gathering, with the fire, a squat table, and people relaxing in a common space, not retreating to their own rooms. The carpets, in particular, seemed to invite sloth. They are movable patches of real estate with twists of maroon and yellow, and knots of purple and blue, that collect people, sand, flies, and time in equal measure. Yet they are capable, as with people and sand, of moving at a moment's notice. There are few things more portable than a carpet that, when unfurled again, can so effortlessly give the feeling of home. Have carpet will travel; have carpet will stay.

Which is why, I was coming to see, reclining is so important to the Israelites. With a limited number of trees in the desert, and thus limited wood, furniture played almost no role in the daily life of wandering tribes. Also, tribes never stayed in one place long enough to require the trappings of permanence. No table is mentioned in Genesis, and only one of any significance appears in Exodus (made of acacia wood and covered in gold, it is designed for use in the Tabernacle). Not one chair is mentioned in the entire Five Books of Moses. No small matter, this absence of home furnishings has religious significance. During the Passover seder, one of the four questions Jews traditionally ask is, "On all other nights we eat sitting or reclining. Why on this night do we only recline?" The historical answer would be, "Because the Israelites, too, would have been lounging on a carpet, leaning to one side, eating with their hands."

The following morning we awoke early once again and, heeding the principal lesson of the desert—perform strenuous activity as early as you can—we decided to climb Jebel Tahuna (*jebel* is Arabic for mountain), not far from Feiran Oasis. Byzantine travelers believed this tiny mountain was the site of Rephidim, where the Israelites camp on their way to Mount Sinai, where Moses draws water from a rock, and where the Israelites wage war with the tribe of Amalek. In the fourth century C.E., visiting monks built a monastery and a cathedral to honor those events and made the small community of Feiran a bishopric. The remains of their town occupy a small tel near Jebel Tahuna, which itself is lined with several ruined churches.

Before starting out, we performed the traditional modern pilgrim's ritual upon reaching a holy site: shielding ourselves with floppy hats and sunglasses, lathering ourselves with sun block and UV lip protector, and arming ourselves with an assortment of Kleenex, insect repellants, and bottles of purified water. For a time, when I started this journey, I felt pampered and a bit sissified to be exbalming myself with such luxuries of the twentieth-century duty-free store, but the more accounts I read of travelers of previous centuries getting sick, lost, or disease-ridden for weeks, the less guilty I felt. Even the great Lawrence of Arabia was often felled in his attempts to help liberate the bedouin by his repeated bouts of sunstroke, malaria, and other maladies of the desert.

We made our way to the mountain and began heading up the narrow, rock-strewn path. No sooner had we begun than we were joined by a swarm of hangers-on, a cluster of barefoot, eight-year-old boys who tugged at our shorts and reached into our pockets, parroting, "Money. Dollars. Pepsi. USA!" We spoke to them, ignored them, sighed at them, turned them down, but still they continued to haggle with us for most of the way to the top. "Money. One dollar. Two dollar. Baksheesh!" Eventually, after half an hour, they changed tactics and elected to hold our hands and sing to us. "At least we have something to sacrifice when we get to the top," I said. Just before getting there, though, Avner showed them his Bible and mentioned that we were going to study. Quickly they hurried down the mountain.

Once the Israelites arrive in the desert, they realize their dire condition—no water, no food, no idea where they're headed. Immediately they start to complain, thereby initiating a cycle that will be repeated for the next forty years: The people protest, Moses becomes exasperated,

God intervenes, and the people are temporarily placated, before starting the process all over again. The first source of grumbling, described in Exodus 15, was the bitter-tasting water, which God rectified by directing Moses to throw a piece of wood into the water. In Exodus 16, the people complain about the lack of food, which God solves by delivering manna in the mornings and quail in the evenings. In Exodus 17 the people complain about having *no* water to drink, which God addresses by instructing Moses to strike a stone with his staff. In each case the people receive God's blessing and continue their trek.

Suddenly, though, in the middle of Exodus 17, a nomadic tribe called Amalek appears and declares war on Israel. Moses asks Joshua to lead the troops while he, Aaron, and Hur, a previously unmentioned aide, climb to the top of the hill to oversee. Once there, a strange development occurs. Whenever Moses raises his hands, the Israelites prevail; when he drops his hands, Amalek prevails. No reason is given for Moses to perform this action, and no explanation is given for its power. Moses grows tired, though, so Aaron and Hur bring a stone for him to sit on. Aaron and Hur then each take a hand and hold it in the air until sunset, when the Israelites finally triumph.

"So what's the purpose of this story?" I said. "What's it suddenly doing in the middle of Exodus?" We were sitting on top of the mountain now, in the apse of a ruined chapel. A modern cross stood on the spot. Down below, several wadis came together at the foot of the great palm forest. At the intersection was a nunnery, built alongside the ancient tel.

"Maybe there's some oral tradition behind it," Avner said. "Maybe the Israelites faced some attacks in the desert."

"And what about the raised arms? What does that symbolize?"

"The nuns say it foreshadows the cross on which Jesus is crucified."

"Really?"

"They also believe the twelve palm trees represent the apostles, and the Red Sea is a kind of baptism."

"Surely the hands form some connection with God."

"Ancient people went into war carrying likenesses of their gods. In this case, it's as if Moses is a likeness for God."

"A living icon."

"And an aging one, too. He's eighty by now, you know."

I asked him what he thought of Moses at this point in the story.

"I have some problems with Moses," he said. "Problems with him as a negotiator between God and the people. He's the one who's carrying the covenant that God gave to Abraham, Isaac, and Jacob, and the Israelites are supposed to follow him. But many times he gives up. 'I'm too tired to continue,' he says."

"But he's given a pretty tough assignment," I said.

"Very much so."

"Jacob couldn't even control twelve sons."

"Sons are always more difficult," he said, chuckling.

"So maybe he's just working out his role," I said. "He doesn't yet have the confidence he does when he goes up Mount Sinai. He doesn't even have the power to hold up his own arms."

"The point is: He never has that power. He's just a middleman. God has the power. The Israelites have that power. But they're both wary. Moses' role is to deliver them to each other."

Back down the mountain we waved good-bye to the boys, who were now idly tossing stones at passing cars, and turned inland. We hoped to make it to Saint Catherine's by nightfall and begin several days around Jebel Musa. The road was climbing higher now and the surroundings growing more severe: The mountains were no longer armadillos, with rounded tops, but rhinoceroses, with rough, angular peaks. The light was brighter, almost a white neon. It was as if we were driving through a pile of discarded bones.

By midafternoon we reached another cluster of vegetation, the Oasis of the Tamarisks of Saint Catherine's. We pulled over for lunch. This oasis was much smaller than Feiran, closer in size to Ain Musa. Only here the majority of trees were tamarisks, a chiefly desert tree, with stringy bark similar to cedar and feathery leaves akin to fir. To explain the concentration of greenery, Avner began constructing another of his models in the sand. He drew a shape that looked like a bottle. He dug out the model several inches deep and then went over to a well and brought back a jug full of water.

"This is a wadi," he said, gesturing to his creation. "Most of the water from the mountains drains down into these basins. But the wadis are wide, so the water is equally distributed on the water table just below the surface." He poured the water into the bottom end of the bottle and it dispersed evenly across the width. "Now watch," he said. "As the water nears the neck, it begins to rise, because the width of the water table shrinks." And indeed the water did spill over at the neck; not with a splash, but with a gurgle. "Where the water bubbles up," he said. "That's where you get an oasis. It's the part where the valley narrows. The water table pushes through the ground, and plants have enough water to survive."

"So where does the word *oasis* come from?" I asked.

"It's Greek."

"What's the Hebrew word for oasis?"

"*Naot midbar,*" he said, "the most beautiful place of the desert."

Once we finished with the model, we turned our attention to the real focal point of the site, the trees. Oases are mentioned throughout the Bible as locations where the Israelites camped. Though tamarisk trees are not mentioned, they, too, may have played a part in inspiring one of the more memorable details of the Exodus story, the "bread from heaven." In their second month on the road, the Israelites complain bitterly about the lack of food, and God promises Moses that he will rain down "bread" from the sky every morning and "flesh" every evening. The flesh turns out to be quail, and the bread a "fine and flaky substance, as fine as the frost on the ground" that the Israelites call manna, from the Hebrew expression they mutter when they first see it, *man hu,* "What is it?" Manna is described as being like coriander seed, white in color, and tasting like wafers in honey, or rich cream. In addition to providing the food, God provides a warning: Each person should take only one portion every morning, and two on the sixth day. There is no manna on the Sabbath. The Israelites, of course, ignore the warning, but they soon find that all their hoarded manna "became infested and stank." Having learned their lesson, the Israelites eat manna for the rest of their forty years in the desert.

The unusual details of the manna story have inspired curiosity since the first days of the Bible. Early rabbis said manna was created between the sixth day of Creation and the first Sabbath. Anyone who ate manna gained the strength of angels, interpreters said, and had no need for bowel movements, since the flaky substance was entirely dissolved into their bodies. Even better, no one ever tired of manna, the commentators agreed, since manna had the ability to adapt to each person who ate it. "One had only to desire a certain dish," wrote one commentator, "and no sooner had he thought of it than manna had the flavor of the dish he desired." To little children, he said, it tasted like milk; to strong youths like bread; to the old men like honey; to the sick like barley steeped in oil and honey. On the Sabbath, the manna saved from the previous day "sparkled more than usual" and tasted even better. One can almost hear the commentators say, "It tasted just like chicken."

While rabbis speculated on the taste of the manna, others focused on what manna actually was. Some commentators said it must be snow, others said hail, ice, or dew. When Byzantine travelers started visiting the Sinai in the fourth century, they realized there may be a natural inspiration for the manna. Tamarisk trees grow in many oases around the Sinai. In spring, two types of plant lice—*Trabutina mannipara E.* and *Najacoccus serpentinus*—infest the stems of tamarisk branches. They suck in the sap of the trees, which is rich in carbohydrates, and excrete the surplus onto the twigs in the form of white, resinous globules. As the text says of manna, these excretions are sweet, edible, and crystallize rapidly in the sun. If they're not harvested in the morning, they quickly dry up or, worse, get devoured by ants. Either way, they quickly disappear.

According to estimates, the Sinai creates about five hundred pounds of tamarisk manna a year. The droplets, which the bedouin call *mann rimth,* from the translation of manna in the Koran, have been a cash crop in the Sinai since the fifteenth century, when a German visitor reported that local monks "gather, preserve, and sell manna" to passing pilgrims. In the nineteenth century, Konstantin von Tischendorf, a Bible scholar, was able to eat the "excrescences like glittering pearls." The thickish lumps were clammy, he said, and had "the same powerful scent emitted by the shrub. I tasted it, and the flavor, as far as I could find a suitable comparison, greatly resembles honey." In the twentieth century, manna was harvested commercially and exported to the West, where it was sold under the brand name Mannite and marketed to what one observer calls "pious gourmets."

These tamarisk excretions are almost surely the inspiration for the manna in the Bible, and suggest, once again, that biblical storytellers had intimate knowledge of the Sinai, most likely passed down through oral tradition. But if manna has such easily identifiable natural roots, does that undermine the role of God in the story?

Not necessarily. As we were lounging in the faint shade of one of the tamarisks, a bedouin man in a flowing cotton laborer's gown came strolling over to our carpet. Avner leapt up and embraced the man fervently, kissing him three times on alternating cheeks and holding his hands. Khaled had worked with Avner when he lived in the Sinai and the two men hadn't seen each other for a number of years. They spent a few minutes holding hands, catching up. Khaled was in his forties, but looked twenty years older. He had a white kaffiyeh around his head and a prominent gold tooth. Despite the heat, he wore black jeans underneath his robe and a gray sweatshirt that said "Winner Casual Wear." Eventually Avner told him about our discussion of the tamarisk trees and asked him what time of year the manna appears.

"Only when the apricots are ripe," he said. "In June."

I asked him what it looked like.

"Like small cotton balls," he said. "In the morning they're liquid, but as the sun comes out, they become fluffy, like fur. By noontime they're dead. They just disappear, melt."

"So how do you collect them?"

He reached down and grabbed some small pieces of granite and a handful of sand. "The manna covers the ground in early morning," he said. "You pick it up, then let the wind take away the dirt." He opened his fingers to let the sand blow away, leaving only the rocks. "The wind sorts it out," he said.

"So what does it taste like?"

"It's very sweet, sweeter than honey," he said. "There's even a special blessing, since it's mentioned in the Bible and the Koran."

"And do you feel connected to those ancient people when you eat it?"

He squirmed momentarily, as if trying to find the right emotion. "It's spiritual to eat it," he said. "It's not like bread or meat. It's kind of a surprise. Some years you have it; some years you don't. And you never know which one it's going to be. It's not like a flower that you know to expect. It's like a person with no children who suddenly becomes pregnant. It's like an idea that comes out of the back of your head and not the front." He stopped for a second and ran his fingers across his teeth. "It's a blessing."

Dusk was descending by the time we returned to the jeep and proceeded southeast for the slow climb to the monastery at the base of Jebel Musa, the second-highest peak in the Sinai. The mountains no longer gently shadowed the road, they now completely overwhelmed it with a range of peaks over seven thousand feet. No longer gray, the mountains were a rich, reddish granite, the color of sweet potatoes. Dense, almost burdened by their bulk, they looked like mounds of slightly rancid hamburger meat waiting to be molded into loaves. With the sun catching the sparkle in every fold of the rock, I felt as if we were driving inside a rust-colored geode.

The southern mountains are the oldest part of the Sinai, having broken from Egypt during the formation of the Great Rift Valley. As Avner explained, the soil in the Sinai gets older the farther south it goes, with limestone and sand on the surface near the Mediterranean, sandstone on the surface in the middle, and exposed granite in the south. In effect, the Sinai is like a giant slice of apple pie where the crust, to the north, is flat, the dough bulges in the middle with a small amount of filling, and finally the wedge spills over in the south with oversized chunks of fruit. If the Israelites did come this way, they must have felt as if the ground was preparing them for something special. Especially for a population that had grown up in the terminal lowland of the Nile Delta, the Sinai would have been a tease. First they would have come upon the dunes of the north, which themselves would have felt large for flatlanders. Then they would have arrived at the central hills, which at two thousand feet must have seemed daunting. And finally they would have faced the southern mountains, a formidable seven thousand feet high, which must have made even the "stiff-necked" Israelites crane with awe—and fear.

And what better emotion to describe this place. All through our journey, I had been fascinated by the ability of the places we were see-ing to evoke sentiments conveyed in the text: from the capricious fertil-ity of the Tigris and Euphrates, to the scorched destitution of Sodom, to the menacing power of the Nile Valley. It's as if the changing dimen-sions of the landscape were somehow reflected in the sweeping range of emotions in the narrative—the Bible as psychological atlas.

This gamut of topographical—and psychological—extremes was starting to have an effect on me, as well. I come from a flat, sandy place, with pine trees, live oaks, azaleas, and daffodils; temperate winters, sunny springs, swampy summers. I realized I had never spent much time in places with exaggerated geography—high mountains, hollow valleys, dense rain forests, desert. The Middle East was by far the most severe place I had ever been in; and within that, the Sinai was the harshest stretch. And inevitably, perhaps, for someone so identified with place, I found these extreme landscapes stirring in me more extreme emotions. It's as if the act of mapping the land was forcing me to remap my own internal geography, suddenly taking into account a broader range of feelings than I had ever previously explored—deeper canyons of confi-dence, perhaps, but also wider expanses of uncertainty and higher eleva-tions of need.

The emotion I felt upon reaching these levels was not all that differ-ent from the emotion I felt upon being in extreme positions at other times in my life, whether it was pulling myself up a rope as a child, climbing a mountain as a teenager, or scuba diving as an adult: fear. Fear that I might lose control. Fear that I might fail. Fear that I might disap-point myself. When your god is self-reliance, and you let yourself down, there is nowhere else to turn.

This reaction, I was coming to see, is the first lesson of the desert: By feeling uneasy and unsure, by fearing that you're out of your depth and therefore might falter, by feeling small, and alone, you begin—

slowly, reluctantly, maybe even for the first time in your life—to consider turning somewhere else. At first that somewhere else is some*one*
else: a Moses, an Aaron, an Avner. But ultimately, maybe even inevitably,
that some*one* else is some*thing* else. For the secret lesson of remapping
yourself, as I was just finding, is that you eventually grow wary of the
flat and easy, the commonplace and self-reliant. You begin to crave the
depth, the height, the extremes. You begin even to crave the fear.

A little after seven we reached one of the few four-way intersections in
the Sinai, where roads come from the north, south, east, and west, con-
verging at the entrance to the high mountains. The air was noticeably
cooler, and as we stopped to pull out our sweaters, Avner suggested we
take in the scene. We were minutes away from Saint Catherine's, the
small village at the base of Jebel Musa that took its name from the
monastery. The red in the landscape had disappeared with the sun, so
the mountains were mostly shadows in the sky. Everything was still.
"When I first came here, in 1967, I was in shock with the beauty," Avner
said. "I could have lived anywhere in the Sinai, but once I saw this, I
knew this is where I wanted to live."

He talked about some of the battles he and his team of archaeologists faced in trying to open up the region to exploration, but also in
trying to maintain its isolation. "For a long time we fought very
strongly, and with some success, not to turn this region into a place that
was built, to keep only a minimum touch with the outside world. But
we did the one thing that almost destroyed the place: We introduced it
to the world. Before 1970, the mountain was almost unknown in the
world. It was unchanged since the Middle Ages."

"And what was that like?"

He went back to the car and returned with a small brown book he
had brought from home. The book was *Egeria's Travels,* the account of a
fourth-century Byzantine nun who ventured through the Near East visiting biblical sites. He opened to the part where she describes coming
upon Jebel Musa, which had just been identified as being Mount Sinai.

We made our way across the head of the valley and approached the Mount of God. It looks like a single mountain as you are going round it, but when you actually go into it, there are really several peaks, all of them called the Mountain of God. And the principal one, the summit on which the Bible tells us that God's glory came down, is in the middle. I never thought I had seen mountains as high as those around it, but the one in the middle was the highest, so much so that when we were on top, all the other peaks looked like little hillocks far below us. And another remarkable thing, even though the central mountain, Sinai proper, is higher than the others, you cannot see it until you arrive at the very foot of it. It must have been planned by God.

We returned to the car and drove down the narrow road to the base of the mountain and the small brick guard shack that protects the monastery. I grabbed my backpack and sleeping bag and we walked up the dirt path to the door of the compound, a crowded sixth-century complex about the size of a city block that contains a church, a mosque, a library, cloisters for housing the eighteen or so monks, a well where Moses is said to have met the daughters of Jethro, and the monastery's botanical jewel, the purported burning bush itself. Though it was only 8 P.M., the entrance was pitch dark by the time we arrived. An almond tree bloomed in the courtyard. One orange lightbulb was the sole source of light. Our plan was to ask the monks if I could spend a night in the monastery, a rare privilege normally extended only to pilgrims on a holy visit. Avner would stay with friends in the village.

We knocked on the wooden door and an elderly monk with a Santa Claus beard appeared. We introduced ourselves and made our request. The man examined me for what seemed like minutes. Finally he spoke. "Are you Greek Orthodox?" he asked in stern, broken English.

"Uhh . . . no," I said.

"Are you *Catholic*?" He raised his eyebrows.

At this point my inclination was to say, "Actually, can we discuss this? I've been traveling through the desert, thinking about . . ." But I caught myself. "No, sir," I said. "I'm Jewish."

"Well, then . . ."

He disappeared inside the door and I looked at Avner as if to say, "Did I give the right answer?" Avner chuckled. "Here it's better to be Jewish than Catholic," he said.

Moments later the monk appeared again in the doorway. "You are invited to stay in the monastery," he said. "Go see Father Paulo. He'll show you to your room."

2. On Holy Ground

I bolted upright the first time I heard the bells—a sound so loud it yanked me from sleep. I held my ears when I realized the clamor was just outside my door. And when the ringing showed no signs of stopping, I stuck my head back under the covers for a few minutes of muffled relief: a carillon fifteen centuries old; a wake-up call older than the clock.

A few minutes later the chimes finally did stop and I emerged from my cocoon. I looked at my watch: 4:25. The room was whitewashed, with a bed, a desk, and a chair. A reproduction of an eighth-century crucifix hung on the wall, alongside a small painting of Saint Catherine, the Egyptian martyr. Before I came to the mountains various people had warned me—"Staying in Saint Catherine's was the longest night of my life," "the coldest night of my life." As a result, I had brought enough equipment for Everest: sleeping bag, gloves, hat, scarf, toilet paper, turtleneck, extra socks. "Would you like a sleeping pill?" Avner had asked. But the room was quite accommodating, with two sheets, a bean pillow, three blankets, and a comforter. There was also a portable heater in the cupboard, a switch for hot water, a toilet, and even, for cleanliness-conscious Muslims or prissy Europeans, a bidet. This was the Ritz for pilgrims, a hermitage with a view.

I slid on my boots without touching the floor and splashed water on my face. The morning service started in five minutes, and I didn't want to be late. Outside, the courtyard was still dark. A rosefinch hopped qui-

etly on the banister; even the birds didn't speak at this hour. I was stationed on the third floor of the dormitory, a dark wooden building with
slabs of plaster that was Tudor not just in appearance. Shakespeare could
have slept here. Across the square was another three-story building that
looked almost Moorish, with stone arches and candles flickering in the
rooms. In between was a jungle of structures with assorted ecclesiastical
purposes—a refectory, a handful of chapels, a library, even a mosque,
built in the twelfth century to appease marauding Muslims. With its
contrasting styles, angled walls, and competing rooflines, the monastery
had the appearance of one of those milk-carton cities children make in
school, then leave in the attic to collect dust and nostalgia and when discovered a generation later seem more charming than ever.

The previous night, after checking into my room, I sat on the banister and admired the timelessness. The place seemed almost haunted,
with cats scampering across the eaves, skeleton keys dangling against
brass doorknobs, and doors opening, creaking, then slamming shut. A
monk chanted evening prayers. It was impossible not to think of *The
Name of the Rose,* with its intrigue and manipulations; death in the
abbey of the Lord. But even in this stew of allure, I felt remarkably
safe. The black cat that ran across my path made me smile, not quiver.
With its church and mosque and bedouin well, Saint Catherine's
touches all bases, even superstition. By 9 P.M. there was a not a person
in sight.

Before going to bed I decided to go for a stroll and visit the burning
bush. The bush, which grows alongside the chapel, is a rare mountain
bramble akin to the raspberry that monks say is the actual shrub in
which Moses first heard the words of God. I went from the third-floor
perch where I was sitting, down across the roof of another building to a
set of stairs that led to the base of the chapel. At the stairs a deep darkness seemed to reach out from below and I realized I was scared, that little boy afraid to go into the attic. Across the alley was a crypt with the
bones of every monk who ever lived in Saint Catherine's, including a
heaping mound of hundreds of hollow-eyed skulls that spill onto the
floor like dry cereal from a box. How many creepy images could this
place conjure up? I wondered. How many childhood anxieties? I opted

to go back for my flashlight. I climbed back to my room, embarrassed, and in my nervousness started to unlock the door adjacent to mine. This made me even more nervous. Was I disturbing some hermit from Greece? By now my hand was shaking. It was less than an hour since Avner had left me alone and I'd managed to work myself into a state.

I retrieved my flashlight and retraced my steps, cursing the creaky floors that seemed to broadcast my every move. I tried an alternate route, climbing down a wooden staircase behind the chapel, but found myself in a dead end, with dark clothes on a line, smoke curling out of a chimney, and a locked wooden gate that squealed but wouldn't open. I backed away, tiptoed through an alley, and found the same stone steps as before. Even with the light they seemed bottomless. I hurried down and tried not to look in any window. On the ground level I exhaled and rounded a corner. A cat was digging in the flower bed like a squirrel. He looked up at me and meowed. I jumped, despite myself, then stopped to feel my heart. How silly.

I took a few more steps and rounded the last corner of the alley. To the right was the back wall of the chapel, about twenty feet high. Directly across the walkway was a rounded stone wall about ten feet high that looked as if it were made of peanut brittle. Sprouting from the top was an enormous, fountaining bush. The plant was about six feet tall, with large, dangling branches like a weeping willow that sprouted from the center like a cheap wig. A white cat with a brown splotch around one eye was perched at the base of the bush, and off to the side was a slightly out-of-date fire extinguisher. *A fire extinguisher?* At first I thought it was an eyesore, but then I realized the unintended humor. Was this in case the burning bush caught on fire?

I sat on a stone bench just below the bush. There was no light in sight, except for the sky, which was indigo, the color of deep ocean. I stayed on the bench for a long time, the bush to my left, the church to my right. After a while I began to feel a certain pressure from the build-ings and I realized that the chapel had been constructed on an angle, so that the back wall sloped away from the building and leaned slightly in the direction of the bush, which in turn leaned toward the chapel. It was as if they were trying to touch, like figures from the Sistine Chapel. The

stars were twinkling now, and without warning, a light came on at the
end of the walkway, illuminating, in perfect silhouette, a wooden cross
about a foot high. There was nothing remotely contemporary about this
scene—the stones, the chapel, the sky, the cross. It reminded me of one
of those medieval paintings where the perspective is all wrong.

And kept getting wronger. The chapel would lean a bit more, the
cross would grow a bit taller, the round fence would bulge at the seam,
and the bush would fountain higher, fuller, until everything else would
have to adjust. It went on like this for a while—lean, step, push, collapse,
lean, push, jump, reach, until all the pieces were moving at once, com-
pressing into one another, pushing back and forth in time and place, and
creating, somehow, out of the combustion, a warmth that filled the
courtyard. The result was a feeling I had sensed before on this trip, a
feeling that the physical components of the environment—the stones,
the buildings, the space in between—were somehow transforming into
a spiritual entity that almost seemed to reach up, tugging at something
inside me. I was just noticing a heat inside my jacket and reached up to
touch my cheeks—was this feeling coming from me or from the place,
or were we somehow bringing it out in each other?—when suddenly
the white cat with the splotch around one eye leapt from the wall with
a screech, landed at my feet, and sent me scurrying back to bed.

By the time I arrived in the chapel it was just after 4:30, and the morning service was under way. The basilica was still dark, except for some
candles above a lectern, where a monk in thick, black robes was chanting a prayer in Byzantine Greek, a mix of Slavic harsh consonants and
Mandarin singsongy vowels. I slipped into a wooden chair along the
outer wall, and even though Father Paulo had invited me to the service
the previous evening, I still felt a bit like a voyeur. In the first few minutes, several monks began making their way around the room lighting
the dozens of brass lamps that hung from the ceiling. Several of the
lamps began to swirl as the monks raised them, lowered them, spun
them, stopped them. Gradually with the glow of the light, like liquid
apricot, the dimensions of the room became apparent.

The basilica, built between 542 and 551 C.E., is small, designed for the monks, not for the masses. The granite walls and pillars are original, as are the cypress doors and ceiling. The expansive mosaic above the apse depicting the Transfiguration of Jesus, flanked by Moses and Elijah, is one of only three surviving Byzantine mosaics in the world. The highlight and by far the dominant architectural feature of the room is a lavish floor-to-ceiling wooden iconostasis, built in the seventeenth century, that's basically a wall-sized picture frame decorated with images of Christ, the Virgin Mary, and a number of saints. It divides the nave from the altar. Altogether, with the scarlet robes on the icons, the green on the ceiling, and the gold on the iconostasis, the chapel looks like a walk-in version of one of those gilded medieval triptychs that fill European museums: one part pedagogical tool, one part inspirational message, one part awesome display of wealth.

The service moved at a measured tempo. A monk would step forward to a lectern, located in the middle of the nave, turn up the flame on an oil lamp, and read a few passages from the text. He would back away and another monk would step forward. Occasionally there would be a call and response, with one monk chanting a passage from an enormous, leather-bound prayer book, and the other monks echoing their responses as they strolled around the chapel or sat in dark wooden chairs in front of the twelve columns in the nave. *Holy! Holy! Holy! Hallelujah! Hallelujah! Hallelujah!* There was not a wasted gesture. As one lectern was temporarily rolled away, another was pulled forward. As one book closed, another opened. The pace was steady, rhythmic, mesmerizing. In a way, the service reminded me of the pyramids in that it was perfectly balanced, reassuring in its proportions, and completely devoid of time. A "living tradition," as the monks like to say.

After about an hour another monk came through the door, kissed a painting of the feet of baby Jesus, and hugged one of his brothers. No monk spoke to another during the liturgy; most seemed lost in private thought. A few remained seated; the majority roamed quietly about, bowing occasionally to an icon, nodding to themselves. If anything, in the darkness, and with the monks dressed head to toe in black, the only way to sense the presence of the others was by heat, or by the sound of their habits brushing against the stone floor. At one point, a particularly tall father encircled the entire basilica waving a brass lantern with incense burning on coals. A sweet, pungent aroma, like singed flowers, filled the hall.

And still the service continued, chanting, praying, pleading. In time, the sheer power of the tempo—and the dedication of those who carried it—began to feel almost overwhelming. How many religious ceremonies had I attended in my life? How many rites and rituals and prayers and benedictions. This was one of the most powerful displays of faith I had ever seen, yet also the least ostentatious. I did a small calculation. Along with this service, which is actually two services in one, there were three others every day, at midday, in the afternoon, and in the evening. Extended back in an unbroken line to the sixth century, this sanctuary had hosted almost three million services—all in the same place, in the same language, in the same manner. A living tradition, indeed.

By 6:15, almost two hours after I arrived, one of the monks unfurled a small carpet on the marble floor and began what would be the most tranquil part of the service, a series of slow, sonorous chants that echoed off every stone. A monk sitting in front of me appeared to drift into sleep and started swaying in his seat. I was struck that like so much of religion, this service was profoundly solitary in nature, yet also deeply communal. There was almost no interaction, but an effortless sense of fraternity. By now the light had begun to change and one of the fathers began to extinguish the brass lamps. Another rolled up the small carpet. On special days, the monks open the iconostasis and allow sunlight from a stained-glass window in the middle of the mosaic to shine into the sanctuary. But on this morning the light had to seep through the window and gradually filter into the room. The faces of the monks were still hidden in shadow, even as the sky was becoming illuminated.

At the end of the service the monks shuffled out as quietly as they had come in, turning to genuflect one last time. Still no one spoke. The last monk out extinguished the final candle and locked the door. Outside, standing now on the stairs I had been afraid to descend the previous evening, one of the monks invited me upstairs and offered a cup of

Earl Grey tea and a piece of coconut cake. The sun was just peeking over the mountain. The bells would soon ring seven.

By the time Avner arrived at nine, I had managed to take a shower and find some additional food, and we set out to explore the monastery. In addition to visiting many of the often sheltered sites that make this monastery so important to the story of the Bible in the Middle East, I also hoped to begin exploring the question of why so many monasteries like this exist in the first place. Why is it that long after religious freedom and political stability made living in the desert unnecessary, so many people, for so many generations, have continued to shuck their fineries and comforts and flee to the barren wilderness?

In the light, the compound was less spooky than the night before, though no less jumbled: a testament to the failures of ecclesiastical urban planning. One reason for all the confusion is that Saint Catherine's is something of an exposed tel. Each generation built on top of the old, though without waiting for the previous layer to be destroyed. It's a house of cards, where the cards never fall. Like so many sites around the Middle East, Saint Catherine's was founded in the fourth century C.E., when Empress Helena took advantage of her son Constantine's hegemonic control over the region to identify places associated with the Bible. Building on a tradition that said the burning bush was located in the valley below Jebel Musa, Helena erected a small church and a tower at the site to protect monks who were already flocking to the area to pray. Helena dedicated the facility to Mary, because church elders believed the burning bush symbolized the Annunciation: Just as the bush was filled with fire, but remained unburned, so Mary conceived the savior, but remained a virgin. Emperor Justinian expanded the facility in the sixth century, surrounded it with granite walls sixty feet high and nine feet thick, and built the basilica. The monks claim the basilica's doors are the oldest functioning ones in the world, and that they lead to the world's oldest continually operating church.

The Monastery of the Burning Bush, as it was called, existed for close to six hundred years but didn't thrive until 1000 C.E., when it became associated with another prominent woman in the region, Saint Catherine. Born to a high-ranking official in Alexandria in the third century C.E., Catherine (née Dorothea) was a woman of exceptional intelligence and beauty. Numerous suitors sought to marry her, but Catherine wanted someone with unchallenged qualities of wisdom and virtue. Her mother, secretly Christian before the religion was accepted in the region, introduced her to an ascetic, who said, "I am acquainted with a unique man who incomparably transcends all those attributes you have mentioned and countless others." Through prayers and visions, Catherine met and mystically married Christ. One of her suitors, Emperor Maximinus, tried to persuade her to renounce the marriage, and when she refused, he ordered her killed. She was attached to four wheels studded with steel blades and sharp spikes that were supposed to mutilate her, though on the day of the execution an angel released her from the device, which spun out of control, mutilating bystanding pagans. Catherine would become the patron saint of clockmakers, carnival ride attendants, automakers, and anyone who works with wheels.

Eventually, Maximinus was able to behead Catherine, whose remains were secretly deposited on a mountain in the Sinai. According to tradition, Catherine's body came to rest not on Jebel Musa, but on nearby Jebel Katarina, the tallest on the peninsula. In 1025, a monk went to visit the remains and while pouring an offering of oil inadvertently broke off three of her fingers, which he then carried to Europe and which miraculously began to heal the sick. The spirit of Saint Catherine ministered to Joan of Arc, among others, and churches in her honor were built in London, Paris, and Venice. Soon a growing number of pilgrims began flocking to the Sinai to see her remains, and the monks, to protect her and to ensure their share of the income that pilgrims would bring, moved her body to a golden casket in the basilica and renamed their abbey the Monastery of Saint Catherine.

For all its elaborate history and geopolitical prestidigitation—the monastery managed to curry support at various times from Mohammed, Queen Isabella, Ivan the Terrible, and Napoleon—Saint Catherine's boasts another direct link to the Bible and to generations of readers who have tried to draw closer to the stories by returning to the spiritual terrain of the desert. The idea of the wilderness as a place of transformation has deep roots in the Bible. Moses first met God after separating himself from Egyptian society. Jesus also passed time in desert quarantine and would recall the lessons of Exodus in fighting back the devil. "Human beings live not on bread alone," he says in Matthew, quoting a line Moses used in Deuteronomy, "but on every word that comes from the mouth of God." Even Mohammed, a devotee of the Bible and the son of a merchant, retreated for weeks at a time to a desert cave near Mecca, where he eventually heard the word of God.

In the early years of the Christian church, a new breed of devotion sprang up in which followers of Jesus heeded his admonition to sell their worldly possessions and seek salvation in nature. The disciples, called hermits, from the Greek word *eremites*, "he who lives in the desert," became spiritual celebrities around the Mediterranean and redefined the architecture of faith in the Judeo-Christian world. They also reshaped the way many people read the Bible.

For the hermits, the best way to express their allegiance to the Bible was by experiencing many of its hardships for themselves. Particularly in Egypt and Palestine, where the movement first gained popularity in the fourth century C.E., the hermits hoped to replace the profanities of urban life with a society based on "wisdom, love, and experience." As Thomas Merton, the twentieth-century theologian, has written: "What the desert fathers sought most of all was their own true self, in Christ. And in order to do this, they had to reject completely the false, formal self, fabricated under social compulsion in 'the world.' "

The experiences of the hermits were in no way unified. A few were completely isolated. Others formed loose-knit communities, or *lauras*. Still more joined early monasteries. As a practical matter, the existence of so many different kinds of religious outposts across the Near East created a physical superstructure along the routes of the Bible. The word *laura*, for instance, means lane, from the lines that connected the hermits' outposts with the central church. But the *lauras*, the monasteries, and the churches did something even more long-lasting: They created a series of lanes across the region that served to bring not only the hermits but also the rest of the world closer to the Bible. In many ways, my trip, 1,500 years later and motivated by different impulses, was made possible by the hermits, who created the notion that the Bible was not merely a book to be read but also a book to be experienced. Perhaps equally important, the monks also left behind actual places—monasteries, monuments, chapels—which people like me could visit.

Avner and I spent the next few hours exploring the monastery. Our first stop was the small spring near the entrance of the compound known as the fountain of Moses, or Jethro's well. According to legend, this is the place where Moses, still a fugitive from Egypt, met Zipporah. The small stone well, square with an old-fashioned iron hand pump, is one of five wells inside the monastery and testifies to the facility's one ample resource, water. This water feeds the garden, which brims with almonds, peaches, poplars, and olives. The olives produce just enough oil to light the several dozen lamps in the church, which hang down from the ceiling on fifteen- or twenty-foot chains. The oil is considered such a delicacy to rodents that each chain is adorned with a whole ostrich-egg shell designed to prevent rats from climbing down for a quick toddy.

Despite its plentiful supply of water, the monastery was otherwise deeply vulnerable, mostly to attack from the numerous invading armies in the Sinai. To protect themselves, the monks sealed off the outside doors and for most of the monastery's history, the only way to enter or exit the compound was in a wicker basket that was lowered sixty feet to the ground, then lifted back up. Avner called it "the first passenger elevator in the world." Since hostile armies could still potentially break through the entrance, the monks built a funnel above the old door, through which they could pour boiling oil—made from their own olives, of course.

By far the monastery's chief curiosity is its so-called burning bush, easily the most famous shrub in the Sinai, and probably the Middle East. According to the monks, the plant alongside the chapel is unique and has been growing in virtually the same spot since the time of Moses. Evidence suggests that the first claim, at least, may have some truth to it. The bush belongs to the species *Rubus sanctus,* which grows in the mountainous areas of Central Asia but is rare in the desert. Avner says he knows of only five other specimens in the Sinai. Beyond its rarity, the reason *this* bush was identified as the burning bush is unclear. Many have suggested the shrub's red berries contributed to the connection by simulating the appearance of flames, but the monastery's specimen doesn't fruit. As for location, the bush was originally situated across the alley from its present site in an outdoor chapel. When monks needed to expand the church in the tenth century, they opted to enclose the outdoor chapel and relocate the bush across the alley. Some monks claim that the root system remained the same, and that the bush merely sprouted up in the new location; most concede that the bush was actually replanted.

One thing everyone agrees on: The bush grows quickly, that bramble in the backyard you can never quite contain. The monks have been known to prune it and give the clippings to visiting pilgrims to take home, which means there may be thousands of baby burning bushes in leftover jelly jars filled with water on sink counters around the world. In 1984, the bush grew so big that it looked "long and sickly," according to geographer Joseph Hobbs, who wrote a book about the area. The monks held an anxious meeting in which they elected to crop the plant close to the roots. On the day of the event, there were more remains than the assembled visitors could cart home, so the monks did what any pious congregation would do to the assembled pile of clippings: They set it on fire. As one wry monk who witnessed the event reported, "Yes, it did burn."

For all the bush's prodigious qualities, it does occasionally require some assistance in the fickle climate of the Sinai. "When I first came here, the bush was just a few feet high," Avner said, "and not doing very well. But with water and fertilizer they managed to nurse it back to life."

"Fertilizer?" I said. "You have to fertilize the holiest bush in the world?"

"You can't be too careful."

"So what kind of fertilizer do they use?"

"Goat droppings."

For all the architectural wonder of Saint Catherine's, as well as the natural wonder that comes from being wedged in a tight valley beneath Jebel Musa, by far the monastery's greatest asset is its collection of religious manuscripts, which is said to be the second most important in the world, after the Vatican's. Following our tour of the compound, we returned to the chapel around midday, where one of the monks, Anastasis, had offered to show us around the library, which is usually closed to visitors. Anastasis ("they call me 'Stasis' ") was a young man, no more than thirty, who had a bit of baby fat on his face and a beard that was so spotty and thin it seemed almost touching in its desire to be taken seriously. As we were walking up the three flights of stairs to the library's main floor I asked him how long he had been at the monastery. "Less than a year," he said, though he noted that he'd been through extensive training at several other institutions in Greece. "And how long will you stay?" I asked. He seemed puzzled by the question. "The rest of my life," he said.

The library's foyer was smaller than I expected, and less ornate. Remodeled in the 1940s, it had the somewhat moldy feel of an Ivy League reading room trying to seem like Oxford. According to Anastasis, the facility contained 4,570 illuminated manuscripts, 7,000 printed books from the late Middle Ages, and 6,000 new printed books. By far the most famous manuscript ever associated with the library was the *Codex Sinaiticus,* the oldest complete edition of the Bible in existence. Written in Greek in the fourth century C.E., the *Codex Sinaiticus* contained 730 leaves and would have required 360 goats or sheep to provide their skins for parchment. The manuscript resided in the Saint Catherine's monastery for 1,400 years, until the German scholar Konstantin von Tischendorf arrived in 1844 and borrowed three leaves for copying. He visited four times in the next fifteen years and finally, in 1859, persuaded the monks to allow him to transport the entire manuscript to

Europe. In the library, on the wall, the monks display a signed copy of a letter by Tischendorf, translated into English, that says Saint Catherine's has handed over to him, "as a loan, a translation of the Old and New Testaments, being the property of the aforementioned monastery."

Once Tischendorf got the manuscript to Europe, however, Czar Alexander II of Russia announced he was keeping it and offered the monastery money, gifts, and jewels in return. Though the monastery accepted the gifts, it never renounced its claim to the text. The *Codex Sinaiticus* remained in Russia until 1933, when Stalin, desperate for money, sold it to the United Kingdom for one hundred thousand pounds. Today it's on display in the British Museum. In 1995, Prince Charles visited the monastery and one of the monks pointed out the correspondence and declared, "The *Codex* belongs here." The prince was polite, Anastasis said, but observed that if the British started returning everything that was taken from other countries, such as the Elgin Marbles and the Rosetta Stone, there would be very little left in the British Museum. "I guess he's right," Anastasis said. "The most important thing is that it has been preserved and has been made available to scholars throughout the world."

The monastery does have a few leaves of the *Codex,* which were found hidden in a wall after a fire in 1975. They are large, folio-sized pages with elaborate, gold-dusted inscriptions around the edges. Following the custom in translations at the time, there are no spaces between the words, which run together in a never-ending stream that made the Bible for so many centuries nearly impossible to decipher. The library also has the *Codex Syriacus,* one of only two manuscripts in the world that preserve the text of the four gospels from the time when they were first translated into Old Syrian in the fifth century C.E. Perhaps the most interesting item Anastasis showed us was the copy of a letter, signed by Mohammed himself, offering protection for the monastery. The prophet never signed his name, though, and used his handprint instead as a guarantor. On the copy, his handprint is bright red and looks like one of those five-fingered *hamsa* amulets that many Muslims and Jews wear around their necks.

After about an hour of looking at manuscripts, we ended up in a dark corner of the library, and I asked Anastasis what was his favorite book in the collection.

"I've seen relatively few of them," he said. "Most of what I've seen is when we've had important ambassadors visiting and I look over their shoulder."

I asked him about the morning service, and why it started at 4:30. He mentioned that he and the other monks had work to do around the monastery, and that if they started at 9:00 they would never have time. "Also," he said, "it's been this way for a long, long time."

"The service seemed more meaningful in the dark," I said. "When the sun came up the mood changed."

"I prefer the dark," he said. "From when I was twelve years old, I liked night better than morning. It's the same with prayer. It's better in the dark."

"And what about praying here?" I said. "Do you feel closer to Moses because you live here."

"It feels a little bit strange," he said. "Because when Moses met God, he did it on this spot. 'This is holy ground,' God said. The ground is much more important than the bush."

"So do you feel closer to God, too?"

"No," he said. "Wherever you are, if you are close to God, you are close. If you are far away, you are far away. It doesn't matter where you live. It matters what you feel."

By the time we got outside the library and Anastasis locked the door, Avner had begun chatting with an elderly gentleman who was waiting to see one of the monks. I went over to join them. Jerry Bracken was from Ireland, a retired farmer, who was making his third trip to the Sinai. He was neatly dressed, in khakis and a green striped shirt, and exuded a casual friendliness, which his sprightly brogue only made more appealing. "I'm bringing some books to Father Justin," he explained. "They are replicas of some of the oldest copies of Genesis ever found."

We leaned against the banister, near where I'd sat the night before, and began talking about the Bible. The conversation had the same effortless intimacy I had experienced at so many times, and in so many places, along my trip. It was as if the Bible were its own kind of lingua franca that opened up instant lines of communication among people who had little in common but a shared interest in the text. Considering that the international language of travel has changed so frequently in the last 2,500 years—Greek, Latin, French, English, American English— and that the stories of the Bible have not changed at all, one could argue that for much of the Western world, those stories form a collective language. Certainly in the Middle East today, with so much suspicion and hostility, a common interest in the Bible can be an immediate source of kinship, much stronger than nationality, denomination, age, or wealth. This is the power of pilgrimage: a willingness to place the spiritual lessons of the past over the political divisions of the present, a desire to connect to a place not for its food, art, golf courses, or even beauty, but for its meaning.

"My principal interest here," Jerry said, "is that we have many early monastic sites in Ireland. I've been trying to see the extent of influence from here on Irish Christianity, which flowered in the seventh and eighth centuries."

We had known each other less than three minutes.

"So what's your conclusion?" I asked.

"That there is a very sound, very strong connection. The style of living, the hermit's way of life, was obviously copied from here. A book by Saint Anthony in the fourth century was widely circulated in Europe and may have been the stimulus for Irish monasticism."

"I can understand the idea of coming to the Sinai to get closer to God," I said. "But how does this work in Ireland?"

"It works the same."

"But Ireland is green and lush," I said.

"Not always. There are many remote islands off the west coast that are difficult to reach. They nourished the hermits' way of life. In fact, Christianity, which almost died out in Europe at one point, was preserved in Ireland because of its remoteness. Then it filtered back again."

"But how did these hermits nourish Christianity?" I said. "They seem like such a limited group of people."

"Because they studied Scripture. Because they copied Scripture. These monks were the main source of literature and culture all across Europe."

I asked him how he got interested in this topic. Did he have a monastic streak in him?

"I'm married and have a family," he said. "I wouldn't make much of a monk. For me it was visiting these little islands off the western coast that stimulated my interest, because you find these early monastic remains—little stone cells, small enclosures—that are right in the middle of nowhere. It's fascinating."

"So what is the connection to the Sinai? Ireland is the greenest place on earth. This is one of the bleakest."

"Sure, the contrast couldn't be more vivid," he said. "This place is so dry my voice has dried up. You hang out washing here and it will dry in half an hour. You hang it out in Ireland it could take a couple of days."

"Then how do you take the lessons of the desert back to Ireland?"

"Look, I couldn't survive here," he said. "I think the people who come to live here are faced with a bleak lifestyle and it shows the strength of their commitment. But the desert is everywhere. There's desert in the cities. There's desert in the countryside. It all depends on your outlook. Christ lived and died in the Holy Land. If you want roots, that's where you go. But the message is universal and applies every- where. Should. If it doesn't, it's not being received properly."

We said good-bye warmly, and Avner and I walked downstairs. The monastery closes to tourists at noon and the monks return to prayer. An echoing solitude hovered over the complex as it had the night before. A swallow sat chirping on a beam. As we found a shaded corner and took a break for lunch—bread, cheese, tuna, honey—I was struck by the ways in which Saint Catherine's, this tiny monastery in one of the remotest parts of the Middle East, a place probably visited by fewer than ten thousand people in its first 1,500 years of existence (before being opened to tour buses in recent decades), embodies so many of the issues, charms, and contradictions I had experienced in other places along the biblical route.

Saint Catherine's is perhaps the best example of not only the living tradition of the Bible but also the living challenge it poses to people who wonder if the text is true. The facility has existed for fifteen centuries largely on the basis of some bedouin traditions, endorsed by Byzantine monks, that it was the place Moses met Zipporah, the site of the burning bush, and the gateway to Mount Sinai. Undoubtedly, most of the monks who ever lived here, and most of the pilgrims who visited here, believed those links were true. Now, of course, we know, through history, botany, geography, and archaeology, that those links may not be true. Certainly most of the visitors who come here today, and certainly most of the scientists who study these matters, believe those links are untrue. But the reality is, neither side knows for sure. For all the scientific exploration of the stories of the Bible—especially Exodus—no one has been able to prove them; but no one's been able to *dis*prove them, either. We simply don't know.

One is left, instead, in a seemingly unbridgeable chasm, away from the firm ground of certitude, faced with the bottomless breach of doubt. About halfway through my journey now, I felt that gap more than ever. Should I dismiss the faithful claims of the monks about their connection to the Bible? Should I marvel at them as at an anachronistic curiosity? Or should I take, from them, a different lesson: that the Bible is somehow deeper than faith or science? That it's something different, a set of stories that transcends most traditional ways of thinking, that somehow finds a way to have something to say to bedouin shepherds, Irish farmers, Israeli archaeologists. Indeed, as I was coming to believe, the power of the Bible to reinvent itself, to withstand the often withering glare of skepticism, to withstand even the sometimes crushing weight of belief, was a beautiful thing, a thing to admire. Maybe that thing is the essence of being divine; maybe it's the essence of being human. Maybe those are the same thing. I didn't know.

I was in the gap now, in that space between where the latent spirit in the places we were visiting and the emerging spirit in me had still not fully connected. I was still in the zone of fear. And the one thing I knew for sure was that I had less and less interest in voices that had all the answers, in people who were sure of their beliefs, who never questioned, or rediscovered. I was drawn instead to a manner of speaking, a tone, a sense of exploration. I was attracted, most of all, to people who wanted to engage the text in a dialogue, in an ongoing conversation. It's what had drawn me to Avner, to Fern Dobuler in Bethel, to Gabi Barkay in Jerusalem. It's what made my conversations with Basem, with Professor Nurel Din, with Jerry Bracken, so satisfying. It's what had made my trip so unexpectedly rich: the contemporary people who lived their lives in perpetual contact with the people of the Bible.

And it happened again with Father Justin.

Even before we arrived at Saint Catherine's, I had heard word that there was an American monk at the monastery, the first in the institution's 1,500-year history. I had asked Father Paulo about him, and Anastasis. Both of them said I was most likely to catch him in the afternoon, before the evening service, when he was doing his chores. We were sitting in the office later that day, Avner reminiscing with one of the monks, when a tall, thin monk in his late thirties walked into the courtyard. I recognized him as the one who had sprinkled the incense in the morning service. I went and introduced myself, and he invited us to join him for a cup of tea in a small antechamber near the basilica.

"Living here has been a profound revelation," Father Justin said. "Especially for an American." He was close to six-five, with long flowing black robes that accentuated his otherworldliness. His face was gaunt, with a gnarled black beard dusted with gray that seemed like a piece of Spanish moss attached to his chin; he wore thin round spectacles. With his earnest manner, deep-set eyes, and his black skullcap, he looked like a character out of *The Brothers Karamazov*.

"Just the services alone," he continued. "If you think that ever since the sixth century they have been going on here. Not just in this place, but within these very walls. There are so many places where you see a few tumbledown stones and you wonder what this place must have been like over the years. What the way of life was like. What were their goals?"

We were sitting in a small stone room with a wooden icon of the Virgin Mary with the infant Jesus. On the opposite wall was a picture of Moses receiving the Ten Commandments on top of Mount Sinai, along with a picture of Saint Catherine being carried to burial by angels. The setting, again, as spiritual forge.

"What's amazing," he said, "is that I see the bedouin girls walking through the mountains, feeding the goats, and I think to myself, 'That's exactly what Zipporah would have looked like twenty-three centuries ago.' Even to this day, the bedouin are building primitive homes and bringing in all the amenities of modern life, but you still see tents. And these tents are exactly like the ones that would have been used in the time of Moses."

"And do you feel isolated by all this tradition?" I asked. "There's a whole world out there you never hear about."

"Who says we never hear about it?" he said. "Some Americans came here about a year ago and said, 'You people need e-mail, because you need to be in touch with scholars all over the world.' "

"You have *e-mail*!" I said.

"They gave us computers and we hooked them up. And they pointed out some Internet search engines where you can look for used and rare books. So all I did was type 'Sinai' for the subject, but so many thousands of books came up that after sixty seconds it just cut off."

"So what's your e-mail address?"

"Sinai@gega.net," he said, spelling it out. "The problem is that sometimes for days on end you can't get through with a telephone or a fax. That's why e-mail has become the easiest way. But usually the telephone lines are so poor that if you try to open up a Web page it will take you two minutes or longer. The worst is when people send us these mammoth files and then you sit there for a whole day and try to get a connection!"

I was stunned: downloading problems at Mount Sinai, the place of the most famous download in history. The irony was too rich to contemplate. "In Jerusalem, they have this service where you can fax a message to the Western Wall," I mentioned. "Can you e-mail a message to Mount Sinai?"

"Why not? What's amazing to me is that I can sit up there in the library working on the computer and look out the window and there's Mount Sinai to my left, a sixth-century basilica to my right, and it's thirty-four centuries between me and Moses."

I asked how he came to be at the monastery, and he began to sketch the story. Like many young believers, Father Justin first visited Jerusalem as a young adult and was transformed. He studied Hebrew, Latin, Ancient Greek, and Modern Greek and joined a Greek Orthodox monastery near his home in Massachusetts. After a decade of service he made a pilgrimage to Saint Catherine's and told the archbishop he would like to become a member.

"He just gave me this icy look," Father Justin recalled. "It's like I asked the wrong question. And then that night he left for Greece. I didn't know what my status was." After three weeks the archbishop returned. "Now that you've seen the monastery without rose-colored spectacles," he said, "do you still want to become a member?" Father Justin said yes.

"Many people come here with idealistic views of what it is to be a monk," Father Justin continued. "It was only after we had gotten to know each other that he was willing to discuss my becoming a member. Even then I had to tell him my whole history and they had to vote. It was a happy moment when they told me I would be allowed to stay."

And now that he lived here, what did he feel about scholars who suggested the events in the Bible, specifically the events at Mount Sinai, may not have happened?

"A lot of people say that what's important is *that* it happened, not *where* it happened," Father Justin said. "We base our confirmation on two things: One is the living tradition. Moses lived in the area for forty years. It's recorded in the Scriptures that he told the people around him what happened and they passed it down from generation to generation. The second thing is research. In the nineteenth century, when they first deciphered hieroglyphics, the French and British did all sorts of archaeology and many, many scholars came to the conclusion that this is the only place that fits every description we have of Mount Sinai in the Bible."

But these days many people question that, I said.

Father Justin was unmoved. "Archaeologists may challenge the connection today," he said. "But you have to remember, history has shown repeatedly that scholars get consumed by fads and that subsequent generations have different fads." In the corner Avner started to nod. "Living here you become intensely aware of the history of the area. You see how many times the church came close to being destroyed, how many times the weather was horrendous, how many times it came close to being abandoned because it was so difficult to bring supplies here. There's been an amazing continuity that defies all human explanation. So the only explanation is that it's a place that has been especially protected by God.

"There's one story," he continued, his eyes brightening. "Centuries ago, when the monastery was in extreme isolation, it was very difficult to bring supplies here. One time the monastery was infested with flies, ants, and fleas, in such numbers that they destroyed the supply of corn. The number of monks had dwindled to just a handful and they were starving to death. Figuring there was no way to survive, they decided to hold a last service on the mountain and then abandon the place. As they were coming down, the Virgin Mary appeared to them and persuaded them of her protection. Once on the ground a caravan appeared on the horizon. 'Who brought these supplies?' they asked the members of the caravan. And the people said, 'This older man appeared and told us to take these supplies to the monastery. Then he disappeared.' When they finally entered the church at Saint Catherine's, one of the little boys who was on the caravan saw the depiction of the prophet Moses and screamed, 'That's the man that appeared. He's the one who sent us.' "

Father Justin crossed his hands on his lap. Though he was of a different generation, a different nationality, and a different religion from Avraham Biran, he had an avuncular tone and a kind tutorial disposition that reminded me of his fellow teacher. The scientist and the theologian, separated by outlook, but brought together in a common quest to understand and explain the same story—and to keep it alive by passing it on.

"There's one more thing I want to ask you," I said. It was almost sunset now, and the next morning we would begin our ascent up the mountain. But one paradox about Saint Catherine's still puzzled me. It was the same paradox that had hovered over our quest from the beginning. Was retracing this route something that the Bible itself demanded, or requested? If anything, the opposite seemed true. Exodus, for example, clearly states that Mount Sinai was so sacred—and so highly combustible—that no one was allowed to climb it, no less touch it, look at it, or sleep on it.

"That's right," Father Justin said. "In the story, when the Israelites first came into contact with the mountain, they marked the whole area off. There was thunder and lightning and thick black clouds. Even the animals were not allowed to go up the mountain. And that's when they heard the sound of trumpets, as if the mountain was on fire. Everyone was terrified. And the people said to Moses, 'If we go up we will surely die, so you go up and speak to God for us.' "

"If that's the case, then how do we justify walking up the mountain today?" I asked.

Again he was serenely confident, even brotherly. "In ancient times," he explained, "a monk would be at the top of the path and he would hear a person's confession to make sure that he was spiritually prepared to be at the sacred place. That's how we justify it. You come to the monastery. You purify yourself. And then you ascend."

"And once you arrive at the top?"

For the first time all afternoon he smiled. He knew what happened to people when they walked in the footsteps of the Bible. "You don't have to prepare for that," Father Justin said. "As the Bible says, 'This is holy ground.' When you get there, your heart will be beating and your head will be light. Just shut your eyes and listen closely. God will tell you what to do."

3. The God-Trodden Mountain

I f I learned anything during my time in the desert it was this: Places have the power to transform—people, nations, even ideas. The Bible understands this implicitly. The story of the Five Books of Moses is the story of the people, the land, and God, and their relationship to one another. Take out the land, and you lose the grounding element in the equation. God could have offered Abraham dominion over any place; he offered him dominion over the land of Israel. The place, in this instance, was inextricable from the people. God could have led the fleeing Israelites directly from Egypt to the Promised Land; instead he led them for forty years in the desert. The place, in this case, was necessary for their development as a nation. And above all, God could have given the Israelites the Ten Commandments wherever he wanted. He chose Mount Sinai. The place, we can conclude, must be vital to the event. And what is that connection? That question was foremost on my mind as I awoke from my second night in the monastery, met Avner at the entrance, and prepared to climb the mountain that lorded over us all.

One possible answer was already becoming clear: A desert is a spiritual enough place; a desert mountain is downright inspiring. Avner Goren was an untested graduate student in 1967 when Avraham Biran asked him to serve as the chief archaeologist of the Sinai. By the time he left fifteen years later, Avner had been transformed into a diplomat, a man of stature. He was a member of the Israeli delegation that negotiated control of the Sinai with the Egyptians. He had received enough gifts from local residents to begin Israel's first-ever museum of bedouin culture. Israeli television aired a documentary on his children called *The Blond Bedouin of the Sinai*. The place, in effect, had elevated him.

That transformation was apparent from the moment we arrived in the small village of Saint Catherine's, where Avner was like a father showing his son the old house where he grew up. "This road wasn't there," he would say. "That building is new. The entire neighborhood has been redone!" I had never seen him more emotional, or engaged, than when we were around the mountain.

Yet for all his nostalgia, he never showed regret. If anything, he was proud that Israel had returned the Sinai in 1982. As he explained during our walk toward the camel-resting area alongside the monastery, "I was among those who always said, 'Guys, we can talk a lot, but one day the Egyptians will get it back. We have to be prepared for that.' The others said, 'What are you talking about? This will stay in our hands.' " Eventually, as part of the Camp David Accords, Israel agreed to give back the peninsula. "A few weeks later Sadat approached us and asked us to let him celebrate one of the holy days of Islam at the mountain," Avner said. "According to the agreement, the Saint Catherine's area should have been given back two months after the feast. But it was his own personal request, and he was so beloved among Israelis for having stepped into the new world of peace, that the government agreed. And I agreed, too, even though for me personally it was one of the hardest things I ever faced in my life."

"What was hard?" I said.

"Withdrawing from here. Leaving the mountain as my home."

"So what happened?"

"I sent my family ahead. But I stayed behind, and the day before Sadat came, a half a day after the Egyptians took control, I waited for a few hours, then started to drive home."

"And what did you do in those few hours?"

He stopped and looked up at the summit. "I cried." Then he caught himself and looked back at me. "But I want to emphasize, that was on a personal level. I do think, even now, that things should be done for peace. Because the Sinai was taken in war, and the war was fought to try to find some way of living together."

Jebel Musa in the morning is like a tiger at dawn, a cat curled up in the shadows, its coat the color of pumpkin pie, its demeanor a misleading message: tame. As we arrived at the small plateau where climbers prep for the hike to come, the mountain seemed almost inert, waiting. At 7,455 feet, it's not a particularly tall mountain: half as high as the tallest mountain in the Colorado Rockies; roughly as tall as the highest peak in the Appalachians. But it is impressive, completely dominating the landscape around it like a mother elephant dwarfing her babies. A mixture of red and gray granite fused together in an imposing, almost threatening mass, Mount Moses rises straight from the ground and softens slightly at the top like a drip castle. Though not as angular as Mount Ararat, nor as tall as nearby Mount Katarina, it still seems like a particularly imposing backdrop, waiting for some particularly majestic drama to take place in front of it. As American visitor John Lloyd Stephens wrote in 1836, "Among all the stupendous works of Nature, not a place can be selected more fitting for the exhibition of Almighty power."

There are two basic ways to climb the mountain. The direct route is the Path of Our Lord Moses, or Steps of Repentance, a near-vertical climb of 3,750 steps hewn out of the rock by a penitent monk. It takes an hour and a half to climb up, nearly twice that to climb down. The longer, easier route is via a serpentine camel path that goes up the east side of the mountain and joins the stairs about two-thirds of the way up. Both paths then converge on an additional 750-step ascent to the summit.

As a former resident (and perpetual romantic), Avner didn't like taking either path. He suggested that we hire three camels—one for each of us, and one for our bags and lunch—start out on the camel path, but quickly veer off when we reached the rear of the mountain. We'd spend the day visiting early Christian holy sites in a secluded part of the mountain once populated by hermits, have lunch in a centuries-old orchard believed to be the place where the Ten Commandments were

given, then climb up the early Byzantine trail, which has been abandoned for decades, before arriving at the peak by sunset.

The scene in the small resting area was chaotic, a Middle Eastern
bazaar, with fifty or so camels and their handlers angling for the services of what, at the moment, was barely a handful of climbers. Avner
had prearranged a ride with a friend and we stepped off to the side and
began assigning our gear. Camels—or in this case, one-humped drom-
edaries (*Camelus dromedarius*)—are curious-looking creatures, around
eight feet tall to the tops of their heads, with sandy-colored hair and
large, shaggy humps that look like marshmallows covered with toasted
coconut. In general, looking at a camel reminded me of looking at a
clown, with everything rather misproportioned, the too-tall legs, the
bony knees, the molded jowls. Clowns design their costumes to accentuate their oddities; camels seem to come that way naturally. The
observer's eye goes directly toward the hump, the loopy neck, the long,
hooked nose that looks like a bunch of bananas, arching down to the
stem. This sense of the absurd is only enhanced by the saddles, large
padded thrones made from a grab bag of anything squooshy: foam,
blankets, plastic garbage bags, old T-shirts, bedouin rugs, pom-poms,
rubber welcome mats. If you find it in the desert, you find it on a
camel.

The reason for all this effort—and iconography—is simple. Riding a
camel is to life in the desert what riding a bike is to childhood: a rite of
passage, a way of life, a source of freedom, a pain in the butt. Almost
anyone who spends time in the desert is forced to confront, in one way
or another, the tyranny of the camel, the only mammal capable of surviving without water for as much as two weeks in the summer, and two
months in winter. Camels don't store water in their humps, as once
thought, but in their tissues and cells. They conserve water by constantly
increasing their body temperature to match the climate (as much as
twelve degrees Fahrenheit), thereby eliminating the need to use water to
cool themselves down. In fact, camels "store" no extra water at all,
drinking only what they require to live. Humans, by contrast, must
maintain a steady body temperature. When we get hot, we use water as

a coolant, evaporating water via perspiration and making our bodies thirsty for more.

Camels have other idiosyncrasies that make them uniquely suited to desert life. Their humps are filled with as much as eighty pounds of fat, which enables them to live without food for long periods of time. They have broad feet that permit them to walk in the sand without sinking, and tight nostrils they can seal off from blowing sand. Their eyes are particularly well adapted, with thick bone visors on their foreheads that block the sun and an extra eyelid that moves from side to side like a windshield wiper to remove sand from their eyeballs. In a sandstorm, camels can actually close this third eyelid and see through it. As further protection, camels also have extremely long eyelashes. I also have long eyelashes, which at the moment I swung atop my camel I hoped would be taken as confirmation that I, too, was somehow genetically aligned with the desert—or at least kin enough not to be unceremoniously flung off.

One reason for my concern is that camels are notoriously nasty, the earliest exemplars of road rage. "Stay away from camels," more than one friend advised. Camels are known to hiss, spit, vomit, shake, and, on occasion, go suddenly berserk. T. E. Lawrence, in his famous book *The Seven Pillars of Wisdom,* wrote that Arabs of means "rode none but she-camels," since they were smoother under the saddle than males, as well as being better tempered and less noisy. Also, they were patient and would endure to march long after they were worn out, indeed until they tottered with exhaustion and fell in their tracks and died: whereas the coarser males grew angry, flung themselves down when tired, and from sheer rage would die there unnecessarily." Emil Ludwig, in his book on the Nile, describes how the skeletons of so many dead camels mark the desert like milestones. "Their shadowy, bleached bones, quickly cleansed of flesh by sun and vultures alike, are the cleanliest remains of organic life, and, if they stood upright, would look like some carefully prepared model in a museum, the Platonic ideal of a camel."

But for sheer directness, nothing beats the story of a friend of mine, who received a postcard from a friend of hers visiting Egypt. On the front was a picture of a camel; on the back was a single sentence: "Whoa doesn't mean stop to a camel."

By nine we were on our way up the mountain. The handlers, teenage boys with red-and-white-checked kaffiyehs and sandals, walked in front of the animals, occasionally swatting them with short sticks wrapped in duct tape. The pack camel went first, followed by me, then Avner. The path was about five feet wide, lined along the edges with red granite boulders about the size of bread loaves. The sand on the trail was also red, the color of ground-up flowerpots, and seemed particularly suited to the gentle gait of the camels, who put one pad in front of the other in a rocking, metronomic rhythm. If anything, the animals seemed almost lulled by the routine. They didn't look around but stared straight ahead, plodding forward like blank-faced Teamsters. They even had their own CB code—a mix of clicks, gargles, and hisses—that they used to communicate with their brethren. No oasis for six hundred miles; no rest stop for forty years.

Sitting on the camel did prove uncomfortable. Despite all the padding, the twin prongs of the wooden saddle—one in front, one in back—still managed to break clear, pressing against my back and groin. Even resting one leg over the neck of the camel, as the bedouin do, only uncovered a new set of citified muscles for the saddle to grate. I felt a bit like a plum being squeezed by a pair of chopsticks. In no time the ride reminded me of one of the worst days of my childhood: spent on a donkey descending the Grand Canyon. The donkey wanted me on his back even less than I wanted to be there. It was a struggle of attrition, which both of us lost.

In a way, the scenery also reminded me of the Grand Canyon, with its palette of rusts and browns, its stratified layers of rock, its complete isolation. The one difference, of course, is that we were going up, not down. Indeed, within half an hour we were high enough on the mountain, and far enough away from the monastery, that the scenery lost all sense of proportion. The sun, by now high into the sky, beat down relentlessly. There was no vegetation visible for miles. The rocks were sharply jagged in places, like scales on a crocodile, and in other places more gently rolling. The tops of the mountains, which had seemed so imposing at dawn, took on a sad, droopy feeling, like melting dinosaurs. With the winding path, the camel, and the steep vertical climb, the scene took on the feel of one of those Chinese scroll paintings, which always include a hut, a bridge, or a path, to stress that nature is more fully realized when a human being pauses to consider it.

The higher we went, the more solitary the atmosphere seemed. A wheatear alighted on a boulder. A flock of doves took off from a ridge. The path grew steeper, the camel a tad more ornery. The air began to pinch my nose. Perhaps it was the bucking of the animal, perhaps the heat, perhaps the fact that we were climbing Mount Moses, but I felt a renewed appreciation—and awe—at the changes the Israelites had undergone during their journey, beginning in Mesopotamia, arcing down through the Fertile Crescent, descending deep into the Nile, and emerging to face an unknown mountain. Not since they passed Syria, almost five hundred years before the Exodus, would the Israelites have faced such imposing peaks. And whatever route they may have taken, this terrain would have been ideal as a place of revelation. Come face-to-face with the high mountains of southern Sinai, and whatever one's orientation, one pauses with anticipation. The Bible says that when the Israelites beheld Mount Sinai they "trembled." At the moment I could understand why.

By a little past eleven we had arrived at an intermediate peak and dis-embarked from the camels to begin our hike. Avner brought over a small piece of stone imprinted with what looked like a fossilized branch of fir needles. "These aren't fossils," he noted, "but minerals—manganese crystals—that accumulated here in this shape." Like the *tafuni,* the weather-worn holes in the rock we saw a few days earlier, these impressions were made when a hard, mineral solution seeped into the cracks and later expanded into tendrils that looked like fragile twigs. "Byzantine visitors decided they were the remains of the burning bush," he said.

"So the burning left this scar on the rock?"

"Remember," he said, grinning, "you are standing on holy ground."

And frightful ground, too. Though the mountain may seem poetic from the path, from on top it can be wickedly cruel. Almost anyone who climbs the mountain at night to see sunrise reports that the experience was the coldest of their lives. An average of ten people die of exposure every year. During Avner's tenure a special forces officer from the Israeli army came one night and announced he was going to climb the mountain. "Don't go now," the bedouin told him. "You won't have enough time." Being from the special forces, he went anyway. "I went home," Avner said. "Put the kids to bed, and one of the bedouin came running. 'Somebody's stuck on the mountain!' " The man had gone up the front of the mountain, reached a dead end, turned around to come down, and become trapped. "Then it became quite cold," Avner said, "and he tried to shout, and nobody heard him." He needed to signal, but had no equipment, so he took his checkbook, ripped out check after check, and set them on fire. "I climbed up the regular trail but couldn't reach him. I had to fly in a helicopter to bring him down. His legs were already quite frozen, and we had to soak him in hot water."

Despite the mountain's ferociousness, it can be hospitable. Jebel Musa is actually made up of a number of small peaks that cover an area of about two square miles, topped by a conelike summit. The lower peaks contain a series of protected plateaus, hidden caves, and isolated nooks that serve to keep out the elements, making the mountain quite friendly to habitation by those seeking to get closer to God. On Ras Safsaafa, the most extensive of the peaks, the granite ridges are filled with man-made remains—dikes, wells, cisterns. There is even an orchard of pear and almond trees. In the early Christian era, monks perfected means of storing water and actually lived for months at a time on the mountain. In one hollow, Avner pointed out a whitewashed structure that monks claim is the Sinai's oldest monastery, built by a nun and her husband (!) during the Roman persecutions of the third century C.E.

This juxtaposition of the barren mountain and pockets of fertility only heightens the sense of otherworldliness that envelops Jebel Musa. It also mirrors one of the tensions in the biblical story of the Ten Commandments: A mountain that seems so terrorizing to the Israelites proves to be so welcoming to Moses; a mountain untouchable to humans succors an eighty-year-old prophet for weeks at a time.

The story of Moses and God on Mount Sinai is one of the most celebrated in the Bible, but also one of the most confusing, with a series of ups and downs that are almost impossible to keep track of. In the third month after the Exodus, the Israelites arrive at the wilderness of Sinai and set up camp at the base of the mountain where Moses first encountered God in the burning bush. The Lord calls Moses from the mountain and asks him to tell the people that God bore them "on eagles' wings" from Egypt and that if they obey him, they will become "my treasured possession." The people agree, saying, "All that the Lord has spoken, we will do!" The Lord then orders the people to stay pure for two days, and wash their clothes, for on the third day he will come down in a cloud on Mount Sinai, in sight of the whole community. The people are not to touch the mountain, and whoever does shall be put to death. On the third day, as morning dawns, thunder and lightning fill the area and a dense cloud envelops the mountain. A shofar sounds. Moses leads the people to the foot of the mountain, which trembles violently. The Lord calls Moses to the top of the mountain, then sends him back down to get Aaron. The two then ascend again, and God reveals his laws.

The Ten Commandments, which the Greeks called the decalogue, or ten words, and the Hebrew text calls the "decade of words," turn out not to be limited to commandments, and not to be confined to ten. The laws, which theologian J. Ryder Smith called "the universal alphabet of religion for all mankind," actually comprise thirteen verses in Exodus 20, which has led to enormous debate over precisely what constitutes the code. The first verse, for example, is not a commandment at all, but a preamble, in the manner of other Near Eastern laws from that time: "I the Lord am your God, who brought you out of the land of Egypt, the house of bondage." Jewish tradition lists this as the first commandment. Most Protestant denominations believe the first commandment also includes the subsequent verse "You shall have no other gods beside Me." Jewish, Catholic, and Lutheran traditions make that verse part of the second commandment, along with the next few verses, which command against making "sculptured images" of God. For everyone, the subsequent six laws command, in order: (3) You shall not swear falsely by the name of the Lord; (4) Remember the Sabbath day and keep it holy; (5) Honor your father and mother; (6) You shall not murder; (7) You shall not commit adultery; and (8) You shall not steal. The last two laws are also apportioned differently in different religions, but command: You shall not bear false witness against your neighbor, and you shall not covet your neighbor's house, wife, slave, ox, or ass.

After God delivers the Ten Commandments, thunder and lightning again surround the mountain. A horn blares and the mountain smokes. But God is not finished. He continues for the next three chapters to deliver a series of regulations on everything from what to do with a slave who doesn't want to go free (pierce his ear with an awl and keep him), whether to use the death penalty for kidnappers (yes), and what to do to a man who pushes a pregnant woman and causes a miscarriage (fine him). Moses repeats these laws, commonly known as the Book of the Covenant, because it amounts to a contract between God and the people, an expansion of the verbal agreement first reached between God and Abraham. To press the importance of these laws, Moses has the population agree to follow them by sprinkling bull's blood on the people. As he says, "This is the blood of the covenant which the Lord now makes with you concerning these commands."

God's revelation of himself on Mount Sinai and his subsequent delivery of a written contract with the people marks the narrative climax of the Five Books of Moses. Up to now, the Israelites have been largely passive—receiving the protection of God, being freed from slavery—but promising little in return. Now they become active participants in the covenant, agreeing publicly to follow the dictates of God. Mount Sinai marks their birth as a spiritual nation, one committed not merely to conquering and holding power at all costs, but to doing so within a strict moral framework. As a result, they would forever alter the course of both political and religious behavior. From now on, nations would no longer say merely, "My god is stronger than your god." They must add, "My conduct is more righteous than your conduct." In this way, at least, the story of Mount Sinai is a monumental achievement. As commentator Gunther Plaut has written, "The story—in all its brevity—achieves its major goal: to convey to some degree the awesomeness of that moment when the Lord of the universe showed His Glory to Israel and when he made his covenant with them, changing their history and the history of all men as well." Revelation, covenant, and law, Plaut says, are the three pillars upon which the structure of Israel's history is reared. "Without them, Israel would have been a nation like other nations; with them, it became a focal point of human destiny."

After a half-hour hike we arrived at the northern ridge of Ras Safsaafa, which overlooks an enormous swath of open terrain called the Plain of ar-Raaha. Seen from above, the plain is wedged in the middle of a hub of craggy mountains and looks like a rare patch of smooth skin on the belly of a toad. At midday the sun bounced off the pale sand as if it were the face of a mirror, creating a blinding glow. Jebel Musa drops straight to the desert floor here, with almost no foothills, thereby giving people on the ground a clear view of Safsaafa's peak. Based on that view, early visitors concluded that the plain must be the spot where the Israelites gathered to watch God reveal himself on Mount Sinai in the form of smoke and lightning. Those visitors named the clearing the Plain of Assemblage. As Arthur Sutton, an English pilgrim, wrote: "So close does the plain of ar-Raaha come to Mt. Safsaafa that one can at once understand why Moses 'set bounds for the people around the mountain' to prevent them from touching it."

Not content with visual identification, some scholars, whom Avner called pseudo-scholars, went so far as to measure the plain in an attempt to determine if it could hold all the Israelites the Bible says would have been there. Using a population figure of two million, the twelve-mile-by-four-mile site could have accommodated each man, woman, and child with 669 square feet, about the size of a New York City studio apartment.

More seriously, the question of which mountain played host to the revelation has been a matter of debate for thousands of years. The Bible is notably silent on the matter, giving no physical description of the mountain whatsoever, saying only that it's in the "desert of Sinai." Josephus, writing in the first century C.E., said that it was "the highest of all the mountains thereabout." A rabbinic midrash, written several hundred years later, offers a different take, saying that the mountains of the world quarreled with each other to play host to God. Each extolled its own height and distinction, except Sinai, which humbly said, "I am low." Finally God announced: "My presence will rest on Sinai, the smallest and most insignificant of all." In its modesty, the rabbis noted, Sinai resembled the humility of Moses who had not wanted to accept the mantle of leadership.

Other commentators were more specific and equally romantic. No fewer than twenty-two mountains have been put forward as the "real Mount Sinai," including candidates in southern, central, and northern Sinai, the Negev, Jordan, even Saudi Arabia. Advocates of the various theories cite everything from soil samples to rock formations, wall carvings to climatic conditions. It must be Jebel Sin Bisher, in the northern Sinai, because it's low enough for the octogenarian Moses to have climbed. It must be Serabit el-Khadim, in the central Sinai, because its rich artwork indicates a ritual importance. It must be Jebel Serbal, in the southern Sinai, because it's holy to the bedouin. It must be Mount Seir, in Saudi Arabia, because the apostle Paul indicated in a letter that Sinai was "a mountain in Arabia."

Even as late as the 1980s, two Americans—Larry Williams, a multimillionaire and two-time Republican candidate for the U.S. Senate from Montana, and Bob Cornuke, a former police SWAT team member—forged passports, hid for weeks in the Saudi Arabian desert, and eventually came upon Jebel al Law, which they believed was the "true" Mount Sinai and would contain troves of undiscovered gold. The gold wasn't there, of course, but they did claim to find the stone boundary Moses erected to keep the Israelites away from the mountain (their interpretation of the "bounds set round the mountain" described in Exodus 19), the twelve pillars Moses erected in commemoration of the tribes, and even an "unnaturally scorched spot" where God must have descended to give Moses the stone tablets. Today, despite their contentions, the mountain houses a $30 million radar station, financed by the CIA.

Though most archaeologists have long since given up pinpointing the mountain, at least one scholar has not. Before leaving for our trip I went to visit Emanuel Anati in Jerusalem. A colorful if controversial figure, Anati, born in Florence, is a self-described humanist and man of culture (he's written eighty books), who trained as an archaeologist in Israel before spending decades doing pioneering work on rock carvings in Europe. Early in his career he discovered similar carvings on a mountain in the southern Negev, close to the border with Sinai. In the 1980s he returned to the mountain and unearthed 230 additional archaeological discoveries, including many with eerie connections to the story of the Ten Commandments, among them twelve pillars at the base of the mountain like the ones Moses is said to have erected, and a cave on the summit like the one he is said to have used for shelter. These findings led Anati to conclude that the mountain, Har Karkom, was a holy place as early as the second millennium B.C.E. Because the mountain is also directly on the path from Midian to Egypt (the central route), Anati believes Har Karkom is the mountain referred to as Mount Sinai. He even got Pope John Paul II to endorse his research, which instantly made Har Karkom, though it's located hours from any road, one of the most coveted adventure sites in Israel.

"So as far as you're concerned," I said to Anati during our conversation, "this will be the last theory. The two-thousand-year search for Mount Sinai has ended?"

"I don't know," he said. "And I don't care. But this is not a theory. I know. And I'm not the only one who knows. Whoever knows what I know, knows."

As charming as it was to meet an old-fashioned romantic purposefully bucking the trends of academia, I ultimately found Anati's theory more enchanting than persuasive. If anything, I came to believe that the search for Mount Sinai misses an important point inherent in the story. The Bible has perfect recall when it wants to. It remembers people, places, things, even dialogue. If it wanted to tell us the exact location of

Mount Sinai, it could easily have done so, as it does for countless other places. Instead the story is vague, and it seems fair to assume that that vagueness is purposeful.

There are many possible reasons for such a lack of specificity. First, Mount Sinai is not in the Promised Land, and the Bible may not have wanted to glorify any location outside its own boundaries. As Avner noted, biblical writers sanctified few places outside Jerusalem. Second, these writers feared fetishism in general and did not want to encourage pilgrimages. In fact, Jews have traditionally been much less interested in identifying holy places than Christians, who didn't really begin their effort until Byzantine times. By then, few Jews lived in the Middle East and Judaism had become a religion based more on prayer and ritual than pilgrimage. Third, as one rabbinic midrash suggests, other nations might have been more inclined to dismiss the Five Books had they been given in Israel. "Therefore the book was given in the desert," the rabbis concluded, "publicly and openly, in a place belonging to no one."

For me, the lack of identifying details points to another, perhaps more consequential, factor: The less Mount Sinai is associated with a physical place, the more it's perceived as a spiritual place. Since the Promised Land is never achieved in the Pentateuch (Deuteronomy ends with the Israelites still in the desert, about to start the conquest), Mount Sinai emerges as the spiritual locus of the story, the pivot on which the Five Books hinge. Indeed the appearance of God on the mountain and the people's ultimate acceptance of the Ten Commandments mark the high point of the story—maybe even the high point of monotheism—when the people and God come together in a moment of unprecedented union. *Sinai,* thus, is not just a place, it's a metaphor for the covenant between Israel and Yahweh. The people are forever bound to that mountain, attached to that rock. And just as the mountain became the symbol of the covenant, the Bible, in turn, became the symbol of the mountain. If the pyramids are the "Bible in stone," as Egyptologists Piazzi Smith and David Davidson said, the Bible is Mount Sinai in words, the living embodiment of the physical link between humans and God.

. . .

We made our way back from the overlook through a fascinating corridor of amber-colored stone, which the wind had carved into a series of undulating forms, a fun house of brown sugar. The formations were like clouds: Stare at them long enough and they became objects. One looked like a cow, another a hopping rabbit, another the hood ornament from a Jaguar. We saw a curled cobra the size of a teepee, and a chipmunk the size of a Macy's Thanksgiving Day balloon. If I didn't know better, with all the animals in stone, I would have thought this was the mountain where Noah's ark landed.

The corridor eventually spilled into a small enclosure near the middle of the mountain. A stone chapel dedicated to Saint John the Baptist sits in the middle of a scene so green it could be in Ireland, with hawthorn, fig, and apricot trees scattered in a small grove. Water, collected by a dam that prevents rainfall from cascading on the monastery below, was so plentiful here that early monks who lived on the mountain were actually able to grow wheat. In the sixth century, as many as three hundred monks resided here at one time, Avner said, and there are countless chapels dedicated to everyone from Saint Gregory, to Saint Anne, to Saint Panteleimon, and nooks and crannies named after Moses, Elijah, Jethro, even the "Virgin Mary's Holy Girdle." According to legend, the mother of Jesus visited a fourth-century ascetic at the site and gave him her belt as a memento of her visit. All in all, the extraordinary array of facilities on the second-highest mountain in one of the most remote places in the world gives the place the feeling of a plush community of devotion, a suburb of the soul.

A few minutes' walk from the enclosure, Avner led us to a sheer cliff overlooking the eastern side of the mountain. The wind had picked up a bit, and the sun was glaring off the red face of the stone. Though it was early afternoon, the air was chilly and bracing. I could only imagine how raw the place must feel in winter. Avner hadn't mentioned where we were going, but when we arrived, he pivoted me around to face a tiny cave, the mouth of which was no higher than my waist. "This is a

Byzantine cave," he said. "A hermit lived here." The space between the top and bottom of the opening was no more than a foot and a half. I had to bend over, squat down like a frog, lean forward even more, and go rear-end-first into the cave, just to fit. Inside I crossed my legs in front of me and managed to sit down. My left knee touched the left wall; my right knee touched the right wall. I could reach forward and touch the front lip; I could reach back and touch the back wall. My head rubbed against the top.

"How long would he have stayed here?" I asked.

"Six days a week."

I closed my eyes. The wind was so loud it seemed like cars whizzing by, and the sensation reminded me of my first day in the desert when the sounds were so loud they had an isolating effect. The wind as white noise. Here, the stimulation came from the front, from this extraordinary window on the world. Thinking back on how I entered the cave, I was reminded of an old Japanese saying that one never leaves a room headfirst, but backward out of deference to the room one leaves behind. Here one enters the room backward out of deference to the landscape. Looking out, I couldn't help wondering what that landscape must have represented to the monks who sat here. Was it a mirror of their soul? A mirror of God? Or are those the same thing? I could see how sitting here hour after hour, week after week, the view through the eye-shaped opening would begin to consume one's imagination. Here you're not on top of the world; you're inside it. You become, in essence, part of the land.

And how better to remind yourself of the lowly qualities of your body, which will ultimately return to the ground, than to return to the ground yourself. What better way to liberate your spirit than to cut off your body from the world. Not until I slid inside that envelope of earth did I realize how much these individuals were reacquainting themselves with Moses, who met here with God; with Elijah, who fled here from Israel; with Jesus, who sequestered himself in a similar location in the desert and was later placed by apostles in a cave outside Jerusalem. A space like this, coupled with strict self-denial, might be as close as a living person can come to the concept of resurrection. If nothing else, it shows the lengths that some people will go to to find a way to enter the Bible. By inserting themselves in the rock, the monks, in effect, were inscribing themselves in stone, aligning themselves, as much as humanly possible, with the word of God.

Back outside the cave we walked back to the chapel of Saint John, where our pack camel had arrived with lunch. We leaned up against the stone wall and ate our daily regimen—bread, cheese, tuna, honey. A lizard scooted by on the ground, stopping to stare at the spread. With the sage, the flowering almond trees, and the total silence, we could have been in any park in the world—except for the stone cliffs all around us, and for the fact that we were six thousand feet high.

We pulled out our Bibles and returned to the story. After the Israelites agree to follow the laws God lays out in the Book of the Covenant, Moses, Aaron, and seventy elders climb back up the mountain, where they are allowed to glimpse God, or at least his feet: "Under His feet there was the likeness of a pavement of sapphire, like the very sky for purity," the text says. The procession of ascendings and descendings gets confusing here, but Moses is called up the mountain again, this time with Joshua, and God covers the mountain with smoke and fire. Moses enters the canopy of smoke, where he stays for forty days and nights, receiving elaborate instructions on how to construct the Ark of the Covenant, a box made of acacia wood, covered with pure gold, and protected by two cherubim with outstretched wings. The ark will ultimately contain a copy of the law, and, like the divine boats used in Egyptian temples, is fitted with rings and poles that allow it to be carried. The ark is to be placed inside the Tabernacle, or Dwelling, which serves as God's residence on earth. The Tabernacle is a blue, purple, and crimson tent, made of linen and goat yarn, roughly forty-five feet long and thirty-six feet wide, about half the size of a tennis court. It has a special inner chamber, the Holy of Holies, separated by a curtain, and containing the Ark. In front of this is a holy area, with a table, lamp stand, and altar.

At the end of these instructions, God gives Moses two stone tablets, "inscribed by the finger of God," containing the Ten Commandments. He begins to descend. In the meantime, the Israelites have become impatient and plead with Aaron, "Come, make us a god who shall go before us, for that man Moses, who brought us from the land of Egypt—we do not know what has happened to him." Aaron instructs them to take off their gold earrings, which he molds into a "young bull," usually called a "calf" in English translations. The bull was quite popular in Egyptian religions and the Israelites, in familiar territory again, rejoice. "This is your god, O Israel, who brought you out of the land of Egypt," the Israelites say. Aaron builds an altar and the people celebrate with eating, drinking, and dancing—an orgy on the desert floor.

God is outraged and enjoins Moses to hurry down the mountain. "I see that this is a stiff-necked people," God says of their unwillingness to bow down in deference to him. He threatens to lash out, terminate the covenant he made with Abraham, and begin again with Moses. "Now, let me be, that my anger may blaze forth against them and that I may destroy them, and make of you a great nation." But Moses, who once said to God on this same mountain that he was a stutterer and not a man of words, uses words to temper God. "Let not your anger, O Lord, blaze forth against your people. . . . Let not the Egyptians say, 'It was with evil intent that he delivered them, only to kill them off in the mountains and annihilate them from the face of the earth.' " God relents and renounces his punishment, and Moses continues down the mountain.

But when he reaches the bottom and sees what God has already seen, Moses also becomes enraged and hurls the tablets from his hands, shattering them at the foot of the mountain. He then burns the calf and grinds the remains into powder, sprinkling the powder into water, which he makes the Israelites drink. Moses then offers a loyalty test. "Whoever is with the Lord, come here!" he says. The Levites come forward, and Moses bids them travel through the throng, slaying "brother, neighbor, and kin." Three thousand people die that day, and the following day Moses returns to the mountain and makes a personal appeal for God to forgive the Israelites for their sin of constructing the golden icon.

God is sympathetic, and he and Moses enter into an elaborate negotiation on the journey to come: Will God go with the Israelites? Will
Moses have assistance? Much of this conversation takes place near the
camp, inside the Tabernacle, "where the Lord would speak to Moses face
to face, as one man speaks to another." This communication, though, is
not enough for Moses, who asks to see God directly, suggesting their
earlier conversation was somehow indirect. God promises to pass before
Moses, but says, "You cannot see my face, for man may not see me and
live." God points him to a cleft on the rock and shields Moses with his
hand. "Then I will take my hand away and you will see my back; but my
face must not be seen." After the viewing, clearly the most intimate yet
between God and the prophets, God asks Moses to write the Ten Commandments on a new set of tablets.

When Moses takes those tablets back down the mountain, he is not
aware that the skin of his face is radiant, sending forth beams of light.
Since the word for radiant, *karan,* is similar to the word for horn, *keren,*
the word was mistranslated by the Latin Vulgate to say that Moses' face
was "horned," which led to the erroneous image in Michelangelo's
statue of Moses with two goatlike horns. Either way, the Israelites shrink
from the radiance of Moses, and the passage at Mount Sinai ends with
Moses putting a veil over his face, shielding himself from his people.
The veil is a fitting metaphor for this string of chapters, for it seems to
capture the change in status that occurs at Mount Sinai: When Moses
speaks directly with God, he removes his veil; when he speaks with the
people, he puts it back on. Moses has become an intermediary—no
longer worldly, not quite divine. In that way, he's like the mountain
itself, a bridge between the people and God, an earthly body infused
with light.

For many biblical enthusiasts, Jebel Musa perfectly captures that mix
of emotions. Avner, in particular, feels this way. As we were finishing, he
told a story about a photographer he brought to this spot many years
earlier. "She refused to get excited," he said. "She insisted on playing it
cool." The day was sunny, with little wind. "We had some chocolate and
some wine with us," he said. "I told her about a monk who came here
and was so moved he stood and shouted part of the liturgy"—Avner

stood himself to demonstrate—" 'Holy! Holy! Holy!' " And the whole
mountain echoed, as it did at that moment, " *'Holy! Holy! Holy!'* But the
monk said, 'Only those who have ears to hear it, hear it.' "

"And did she hear it?" I asked.

"Do *you?*" he said.

The last words were just drifting away.

By the time we finished lunch, it was time to climb to the summit. We
walked a few minutes along Ras Safsaafa and passed through the Basin
of Elijah, a small depression containing a five-hundred-year-old cypress
tree, which is said to be the place where the prophet Elijah, according to
1 Kings, flees from the wrath of Queen Jezebel and is rewarded by having his own vision of God. From there we turned to the west and the
path to the top.

The summit of Jebel Musa is a geological oddity, a large, angled
mound of dark volcanic rock perched like an upside-down ice cream
cone on top of the other ridges. The summit itself occurs on a fault line
and is the neck of an extinct volcano that washed away. In the nineteenth century, historian Arthur Stanley called it a "bosom" of a mountain; clergyman Edward Robinson described it as a black and desolate
hump, "rising perpendicularly in frowning majesty." For centuries, the
main route to the peak has been the 750-step footpath, which weaves
around the nooks and fissures like the spiral on the outside of a conch
shell. When Avner and his colleagues were excavating the mountain in
the 1970s, they uncovered a previously unknown path up the far steeper
western side that was built by Byzantine monks. This would have been
the path that Egeria, the Byzantine nun, used to climb the mountain in
the fourth century, and Avner suggested we use it ourselves.

As we paused to tie our shoes and take a final sip of water, I asked
Avner how many times he'd been up the mountain. "Many, and not one
time less than that," he said.

"So what advice do you have for someone going up for the first
time?"

"Do you have something warm?"

The bottom part of the path was well hewn, with the steps carved out of the rock. But the higher the path rose the more it began to disintegrate, until finally the steps were all but invisible. After twenty minutes, I was crawling on all fours, like a squirrel on a tree. I would grab onto a boulder with my left hand, put my right leg on another boulder, wait to see if it would hold, then propel myself up with a mixture of torque and hope, or maybe that's faith. Climbing this gorge, with its overturned stones and spilling of shale, was like climbing an avalanche of overgrown popcorn, with an occasional kernel getting stuck in your knee, producing a wince of pain. When I mentioned this analogy to Avner, he said that when he was a child Israelis referred to popcorn as "American manna."

"I can't believe Moses made this walk in sandals," I said.

After a while I was sweating through my windbreaker and almost completely out of breath. I pulled myself up one last boulder and came to rest on a flat area that seemed to mark an end to the cataract. About fifty yards higher was the summit, topped by a few buildings that were just visible from this angle. The blush of sun was gentle at this hour, and the air contained a hint of the cold to follow. After waiting a bit for my pulse to calm down, I was joined by Avner and we climbed the remaining steps of the mountain, taking advantage of the now solid rock to scamper far more quickly to the top, a rush of excitement pushing us the final few feet. The surface of the mountain here wasn't like popcorn but was a chocolate-colored dollop of igneous rock that up close had lots of hidden divots and folds but from afar would look perfectly smooth and delectable.

The summit itself was surprisingly crowded, with a chapel, a mosque, and a bedouin rest tent all in a space less than one hundred feet long and thirty feet wide, an ecclesiastical strip mall on top of the world. The church, dedicated to the Holy Trinity, was built in the 1930s on a spot that has been almost continually occupied since the fourth century, when Egeria described a church in the same location that was not great in size but "great in grace." Egeria said the facility was built on the place where Moses received the Law from God; later monks escalated that, saying the rock beneath the church floor contained the imprint from Moses' knees where he bowed down to God; monks today go even further, saying their church sits on the very rock from which God chiseled the tablets. I half expected to see a sign that said MOSES SLEPT HERE. As it was, Avner pointed out a large rock just to the west of the church that monks claim has the cleft where Moses hid his face from God. Edward Palmer, an American scholar who visited in 1872, described seeing in this cleft "something like the impression of a man's hand and head left there by Moses."

The buildings, though, are overshadowed by the view, a 360-degree panorama of blood-colored mountains, which in the long shadows of late afternoon seemed even more menacing than earlier. With the jagged mountains confined to a large ring of southern Sinai, they seemed like the head of a giant lion roaring up in the middle of the desert, each of the peaks another tooth tearing at the sky. "Nothing can exceed the savage grandeur of the view from the summit of Mt. Sinai," wrote English naturalist Edward Hull. "The whole aspect of the surroundings impresses one with the conviction that he is here gazing on the face of Nature in one of her most brutal forms." As French artist Leon de Laborde put it, even more breathlessly: "If I had to represent the end of the world, I would model it from Mt. Sinai."

This combination of raw beauty and pure emotion has made Jebel Musa a requisite layover for naturalists and pilgrims alike. Avner and I were admiring the view from the western side of the church when I began to hear singing from the other side. I peeked around the corner, where a dozen or so travelers in bright yellow caps were singing "Amazing Grace." They were the only other visitors on the summit. When they finished, one of the members said a few words, and the group held hands and began chanting the Lord's Prayer. After they were done, I spoke to one of the men, an engineer in his forties from Vienna. The group was on a pilgrimage, he said, from Jerusalem, to the Galilee, to Bethlehem, to Mount Sinai.

"Was the experience meaningful?" I asked.

"I'm Catholic, though not a very good one," the man explained. "I believe in God. I believe all the stories. But I don't like public religious things. I prefer to have religion inside, alone. Inside you have silence and mysticism."

"And do you have such feelings here?"

"Here you have the whole story," he said. "You have the view. You have the mountain. It doesn't matter if it's the real mountain. What you have is a memory—a real memory—of what happened here three thousand years ago."

I walked the few steps to the bedouin tent, where Avner was chatting with an old friend, who sat with an unfiltered view of the Sinai, selling drinks and snacks to visiting pilgrims. A cardboard sign behind him read WE HAVE BLANKETS, WE HAVE TEA, WE HAVE HOT CHOCO-LATE AND WOARM PLACE TO SLEEPP. He also had a small water dish next to his hands where birds stopped for a drink. "Sunset and sunrise are the most beautiful time," he said. "But at lunchtime there's nobody here, and that's also a great time."

I asked if he had a particular spot where he liked to go.

"There's a cistern a few steps down," he said. "I built a small chapel there. I go there for three or four hours during lunchtime, alone and quiet."

"And what do you see when you look out from there?"

"I see a lot of calmness," he said. "When the site is very clear, when you have six-by-six sight"—six-by-six is the bedouin equivalent of twenty-twenty, Avner explained—"what you see is not important. It's what you feel that's important."

"And what do you feel?"

"Peace."

I let Avner and his friend continue their conversation and stepped out to the ridge. A late afternoon haze had settled over the mountains. The sun was still yellow despite the dust. As I looked out over the plain—the mountains, the sand, the Gulf of Aqaba, which was now becoming visible on the horizon—I was struck by the similarity of what the engineer from Vienna and the bedouin from the desert had said. Both enjoyed the mountain for its silence, for the feeling of being alone. And yet both were drawn here by others—in the case of the engineer, by the many people who made a similar trek over the centuries, making it such an accessible holy place; in the case of the shopkeeper, by the thousands who continued to come, looking for a moment of peace. And it's that tension—between being with others and being alone, between reaching salvation within a sometimes unruly community and seeking enlightenment on your own—that lies at the heart of the story of Mount Sinai.

At the beginning of Exodus, Moses goes into the desert to escape his community (and his own murderous behavior), but God, speaking to him from the burning bush, at the base of Mount Sinai, sends him back to lead his community. Once he arrives back at the mountain, with the people in tow, the pattern continues. Moses goes off alone, encounters God, then returns to convey God's message, and bring the people along. Once, twice, three times this happens, before the people, thinking Moses has abandoned them, abandon him. And at that moment comes the test. Will Moses follow God's wishes and abandon the people? Will he go off alone and father another great nation, as God offers? The answer, glorious, is no. Moses knows, even more than God seems to know at that moment, that a leader, no matter how great, is nothing without his people. That an individual cannot reach salvation without a community. That the only way for the story to work is for Moses to lead—to inspire—both the people and God. And in that way, the triumph of Mount Sinai is that Moses, in the end, becomes the mountain himself, the link between humanity and the divine.

Equally stunning is that today, three thousand years after the events on Mount Sinai, the legacy of that encounter still manages to thrive on a mountain in the southern Sinai peninsula. In the Bible, Mount Sinai is a physical place that serves as a spiritual emblem. Jebel Musa, regardless of its archaeological pedigree, is the same thing, a physical place that serves as a spiritual symbol. That symbolism is only deepened by the layers of devotion that enshroud the mountain: the monastery at the base, the hermit caves on the side, the chapel on the summit. And perhaps it's those shrines, perhaps the memory of Moses, or perhaps the lingering presence of God, but the place does have a spirit. It's the spirit of the people who came here, struggled to survive, and managed to find a way to believe.

And deep into my trip now, I realized that spirit was unlocking something within me, something that I hadn't even known existed. It was the feeling of the land reaching up to me that I first felt in Turkey. It was the feeling of myself reaching out to the land that I first felt in Karnak Temple. It was the feeling that the spirit in the places and the spirit in me were somehow colluding with one another to circumvent my better judgment and bring me to an entirely different place, a place that seemed, if nothing else, beyond my control. Where was this place?

At the moment, standing on that mountain, staring out at what a pilgrim once called the "sea of petrified waves," I had no idea. I also, for the first time, felt any fear of that place drift away. I watched, instead, oddly comforted, as the sun set behind me and the shadow of the mountain stretched out before me, drawing slowly, slowly, over the cliffs, onto the sand, and finally to the water's edge, pointing ever so slightly toward the northeast, and to the promise to come.

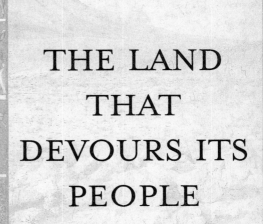

Book IV

THE LAND
THAT
DEVOURS ITS
PEOPLE

1 . Wandering

Firrst, you get thirsty. You wake up thinking about water. You go to bed thinking about water. You walk, talk, and eat thinking about water. You dream of water. You wonder, "Do I have enough water?" "Am I drinking enough water?" "Where is the water?" But you stay calm. You know water. You know how much water you need. Twelve liters a day. Or is that thirteen? And what if it's hot? Does that mean more? What if it's windy, does that mean less? Just drink. Drink when you're thirsty. Drink when you're not thirsty. Because *"If you're thirsty, it's too late."* And you're thirsty. So that's bad. But you know yourself. And you know water. So you tell yourself, "I can go longer than most people." But you're wrong. Everybody needs water. Needs it now. Go wandering in the desert, for days, weeks, or forty years at a time, and water becomes the most important thing, the only thing. Water becomes life. Becomes salvation. "The fountain of wisdom is a flowing stream," says the Proverbs. "With thee is the fountain of life," adds the Psalms. Or, as God puts it, in Isaiah 55, "Oh, all you who thirst, come to the waters . . . incline your ear and come to me."

Next, you get hungry. And you stay hungry. Your first few days in the desert, you have remnants of the city, a bit of chocolate, a cookie, an apple. You eat these in diminishing portions, and with increasing relish. You've outwitted the desert. You've brought the fleshpots with you. But then the desert wins. That piece of chocolate you've been saving melts. The cookie crumbles. The apple rots. You're left to the ground, which is a cruel resort. You're left to your provisions. You eat breakfast—bread, cheese, tuna, honey. You eat lunch—honey, tuna, cheese, bread. You eat dinner—the same. Traveling in the desert would be ideal for five-year-olds: Every meal you eat is identical. Inevitably, though, the routine tires. The sameness grates. It's then, as with water, that food becomes more. It becomes metaphor. "They asked, and he brought them quail," says the Psalms, "and he gave them bread from heaven." Food, like water, becomes a way to salvation. As Philo notes, "The soul is fed not with things of the earth, which are perishable, but with such words as God shall have poured like rain out of that supernal and pure region of life to which the prophet has given the title of 'heaven.'"

Finally, you get tired. You get tired of the heat. You get tired of the cold. But mostly you get tired of the sand. Sand is relentless. It goes through your shoes, through your socks, and lodges in between your toes. It seeps through your pants, through your underwear, and gloms on to places it ought never to see. It penetrates your windbreaker, gets under your shirt, and sticks to anything with hair. It infiltrates your food, sticks onto your teeth, and passes eventually into your stomach. And as a result, whenever you expel anything from your body, it comes with a blasting of sand. Sand in the desert is like rain in Britain: Sometimes it storms, sometimes it sprinkles, but most of the time it just hangs in the air and waits for you to walk into it. Thus, sand, like water and food, becomes cause for misery. And out of this agony comes meaning. "The wilderness is the most miserable of all places," the sages said. "Having received the Torah there, Israel could take it to the deprived of the earth, and from lowliness ascend to the heights." Who preserves the Torah? the sages asked. "He who makes himself like the desert: set apart from the world."

Spend enough time in the desert, and you begin to see that nothing is quite what it seems to be. Water becomes wisdom. Food becomes salvation. And sandstorms become poetry. Everything, in other words, becomes grist for allegory. As Moses tells the Israelites near the end of their journey: "Remember the long way that the Lord your God has made you travel in the wilderness these past 40 years, that he might test you by hardships to learn what was in your hearts." Today, almost three thousand years since those words were written, the appeal of the desert remains the same. By its sheer demands—thirst, hunger, misery—it asks a simple question: "What is in your heart?" Or, put another way, "In what do you believe?"

Those questions would dominate the last half of our trip, as they dominate the last half of the Pentateuch. The final three Books of Moses—Leviticus, Numbers, Deuteronomy—tell the story of the forty years the Israelites spend in the desert following their receiving of the Ten Commandments. These books contain far less narrative than Genesis and Exodus and far more discourse on how to behave. Leviticus is given over entirely to a seemingly interminable litany of laws covering such topics as how long a woman must remain segregated after giving birth—seven days for a boy; two weeks for a girl—to how one should dispose of a bull after sacrificing it to the Lord: "The priest shall remove all the fat from the bull: the fat that covers the entrails and all the fat that is about the entrails; the two kidneys and the fat that is on them; and the protuberance on the liver, which he shall remove with the kidneys. The priest shall turn them into smoke on the altar of burnt offering." But the hide of the bull, it continues, "and all its flesh, as well as its head and legs, entrails and dung, he shall carry to a clean place outside the camp, to the ash heap, and burn it up with wood."

The Bible, in other words, which contains some of the most moving narrative passages in the history of literature, suddenly slows to a dead stop, a filibuster of legislative minutiae. As commentator Everett Fox has written: "It is as if a history of the American Revolution contained all of the debates on and drafts of the Declaration of Independence and the Constitution, as well as accounts of battles and biographies of key personalities." That such an approach parallels neither Homeric epic nor other ancient texts is precisely the point, Fox concludes. "We have here a new genre of great complexity and richness, in which narratives exemplify laws and laws follow narratives. The result is truly a torah, a 'teaching' or 'instruction.' "

The narrative resumes in Numbers as the Israelites depart Mount Sinai and begin the long trek toward the Promised Land. Our plan on this leg was to follow this path by moving north from Jebel Musa into the central zone of the Sinai, the so-called Wandering Plateau, before proceeding into the Negev. We left Jebel Musa at dawn and began our gradual drive northeast. The mountains, bulging like potato sacks, began to thin and shorten a bit. The big sky returned, once more dominating the landscape like one of those children's drawings with sky and clouds covering most of the page and a thin line of ground along the bottom. Close to midday now, and several hours from Saint Catherine's, we pulled to a stop on a charred plateau just off the highway. Small pieces of flint covered the ground like debris cast off from the carving of an oversized sculpture. Avner picked up a piece, which was smooth on the top and sharp on the edges, like an arrowhead. He tossed it about twenty-five yards toward the open terrain. It landed with a tinkle and came to a stop. "See anything special there?" he asked.

"No," I said.

"Look again."

Stepping forward, I began to detect a gathering of large, standing stones emerging out of the landscape like a family of deer materializing out of the brush. The five stones averaged about six feet tall, with the middle one slightly taller, and were arranged in a half circle like basketball players waiting for the tip-off. The effect was like Stonehenge, only smaller. "This is a cult corner," Avner explained. "It's probably a sacrificial site for people who buried their dead nearby." But for our purposes, he said, it's even more important. These stones are what the Bible calls *matzevah* (or *matzevot,* in the plural), which translations refer to as stelae or pillars. They appear in various places throughout the Bible and embody one of the more vexing struggles in the biblical narrative: the battle between monotheism and paganism.

The delivery of the Ten Commandments on Mount Sinai has always been understood as the crowning achievement of monotheism, the final sealing of the bond between the people of Israel and their God. But like all matters related to the Bible, the truth is not that simple. As many commentators have noted, a close reading of the text suggests there were two principal phases in the development of Israelite religion: the patriarchal phase and the Mosaic phase. In the first phase, the patriarchs most likely viewed their god, Elohim, as being similar to El, the primary god of Canaan, who appears to the patriarchs as a friend and sometimes even assumes human form.

The God of Moses, by contrast, whom the text refers to as Yahweh, is a much more violent and stormy deity, who appears in the guise of smoke, fire, and lightning. While the God of Abraham destroys the city of Sodom, the God of Moses reaps havoc on the entire *country* of Egypt, later gives the Israelites permission to do the same in Canaan, and in between is forever threatening to vanquish the Israelites and begin anew with a different people. Several times he exacts a demanding purge on his own chosen people.

There is another change from the patriarchs to Moses. Whereas Genesis makes no mention of tensions between the patriarchs and their neighbors over religion, Exodus explicitly says that God is in competition with other gods. With the plagues, for example, the war on paganism becomes paramount, as God promises to mete out punishment to the "gods of Egypt." This conflict is deeply embedded in the Ten Commandments, which clearly assume the presence of other gods. As God states: "You shall have no other gods beside Me. You shall not make for yourself a sculptured image, or any likeness of what is in the heavens above, or on the earth below, or in the waters under the earth. You shall not bow down to them or serve them." There would be no need for this commandment if this practice were not common at the time.

Even the *shema*, the holiest words in Judaism and what one commentator calls "the great text of monotheism," seems to imply that other gods exist. The traditional translation is "Hear, O Israel! The Lord is our God. The Lord is One." But the words, which come from Deuteronomy 6, are considered vague by Bible scholars and are often translated today as "Hear, O Israel! The Lord is our God, the Lord alone." God, the words suggest, should stand apart and above other gods, meaning he is the superior god but not the *only* god.

The ever-shifting interaction between the God of Israel and the gods of neighboring cultures is embodied by the *matzevot,* the standing stones. The ones we were viewing date from the fourth millennium

B.C.E., but the Bible uses them later, during the time of the patriarchs. In Genesis, after Jacob has the dream in which he sees the angels on the ladder, he erects a *matzevah*. "And this stone, which I have set up as a pillar, shall be God's abode." He repeats the gesture later, when God renews his promise to bestow the Promised Land to Jacob and his descendants. "And Jacob set up a pillar at the site where He had spoken to him, a pillar of stone, and he offered a libation on it and poured oil upon it." In these stories, Avner noted, the stones mark a holy location, a sort of notarization of the communication between God and Jacob.

"Isn't this pagan?" I asked.

"I wouldn't say that. I would say that this is part of a language used by all the people of the Mediterranean. Therefore it appeared in the Bible."

"But these stones are essentially the land," I said. "These are rocks. That's the ground. And they become symbolic of God. That's pagan, isn't it?"

"Yeessss," he said, tentatively.

"Isn't the whole point of the Ten Commandments 'Don't make graven images of God'? Leviticus explicitly warns against constructing *matzevot*."

"That's why in the text it never says that such stelae should represent God. But the reality is, sometimes they did, even after the Ten Commandments were given."

"So as a practical matter," I said, "these *matzevot* are a transitional step between paganism, which said that God existed in the rock, to something more abstract, which said that God needs no representation."

"You must remember," Avner said, "monotheism went one step beyond the existing understanding of God, but it didn't change the whole concept of daily life: that the world was created out of water, that it was created in a certain order, that a flood followed. Those details show that certain features were shared across the area by all people of the region. So the Israelites, even when they became monotheistic, did not pull themselves out of the world entirely. They were part of the world. They just trumped the world with the larger idea of God."

As he spoke, I began to realize how much conversations like this had altered my view of the Bible. On the one hand, they shattered a host of childhood myths I still clung to about the story—that Noah put all the animals into the ark, that hundreds of thousands of Israelites crossed the Red Sea, that the patriarchs believed in only one God. On the other hand, those myths were being replaced with new ideas, far more complex, but no less compelling. If anything, this new framework made the Bible *more* intriguing to me as an adult. Flood stories exist in many cultures; the Bible simply recast its version to include God's disappointment with humanity. The Exodus may have involved a smaller number of people and occurred over a longer period of time, but its historical significance is in no way diminished by this fact; and its literary significance may even be magnified. Dispelling childhood illusions may have been painful, but discovering adult nuances can be palliative—even restorative. I didn't have to feel juvenile, or willfully naive, to be interested in the Bible. I could embrace it as a sign of health—and maturity.

This was nowhere more true than with the issue of the Israelites and their monotheistic God. "One of the things I've taken away from this whole endeavor," I said to Avner, "is that the Bible is not a direct line: the triumph of the Israelites, the rise of monotheism. Instead, it's one step forward, two steps back. Three steps forward, two steps back."

"True for today as well."

"But why?" I said. "Why was it so hard to accept the notion of an abstract God?"

"Because you have to be capable of having such an abstract notion *and* living with it daily. That's not always so easy. Look at today. In Christianity and Judaism, there are many examples of representations of God: building sculptures of Jesus, putting faxes into the Western Wall. Are you faxing your prayer directly to God?"

"Not necessarily," I said. "You're not worshiping the stone. The stone is just the representation of a holy place."

"Okay, that's a nice way to put it. So it is with the *matzevot*. Even monotheism needs its monuments."

We drove north to the Ain Khudra Valley, a wide, winding former riverbed dominated by a sandy floor with sheer sandstone walls on either side. The crumbling brown cliffs reminded me of one of those ready-made graham cracker piecrusts. We unloaded at an oasis and decided to hike across the valley floor, eventually climbing up a steep path to visit the Written Stone, a free-standing rock with numerous inscriptions in Nabatean, Greek, and Latin. There we would meet up with our jeep and camp for the evening.

Compared with the mountain air, the atmosphere was thick, filled with heat and dust. Also the glare was more pronounced, as the light bounced off the sand in starbursts. The desert was not only one of the least quiet places I'd ever been but also one of the most alive, with particles leaping and jumping, as if they wanted to transform themselves, kaleidoscope-like, into a different formation. Look long enough at one patch of sand and the effect is like watching an ant colony under a strobe light. Before long, you find yourself asking: "Is it really changing, or am I?"

In time we reached the end of the valley and began climbing the path, which was like a scratch of white on the otherwise sandy cliff face, as if someone had taken a knife and carved an S in the skin of a Bosc pear. This was a camel path, Avner said, as opposed to one for donkeys or goats. Camel paths are less steep because of the animals' size and deeper because of their weight. Camel dung is also bigger—and lighter—than that of donkeys and goats. When all else fails, follow the camels; they're blazing superhighways through the sand.

We reached the top and settled onto a rock. It was clear we were now in a transitional area. The granite mountains of the south were behind us; the sandstone cliffs of the center were around us. Soon we would enter a flatland, with few of the extremes in height or climate, but none of the water runoff from the mountains, either. Here was the broad emptiness of the desert; here, for travelers, is the true test of the land.

Considering the drama the Israelites had already faced by this point—crossing the Red Sea, receiving the Ten Commandments, implementing the laws—it seems surprising to read at the beginning of Numbers that they have been in the desert for only little more than a year. Specifically, on the twentieth day of the second month of the second year since the Exodus, a cloud that God has been using to shelter the Israelites lifts from the Tabernacle, and the population sets out on its journey from Mount Sinai. The group marches according to tribes. There are twelve tribes in all. Ten of them—Asher, Dan, Naphtali, Issachar, Judah, Zebulun, Gad, Reuben, Simeon, and Benjamin—are sons of Jacob. The final two—Manasseh and Ephraim—are sons of Joseph. (The descendants of Jacob's other son, Levi, serve as priests.) The tribes carry the Tabernacle, which contains the Ark of the Covenant. Whenever the Ark sets out, Moses proclaims, "Advance, O Lord! May Your enemies be scattered, and may Your foes flee before You!"

No sooner do the Israelites begin their travels than they begin to complain—to Moses, to God, to anyone who will listen. This act of grousing begins a distinct cycle in the Book of Numbers, generally called the rebellion narratives, in which the Israelites proceed through a series of attempted coups d'état—six or seven, depending on how you count—that will dominate, and ultimately lengthen, their trek to the Promised Land. In the first of these incidents, no reason is given for the Israelites' grumbling. Nonetheless, God becomes incensed and sends a fire that ravages the outskirts of the camp. The people cry out to Moses, who prays to God for peace. The fire retreats. "That place was called Taberah," the Bible says, from the Hebrew word for burn, "because a fire of the Lord had broken out against them."

"Now look around," Avner said. He pointed to a few of the cliffs on this upper shelf above the valley, which were coated with what looked like a wash of India ink. The debris at the base of these cliffs looked especially dark. "Early visitors said this must be Taberah," he said.

"This place does look like a pretty burnt landscape," I said.

In no time the Israelites find another reason to complain: They're hungry. The "riffraff" in their midst feel a gluttonous craving, crying, "If only we had meat to eat!" They remember the fish they ate in Egypt, along with the cucumbers, melons, leeks, onions, and garlic. "Now our gullets are shriveled," they shriek. "Nothing but this manna to look to!" Moses, feeling the plight of his people, appeals to God, saying, "Why have You dealt ill with Your servant, and why have I not enjoyed Your favor, that You have laid the burden of all this people upon me?" Where can he get meat for his people, Moses asks. God appears to relent, instructing Moses to gather seventy elders and to tell the people that the next day they shall eat meat; but God gets angry. "You shall eat not one day," God says, nor two, five, ten, or twenty, "but a whole month, until it comes out of your nostrils and becomes loathsome to you. For you have rejected the Lord, who is among you." Moses questions God's ability to provide enough meat for the entire six hundred thousand men, but God retorts, "Is there a limit to the Lord's power?"

God summons a wind, sweeping quail from the sea, and strewing them over the camp, until they cover an area that's a day's walk in either direction and two cubits deep, or about three feet. The people gather quail for two days, until each gathers ten *homers,* an amount estimated at between fifty and one hundred bushels. God is outraged by their gluttony. "The meat was still between their teeth, not yet chewed, when the anger of the Lord blazed forth against the people and the Lord struck the people with a very severe plague. That place was named Kibroth-hattaavah"—the Graves of Craving—"because the people who had the craving were buried there."

The phenomenon of the quail, Avner noted, like manna, has a curious natural correlative in the Sinai that suggests the story may have roots in reality. Huge flocks of quail, *Coturnix coturnix,* migrate every autumn from Europe to Central Africa and return in the spring. The birds are often so exhausted by this flight that they drop, near-dead, in the hundreds along the northern coastline of Egypt and the Sinai. Diners at sidewalk cafés in Egyptian coastal towns like Alexandria and Port Said occasionally report being "invaded" by quail, and bedouin in the Sinai report that the quail occasionally land so thick on the ground there is no room for more, unless they alight on others' backs. Avner told of seeing bedouin setting up elaborate nets over the shore to catch the falling birds before they could get waterlogged. Given this phenomenon, some scientists have suggested that the death of the Israelites after eating the quail can be attributed to a rare ornithological disease the birds carried after ingesting a poisonous fungus in the Nile Valley.

Regardless, it seems safe to assume that biblical storytellers knew about this occurrence—either because they passed through the northern Sinai, or because they lived in the Delta for hundreds of years and witnessed it there. "It did come every year," Avner said. Still, the birds rarely reach this far south, he noted. "If you believe the quail are based in reality, you really shouldn't believe that Jebel Musa is Mount Sinai."

"Not necessarily," I said. At this point, I was less inclined to accept a sterile, naturalistic explanation for every event, particularly when it threatened to undermine the meaning of the story. I was more interested in how the writers took possibly factual occurrences and shaped them with spiritual objectives. To overlook those objectives was to overlook the stories' undeniable source of power. As a practical matter, Avner may not have changed, but I had, in effect, slid around him and was now having conversations from a new point of view. While I didn't necessarily *believe* every story, I had become, in essence, a defender of the story, particularly its moral imperative. I had become an advocate of God.

In the case of the quail, that meant going back to the Bible and noticing that the text implies that the deluge wasn't *entirely* natural, and that God played a pivotal role. "The story says God summoned a wind," I said, reading now from the page, "'swept the quails from the sea, and strewed them over the camp.' If the Israelites were in the north, where the quail fall anyway, the wind would not have been needed. Divine intervention is key to the story."

"Okay," Avner said. "Plus, this top layer of rock does look like charcoal here, and it doesn't up north."

"If you didn't know it was igneous rock, you might think it's burnt rock."

"Burnt by God."

We packed up our Bibles and set out through the sand for the Written Stone. The ground was coarser here and sparkled less than the floor of the valley. The sun was starting to set. In the distance were some small bedouin huts. We walked about fifteen minutes when suddenly a small stream of people came pouring out of the huts—first children, then teenagers, finally some older women with toddlers on their hips. *"Abunar!"* they shouted. *"Abunar! Abunar!"* It was the call I had seen numerous times before—in the desert, in oases, in villages. Once a car passed us on the road going seventy-five miles per hour, came screeching to a stop, then turned around and chased us for several miles—just so one of the people in the truck could give Avner a kiss hello. Even twenty years after he left, in an open election for president of the Sinai, Avner would win hands down. The reason, I was coming to see, was that he respected the bedouin, gave them work, dignified their culture, and, simply, listened. And he did it with a grace that few before, and certainly fewer after him, had shown. Avner didn't need to pretend he was one of them, as Lawrence had done. He simply became a part of their world.

Within seconds of greeting us, the women insisted we stop for tea, and we walked the short distance to their small huddle of homes. Having invited us, however, the women promptly disappeared out of custom, and we proceeded toward the fire, where a small handful of men, ranging in age from forty to seventy-five, were gathered in evening senate. Their faces were rich with weather and age, with skin the color of cordovan, and whiskers that sprouted black and white in thinning mustaches or faint goatees. None had more than a few teeth. We shook hands, kissed on the cheeks, and sat down. Dusk enveloped us.

Though desert gatherings like this happen spontaneously, they still have a strict choreography, as nuanced as a Japanese tea ceremony. The oldest man in the group, with black sunglasses held together by a rubber band, picked up a few glasses that were slightly larger than shot glasses, though more ornate, the shape of morning lilies. He tucked the glasses in between the fingers of his left hand, plucked the teakettle from the fire with his right hand, and poured a small bit of tea into one of the glasses. After replacing the kettle, he rubbed his callused fingers around the rim of one glass to clean it, then poured the backwash tea into successive glasses, repeating his ablution like an elaborate fountain-cum-dishwasher that in its ability to keep the glasses apart and not spill the tea seemed akin to baton twirling. When he finished, the man splashed the used tea onto the sand and handed me an empty glass. "Don't pass it," Avner whispered. I held it just above the sand and waited for the others to receive theirs, at which point the man reclaimed the kettle from the fire and began to pour the tea, starting with me and moving in the same direction as he had distributed the glasses. The kettle was made of brass, lined with tin, and was dented in various places. It was also entirely covered in soot, the color of perpetual use.

When each of us had his serving, the old man replaced the kettle on the fire, mumbled a brief blessing, and we drew the glasses to our lips, sipping the piping hot liquid, which had the consistency, and taste, of maple bouillon. Molten manna would not be sweeter. Since no one could tolerate more than a few sips at a time—either for the heat or for the sweetness, I could never tell—the older man buried his glass a half inch in the sand and the rest of us followed. For twenty minutes no one spoke. Instead we just watched, and listened to, the fire. It was the most economical fire I had ever seen, with two wormwood logs the size of hot dog buns, flaked with white charcoal like dandruff, and barely concealing a searing red core that instead of emanating heat seemed to draw us closer, as if drawing heat from us. If most fires seem confident, this one seemed tentative, as if to ask, "Will I make it through the night? Do you have enough wood for me?"

The answer, of course, was not really. Wood, like most resources in the desert, is almost impossible to find.

The life of the bedouin in the modern Middle East—in the Sinai, the Negev, and Arabia—is a study in what it means to exist in the breach between urban and desert environments, and may be as close as contemporary observers come to understanding what the Israelites must have experienced during their two generations in the wilderness. The bedouin—who number about sixty thousand in the Sinai, one hundred thousand in Israel, and more in Saudi Arabia—are pure Arabs, descended from tribes of the Hejaz, the western region of the Arabian peninsula along the Red Sea. Traditionally, they move in tribal groups, search for grazing areas in the desert for their animals, and settle around oases. They're not pure nomads, who wander continually without pattern. Instead they're pastoralists, who move into the desert following the spring rains, when there is more vegetation for their goats, then drift back into settled areas in autumn, when they must rely on stable sources of water.

As Emanuel Marx, Israel's leading expert on bedouin life, explained to me, the bedouin are entirely dependent on settled areas for trade, income, and many of the staples of their daily life, especially the grains that make up the bulk of their diet. If anything, they are urban satellites, he said, more accurately viewed as tangents of city life than residents of the wild. In some cases they sell their meat and wool to the cities in return for provisions. In other cases they actually work in economies that link the desert to the settled areas, such as tourism. "You think that these are people living in the desert, which they aren't," he said. "You think that these people are only raising animals, which they don't. You think that these are people who are self-sufficient, but they're not."

Because of their intimate relationship with the land, the bedouin view of the desert is much different from ours. "What they call the desert," Professor Marx said, "is a place where resources are in different places. You walk in one place. You graze in another place. You raise date palms in a third. They think of the desert as a place they can always fall back on. It has a lot of range, and a lot of resources."

"So the Western notion of the desert as emptiness would seem to them . . ."

"They would consider it very strange," he said. "Even the Hebrew term *midbar,* which is translated as wilderness, is derived from the word for grazing. So in bedouin terms, the desert is a land where you graze animals. If you translate it as savanna, it would make much more sense."

"So you're saying that the bedouin term for desert is closer to the English word *savanna*?"

"In terms of inner meaning, yes."

"But when I think of a savanna I think of a grassy plain. Certainly none of the places we're talking about—the Sinai, the Negev—is a grassy plain."

"We also call savannas places where there are trees, spread widely over an area. In this part of the world, that's a desert."

This cozy feeling toward the desert exists, in part, because the bedouin have developed extraordinarily sophisticated ways of thriving in that environment. In effect, the bedouin have learned to read the desert. Hares and foxes lead them to water; jackals and hyena lead them to higher ground. They also know how to whittle the environment into

daily tools. Goatskins make good canteens; hyrax skins make good cur-
dling bags; almond, castor, and quince wood make good camel saddles.
Desert plants also produce powerful medicine. Boiled lavender tends to
eye infections; wild mint balms earaches; wormwood broth is good for
headaches. Perhaps the most elaborate desert cure is that for rheuma-
tism, which the bedouin address by cooking the meat of hyenas. The
full treatment involves enclosing the patient in a tent in which hyena
meat and bones are burned. The patient drinks the broth of the meat,
covers himself in blankets until he sweats profusely, then emerges
twenty-four hours later, able "to climb mountains with ease."

Perhaps more important, the bedouin respond to the harshness of
desert conditions with a fulsome tradition of hospitality. As one
bedouin saying goes, "Had I known that you would honor me by walking this way, I should have strewn the path between your house and
mine with mint and rose petals." The bedouin philosophy of hospitality
is simple: host first, ask questions later. This custom is reflected in several
places in the Bible, notably in Genesis just before the story of Sodom
and Gomorrah, when Abraham invites the three unknown visitors into
his tent and asks his wife to welcome them with provisions. Not until
later does he realize they are emissaries from God.

Bedouin hospitality customarily lasts for three days (which today are
sometimes simulated with three glasses of tea). The first stage is called
salaam, or greeting; the second *ta'aam,* or eating; the third *kelaam,* or
speaking. Though this welcome mat is laid out without condition or
prejudice, before the rising of the morning star on the fourth day hosts
help their guests prepare for departure. Tarriers who linger beyond the
drying of the dew are "as welcome as the spotted snake." Such openness, inevitably, comes at a cost, particularly with precious resources.
When our hosts that afternoon insisted we stay for dinner, Avner would
agree only if they promised not to slaughter a lamb, a traditional but
costly expression of respect. The men insisted, Avner remained firm,
and fifteen minutes of peacock preening later, they finally agreed to his
request. Dinner was a large platter of rice, with mushrooms and vegetables, which we plucked with flatbread, using only our right hands. "You
eat like bedu!" the men cheered.

And sleep like them, too. By the time we finished dinner the familiar chill of the desert had returned, and we all had reclined somewhat in our places, drinking our bottomless glass of tea. The circle had expanded somewhat, with several more men and some boys joining us for dinner, as well as Yusuf, our driver. The women remained out of sight. Nearby, a few camels were eating barley out of sacks around their necks. Eventually, when we made noises about driving a few miles away to a campsite, one of the men, Ahmed, insisted we stay with him. Again a brief Kabuki followed, but this time Avner agreed. We said good night to the others, walked the short distance to Ahmed's home, and began to unload our bags. As we did, Ahmed went inside to inform his wife.

For generations, bedouin lived exclusively in goat-hair tents, called *beit shaar*, or "house of hair," which they took with them as they migrated from location to location. Women have traditionally been responsible for the tents, their weaving, striking, packing, and erecting. In bedouin divorces, the husband keeps the animals, the wife keeps the tent. In recent years, some bedouin have been taking the money they receive from work as migrant laborers or in the tourist trade and begun building modest homes. Ahmed's home was a prime example of this shift toward more permanent habitation. It was small, about the size of a two-car garage, but well constructed, using unpainted concrete blocks and tin roofing. Half the house was taken up by an open-roofed living area that had only sand for a floor, and the other half taken up by a small kitchen area and two raised bedrooms, one for the man and his wife, the other for their five children. This area had a cement floor and a tin roof.

After rooting out the kids and sending them to a neighbor's, Ahmed sat with us on the step to his bedroom and discussed his masterwork, now just two years old. He was a slight man, wearing flip-flops and a thin white robe. He wore one white kaffiyeh around his head, and another around his neck, as a scarf. I asked him how he had chosen this spot.

"I had a house next to my father, in another area," he said. "About ten years ago there was a strong flash flood and the whole valley flooded to the level of two meters. Lucky for us, it came during the daytime and no one was home, or they would have been washed away. If it had come at night, we would have died."

Ahmed decided to move, and chose this spot because it was high enough that it would not be imperiled in a flash flood. He marked the area, laid out the walls, and brought a builder to help construct it. He built a foundation of limestone, on top of which he placed cement, which he purchased in forty sacks from the city and mixed with water from the well.

"It's become more and more expensive to build in the open valley, away from the cities," he said. "A house like this costs two thousand Egyptian pounds," or about $750.

Every house has the character of the person who designed it, I suggested. How did his house reflect his character?

"In the old days, when my father was young, there were no houses. Only tents. Tents meant moving from place to place. They were not a stable place to stay: Today you were here, tomorrow you were there. But now you have a stable, sturdy place. I think we are a more stable people."

"But is that bedouin?" I asked.

"Sure," he said. "Being bedouin is not about moving all the time. It's about being open to nature. It's about being open to people. Look at this house. It's open. In the morning and the night it is open. In the summer and the winter it is open. We are always open."

"So what feature of this house are you most proud of?" I asked.

He chuckled. "Maybe you understand," he said. "If you have such a house, your wife is pleased, so you are pleased. I think it's the same everywhere you go."

We spent the night on the floor of Ahmed's second room, and the following morning lingered over a traditional bedouin breakfast—bread, cheese, honey, tea. They seemed not to favor canned tuna; or maybe we had depleted the Sinai's reserves. Either way, by the time we viewed the inscriptions of the Written Stone, which early scholars also attempted to attribute to the Israelites (although its inscriptions turn out to date from much later), it was nearing noon. We were late getting started for a daylong hike that Avner said might be an elaborate detour, but proved to be an unexpected looking glass through which to catch a glimpse of ancient Israel.

While he was chief archaeologist of the Sinai, Avner initiated a variety of projects. Many involved excavating and restoring known archaeological sites like Serabit el-Khadim, the pharaonic temple near the turquoise mines. A few involved preserving historical sites like Saint Catherine's. On one occasion, though, he discovered a site of such profound historical and archaeological importance that it not only challenged conventions about the Bible and the ancient Near East, but also raised provocative questions about the course of human evolution.

The discovery almost never happened. One day some bedouin whom Avner knew in the area came to him and announced, "We have found this magical place." With the bedouin, of course, this could have meant almost anything—a mountain, an oasis, a cave—but Avner knew enough to follow their hunch, and the place they led him to proved to be an unknown gem of early man, overlooked by hundreds of years of explorers. Petrie, the great Egyptologist, had been two hundred yards away, but had never made it to the cliffs overlooking an isolated plateau. It's possible the bedouin knew of the site for decades but waited to tell someone they trusted. By the time we arrived, I could understand their protectiveness. Even after weeks of inaccessible sites, this was one of the more inaccessible. The terrain had a dusting of chipped stone, like burnt almonds, similar to the ground around the *matzevah*. In late afternoon, the sky had a pearl sheen to it, like the inside of a shell, light along the horizon, darker on the top.

As we approached, nothing appeared distinctive about the site. But once we climbed up the small cliff, a remarkable scene unfolded, with two dozen round huts, like stone igloos, spread out over an area the size of two football fields. Each hut was about shoulder high, constructed with overlapping slabs of sandstone, with an open mouth like a doghouse. The sides were constructed with corbeled stones that supported a stone roof. From afar, each shack looked like a giant hamburger, or, more accurately, the contents of a can of tuna. I had never seen anything like them.

Nor had anyone else, it turns out. The bedouin name for these con-
structions, which were duplicated in several nearby sites, was *nawamis,*
which means mosquitoes. The bedouin told Avner they were constructed by the Israelites during the Exodus when they needed a place
to escape the mosquitoes. Excavation, however, revealed that the
nawamis were far older, from the mid-fourth millennium B.C.E., a thousand years earlier than the pyramids, and 2,500 years before the Israelites
passed anywhere close. The *nawamis* are now considered the oldest
structures with intact roofs ever found on earth, perfectly preserved
remnants of a six-thousand-year-old culture that may represent the
world's first pastoral society.

The purpose of these structures, Avner and his team concluded, was
not residential, but funereal. Since pastoral tribes never stayed in one
place for very long, members temporarily buried their loved ones in the
desert where they died. The tribe would then return the following year
to claim the bones and move them to a permanent burial spot. These
bones were then interred in the *nawamis* in family groupings, along with
ostrich-egg jewelry, small jugs of oil, and other household items. The
deceased would have needed these commodities, Avner said, because
the afterlife was considered a physical continuation of life on earth. Six
thousand years later, the bedouin continue to honor the memory of the
deceased: During Avner's excavation, his workers refused to enter the
tombs.

We did enter, though. Avner went first, and I followed. As with
the hermit's cave on Jebel Musa, I had to back in, squeezing my backside
in first, then my torso and head, and finally my legs. The ground was
sandy inside and the space barely large enough for two men to sit cross-
legged. The construction was remarkably tight, and may have been
waterproof had there been any water. As it was, almost no light seeped
through the cracks in the layered stone walls or roof. The structure
could have been on the cover of an *Architectural Digest* special issue,
"Best Buildings Before Buildings Were Invented."

Once inside, when my heart stopped racing, Avner began to explain
how discovering the *nawamis* had changed his view of ancient history
and, in turn, the Bible. As a student at university, he said, he had learned

that evolution was a largely linear process, with mankind progressing from nomadic hunter-gatherers to settled, farming populations around the time of the agricultural revolution about eleven thousand years ago. This was true, he noted, for all areas where populations had regular access to water and could raise crops. Some areas of the world, though, were only semiarid at the time; they could support grasses and other vegetation, but not large-scale cultivation. In succeeding millennia, because of climatic changes, these areas became deserts. In the Near East, people who were obliged to live in these areas—usually because they were denied access to urban communities, or because they never learned how to farm—were forced to develop alternate means of survival. The easiest way was to learn to raise animals in the desert, usually goats, and trade the by-product, wool, with the settled areas in return for provisions.

"For the first time in the history of mankind," Avner continued, "there was this split among people. There was a society of farmers; there was a society of pastoralists. This view goes against the theory that evolution in society is linear."

Each group related to the environment in different ways. As Avner summed up the divergence: "Those in agricultural areas used technology to change the world around them. They changed it by plowing, seeding, planting, domesticating animals. The strategy of the pastoralists was to adapt themselves to the environment. That's why all their tombs face east, for example, to get warm as early as possible in the morning."

Also, they developed strong tribal bonds—bonds that can still be seen in desert cultures of today. "I don't know if I ever told you," Avner said, "but when I was in the Sinai, we made a documentary about the bedouin legal system. We asked one person to play the judge, and another the judged. One man volunteered to play the criminal, and we asked, 'What ill have you done?' He said, 'I approached a girl while she was grazing goats.' 'And what did you do?' we asked. Well, he didn't hug her, or rape her, or anything. He asked her to make him tea!"

The point was, Avner said, the man had embarrassed his family by his action. He had behaved in a non-bedouin way: being selfish at the expense of customary rules for interaction. "When you live in the desert," Avner said, "there is no way to guarantee that once you leave your community, no one will come steal your animals, or stab you. But no one *will* do that, because that bedouin is not alone. Even though he's physically walking alone, he's under a huge umbrella of his brothers, his uncles, his nephews. He's in the middle of a pyramid of five generations. If there's an evil done by anyone, you could endanger not only yourself but the whole group."

In the end, it's that quality of desert culture—its community, its stickiness—that is most striking to an outsider, and the most inspiring. It's also the part of living in the desert that emerges most powerfully from the stories of the Bible. The desert is somehow *necessary* for the Israelites. Viewing the *nawamis* offered one powerful reason why. Abraham likely lived his life as a pastoralist, moving from settled areas into unsettled areas and back again in a never-ending stream. In his case the settled areas were not always the same—he spent time in, among others, Ur, Harran, Shechem, Beer-sheba, and Gerar—but the basic outlines of his life were pastoralist, involving herds, tents, and grazing conflicts with the settled communities. (Some scholars use the term *pastoral nomads* to describe the patriarchs, since their lifestyle includes some element of nomadism—linear wandering—with the seasonal migration patterns of pastoralists.) Isaac and Jacob follow similar paths.

With Joseph, though, and his offspring, the Israelites become fully settled in Egypt. After their escape, but *before* they are allowed to settle their own society, God forces them to spend forty years—two generations—in the desert, moving in a cycle of wandering and settling that are also clearly pastoralist in nature. By forcing the Israelites to pass through this phase, God, in essence, interrupts the linear flow of evolution, reversing the Israelites' seemingly inexorable rise to nationhood, and making them revisit—and *reclaim*—some of the wisdom of their desert forefathers.

This act of reconnecting with the past, I was starting to realize, is largely what I was undergoing on my trip through the desert as well. I was wriggling free from the firm grip of modern life and inching toward something else, something more instinctive and untaught. I was breaking away from modes of thought I had used since I was a teenager—reason, skepticism, logic, *learning*—and moving toward modes of relating to the world—emotion, intuition, trust—that I probably hadn't relied on so much since I was a child. In doing so, I felt myself slide farther away from the rigid, controlled person I was at the beginning of this process. I was less of an upright wooden chair, to use the local vernacular, and more of a roll-out carpet. I was conforming to the land.

I could see this change in how I related to the text. In the early months I was consumed with the factual foundations of the stories—Near Eastern mythology, land routes from Egypt to Mesopotamia. Then I moved toward trying to understand the power of the stories, the motivation of the characters, and their evolving relationship with God. Now I was in a different place entirely. I was much more interested in trying to grasp the underlying, raw human emotion involved in being in a stark place, confronting the limitations of one's upbringing, and trying to forge a new identity in the midst of a difficult, transforming journey. Understanding this transition—which, after all, lies at the heart of the Five Books of Moses—required, for me at least, a new approach. I couldn't quantify whatever I learned; I couldn't prove it, or even document it. I could only feel it, and hope that by experiencing it myself—however superficially—I might reach some deeper insight into the story.

Yet as comfortable—and as natural—as this process felt, I could only wonder how long it would last. Would I succumb to city life once I returned home? Would I forget what happened to me in the desert? Would I forget what happened to the Israelites? This anxiety, I realized, is yet another reason to be thankful for the Bible: It serves as a living testament to the Israelites' life in the desert, to their struggles with the Almighty that took place there, and to the covenant of laws they received there. In performing this function, the Bible serves as a sort of universal literary moonrock—a souvenir of the desert that allows each of us to feel as if we've touched it ourselves. Readers of the Bible may not be able to visit the desert themselves, but by embracing its stories, they have tangible evidence of the power of the wilderness as a spiritual foundry.

To be sure, there is an element of romance in this view—that experiencing the desert can offer spiritual guidance to residents of settled areas. But one thing I learned during my trip was never to underestimate the power of the desert to serve as a metaphor, not just to people who are born in it, but even more to people who are not—people like retired Irishman Jerry Bracken, Father Justin, Avner, or even me. Before we left the *nawamis,* I asked Avner if he would like to be buried in one of these tombs. He thought for a second, then said, "Sure. I would love to be among these people. I'd love to be forever in the Sinai."

By the time we emerged from the tomb, evening had set, and I had that disorienting feeling one has upon going into a movie theater during daylight and emerging after dark. It was as if we'd missed some moment of transition and were left in a breach. "Excuse me, what millennium is it?"

We started down the hill to the place where we had arranged to meet Yusuf, when we noticed another jeep speeding across the desert floor, sliding back and forth like a water-skier, in that way desert drivers have of not getting bogged down in the sand. The jeep came skidding to a stop not far from where we were standing, and a bedouin driver jumped out. He was shorter than some of the men we had met, and more highly strung. He had a tight red-checked kaffiyeh wrapped around his head and no shoes. *"Abunar!"* he cried. *"Abunar!"*

"Ramadan!" Avner echoed. "Ramadan!"

The two men sprinted toward each other and embraced, kissing three times on the cheeks and holding each other's hands like schoolgirls. A few minutes passed and they kissed again, as if to convince themselves they were actually together. Eventually, introductions were made. Ramadan had been the guard and chief aide-de-camp Avner employed to watch over the *nawamis* during the five-year excavation. He had been like an older brother to Avner's two children, Smadar and Ido, and Avner, in turn, had been like a father to him.

In no time the two had rerouted our schedule; instead of spending our last night in the Sinai outdoors, we would spend it with Ramadan and his family. We drove across the desert, met up with Yusuf, and made our way to a small bedouin community located at the junction of two dried riverbeds. This village was more organized than the one in which we had spent the previous night, and the houses sturdier. Ramadan led us through a small gate and a yard cluttered with chickens and discarded tires. His house was smaller than Ahmed's, but more elaborate. The main living area was about the size of a crowded hospital room. Assorted mats and blankets covered the floor, making it look like a Mondrian painting; a fabric decorated with gray whales was draped like a canopy from the ceiling in a manner reminiscent of a bedouin tent. The walls were equally ornate, in a teenage bedroom sort of way. One wall was painted with fake flowers and a giant pheasant. Another had a painting of an elk in front of snow-covered mountains. The biggest wall was covered with six dime-store posters of plump infants with slogans like "Delicious" and "I Feel Cold." Why these babies? I asked. "Everybody loves children," Ramadan said.

By far the dominant, and most surprising, feature in the room was a twenty-inch color television set, the first Avner had ever seen in a bedouin home. Less than a year old, the set received only two Egyptian channels, but coupled with radio reception, it had created quite a stir. Ramadan said he watched television six hours a day and listened to radio twelve hours a day. As he was demonstrating the television, his sister arrived, dressed far more elegantly than other bedouin women we had seen, in a shimmering purple and maroon robe. She said, "When he goes to bed he switches from TV to radio." She rolled her eyes to indicate her frustration. The two of them, together with their mother, his wife, and their child, all slept in this one room. When the sister, and later the mother, joined the edges of our gathering, and especially when the sister said that she had found work outside the home, I realized we were seeing that moment of transition when the bedouin meet the world. Did that mean, for them, that the desert had lost its appeal? After dinner around a communal plate of rice, lentils, and bread, I asked Ramadan that question.

"I like to have electricity," he said. "I like to have television. But I wouldn't like to have all the chaos of the city. I wouldn't want to have all the tall buildings. I like the desert."

What did he like about it?

"First is the sun, which is always here and always reaches the ground. There is no pollution. Second is the wind. Third is the environment, the mountains, the trees."

"What about water?"

"Water is not a problem. Now we get water from a government cistern."

"So can someone like me, who grew up in the city, learn to love the desert?"

"Everybody has a spirit, a dream, of being calm and quiet, at peace with himself," Ramadan said. He was seated at this point on the edge of his room, with the rest of us gathered in a small circle. In the middle was a ceramic stove, an electric campfire, on which he was boiling a kettle of tea as beat-up as the one from the previous night. The intensity I had noticed earlier only grew as he spoke in slow sentences, running his fingers over his lips as if drawing out every word.

"People coming to the desert discover that they are drinking from truth," he continued. "And people become at peace with themselves because of this truth, this quiet. It's something that's built into the spirit of people, and it's waiting to be discovered, sometimes maybe without their knowing it. The nature around here, it's not me who built it, or you. It's God, the all-knowing. This is the greatness of God, and it infects everyone who comes here. It's like me and Avner, we can sit one next to the other, sometimes without even talking, and it brings joy in common to both of us. It's the same with the desert. It finds a way to bring out peace."

He began to tell a story.

"There was this American lady," he said, "a dancer. She lost her husband to cancer. People told her, 'Your husband will come back as another star, but he won't come here. You should go someplace open, where you can see the sky.' She went to Turkey and Greece, but she didn't find the other star. Then she came to Egypt. She stayed in Cairo for three days, she went to Luxor and Aswan. She went to Saint Catherine's, then she came here. She stayed across the street, under the trees in the oasis. She told me her story, and she said, 'Here I am, and my husband is not coming.' And every time she would see a falcon, or a dove, or another bird, she followed it. 'Maybe there's a message coming from the other star,' she said. But nothing happened.

"I started to talk with her and tell her that the way to see that other star was not to wait for something to happen, but to build up her home in this area. And she would start to be at peace with herself, and find something inside her, and that would be her other star.

"And she did this. But soon she discovered that life here is not so easy, not like dancing and singing as she was doing at home. Life is hard here. You have to work hard to collect food, to gather wood for the fire, to plant tomatoes or potatoes to get something to eat. But she did this work. She thought that she would physically find her way to the other star. And she was right. She used to write letters home, but once she reached here she stopped writing. She found a new life, a quiet space in the corner, and this was the other star.

"And then something happened that made us know," Ramadan said. "Her family didn't know what happened to her. She had disappeared. So they came to Cairo and searched for her. They asked about her, and nobody knew. Finally they published a note, with her picture, in a newspaper. The paper arrived here. Immediately we understood what happened, and we called the reporter in Cairo. The day after, her parents came to see her. 'Come back home,' they said. 'No,' she said. 'I'm staying.' "

Ramadan paused even longer than normal, before adding, "That's my answer for the first question you asked about the spiritual meaning of the desert."

"So what happened?" I said. "Is she still here?"

"She stayed for a half a year," he said, "and now she's in Cairo for two months. It's too cold to stay in the shade, and she didn't want to stay in a room. She's left, but she's coming back."

"But why?" I said. "Why did she do it?"

"Because when she came here, she felt as if she was coming into her own home. That's because since the early times, the Sinai is a place that all the prophets, and all the spiritual people, are linked to. Everyone is home here."

"And why is that?"

"Because everyone can find their other star here."

"Is that star out there?" I said, pointing to the air. "Or in here?" I pointed to my chest.

He thought for a second. "There are some things I don't know," he said. "There are some things we might never know."

2. And the Earth Opened Its Mouth

For as long as we were in the Sinai, we talked about food. We talked about the food we were eating. We talked about the food we wanted to eat. And mostly we talked about how we couldn't complain about the food we were eating because that would make us too much like the Israelites. Misspeak and we'd be eating manna for forty years.

With that in mind, early on in our trip, I made a rogue prediction: Before leaving the Sinai we'd have an experience involving quail. It became something of a running joke. Everywhere we went—with the farmer in the Oasis of the Tamarisks, with the monks in Saint Catherine's, with Ramadan—I asked if any of them had ever eaten quail in the Sinai, ever seen one fall from the sky, ever gone out into the desert one morning and seen them stacked knee-high, one on top of the other, as on a Thanksgiving table. None had. Quail were as elusive in the modern Sinai as archaeological evidence of the Exodus. "Don't worry," I said, mockingly by now. "God will provide."

By our last morning, when we left Ramadan's house and drove northeast along the coast of the Gulf of Aqaba toward the border with Israel, where we planned to pick up the Israelites' wandering by spending a few days in the southern Negev, my taunt had lost a bit of its swagger and Avner was polite enough not to rub it in. In midmorning, we stopped in one of the beach towns where intrepid Germans and hippie Israelis seek refuge in grass huts to smoke dope and scuba dive.

Yusuf went to get gas, and Avner and I walked across the street to the first market we had seen in the Sinai. Suddenly we were boys in an arcade, as we ran around the aisles grabbing anything that wasn't bread, cheese, tuna, or honey. In a matter of seconds we had the least-balanced food basket I'd ever assembled: fig bars, Cadbury chocolate milk, guava juice, raspberry juice (which Avner called "burning bush" juice), peanuts, butter cookies, and two dozen miniature bananas, still green, but we didn't care.

After twenty frantic minutes, I stood staring at one of the refrigerated bins trying to decipher the fruit drawings on the yogurt canisters, when suddenly I noticed in the corner of the bin a plastic container crammed with about eighteen eggs. Only these weren't normal-sized eggs, they were tiny and speckled with brown. They couldn't be chicken eggs, I thought. What could they be? Maybe quail eggs. That's it: *quail eggs!* I called Avner over and he started giggling uncontrollably. He checked with the store clerk, who verified the ornithology. An hour later we sat on a deserted beachfront of the eastern Sinai, made a small fire out of wormwood, and ate the most pleasing meal of our trip: chocolate milk, unripe bananas, two kinds of cookies, and hard-boiled quail eggs, which once we peeled away the shell were roughly the size of globules of manna.

"As you often say," I said to Avner, raising a toast of burning bush juice, "how can you spend any time in the desert and not believe in miracles?"

Miracles aside, arriving in Israel from the Sinai is like arriving in Disney World from the Middle Ages. The sudden concentration of prosperity that hits one immediately upon crossing the border into Eilat is as disconcerting as it is relieving. Legend holds that after Creation, when the angels were painting the earth, they got tired and spilled their paints: The blue became the waters of Eilat, and the other colors its fish and corals. Some of those colors must have been saved for the topless bikinis and umbrella-festooned drinks that adorn the beaches today. In a way it seems only fitting that Eilat, one of those strategically placed Middle

Eastern locations that was occupied by a different power every two generations, has now been taken over by the twelve tribes of modern Israel: Ramada, Radisson, Sheraton, Holiday Inn, Days Inn, Howard Johnson, Ambassador, Princess, Neptune, King Solomon's Palace, Aqua Sports International, even Club Med. The only milk and honey here are served in fake crystal goblets in dining halls of brass and glass overlooking the most crowded beaches between Cannes and Kuwait. In essence, Eilat is a Vegas-style, mirrored disco ball at the union of three deserts—the Sinai, the Negev, and the Arabian. Shake this plastic city and it won't be covered by snow but by sand.

Having just sated ourselves across the border, we decided to pass through "the Riviera of the Middle East" as quickly as possible and head into the Negev, which the Bible calls "the land that devours its people." Our plan for the next few days was to finish working our way through the rebellions that fill the bulk of Numbers and further press the question of what these repeated challenges to Moses' authority meant to the Israelites in the desert.

For this trip, we were joined by Avner's son, Ido, a tall, hawk-eyed twenty-five-year-old with a ponytail and surfer glasses. He had broad shoulders, like his mother, and the gentle demeanor and wry humor of his father. He could have been a California beach dude—except who needs the waves: The sand is enough. Early in our drive, when we veered off the highway and onto an off-road that Ido, a desert tour guide, preferred, I asked him the difference between driving on the highway and in the desert. "First, you don't need seat belts," he said. "Second, there are no police, so you can drive as fast as you can. Third, well, the view."

And what a view it is. The Negev, which means "dry south country," is the Siberia of Israel, a region of vast emptiness and barren beauty that has both fascinated and repelled observers since the days of the Bible. Shaped like an arrowhead pointing south, the Negev is bordered by Jordan to the east, the Sinai to the west, and the vast developed center of Israel to the north. Today its four thousand square miles represent 60 percent of the landmass of the State of Israel but hold only 6 percent of the population. Far from isolated, though, the Negev is actually part of a broad belt of deserts, including the Sahara, the Sinai, and the Arabian, that girds much of the world. How much of the world? I asked Avner.

"Most of the subtropical area," he said.

"Does this belt have a name?"

"The Subtropic Desert Belt."

"*The Original Bible Belt.* Now there's a name."

Avner was actually apologetic about the Negev. "I wish you had seen it before the Sinai," he said. But the Negev has its own dramas. Within minutes of leaving the blacktop, Ido was driving two-handed and two-footed over some of the rockiest terrain I'd ever crossed in a vehicle, using some of the most acrobatic driving I'd ever experienced. His technique involved a combination of leaning forward, rolling down the window, standing to peer over the hood, opening the door to pop out onto the running board, stopping temporarily to stack a few rocks into a pothole, then returning to spin his wheels, back up, lunge forward, and sprint into the open. At one point I realized that I was holding on to the handle above me with two hands, as if on an amusement ride. That was jolting enough, but when Ido reached over during one vertical lurch and grabbed the same handle, I knew we were at our most perilous. The whole experience reminded me of my first flight in a single-engine plane when I was twelve and the pilot reached under his seat during one particularly brutal patch of turbulence and strapped on his parachute, unconcerned that those of us in the back didn't have that option. Ido's rules notwithstanding, you do need seat belts in the desert just to stay in your seat.

After several hours, the road began to smooth a bit and we pulled into a clearing. Ido parked the jeep and we eagerly sprung free. In my haste I hadn't noticed that we'd arrived at the edge of an astounding geological site. The Ramon Crater is a giant pockmark on the face of the Negev, a heart-shaped hole twenty-five miles long, six miles wide, and a quarter mile deep that looks like an oversized sand trap. Part of a geological phenomenon unknown outside Israel and the Sinai, the Ramon is the largest of three such gorges in the Negev that are commonly referred to by the Hebrew word *maktesh,* meaning mortar, as in mortar and pestle. Unlike the Grand Canyon, say, which is ten times longer and four times deeper, and was formed by a river eroding the earth, the Ramon Crater was formed by collapsing earth following the creation of the Rift Valley hundreds of millions of years ago. The rift, by generating such a huge valley along the eastern border of today's Israel, caused rivers that had drained to the west to shift to the east. This drainage slowly ate away the sandstone hill that once stood here. The hill actually consisted of a sandstone core underneath a limestone crust, and when the sandstone was depleted, the limestone collapsed like a soufflé, creating the crater.

"Don't tell me, this is the largest such crater in the world," I said to Avner.

"I'm afraid so," he said.

With its layered walls and smooth sand floor, the crater is like a book that lay unread for generations. British aerial surveillance overlooked the formation, and not until 1948 did most people realize the crater existed. The Romans knew, of course; the crater floor is marked with milestones where an ancient road dissected the site. The effect of all this untouched grandeur is captivating. "This is the most beautiful place I've been in Israel," I said.

"That's quite a statement," Avner said.

"Can you think of one more beautiful?"

"It reminds me of a poem by Abraham Shlonsky. 'There may be a more beautiful place than this. There is no place more beautiful like this.' "

This being Israel, though, beauty is rarely enough; it comes with a potent buffet of politics, religion, and, inevitably, the Bible. In the nature reserve overlooking the crater, we ran into a pal of Avner's who had worked at the site for sixteen years. Dafna was born in the north of Israel but now couldn't imagine living in its grassy hills. She'd become a disciple of the desert, and, by dint of her job, a passionate defender of geology. The video the center plays for tourists to describe the crater, she explained, says the earth was created four billion years ago, a relatively safe statement in the scientific community. Over the years, however, some Orthodox Jewish visitors have emerged from viewing the video and spit on her. "The world was created 5,700 years ago," they insist, using the traditional calendar that dates the start of the world from the Creation story in Genesis.

"So what do you do?" I asked.

"I say, 'Don't bother me. That's what you believe; I believe something else.' "

"And would you consider changing it?"

"Why? If you want to learn about religion, you go to synagogue. Here you learn about science. I can't change that, so they shouldn't change this. I accept religion; they should accept science."

"But how can you say religion is not connected to science?"

"I don't say that. For me, the Bible is mostly a historical book. I believe it's written by human beings. But I'm not ignoring it. I don't know if there's a God, but neither am I sure about science. But I am sure this crater is more than 5,700 years old. I've seen bones older than that."

"So did God create the crater?"

"No, the water did."

"Then it's not a miracle."

"For me, no. For you, maybe yes. Maybe God sent the water."

Back in the car, I was struck that Dafna, like many people we'd met, defined herself as a person of the desert, a person who chose to be in the wilderness not necessarily because of its association with religion (as, say, the hermits), but because of its natural beauty. Ido was clearly a member of this group. On our drive toward a secluded stretch of the Egyptian border, where we were going to stay with some friends of Avner's who were squatting near the site associated with the biblical city of Kadesh-barnea, I asked Ido if he thought it was connected to his upbringing.

"My greatest memories are from the desert," he said. "From the years we lived with the bedouin in the Sinai." When he left the Sinai as a boy and moved to Beer-sheba with his mother, Ido found the transition almost unbearable. "It was very hard for a seven-year-old kid, who didn't know what television was, or telephone, or electricity, to suddenly be in the middle of things. I had no idea how to live my life in a normal place.

In the Sinai I could do whatever I wanted. I ran around by myself since I was three. No fears. My friends in Beer-sheba never left the house."

Ido's response was to flee, to return to the desert, to go outside and play.

"The best place to be is the desert," Ido said. "It's where my happiest times as a child were. It's where I want to raise my kids. I spent three years in the army, in Lebanon. I did what I had to do for my country. Now I just want to live my life."

"What about the future of the country?"

"I don't really think of myself as an Israeli," he said. "I don't really care about my nationality. The desert is important to me as a person— not to me as an Israeli, just to me as a human being."

"So this feeling," I said, "is it connected to religion at all?"

"To me the connection is to the fact that I was here, that I have memories of the desert. There's an energy. I can understand how people connect it to religion. I just don't."

"If you go into a room, say a wedding, and there are five hundred people there, how long does it take you to find the other desert people in the room?"

"Not too long."

"How can you tell?"

"You can tell. You can see, the way they walk, the way they talk. Usually they try to escape and go outside."

"Do you go talk to them?"

"Usually I do. We find each other. That's what the desert does. It sticks to you. It stays in your mind. It goes with you wherever you go."

I chuckled. "It's the same thing people say about the Bible."

"Maybe that's why they're so similar."

We got up to go. "By the way," I said. "Is there a secret handshake among desert people?"

"No," he said, "but even if there was we wouldn't tell you."

We continued driving along paved but increasingly empty roads toward the most isolated part of Israel. The desert may have appeal as a play-

ground, but few people want to live here, particularly in the highly fortified zone along the Egyptian border, which is home to secret military
bases, intelligence listening posts, and sensitive archaeological ruins. Har
Karkom, the mountain that archaeologist Emanuel Anati says is Mount
Sinai, is located near here, as are seven stations on the legendary
Nabatean Spice Route, on which traders ferried frankincense from Arabia to the Mediterranean.

The night had turned black—no road signs or car lights for miles—
by the time we pulled onto a dirt causeway that led to a small campsite.
The campsite was tended by Avner's friend Ofer, who lived in the
nearby village of Ezuz, population: twenty-five. Ofer was an Israeli but
looked like a bedouin, with leathery skin, deep wrinkles around his eyes,
and a whispering, inward manner. If there were a desert handshake he
would have known it without being taught.

Sitting around a small fire underneath an acacia, Ofer explained
how he came to live in this outpost. Thirteen years ago, newly married
and having traveled around the world after the army, Ofer and his wife
wanted to help colonize the Negev, an area that had been mostly
ignored in Israel's early rush to settle the waistline of the country. Ofer
and his wife chose this spot, which at the time had two and a half families, because it had water, a well dug by the Turks. "You can live without electricity," Ofer said. "You can live without people. But you can't
live without water."

"And how did you intend to make money?" I asked.

"We didn't really know. We lived almost without money."

"Really?"

"The money was not the problem. The problem was we didn't have
a cow, so if we wanted to buy milk it was 110 kilometers," about seventy
miles.

"You came here without a car?"

"Oh, no, we had a car, but she broke after one month and we didn't
have money to fix it."

"So how did you go shopping?"

"We walked to the nearest town by foot. We took a bus to Beer-
sheba. We shopped, took the bus back, and walked home."

"How long did that take?"

"Three hours each way."

I looked at him. "What did your *mother* say about all this?" I asked.

He grinned. "Good luck."

In time, Ezuz started to grow. Ofer and his wife had two kids. Eight other families moved in. The community flourished as a desert hideaway, a shining village in the sand, with a naturalist, two potters, a philosopher, a French cheesemaker, and Ofer, who started running ecotours of the region. Didn't his kids resent not being in the city with easy access to pizza and movies?

"We recently made a donkey trip for three days with my children and the children of my neighbors," Ofer said. "We were sitting one night around a fire like this, and one of my boys said to his friends that we were planning to grow the community, to add another twenty families. And my boy said, 'You know, if our parents are going to continue with this thing, bringing in too many families, I don't want to stay.' And his friend said, 'Yeah, maybe we'll speak with our parents and we'll close the town before it becomes a city.' "

"You must have been happy about that," I said.

He smiled. "We've tried to give them a good life," he said. "The desert's a special place. It's my place."

"So where does that come from?" I said. "From history? From your parents? From the Bible?"

Ofer suddenly got very still, as if he were waiting for the answer to come up through the ground. "The feeling doesn't come from the Bible," he said. "But it's *described* in the Bible. There is a lot of mysticism around the desert, and around this place especially. The Bible talks about that. But the Bible did not invent it.

"Look," he continued, patting the ground. "I don't want to say that this was the place that Moses walked or slept or talked to God. But I believe Moses was here. Tomorrow you're going to go to the border, to the place where Moses may have stood and looked over the Promised Land. I see this road seven times in the week, and every time it's different—because the sun hits it in a different place, because I am in a different mood. And for me it's always new. I don't feel this when I go to other places. I feel it only when I'm here."

We slept around the campfire that night and when we woke the following morning, the valley was covered in a dense swell of fog. It was like waking in a meringue. Unlike northern Sinai, which is low and flat, this part of the Negev is four hundred feet above sea level and gets over two hundred days of dew a year. "That's why even desert plants are green," Avner said. "It's not the rain, it's the dew." Nearby, you could see the symbiosis at work. Dew that collected on the leaves of the acacia would drop to the white broom bushes, then in turn drop to the ground, where little yellow flowers sprung up in a circle like a wreath.

Slowly, as the sun grew stronger, the fog began to dissipate, revealing a vast, open valley where we'd been sleeping. Six hundred thousand people could have slept here. To help determine whether they did, we were joined over breakfast by the resident naturalist of the area, Doron, the lone bachelor of Ezuz and the "half a family" Ofer had referred to the previous night. An Israeli of Yemeni descent, Doron had dark skin, hardened cheeks, and the kind of stony, impassioned eyes that could stare down an animal peering through the darkness. The symbol of native-born Israelis is the sabra, a prickly pear that's spiny on the outside and sweet on the inside. Doron was closer to the *maktesh,* a cracked limestone exterior and a sandstone heart. He, like Ofer, was made of the land.

Plus a generous helping of rock and roll. Five minutes after arriving, Doron apologized for the quality of his speech. "I'm afraid my speaking is not very good," he said. "I learned English from the Beatles, the Rolling Stones, Stevie Wonder, and Aretha Franklin."

"So you must speak city English," I said. "I don't think any of those people ever set foot in the desert."

Our plan was to drive across the valley and visit an abandoned Israeli military outpost on a mountain that may have been the one Moses used to survey the Promised Land, overlooking the oasis that might have been the one where the Israelites lived for thirty-eight of their forty years in the wilderness. I joined Doron in the front seat of his government-issue jeep, which was equipped with two telephones, several packs of cigarettes, and a copy of the Wayfarer's Prayer, the one I had heard on the way to Hebron.

For most of the next few hours we made our way south-southwest over a series of escalating passes, on a succession of deteriorating roads, toward the border with Egypt. Every now and then we'd stop, get out and explore a site, fill a pothole in the road with boulders, or just take a break, before continuing again. At one point Doron slowed the jeep to a stop and pointed to the horizon, where a small family of gazelles—a male, a female, and two calves—was grazing. They looked like they were made of sticks. These were Negev gazelles, Doron explained, able to survive without drinking water, getting all the moisture they needed from plants. "When you say *desert,* the usual interpretation is that it's an empty place, with no life," he said. "But in this desert, it's full of life—birds, animals, bugs."

I asked him what was the most exciting animal life he'd seen, and he told me the story of tracking the rare Negev leopard. Recently, the radio beacon Doron and his colleagues had placed around the neck of one of the leopards broadcast from the same place for forty-eight hours. They went to see her, and found her dead. In her heart was the needle of a porcupine. "Porcupines have a wise strategy for protecting themselves," he said. "They let the predator run after them for a while, then all of a sudden they stop. The predator—in this case, the leopard—runs right into the needle. When it sticks, the porcupine releases the needle from its body."

Doron didn't act particularly excited when he told this story. He didn't act excited when he told any story. He had that peace that comes from being comfortable in his own skin. But unlike other confident people I'd known, Doron had a quality I'd noticed elsewhere in the Middle East, in Father Justin, in Avner. It was the feeling of being comfortable across time—in the present, the future, the past. Ground yourself in this part of the world, and you may find yourself sprouting up at any moment from the third millennium B.C.E. to today. It's as if by fol-

lowing a simple rule of design—broaden the base of an object in order
to increase its stability—they had strengthened their lives. Perhaps that's
why time moves more slowly here: When you use ten thousand years
ago as your starting point, your life seems awfully short.

One factor in this equation, of course, is the Bible. When I first set
out on this trip, I expected—or at least hoped—to find the Bible in the
places that I looked. What I was unprepared for was how easily I found
the Bible in the people that I met. Almost all the people I encountered—especially in Israel—carried the biblical stories in their head like
some cornerstone against which they measured their lives. To be sure,
not everyone took the same lessons: To some the Bible was a measuring
stick of faith, to others character, to others history. But everyone seemed
to find a way to relate the stories to his or her own experience. Doron
was a particularly unexpected example.

At one point in the afternoon we pulled over to view an ancient
bedouin burial site, similar to the *nawamis,* only these weren't buildings
but rings of stone that had been untouched in the six thousand years
since they were built. A few minutes later, back in the car driving toward
the Kadesh-barnea lookout, we passed a homemade stone monument to
a motorcycle driver who had been killed on the road. "That's new!"
Doron said, screeching to a stop and going back to inspect it. "It's only
two or three days old. You can still see the oil stain on the road." As the
area's naturalist, he would have to decide whether to keep the ring of
stones, which had been painted fluorescent orange, or remove it. He said
he would try to find a way to preserve the memorial, only make it more
tasteful. I mentioned that I had never seen so many roadside memorials
as I had in Israel, and asked him why.

"This is a small country," he said. "The population is getting larger.
More people are dying in accidents."

"But that doesn't explain why there are so many memorials."

"Jews like memorials," he said.

"So is there a connection between a stone memorial built six thousand years ago and one built three days ago?"

"Sure, it's the same thing," he said. "In the Bible, Solomon says,
'There's nothing new under the sun.' "

"I thought that was the Beatles," I said, half joking.

"If so, they took it from Solomon."

"Wait. I can accept that Israel comes from the Bible, that the Ten Commandments come from the Bible, that monotheism comes from the Bible. But the Beatles?!"

"If you check their songs, their ideas, you'll find a lot of things from the Bible." He thought for a second. "Like 'All You Need Is Love.' It's the same thing Rabbi Akiva, the famous sage, said. When he was asked to summarize the Bible in one sentence he said: 'Love your neighbor as yourself.' That's not an exact translation, but it's similar."

For the first time on the entire trip I could think of nothing to say.

"There's another song," Doron said, "on the *Abbey Road* record, the song before the last. 'And in the end, the love you take is equal to the love you make.' Also from the Bible."

He went on like this for the next twenty minutes, pulling lyrics from his memory and aligning them to biblical verses. It was the most awesome display I'd yet seen of the Bible's ability to reinvent itself for every generation. One person's daily inspirational is another's Woodstock primer.

"And another example!" Doron said. "The whole point of the Bible is that you keep reaching for the perfect world but never reach it. It's like Paul Simon said, 'The nearer your destination, the more you're slip-slidin' away.' "

"You should do a compilation," I said. "Doron's Biblical Guide to Pop Music."

He beamed.

"Which reminds me," I said, "which do you know better: the lyrics of the Beatles or the lyrics of the Bible?"

Now for the first time *he* was quiet, before finally adding, "Is it okay if I don't answer that question?"

Eventually we emerged from the mountains into a clearing. We were in a wide valley now with soil white like beach sand. To our right and left was a vast, open plain, but up ahead were several small mountains. "Do you see those two breasts," Doron said, pointing out two hills that rose alongside each other. "They mark the border. The right breast is in Egypt, the left in Israel."

We were headed to the hill on the left, the highest point along the border, and the best vantage point to see Ain el-Qudeirat, the northern Sinai spring commonly associated with Kadesh-barnea. Far from a passing reference, Kadesh-barnea is central to the story of the Israelites' time in the desert and the dominant location in the second half of the Five Books of Moses. Following the rebellion over the quail, the Israelites once again set out in the direction of the Promised Land. Another rebellion ensues, in which Miriam and Aaron, Moses' siblings, speak out against their brother because "he married a Cushite woman," an apparent reference to the land of Sudan or Ethiopia, meaning they were upset that the woman was black. God swiftly intervenes, scolding Miriam and Aaron and saying, "Moses is trusted throughout My household." In further punishment, God inflicts Miriam with "snow-white scales," or leprosy. Moses appeals for her recovery, but God insists she be exiled for seven days, at which point she is readmitted and the Israelites set out for the wilderness of Paran, an area believed to correspond to the southern Negev.

For the first time since leaving Egypt, the Israelites are now at the brink of the Promised Land, in a place the Bible refers to as "Kadesh in the wilderness of Paran." God asks Moses to send a legion of spies to scout out the Promised Land. They return after a little more than a month, saying the land is too strong to conquer, and the Israelites once again rebel, crying, "If only we had died in the land of Egypt, or if only we might die in the wilderness." It is this act of hostile doubt that prompts God to forbid this generation of Israelites from ever entering the Promised Land. "None of the men who have seen My presence and the signs that I have performed in Egypt and in the wilderness, and who have tried Me these many times and have disobeyed Me, shall see the land that I promised on oath to their fathers." Your carcasses shall drop in this wilderness, he says, while your children roam the wilderness for forty years. "You shall bear your punishment for 40 years corresponding to the number of days—40 days—that you scouted the land: a year for each day."

The Bible implies that the Israelites spend the next thirty-eight years living in this location, which it refers to as Kadesh or Kadesh-barnea. The word *kadesh* derives from a Hebrew root meaning holiness or separateness; the word *barnea* is of unknown origin. In part because of the vagueness of this term, and in part because of the inexact description of the place, a precise identification of the location of Kadesh-barnea has been difficult to make. In the nineteenth century, the search for Kadesh-barnea focused on the Jordan valley, since the text suggests the site is on the border of Edom, which was located in the mountains of today's Jordan. In the early twentieth century, archaeologists focused on locations in the northern Sinai. In 1914, Leonard Woolley, who later excavated Ur, and T. E. Lawrence, then an archaeologist/spy, declared that Kadesh-barnea was Ain el-Qudeirat, the largest water supply in the Sinai and thus the place most likely to be able to support a large population for decades at a time. Their identification has largely been accepted ever since.

We arrived at the summit of the mountain and disembarked. With the two neighbors—Egypt and Israel—face-to-face on the tallest peaks along the border (2,100 feet), each side built a sentry tower. Later, when the two signed a peace accord, the posts were abandoned, though not dismantled. "It's a disaster," Doron said. "These buildings remain to damage nature and nobody cares." The Israeli site had a run-down steel observatory, which we climbed to get a better view. From the top, the scene was panoramic. To our right we could see the dunes of northern Sinai and the Mediterranean; to our left the mountains of southern Sinai; to our rear much of the Negev. Had Moses stood here, he might have rebelled himself: desert in every direction; no milk or honey for days.

The only source of green in the area was a small cluster of trees, much smaller than Wadi Feiran, on the other side of a small ridge. "That's Ain el-Qudeirat," Avner said.

"It hardly seems grand," I said.

"It's not like the great oases of the southern Sinai," he said.

The most notable feature of the area was the empty plain surrounding the spring. "In the ancient world," Avner noted, "the road from the Mediterranean to the Gulf of Aqaba went through here. That's why the modern border is here." That border, like most in the region, is fraught with intrigue. The Negev side is hilly; the Sinai side is flat. Before World War I, the British, who exercised imperial control over Egypt and the Sinai, drew the border with the Turks. Because the British had done extensive spying in the area, they knew that the chief water supply, Ain el-Qudeirat, was in the hilly area, so the otherwise straight line between the Mediterranean and the Gulf of Aqaba includes two brief detours, which the British referred to as Winston Churchill's knuckles, after his role in the negotiations.

The strategic prickliness of the area has hardly diminished since then. Ain el-Qudeirat was the one place on our entire itinerary that we wanted to go but couldn't. The Egyptian Army refused us access, citing intelligence concerns; the government's main military post of the region is located near the spring. As it happens, the reason we weren't allowed to visit—the area's strategic importance—is one of the principal reasons to doubt the link between this site and the Israelites' route.

In the world of biblical studies, the identification of Ain el-Qudeirat as Kadesh-barnea is viewed as a virtual certainty. Almost every article—professional or amateur—that discusses the Israelites' route through the desert assumes as fact that they lived thirty-eight years in this region. This historical identification, though, is by no means certain. First, the spring, while the largest in the area, is nowhere near large enough to support the needs of six thousand people, no less two million. Second, the original link between Ain el-Qudeirat and Kadesh-barnea was made by Woolley and Lawrence in 1914. It turns out they spent only *three days* in the area. Subsequent excavations produced not one shred of evidence that the site was occupied between the third millennium B.C.E. and the middle of the first millennium B.C.E. Third, and even more devastating, the spring would have been strategically important even then. If the Israelites were trying to evade the Egyptians, they hardly would have stayed for almost *four decades* less than a day's walk from where the Egyptian Army controlled the main road of the world, the Via Maris. Even Exodus mentions the Israelites had not taken that route to begin with, presumably because it was well fortified.

"If you're trying to convince me that the argument is not very convincing," Avner said, "I agree with you. They'd be very vulnerable. Plus, it's a very naive approach to suggest that if we find a place of water we'll find the people. The view of the Israelites living together in a well-organized camp is also naive. It's more likely that they lived in smaller groups all over the Sinai and the Negev."

The stories, in that case, were probably a compilation, a "telescope" to use Avner's word, of a series of events that took place over a wide area and a long period of time. That doesn't mean the stories were made up. If anything, they appear to have deep roots in the desert and deep knowledge of the geographic personality of the region. To explore that side of the story, we pulled out our Bibles to read one of the events that takes place in Kadesh-barnea.

Following the return of the spies, Numbers 16 and 17 tell the story of another revolt, led by Korah. Commentator Gunther Plaut calls this event "the most serious rebellion that faced Moses and Aaron." Korah, a nobleman, rouses two other men, Dathan and Abiram, along with 250 Israelite chieftains, and complains that Moses and Aaron have raised themselves above the Lord's congregation. Moses promises that God will decide who deserves to be leaders. The next morning, Moses instructs the men to take copper fire pans and burn incense before God. Aaron also makes an offering, to give God the choice. God appears and tells Moses and Aaron, "Stand back from this community, that I may annihilate them in an instant!" Suddenly, the earth opens its mouth and swallows up all three men and their families. "They went down alive into Sheol," the Bible says, a reference to the abode of the dead, and then God sends a fire that destroys the other 250 men.

The following day the "whole Israelite community" rises up in anger against Moses and Aaron for bringing death to the community. God, incensed again, sends a plague to annihilate the entire population, but Moses instructs Aaron to burn incense before the Lord to expiate him. The plague is checked, but not before 14,700 people are killed, five times more than in the golden calf episode.

In many ways, the most memorable detail of this rebellion is not the crime but the punishment. As Pseudo-Philo, the second century C.E. Greek commentator, noted, by having Korah swallowed up by the earth, God seems to be administering the ultimate punishment, the direct inverse of creating Adam out of the soil. I asked Doron if he knew any examples of people getting trapped in quicksand, as happens in a famous scene in the film *Lawrence of Arabia* when one of Lawrence's bedouin companions is sucked to his death in the Sinai.

"No," he said. "But there is an area of dry sand on the other side of the spring where you can sink to your chest."

"Quicksand?"

"Closer to a dune," he said. "The wind brings sand and it gathers in loose mounds. If the story takes place there, it's possible for someone to sink in the sand."

"But not to their death," Avner said. "Only to their shoulders."

"But people were shorter then," I joked.

"There's another connection," Doron said. "Behind us you can see a big mountain, Jebel Harad. Along that ridge there is a geological fault line, one of three in the Negev. There are places you can see where the ground collapsed, leaving a huge hole. A few years back, one of these holes suddenly appeared without warning, and people started falling inside. Trucks fell inside. Geologists were very surprised. It wasn't an earthquake; it was something else. They still don't know what happened."

The fact that so many unique phenomena—collapsing holes, the *maktesh,* the Dead Sea, the rift—all existed in one place may be one reason the Bible includes such vivid geographical details in its stories. If nothing else, the details were sure to capture the imagination of a population curious—and perhaps concerned—about the world around them. "This may be another example," I said, "like Sodom and Gomorrah, where biblical storytellers were aware of an occurrence and used their story to explain how it proved the power of God over nature."

"From my point of view, there are three possibilities about the sto-

ries in the Bible," Doron said. It was late afternoon now and we were sitting on the edge of the sentry post with our feet dangling over the side.
The bright white heat of midday had diminished. Our conversation had
grown more personal. These were the moments I once avoided; now
they were the ones I most craved. "First, things happened as they are told
in the stories. Second, some things happened as they are told; others
were made up. And third, a very, very clever man made the stories up."

"So which one do you believe?" I asked.

"In some ways, it's my personality to believe the religious way of
thinking. In other ways it's my personality to believe that somebody
made it up. I don't have a concrete opinion. And that's the nice thing
about the Bible. You can take it however you want. What really matters
are the clues within the stories about how to behave."

"So one, two, or three, in the end they're all the same."

"The basic message is the same. It's solid truth."

Driving back to the campsite, I thought about Doron's comments. Here
was a man, as dry and scientific as any I had met, who viewed the Bible
as offering him some higher meaning. In many ways, Doron's attachment meant more to me now than that of the people I had met during
our earlier stops in Israel. It seemed to confirm my own evolution, my
embracing the story for its emotional resonance, regardless of its factuality. I could accept the story for its moral code, even as I struggled to
identify its grounding in reality.

Still, I wondered how far I could carry my own growing identification
with the text. Specifically, could I carry it to the point of openly connecting myself to the God—the unforgiving God—we were reading about at
this point in the narrative? How could I root my identity in such a capricious source, such a violent source? How could I embrace a presence that
responded to a challenge to its authority by opening the earth and swal-
lowing a volume of people one-tenth the size of my hometown? Was this
act so ferocious—so *inhuman*—as to undermine my own growing respect
for the *humanizing* force of the story? In short, did God go too far?

Back at the campsite we were joined by Ofer for dinner. This meal

was a little more elaborate than what we had been eating in the Sinai—
we had tomatoes, for one, as well as chicken—but the staples were the
same. Ofer began baking what he called traveler's pita, a simple bread
made without a pan; matzoh with leavening. He brought out a blob of
premade dough, dug a small pit in the ground beneath his tidy, bedouin
fire, and placed the dough in the pit, which he covered with dusty
embers. "We're going to eat this?" I asked.

"In about twenty minutes," he said.

"And not get sand in our teeth?"

He chuckled and continued spreading the coals, until the dough was
completely out of sight. As he did, I began to see the parallels—and the
differences—between him and the bedouin we had met in the Sinai.
The bedouin, longtime desert dwellers, were adopting many of the
traits of city folk. Ofer and the others in Ezuz were moving in the
opposite direction: leaving the city behind for the desert. In some ways,
they were closer to the Israelites in the Bible, trying to find in the liberation of the wilderness a richer, more meaningful life.

"There's a reason that all the people who want to speak with God
go to the desert," Ofer said. "It's easier to see."

"But isn't it difficult, too?" I said. "Aren't there things you dislike
about living here?"

"At first you don't like the fact that you can't get what you want,
when you want it," he said. "In the settled areas people are spoiled. I was
spoiled. When you live in the city you can control everything. You control the temperature, you control the food, you control the water. In the
desert, you have to take things as they are. You don't live in this area in
August and have air-conditioning so you think it's winter."

"So why stay?"

"Because we *don't* control everything. When you live in the bubble,
you see just what human beings make. When you live here you see
things other people don't. It's difficult. Sometimes you get frustrated.
You *want* to press a button and make things better. But you can't. I invite
you in the winter, to see a flood, and you will see that we are not masters of the world. It's the most destructive thing I've ever seen, and the
most beautiful."

"How is it beautiful?"

"It comes out of nowhere. No signal. No warning. Just suddenly the skies open and the water starts to fall. And fall. In Avdot, just north of here, I saw water running so hard off the top of the cliff that it continued in midair for twenty meters before it fell to the ground. I almost cried. I knew all the things it was washing away. The bedouin tents, the newly planted trees, the soil. But I also knew what it would bring in the spring."

And therein lies the tension. The flood is beautiful but destructive. The desert is cleansing but calamitous. The people are regenerative but resistant. This struggle, I now realized, dominates the Israelites' time in the wilderness and is the chief story line of the second half of the Five Books of Moses. In many ways, Numbers mirrors what happens in Genesis. At the beginning of the Bible, God's task is to create humanity and he follows a vicious cycle of creation and destruction: First he gives life to Adam and Eve, then they disappoint him, and he banishes them from his garden, forcing them to start from scratch. Adam and Eve go on to spawn humanity, who also disappoint God. He destroys them and starts over with Noah.

A similar, if more elaborate pattern takes place in the desert. God gives life to the Israelites by freeing them from slavery, then they disappoint him, and he strikes out in anger. In a seemingly intractable pattern, God performs miracles—brings water from the well, rains manna from the heavens, delivers the Ten Commandments—and the Israelites react in ungrateful ways. Repeatedly God threatens to kill them and start over with Moses, as he had with Abraham, as he had with Noah. In each case God is mollified, though not before exacting a huge price from the Israelites. He may not destroy the whole population, but he destroys scores of rebels here, hundreds there, until he reaches the bloodcurdling number of 14,700 at Korah. As Jack Miles, author of *God: A Biography,* has noted, if God created man in his own image, the Israelites' behavior in this part of Numbers must be seen as a reflection of the competing qualities of creation and destruction inherent within God's personality. It's as if the two central players—God and his people—are trapped in a downward spiral of immolation, a phenomenon that during the Cold War was called Mutual Assured Destruction. Each unfortunate event triggers an escalated response in the other side, until neither side knows quite how to break the pattern.

As Miles concludes: "God is not a stoic, does not teach stoicism, does not honor or encourage resignation or acceptance, and is, by and large, impossible to please. In each of these regards, Israel is made in his image." From the outset, Miles says, a certain symmetry is apparent, as Israel complains about Moses, Moses complains about Israel, God complains about Israel, Israel complains about God, God complains about Moses, and Moses complains about God. "That such a narrative should have been preserved and elevated to the status of sacred scripture and national classic was an act of the most profound literary and moral originality."

This image of God and the people struggling to find a way to relate to each other is the perfect allegory for what I was going through, I now realized. I could shuck many of my citified conventions. I could embrace the openness—and the devotion—of the place. I could even become an advocate for God. But I still couldn't cross the line to where I completely gave myself over to God. I still resisted many aspects of his character, at least as it's defined in the Pentateuch. If obliterating humanity for no apparent reason was part of the definition, then part of me wanted to reject any nascent appreciation I might feel toward God and assign my newfound openness to something else, like a love of the desert. As quickly as I developed these feelings I could destroy them. I could become an antagonist of God.

The Bible, in many ways, seems to anticipate this dilemma by offering up a creative way to bridge the growing chasm between the people and God. As is the case in international relations, the only way to stop a downward spiral is with enlightened leadership, and Moses, even in his most trying times, emerges as an enlightened leader. Specifically what Moses realizes is that God and Israel need each other, and that it's his role to make sure that happens, to play peacemaker. Time and again throughout the rebellions, Moses pleads with God to forgive the people, then turns around and pleads with the people not to be so hardheaded toward God. What Moses does, in effect, is to tug each side back to the altar, reminding them of their public commitment to each other, and forging out of their reluctance an even deeper bond. On a more figurative level, what he does is loosen the stiff necks of the Israelites. The term *stiff-necked* is a reference to an ox that refuses to lower its neck, which it must do to be properly fitted into a yoke. What Moses does is teach the people to bow down before God, which is what God has wanted all along.

Not surprisingly, it's the part of the story—the role of Moses as power broker—that Ofer most identified with. "My main issue with the Bible," he said, "is not how many Israelites were in the Exodus, but what the story means to contemporary Israelites, to people like me—and you." Twenty minutes had passed since he first placed the dough underneath the coals, and he was now poking it with a stick to see if it was done. Convinced that it needed more time, he flipped it over and recovered it with coals.

"Exodus is not about God, or the Israelites," he continued. "It's about how they learned to get along. It's about how a group of people travels in the desert. How you can't travel more than about ten kilometers in a day. How you have to live and work together. How you have to have *leadership*." He paused for a second. "I want Moses to be the symbol of leadership for modern Israelis."

"And how do you achieve that?"

"You give people the experience of going into the desert. You invite schoolchildren. You invite adults. We had a great example with this march we took last year. Avner was there. It took only nine days, and most of the people knew one another very well and loved one another. And still, how many problems we had! How many hours did we sit around discussing what to do, how to do it, how to solve the tensions among us."

"So what's the principal leadership lesson of Moses?"

"That nobody can survive alone in the desert, not even a prophet. Moses could easily have gone to the Promised Land with God, but without the people. He could easily have gone with the people, but without God. Instead he chose to go with both, and the only way to do that was to stay in the desert until both sides learned to get along. That's why they stuck around for forty years: It took that long for the people and God to learn to live together."

Ten minutes later the bread was ready to eat. Ofer pulled the pita from the embers and set it on the soil. At this point it was impossible to distinguish the ashes from the bread; both were the color of dusk. He took a stick and began beating the loaf like a dirty rug. Dust flew everywhere. After a few seconds, the loaf was clean enough and he pulled off a piece, breathing steam, and handed it to me. I tossed it around my fingers for a few seconds, then put it in my mouth. There was a small coating of sand around the crust, but I no longer cared. And that's when I realized how far I'd come during my time in the desert. I no longer craved the apple, the cookie, or the chocolate from my earliest days. I no longer needed cheese, or okra, or tuna. I didn't even need honey. Bread was flavor enough.

3. The Land of Milk and Honey

Two days later I stood with my bag at the entrance to a large yellow security gate in one of the more unusual communities tucked away in the Negev. Midreshet Sdeh Boker is not so much a town as an experimental community, a living Walt Disney–like EPCOT dream, one part optical illusion, one part kibbutz, one part futurama. The community, which contains a research institute, a high school, an army camp, the largest solar dish in the Middle East, and an entire neighborhood in which every home is constructed to sci-fi-level solar standards, was founded in 1963 as the region's only high-tech village designed exclusively to study the desert and how human beings interact with it. Today Sdeh Boker serves as the epicenter of a particular Israeli dream: the desire to root the country in its biblical desert past, while preparing it for an equally prophetic desert future, one with perpetual energy, perfect tomatoes, and no sunscreen. If Moses went into the wilderness for forty years today, he'd come here first.

Which is why I decided to visit. Having arrived at the part of the Bible in which the spies venture into the Negev to scope out their future land, I decided to step away from the second millennium B.C.E. for a few days and explore what had become of that land today. Avner and Ido dropped me off at the gate on their way back to Jerusalem, and I walked down a narrow street that in its tidiness reminded me of a 1950s sitcom—*Leave It to Beaver* or *Father Knows Best*—but whose dustiness reminded me of a Wild West ghost town in *High Noon* or *Shane*.

Kids wobbled by on tricycles, followed by dogs and older siblings. A family of ibex wandered around a small garden, nibbling on the meager shrubs. After a few minutes a woman came out of her one-story home and swatted at the stubby horned animals with a broom.

My destination was the field school, a small, cinder-block facility with classrooms and bedrooms where every Israeli student in the country is expected to come during his or her education to study the desert. "Can you think of anyplace in America where every student goes?" asked Raz, the thirty-four-year-old director who would be my host for the next few days. He was short, taut, and friendly, with deep, sun-hewn lines around his eyes that made him appear older than he was.

"Maybe Washington, D.C.," I said. "But not everyone goes there."

"Here, everyone goes to two places," he said. "Jerusalem and the desert."

The first place Raz sent me was nearby Kibbutz Sdeh Boker, one of the earliest kibbutzim in the Negev and the onetime home to Israel's founding father, its first prime minister, and the greatest champion of what might be called desertopia. David Ben-Gurion was born David Gruen in Poland in 1886 and adopted a Hebrew name after moving to Palestine in 1906. In no time he became an early leader of Zionism, the movement to reclaim the land of Israel for Jews that took its name from the biblical term for Jerusalem's westernmost hill, Mount Zion.

Ben-Gurion, a socialist, was the person who declared Israel's independence on May 14, 1948, led the country through the war that followed, and spearheaded the absorption of hundreds of thousands of immigrants. A short, stocky man with an Einstein-like shock of hair and an insatiable intellect (he had twenty thousand books in his library), Ben-Gurion towered over people who disagreed with him. Shimon Peres, his protégé, who later became prime minister, wrote of his mentor, "He was not an easy person, or a congenial one, or a person who strove to be liked by others. His personality was very complex, distinguished as it was by an exceptionally strong character, tremendous willpower, and stubbornness." But, Peres noted, Ben-Gurion challenged

Jews to believe that they could be a nation of farmers, not just scientists and intellectuals. "He decided that the time had come to establish a Jewish state, yet once it had been founded, he was not satisfied—it must be an exemplary state, a chosen state."

Time and again, Ben-Gurion relied for inspiration and guidance on the Bible, which he viewed as a blueprint for Jewish life in the Promised Land. "It is not the Mandate which is our Bible," he told the British in 1937 of their rule over Palestine, "but the Bible which is our Mandate." Far from commonplace, this was something of a revolutionary position at the time, even among Jews. What Ben-Gurion did was say the Bible should be taken not just as a spiritual text, viewed as a product of the ancient world, but as a *political* text, applicable even to twentieth-century realpolitik. Wherever he went, Ben-Gurion read the text, quoted the text, challenged conventions about the text (he believed far fewer than six hundred thousand men participated in the Exodus), and used the text as a guide to his every decision. Though critics accused him of delusion, utopianism, or even "Bibliolatry," Ben-Gurion refused to back down.

Eventually Ben-Gurion took his fascination one step further, by endeavoring to enter the Bible himself. In the summer of 1953, while on an expedition in the Negev, Ben-Gurion came upon a handful of pioneers working in a brand-new kibbutz called Sdeh Boker, or Plain of Cowboys. Ben-Gurion stopped his chauffeur-driven car and spoke with the workers. The following day he called a meeting of his advisers. "I am jealous of these young people," the sixty-seven-year-old leader said, "what a wonderful experience!" And that December he did something even more remarkable: He resigned as prime minister of the five-year-old country and moved his wife, his life, and five thousand of his books to a small bungalow in Kibbutz Sdeh Boker, where he went to work as a sheep farmer.

The following March, Ben-Gurion wrote an article in the *New York Times Magazine,* called "Why I Retired to the Desert." After emphasizing that leaders have a moral responsibility to step away from their countries to help build confidence among the people, Ben-Gurion stressed he was driven to the desert by a desire to draw himself closer to God. "It is no accident that the Law of Israel, the Torah, was given in the desert, and that the greatest teacher in our nation, Moses, was the leader of the nation in the wilderness. Here man sees the creation of God as it was in the beginning: rough, wild, and as unyielding as ever. And he finds in himself the forces needed to adapt it to human needs."

I had heard parts of this story before, but not until I hitchhiked the few miles to the kibbutz from the field school did I realize how dramatic an act of biblical devotion Ben-Gurion had performed. His wooden bungalow, prefabricated in Sweden and preserved today as a museum, was a mere 810 square feet, with two bedrooms—one for him and one for his wife, who hated being there—a living room, a small kitchen, a bathroom, and an office. In the sitting area was a copy of the Declaration of Independence. The biggest item in the house was a giant globe given to him by U.S. General Omar Bradley. In his bedroom, where Ben-Gurion reportedly slept only three hours a night, was a cot, a stack of books, a pair of slippers, a photograph of Mahatma Gandhi, and a sketch of the burning bush.

Even more telling was Ben-Gurion's office, which was twice as big as the two bedrooms and kitchen put together. In addition to the books, Ben-Gurion had three miniature statues. On his desk were busts of the Greek philosopher Xeno and the Buddha; and directly across from his chair was a replica of Michelangelo's *Moses*. Also on his desktop, tucked underneath protective glass, were a half dozen biblical passages, most from the Book of Isaiah, from which Ben-Gurion claimed the origin of his plan to "make the desert bloom," to turn the Negev into a Garden of Eden. "For the Lord will comfort Zion," read one citation, from Isaiah 51:3. "He will comfort all her waste places; He will make her wilderness like Eden, and her desert like the garden of the Lord; joy and gladness will be found in it, thanksgiving and the voice of melody."

Walking around the house, I was amazed by the spartanness. It was as if Franklin Roosevelt, having won the war, had decided to go back and live in Lincoln's log cabin. Though Ben-Gurion did return to the prime minister's office from 1955 to 1963, Sdeh Boker would always remain his home, and it was his vision that led to the formation of the Research Institute, which he called a "Hebrew Oxford in the desert." Even more impressive was the greenness of the place. The house itself, which was painted the color of wintergreen, with forest green shutters, was shrouded with pepper trees and ficuses and boasted geraniums up to my waist.

"I have a lot of respect for Ben-Gurion," said an elementary-school teacher from the kibbutz who was walking her dog outside. "He was right about settling in the Negev. In the Gulf War we almost lost the country because so many people live in Tel Aviv. The Scuds could have killed the entire population." Also, she said, this place *was* closer to God. "I went to Greece recently, and it was beautiful. But when I came back, the first thing I did was come here. It was the right time of day, the light was perfect. I just stood here for a while." She paused. "It's good for the soul."

While residents of Sdeh Boker may deem Ben-Gurion a hero for glorifying their life in the desert, many scientists have long dismissed his notions of transforming the desert into a garden as naive or, worse, ruinous. After my visit to Ben-Gurion's house, Raz directed me to the home of Yoel De'Malach, a farmer, researcher, and winner of the prestigious Israel Prize, the country's highest honor, for his work in revolutionizing the role of water in the Negev.

At seventy-five, De'Malach was a slight man whose stooped shoulders and hesitant step belied his flickering eyebrows and crackling wit. He reminded me of an old European clown who refused to stop joking even after his acrobatic days were behind him. Born in Florence, De'Malach came to Palestine in 1944 and was sent to the Negev by the Jewish Agency, the organization run by Ben-Gurion that organized the resettlement of the country. What did De'Malach think of the task of transforming the desert? "Experts had enormous faith," he said.

Actually, even that wasn't true. The centerpiece of Ben-Gurion's plan for the Negev was to pump water into the area and reclaim the wasteland as arable soil. Despite his adoration of the Bible, in effect he wanted to *undo* the desert as a spiritual foundry, and make it an agricultural one. He even proposed paving over the two giant craters and using them as reservoirs. Few thought it was a good idea. During one trip to the Negev, Ben-Gurion stood in front of what's called the Small Crater and proclaimed, "I want to fill this crater with water." His advisers responded, "It can't be done," to which Ben-Gurion replied, "Who said so?" "The professionals," they said. "In that case," Ben-Gurion said, "give me other professionals."

De'Malach didn't need professionals to tell him what he soon discovered: that even with water pumped south from the Sea of Galilee, the Negev was too dry for farming. But the public didn't want to hear it. "There were young people crying, 'How can you say this! You are reducing our hopes!' Children, I am sorry, but I cannot change the world. We have to compromise our dreams." He added, "Don't think we didn't have any feeling for the Bible. On the contrary, I think that we held the Bible in higher regard than Ben-Gurion, who was stuck in Tel Aviv all those years. We lived here, in the desert, in the same place where the patriarchs lived, so we believed we were close to the ancients."

For twenty-five years De'Malach and his colleagues struggled to survive, caught between the parched land on the one hand and the unrealistic expectations of the country on the other—until a discovery in 1969 opened the door for a possible reconciliation. Drilling more than half a mile below the Negev, scientists uncovered a previously unknown aquifer, full of brackish water, ten times saltier than drinking water but only a tenth as salty as seawater. It might not have been as miraculous as Moses tossing a log into the bitter waters of Marah, but in the long run it might prove more significant. If scientists could figure out how to use it, the brackish water could reduce the country's dependence on rainfall.

For decades, De'Malach and his team tried growing produce with the water, with mixed results. Pomegranates and grapes were successful; mangoes and oranges were not. In products that worked, the yield was diminished, but the quality improved. The reason, he explained, is that plants overcompensate for the salt by generating more sugar. "Our tomatoes are the best in the world," he boasted.

"Wait! You're Italian and you're telling me that this image of a big Italian grandmother making spaghetti sauce is going to be replaced with a woman from the Negev?"

"I don't believe that Italians will start to buy Israeli tomatoes," he said. "This is too much! But ours are better."

"So Ben-Gurion would be proud."

"Maybe, maybe not."

"But you're proud."

"When we started, nothing was here," De'Malach said. "Now look what's here. We're selling tomatoes all over the world. And we did it with our own hands. So yes, I think I can be proud."

The next person I went to see was David Faiman, a physicist, weekend biblical historian, and another European immigrant, in his case from London. Faiman was a charismatic person with a trimmed black beard and meticulous speaking voice that reflected his Oxonian past, and sandals and colorful shirts—bright orange today—that reflected his Israeli wife, an actress. I arrived in his office at the edge of the Research Institute, in an area devoted to the more futuristic aspects of the facility: pumping water through buildings as a coolant, growing algae for eating, and trying to solve the puzzle of how to use the sun as a viable source of energy. He showed me around his compound, which looked like a giant outdoor fun house, with mirrors sprouting in dozens of shapes—circular, rectangular, spherical, and conical—all angled toward the sky. The dominant structure was the four-story dish, like a giant metal oyster lined with mirrors, that was Faiman's bid to solve the solar puzzle. "I've had quite a breakthrough in the last few months," he explained. Some businessmen from Germany were arriving within the week to consider investing.

After the tour we sat in his office and Faiman explained that he admired Ben-Gurion, despite his cockamamie ideas for the desert. "Ben-Gurion wasn't a scientist. He wasn't aware of the climatic and geographical factors having to do with the shape of the earth and its orbit around the sun that are responsible for this place being a desert. Now we know better. Now we try to work with the desert, not against it."

Faiman moved to Israel in the 1970s and has since taken sabbaticals in the United States and Australia. He and his wife raised three children in Sdeh Boker and eventually built a dream home in the solar suburb, which included windows facing east, to heat up the house in the mornings, and a special chimney for naturally funneling heat out during the day. I asked him what his dream for the Negev was.

"The dream would be to introduce a serious rail system in this country. The country is designed for it. The New York subway system could very easily cover all of Israel. Then you could settle the Negev in an ecologically responsible manner. Some areas would be nature zones; others would be for nonpolluting industries. You could even do some market gardening. You can grow out-of-season orchids and fly them into European markets. If you did this, you could move people here from Tel Aviv and restore farmland. The best agricultural land in the country is now covered by cities, and here we are trying to develop agriculture in the Negev, when the Negev is the most wonderful place to live imaginable."

I asked him if his vision, like that of Ben-Gurion, was tied to the Bible.

"Obviously they are related, otherwise I wouldn't have come here. My whole philosophy is strongly influenced by the Bible. What is clear to me is that there is a physical world and a spiritual world, and I am saddened that our perception of the spiritual world is very primitive. It hasn't evolved at the same rate as our perception of the physical world."

"Has living in the desert affected your spiritual life?"

"For one thing, I think it deepened my understanding of the Bible enormously," he said. "Simply because the Bible always meant a lot to me, but through British eyes. Living here, among the bedouin, seeing how they live, has brought home to me that many episodes written in the Bible were not written by European rabbis. They document events that have their very core in the desert, far away from urban life."

"So are you a desert person?"

"I feel I'm a Negev person. My roots are here. I have enjoyed visiting deserts in Australia and the United States, but I never felt I belonged there the way I feel I belong here. It's part of my tradition."

"And do you feel your work here is part of that tradition?"

"I feel that I've been a useful part of the process," he said. "That I came to this place, and made it work for us, but that when we were finished, we shared our technology with the world. It's the same with the Bible. It was originally given to us. Now it's part of the world."

On my last afternoon in Sdeh Boker I went with Raz to visit Ben-Gurion's gravesite, a tasteful enclave overlooking the desert, shrouded with pistachio trees and lined on the ground with flagstones and yellow flowers. In the center were two tombs of Jerusalem stone. One for Paula Ben-Gurion, who died in January 1968; the other for the "Old Man," as he was lovingly called, who died in December 1973. Though set up as a triumphant spot, including an amphitheater for visiting school groups, the place seemed sorrowful.

"Among my generation, it's not popular to say we are Zionists," Raz said. "Israel, as a nation, has lost much of its romantic appeal. It's the same with the Negev. Once people came as pioneers. Now, they come for selfish reasons. They want to be closer to nature. They want to raise their children in the open."

"And that's sad?"

"A little. It's sad because people don't care about the communal parts of the country—education, what streets should look like. People of my generation are interested in how much money they can make, their work, their immediate family. Not even their parents. I don't call my mother and father every day. It's a fact. My father is furious with me for not being involved enough in politics, in religion."

What he is involved in, he tells his father, is trying to change the image of the desert—from a place to be afraid of to a place to be enjoyed.

"People are scared of the desert," he said. "It's far away, it's brown. There's no place to swim."

"And where does that come from?"

"It comes from the Bible. 'The people of Israel suffered in the desert,' it says. We read it in the first grade and never forget it."

"But you can't compete with the Bible," I said.

"Some friends told me I should rewrite the Bible in language we could all understand."

"You'd have to rewrite the history of modern Israel, too. The desert was the enemy for Ben-Gurion as much as for Moses."

"My principal message is: 'Don't be afraid. This is the best climate to live in. It's dry. There are many places to hike. There are many ways to make money.' "

"So if the old slogan was 'Make the desert bloom,' what should the new slogan be?"

" 'Make the desert fun.' "

I thought about these conversations on the way back to Jerusalem. It was clear that Ben-Gurion had achieved one central part of his dream: making the desert central to the identity of the Jewish people, particularly to the State of Israel. He did this through his speeches, through his push to settle people in the Negev, and through his personal example of living in Sdeh Boker. But in achieving these goals, Ben-Gurion had lost a central tenet of his Negev dream: turning the desert into a Garden of Eden. Ben-Gurion's inspirational slogan, "Make the desert bloom," which I recall hearing as a child, is now recalled as little more than Zionist propaganda. Israel did make the desert habitable; it made portions of it arable; in the future it will make even more of it profitable. But it didn't make it green, nor should it have. As Ben-Gurion himself said in the *New York Times*, the true appeal of the desert is that it brings one closer to the divine. "Here a person sees primeval nature in all its strength, unchanged and undisturbed by human hand; he does not give up in despair but finds within himself the vigor to meet the challenge and to strengthen his own powers of creation."

And, as Ben-Gurion anticipated, bringing people closer to the desert also brought them closer to the Bible. Everyone I met, from Yoel De'Malach to David Faiman to Raz, mentioned that spending time in the Negev had strengthened his or her attachment to the text. In the end, this may be Ben-Gurion's greatest achievement: rebinding the Jewish people to the Bible, saying that even in a world dominated by politics, nuclear weapons, and international alliances, the desert stories of the past still have a role. "Two things have to be fundamental in our education," he once said. "Science, as a means for knowing nature and controlling nature, as well as obtaining technical and economic mastery, and the Bible, as master guide for human and Jewish upbringing, shaping our social and ethical choices, relating to man and humanity."

So how big an accomplishment was this? To answer that question I went to a skyscraper in downtown Tel Aviv to meet Ben-Gurion's one-time chief aide-de-camp and one of the most recognized Jews in the world. Shimon Peres was not as colorful as his mentor, nor as voluble. He was a technocrat to Ben-Gurion's pioneer, the coolheaded number cruncher to the impulsive entrepreneur. Peres never developed the personal connection with the public that Ben-Gurion had. Four times he ran for prime minister; four times he failed to win. The two terms he served in the role were under less-than-glorious circumstances. First, in 1984, in a power-sharing arrangement with right-wing leader Yitzhak Shamir; and second, in 1995, following the assassination of Yitzhak Rabin.

What Peres did have was a deep intellect, and a sharply analytical mind. For years he ran the country's clandestine program to develop nuclear weapons, and in 1993 he spearheaded the secret talks with the Palestine Liberation Organization that led to the Oslo Peace Accords, an accomplishment for which he, Rabin, and Arafat were awarded the Nobel Peace Prize.

I first had the idea of meeting Peres when I learned that he had led a three-week espionage mission to scout out the Negev in 1944 that had remarkable similarities to the spying episode described in Numbers 13–14, in which Moses sends a team of a dozen Israelites to survey the Promised Land. Peres's expedition involved fourteen men who ventured south on camelback from Beer-sheba toward Eilat with the goal of plotting the land, then under British control, for an eventual takeover by the Jewish state. At the time, Jews were forbidden to travel in the Negev; they were also forbidden to carry arms, which the group had brought along, hidden in large canteens. "A tale of fourteen youngsters who longed to dip their toes in the waters of the Red Sea" is what Peres had said at the outset of the trip.

But they never made it that far. After twenty-two days, and only twenty kilometers from the gulf, the group was surrounded by British and Arab soldiers, arrested, and carted back to Beer-sheba, where they were thrown into jail. Peres was sentenced to a month behind bars. One day during the expedition, the Polish-born Peres, who at the time was still called Shimon Persky, spotted a large bird's nest in a tree. Shinnying up to see the nest, he disturbed a large eagle, which took flight. "That's a *peres*," the ornithologist in the group declared, using the modern Hebrew name for eagle that had been borrowed from Leviticus 11. "An immediate consensus evolved that as my 'Diaspora-sounding' name Persky was close to the name of this bird," Peres wrote in his memoirs, "I ought to adopt it henceforth as my new, Hebraicized name." (As it happens, the *peres* actually appears in Leviticus on a list of birds—including vultures, kites, falcons, ravens, ostriches, seagulls, hawks, cormorants, owls, pelicans, buzzards, storks, hoopoes, and herons—that the Bible says are not to be eaten. No reason is given, though interpreters later concluded that these were all birds of prey, and thus unclean.)

When I met Peres in his office, in a meeting arranged through one of Avner's friends, he was mostly dismissive of the event. "Yes, it was daring," he admitted. The maps, he said, were later used by the army during the War of Independence. But what Peres most wanted to talk about was Ben-Gurion and how he changed the role of the Bible in contemporary Jewish life.

The foyer to Peres's office suite was heavily guarded and extensively decorated with mementos from his travels. On the wall was a large photograph of Peres signing the Peace Accords on the grounds of the White House, as well as a bronze dove and a quote from Isaiah 2:4: "They shall beat their swords into plowshares, and their spears into pruning hooks; nation shall not lift up sword against nation, neither shall they learn war anymore." Over the copy machine was a photograph of Peres and Ben-Gurion, in which the protégé was a full head taller than his mentor.

Peres's private office was sunny and lined with books. There was an air of importance in the room, but it was tinged with melancholy, sort of like a musty beachside hotel. Peres, in his late seventies, was dressed in white trousers and a pink Oxford-cloth shirt with silver cuff links. On his desk was a stack of books in English, including two by Carlos Fuentes and one on Israel and the bomb. His shelves were filled with pictures, including one with him and Hillary Clinton. Next to it was a bulb-headed doll of Ben-Gurion that reminded me of a dashboard icon. I began by asking how much credit he thought Ben-Gurion deserved for making the connection between Israel and the Bible.

"I would give him the lion's share," Peres said. His voice was deep, but so soft it was almost impossible to hear. Not a muscle in his face moved when he spoke. Twice I had to move my chair closer to his desk, until, by the end of our talk, I was practically leaning over into his lap. He spoke perfect English, in perfect sentences, with a deep Polish accent despite six decades in the Middle East.

"First, there was a great deal of shame that had developed among Jews in the Diaspora," he continued. "The exile had introduced some unwelcome insecurities. His goal, intellectually and historically, was to bring back the Bible, instead of concentrating so much on the Talmud," which had become the dominant text in Judaism by the Middle Ages by compiling commentaries on the Bible and other aspects of Jewish law. "On the other hand," he continued, "there was a great debate going on about social democracy, communism, and the Soviet Union. He drew a line against that kind of talk and said our social orientation should be from the Bible, not from Marx, not from Lenin, not from Trotsky."

So what social message did Ben-Gurion draw from the Bible?

"It was a double-edged combination," he said. "He believed that what was unique about Jewish life was that in addition to the historical side—the kings, priests, and officers—we had the prophets. The prophets represented the moral side of our story. The Bible is history, and the prophets are vision, and it's combined. So intellectually, you have double the standing."

"Was this view somehow in the background," I asked, "or did you practice it every day?"

"First of all, Ben-Gurion never gave a speech without quoting the Bible. Secondly, at his home, he had sessions every Saturday and Sunday reading the Bible. Thirdly, he organized what he called the Bible Puzzle, an annual national quiz on Independence Day that continues today. Finally, he just talked about it all the time. When he developed a theory about the Exodus, he held a *press conference!*"

"Were there people who resisted?"

"There were two camps who opposed him. One was the religious parties, who were very mad with him for downgrading the Mishnah and the Talmud. The other was the Socialists, who were unhappy that he downgraded socialism."

We started talking about the Negev, and I asked him if he would describe himself as a desert person like Ben-Gurion.

"Yeah, I spent some time down there," he said dismissively. "But basically, I would describe myself as future-oriented. I think the desert presents an offer for the future. It's an opportunity to take the sand from the land, the salt from the water, the wilds from the people."

"But I thought that view was no longer in favor now. People down there now say, 'Let's respect the desert. Let's keep the desert as a desert.' "

"It's fashion," he said. "They want to keep the environment, but there are two problems. One is how to keep the air; the other how to keep the land. It's a contradiction. Because for clean air maybe you need more trees, which destroy the desert. Most of the people in the desert care more about tomatoes than people."

"So in the future, do you see the desert as green or brown?" I asked.

"Green, green!" he said. "Who wants to live on sand? The desert should be full of trees, leaves, plants."

In a way it was touching to hear the prodigy defending the dream, but Peres, on this matter, seemed out of touch, and a bit uncomfortable. Sensing my time was coming to a close, I brought the conversation back to the Bible and mentioned that in the country today one didn't hear politicians quoting the text.

"Today politicians are victims of television, instead of being students of the Bible," he said, in what was no doubt a reference to his defeat by Benjamin Netanyahu, a master communicator, in the 1996 race for prime minister. "Everybody wants to be a star: his face, his show, his sound bites. But there is a world behind the televisions. There is a world that lasts forever."

"Now that Israel is mostly secular, do you think the Bible can survive the onslaught of television?"

"Yes," he said emphatically, and for the first time all morning he showed some passion. "The Egyptians have the pyramids; we have the Bible. The pyramids are getting old, they're suffering from neglect. Our monuments are words, not bricks. And words last longer."

A few days later, I met up with Avner to discuss the conversations I had been having. One view came across loudly: The Bible is alive and well in Israel, the uncredited national anthem. But there seemed to be confusion about what role the desert should play in this vision. Why did some people want to eliminate it, and others want to embrace it? When I asked Avner this question, he popped open his cellular phone, hit one of his speed-dial entries, and whispered a few words to the person on the other end. "I'll pick you up at seven tomorrow morning," he said.

We drove southwest from Jerusalem, past Hebron and Beer-sheba, to a mostly unsettled corner of the Negev, not far from the Palestinian-controlled Gaza Strip, where we met another of Avner's circle of desert missionaries. Rami Haruvi was taller than Ofer, more kempt than Avner. Dressed in a neatly pressed mustard shirt, he looked like a retired basketball player trying to make a bid for middle-aged modeling. He was also, like his friends, a talker. Early on he told me that after his wife got cancer he went to see a therapist. "The first thing I told him was that when I visit I want to be his last client of the day, because once I start talking, it's hard for me to stop."

Rami met us in an abandoned, two-story concrete building on the outskirts of Kibbutz Be-eri. He had spread out a table with an elaborate breakfast, including rolls, cheese, hard-boiled eggs, tomatoes, tea with mint, and coffee with cardamom. "Kibbutzniks know how to eat breakfast," Avner said. Rami's father helped start this kibbutz in 1946. "When he came here, there was nothing, *nothing*," Rami said. "Imagine a convoy of immigrants from Tel Aviv, with Jews from Venezuela, Africa, Europe. After an hour they came here and had to make a home for themselves." Within two years they had built a small community. When war broke out and the Egyptian Army came sweeping up from the south, they quickly erected this building for safety.

"I once asked my father, 'What did you think at this moment?' " Rami said. " 'You, alone, with your body, with thirty people here, with a few pistols. Not even one cannon.' And my father said, 'We believed.' "

"So what happened?" I asked.

"They were blessed," Rami said. "They defeated the Egyptians. The Negev was included in Israel. And Kibbutz Be-eri went on to become one of the most successful in the country."

After breakfast we went out and began exploring the area, visiting a series of abandoned Ottoman factories, British sulfur mines, and Israeli Army barracks that testify to the area's many changeovers during the wars of the twentieth century. This part of the Near East has always been something of a strategic nexus: Just to the north are the habitable central hills; just to the east and south is the desert; just to the west is the sea. Gaza, the city that controls this hub, has been one of the most important urban areas in the world for five thousand years.

At one point Rami led me into a network of concrete bunkers, dating from the early twentieth century. "Now you are exactly like someone named Archibald Murray," Rami said.

"I always wanted to be like Archibald Murray," I replied. "Who is he?"

"Archibald Murray was here in 1917, during the First World War. The British were trying to take Palestine from the Turks. They came from the south, from Egypt, and wanted to go to Jerusalem. To do so, they had to cross this area. It took them three months to come all the way from the Suez Canal to here. They built a train. They built a road. They built a pipe. They brought water all the way from the Nile, because they needed steam for the train and water for thousands of horses. *In three months!* But they had to get through Gaza, which was controlled by the Turks. And one famous general helped them do that. Do you know which one?"

"Allenby?"

"Ah, you made a mistake."

"Archibald Murray!"

He grinned.

"But I've never heard of him," I pleaded.

"That's the point," Rami said. "One of them is famous, one of them is not. General Murray got the British Army here in three months from Egypt, but then they bogged down for *eight months*. Twice they attacked Gaza, and twice they were defeated, despite using tanks and gas shells. Over eleven thousand British soldiers died. Finally, General Allenby arrived and hatched a plan. The British dropped cigarettes on Gaza with propaganda on the packages. The Turks said, 'Who cares about the propaganda, we want the cigarettes!' " For weeks they smoked free British cigarettes, but the day before the attack, the British laced the cigarettes with opium. On October 31, 1917, the British finally conquered Gaza. "Three months to come all the way from Suez," he said. "Eight months to go three kilometers."

"And as always, Gaza was the key," Rami said. "Take it and you take the land. Six weeks later he took Jerusalem."

"So if what you're saying about this area is correct," I said, "then what they said in the Bible is correct."

"And what did they say in the Bible?" he said, delighted by the point.

"They sent spies from Kadesh who said the Israelites couldn't take Canaan."

"And what did they *do* in the Bible?" he asked, in the manner of a lawyer asking a leading question.

"They decided not to come from the south."

"And where did they go?" he said. "Aaaaallllll the way around." He swung his arms in a giant windmill to reflect the Israelites' journey across the Jordan River, up the east bank of the river, to the central mountains of Jordan. "And where did they attack the Promised Land from?"

"Jericho," I said.

Rami was smiling from ear to ear. "Hard to believe," he said. "But it's the same thing that happened in World War I. It's all but impossible to conquer Israel from the Sinai."

We drove a few miles to a large concrete memorial, about two stories high, in the shape of a giant *A,* built to commemorate the ten thousand soldiers of ANZAC, the Australian–New Zealand Army Corps, who died in the 1917 attacks on Gaza. From the overlook we had a clear view of the surrounding area: Gaza, the Mediterranean, the Sinai, the Negev, the mountains around Hebron. The afternoon light was changing to dusk, and the colors—pale yellow, powder blue, eggplant purple—reminded me of the Nile.

After a while we pulled out our Bibles and finally read through the story of the spies we had been referring to for so long. In Numbers 13, following the first few rebellions of the Sinai, but before the incident with the earth opening its mouth, God instructs Moses, "Send men to scout the land of Canaan, which I am giving to the Israelite people; send one man from each of their ancestral tribes, each one a chieftain among them." Moses gathers the men and instructs them, "Go up there into the Negev and on into the hill country, and see what kind of country it is. Are the people who dwell in it strong or weak, few or many? Is the country in which they dwell good or bad? Are the towns they live in open or fortified? Is the soil rich or poor? Is it wooded or not? And take pains to bring back some of the fruit of the land." The spies set forth through the Negev, along a route that probably had them brush alongside Ezuz and the Ramon Crater, as well as where we were now standing, before arriving in Hebron, where the patriarchs were already buried.

The spies make this trip "in the season of the first ripe grapes," which Avner said probably meant late July. Fittingly, the only thing the text says they actually *do* in the Promised Land is harvest some pomegranates and figs, as well as cut down a branch with a cluster of grapes, which they carry back on a pole stretched between them. This image of

two men carrying grapes has become so famous a symbol of the Promised Land that the Israeli Ministry of Tourism uses it as a logo.

After forty days, the scouts return to Kadesh and give their report.
"We came to the land you sent us to; it does indeed flow with milk and
honey." This term probably refers to goat milk and bee honey, Avner
said, though some commentators suggested the honey could be referring to nectars from fruits like figs or apricots. Another line of thought
suggests the term *milk and honey* is metaphoric, meaning the country
enjoyed an abundance of animals. Either way, the first report is bearish.
"The people who inhabit the country are powerful," they report, "and
the cities are fortified and very large; moreover, we saw the Anakites
there," a name that is derived from the Hebrew term meaning long
necks and has long been interpreted to mean giants.

Still, as would be the case with countless espionage missions
throughout history, different spies interpret the information in different
ways. Caleb, one member of the team, rises to give his spin, saying, "Let
us by all means go up." Surely we can overcome any obstacle, he says.
But the majority of his colleagues disagree, saying, "We cannot attack
that people, for it is stronger than we." The Israelites break into cries
upon hearing this report, and weep half the night, eventually railing
against Moses and Aaron: "It would be better for us to go back to
Egypt!" Joshua and Caleb rend their clothes in frustration and exhort
the community, "The land that we traversed and scouted is an exceed-
ingly good land. If the Lord is pleased with us, He will bring us into that
land, a land that flows with milk and honey, and give it to us."

As the community threatens to pelt them with stones, the "presence
of the Lord" appears before the people. Once again God threatens to
destroy the people, and Moses talks him out of it, saying, "If then You
slay this people to a man, the nations who have heard Your fame will say,
'It must be because the Lord was powerless to bring that people into the
land which He had promised them.' " The Lord pardons the people, but
punishes them: Everyone above twenty years old will die in the wilderness. "Not one shall enter the land in which I swore to settle you," save
Caleb and Joshua, who are rewarded for their optimism. The other spies
are killed by a plague sent by God. The Israelites, however, promptly

ignore God's warning and march by themselves—without Moses and without the Ark—to the crest of the Promised Land, where they are "dealt a shattering blow" by the Anakites and the Canaanites, just like the British at the same place three thousand years later.

Standing near that spot, I began to understand the significance of the spies. After resisting God for two years, the Israelites, at this moment, finally decide they are ready to conquer the land that God promised them. *This* is their manifest destiny, they conclude. But by going forth to claim their destiny without their manifest, the Israelites learn an even greater lesson. The covenant is a triangular relationship among the people, the land, and God. Without God, the people do not deserve the land and can't conquer it. Without the Ark—and the commandments within it—the people are helpless.

And this, I finally realized, points to the major lesson of the first half of Numbers and what I had been hearing in my conversations with Ramadan, with Ofer, with Rami: The desert is a cauldron where the Israelites must coalesce. The desert not only cleanses, it constructs. In Exodus, the desert is a vast sea of sand, a pool in which the Israelites rid themselves of their shackled past and receive the written law from God. Numbers tells a more complicated story. The Israelites begin their trek to the Promised Land, but at each step along the way they resist putting their faith in God. Finally, after the spies, God gets so fed up that he lashes out. And what punishment does he levy? He doesn't kill them. He doesn't send them back to Egypt. He doesn't even rescind his oath of land. Instead he banishes them to *four decades in the desert*. Only by spending that additional time in the wilderness will they fully purge themselves of their past and become a nation of God. Only then will they become worthy of their corner of the triangle.

The rebellions thus become an important turning point in the Pentateuch, the crisis that marks the end of the second act. The final third of the story, including the rest of Numbers and the entire book of Deuteronomy, will be devoted to the story of how the Israelites finally become a people. The desert, having given the Israelites life, must now take their lives, so it can give life to a new generation. It's the oldest cycle in the Bible: creation, destruction, re-creation. And it's those seemingly bifurcated roles, which directly mirror the split functions of God, that Ben-Gurion seems to have understood about the desert: Because the place is demanding, it builds character; because it's destructive, it builds interdependence; because it's isolating, it builds community.

Because it's the desert, it builds nations.

Book V

TOWARD
THE
PROMISED
LAND

1. The Wars of the Lord

Crossing the border from Israel to Jordan is even more complicated than crossing the street in Cairo. Only here there aren't any cars or buses or people around—just decades of distrust.

It was early summer when Avner and I arrived at the Arava border crossing north of Eilat, one of only two land crossings between the former enemies, and prepared to set out on the last leg of our trip, retracing the final third of the Pentateuch up the east bank of the Jordan. The Arava crossing is an isolated outpost in a dusty valley, with a large paved area and several industrial buildings, sort of like a Wal-Mart in the middle of the desert. Arriving from Eilat, one first has to pass through the legendary Israeli security system, which involves relentless prodding of one's luggage, passports, travel plans, and personal history. "Why have you made so many trips to Egypt?" "Where did you sleep last night?" "Please take off your sunglasses so I can see your eyes." The longer I traveled in the Middle East, the more passport stamps I gathered from Arab countries, and the more closely I was scrutinized at Israeli border crossings. "Are you Jewish?" "Do you speak Hebrew?" "Were you bar mitzvahed?" On this morning the questions seemed more intimate than usual—"Do you go to synagogue?" "Do you light candles on Shabbat?"—when suddenly the female security officer asked me a question that, given my recent travels, seemed more provocative than usual: "What is the meaning of Passover?"

I was startled, and a bit annoyed. "It celebrates the Israelites' journey from slavery to freedom," I said, adding for good measure that if she wanted to learn more about it she could read Exodus chapters 12 through 15. "But I don't believe there were six hundred thousand men," I said.

If the Israeli side is prying, the Jordanian is plodding. Once you pass through the barrage of Israeli questions, unpackings, repackings, X-ray machines, and computer scannings, then carry your bags across the border, you are greeted by a wall of inefficiency, softened only by Arab hospitality. One undeniable reality of traveling in the Middle East is that the gross domestic product of Israel is roughly equal to that of Egypt, Jordan, the West Bank and Gaza, Lebanon, and Syria combined. As a result, of all the places along the biblical route, the Promised Land, even for its difficulties, is by far the easiest to maneuver. At the Arava crossing, for example, the Jordanian side has a series of small, concrete-block offices—one for applying for a visa, one for paying for a visa, one for receiving a visa, one for paying the entrance tax, one for inspecting passports, one for inspecting luggage, and one for selling soft drinks, ice cream, and duty-free cigarettes. On this morning, four guards were manning all seven offices, which meant, as a practical matter, that three were closed at any given time, except for the duty-free, which always remained open.

Even animals can get caught in the morass. In 1992, before Israel and Jordan signed their peace treaty, a gray gelding belonging to Crown Prince Hassan, the brother of King Hussein, tossed his trainer during a run on the beach of Aqaba, swam a few hundred yards across the gulf, and walked ashore in Eilat. Israeli officials, not knowing the animal's pedigree, transported him to a nearby kibbutz, where the stray pony became something of a celebrity among local schoolchildren, who combed, rode, and fed him. When word reached Israel that the horse belonged to the Jordanian prince, the government, fearing a diplomatic disaster, sent special veterinarians to watch over the animal and began trying to arrange a discreet handover across the border. Two days later, the Israeli Army drove the horse twenty-five miles north of Eilat and gave him to officials of the UN, who walked him across a specially arranged opening in the border, where officers from the Jordanian

Army were waiting. In a brilliant act of public diplomacy, the "petulant royal polo pony," as the Israeli press dubbed him, took along hand-painted messages from Israeli schoolchildren pleading with the prince for peace.

These days, peace is nominally at hand, and a visitor arriving from Israel is expected to come bearing cigarettes at least. Having made this trip many times, Avner knew the drill and presented our Jordanian guide, Mahmoud, with a red-and-white carton fresh from the duty-free. "But they're not Marlboro," Mahmoud said. "They're Gold Coast." His disappointment at the cheap imitations was palpable, so Avner walked back through the security gate and to the border itself, only to arrive back fifteen minutes later, unsuccessful. "Oh, well. It's all poisonous just the same," Mahmoud said, and we were on our way.

The Hashemite Kingdom of Jordan is a water-poor, desert-rich country of five million people in an area slightly larger than Portugal and slightly smaller than Indiana. The country's per capita consumption of water is 200 cubic meters a year, compared to 1,800 in Syria, 7,700 as the world's average, and 110,000 in the United States. That means the average American uses 550 times more water a year than the average Jordanian. The main reason Jordan uses so little water, of course, is that it has so much sand: Only 4 percent of Jordanian territory is arable, and that's concentrated in the north, around the capital. Jordan is shaped like a pistol, with the trigger being the area around Amman, the handle jutting hundreds of miles eastward toward Iraq, and the barrel pointing downward toward the Gulf of Aqaba. In this scheme, the trigger represents most of the habitable land, while the handle and barrel contain little but dust.

In part because of this inhospitableness, the land that is today called Jordan has been mostly overlooked since history began. The area didn't even have its own name until the twentieth century and was called (since Ottoman times) Transjordan, a name that means "across the Jordan river" but that implies "the other side of the tracks." In the Bible, the area has a split role. Parts of it—the fertile hills around Amman—are included in the Promised Land. It's there, in the valley of Jabbok, where Jacob wrestles with God's messenger and receives the name Israel. By contrast, other parts—namely, the desert—are treated with contempt.

The first indication of this contempt comes with the story of Abraham and Lot. Earlier, Genesis explains how Lot flees Sodom and Gomorrah to the mountains of Jordan and gives birth to two incestuous sons, who grow up to head the nations of Moab and Ammon. Centuries later, in Deuteronomy, the Israelites under Moses encounter these two nations on their final trek up the east bank of the Jordan. Though these two nations are technically descended from the same family as Abraham—Lot being Abraham's nephew—they are now rivals of the Israelites.

Another enemy the Israelites encounter on their northerly trek also has patriarchal roots. Ishmael and Esau, of course, are the banished first sons of Abraham and Isaac. In a little-noted twist that links the two outcasts, Esau marries the daughter of Ishmael, his cousin Basemath. Their descendants (along with those from Esau's other two wives) eventually settle across the Jordan River and become the clan of Edom.

What Lot, Ishmael, and Esau have in common is that all are disaffected family members, separated from the tribe, who ultimately give rise to nations that become antagonistic toward their forebears' descendants. That all three nations are located across the Jordan seems to confirm that biblical storytellers viewed this territory as a particularly poignant mirror image, one that looks identical to the Promised Land, is settled with nations that are directly *related* to the inheritors of the Promised Land, but that for some reason were not chosen to live in the Promised Land. In the case of Lot, his fate seems to come from associating himself with the lascivious inhabitants of Sodom. By contrast, there is no comforting explanation why Ishmael and Esau end up across the river, permanently ostracized from the land of milk and honey. Ishmael, to be sure, was the son of a concubine, but such unions were considered legal at the time; plus, Sarah sanctioned it. As for Esau, he was merely the wronged older brother of Jacob.

The only consolation seems to be that God allows both Ishmael and Esau to father a people. This is subtle storytelling: God's chosen people may be the most elite nation in the region, but God also creates other nations—spin-offs, if you will—that still warrant a watered-down version of his blessing and serve, in a geographic sense, as buffer states around his chosen lot. These semichosen people are hostile to the children of Israel, but forever attached to them, too; blood rivals living just across the street.

This intimate connection between both sides of the Jordan has never disappeared. Since biblical times, the fate of Jordan has never been removed from the fate of Israel, making the two lands the Siamese twins of the Middle East, joined at the head and hips by a single river often no more than a few feet wide. David, the first king of Israel, conquered parts of Jordan; and the two places together were subsequently overrun by the Babylonians, Persians, Greeks, Romans, Umayads, Mamluks, and Turks. The interconnection became particularly intense in the twentieth century. During World War I, the British recruited Sharif Hussein, a bedouin emir from Arabia (and a purported direct descendant of Mohammed), to help oust the Turks from the Middle East. In return, the British promised to promote Arab independence. Hussein and his two sons, Abdullah and Faysal, led the so-called Great Arab Revolt, spurred by a British information officer and onetime archaeologist, T. E. Lawrence. The revolt appeared to be a success, as Faysal and Lawrence led a band of bedouin guerrillas from Medina to Aqaba, and later to Damascus. In 1920, Faysal declared himself king of Syria, while Abdullah was named king of Iraq.

Their independence proved to be a chimera. The British had, indeed, promised to help the Arabs gain sovereignty, but they had also promised to help the Jews carve out a homeland, and were simultaneously colluding with the French in the Sykes-Picot Agreement to keep the Middle East under European control. In the end, loyalty to their colonial partner proved deeper. Faysal was ejected from Damascus, and Abdullah was barred from Iraq. Abdullah was then offered a golden parachute, a job no one considered of much importance, head of the Emirate of Transjordan, a completely fabricated state drawn up by Colonial Secretary Winston Churchill.

Abdullah ruled the colony for more than twenty-five years, at which point the British finally granted him independence. In 1946, the emir became a king, and Transjordan finally lost its pejorative prefix *Trans* and became the Hashemite Kingdom of Jordan. (The term *Hashemite* refers to Abdullah's family lineage.) In no time, the rivalry between Jordan and Israel reignited, as the new kingdom controlled much of the West Bank of the Jordan and half of Jerusalem. Palestinian residents of the West Bank were frustrated, too, since they wanted a homeland of their own, and in 1951 a Palestinian walked up to King Abdullah while he was visiting the Temple Mount and shot him dead; a bullet intended for the king's fifteen-year-old grandson, Hussein, ricocheted off a medal on the boy's chest. Abdullah's son Talal had schizophrenia and was unable to rule, so Hussein became king. He ruled until his death in 1999 and was succeeded by his eldest son, who, in a fitting emblem of the convoluted politics of the region, had a British mother, an American education, a Palestinian wife, and the name of his great-grandfather, Abdullah.

King Abdullah II had another remarkable genealogical claim that linked him to the literary tradition at the root of the region: the Bible. Abdullah's great-great-grandfather Hussein held the title of sharif, or nobleman. Sharifs had ruled Hejaz, the region of Arabia around the holy cities of Mecca and Medina, for over one thousand years, with Hussein's branch maintaining control since 1201. The first sharif was the Prophet Mohammed's elder son, which means, as a matter of tradition, that Abdullah II is a forty-third-generation direct descendant of the founder of Islam. The lineage doesn't stop there, though. Mohammed's great-grandfather Hasem, whose name is the root for Hashemite, was a member of the tribe of the Arab chieftain Quraysh. Quraysh claimed to be descended from Ishmael. If true, this would mean that today, more than three thousand years after Moses first set foot in Transjordan, and four thousand years after the patriarchs passed through here, the current king can trace his family tree back to Abraham himself.

One consequence of this pedigree is that two tiny nations, Jordan and Israel, already bound by geography, climate, and history, also share national story lines that bind them to one of the oldest stories ever told: Abraham and his son. In the case of Israel, the son is Isaac; in the case of Jordan, the son is Ishmael. This difference, seemingly minor, has actually made one of the narrowest rivers in the world seem like one of the widest.

As we drove north on the only highway of southern Jordan, a single-lane road that bisects the reddish desert, I explained to Mahmoud the nature of our trip. He brought out a notebook and occasionally diverted his eyes from the road to jot down notes. Of all our guides, he was clearly the most studious. About forty, with eyeglasses and an accountant's meticulousness, Mahmoud described himself as a student of the holy books. I asked if that included the Bible.

"In Islam we believe in all the holy books," he said. "Mohammed tells us, 'Don't refuse all the Bible, and don't accept all of it.' "

"So how do you know what to accept and what not to accept?"

"We don't know. We should compare it to logic, to the Koran, and so on."

"So have you read the Bible?"

"In Arabic, yes."

"What was that like?"

"From the central points, it's the same. But from the religious points, it's completely different. Because the Koran, we believe, is the last book, it's our holy book. Every sentence is important because it came from Allah to the Prophet Mohammed. But the Bible—we believe that some parts of it are not the original ones."

"When I look through the Koran, I notice that there are far fewer details about places," I said. "The writing seems more poetic."

"Here is the main point. To understand the Koran you should read it in Arabic. You can't translate it. There are some sentences in the Holy Koran, for example, that the Prophet Mohammed made us promise would be kept in Arabic writing."

"So do you find the Bible beautiful?"

"In the Bible, as I told you, there are a lot of things which are useful. It's one of the great books for a lot of things. For example, I am interested in botany. There are lots of plants mentioned in the Bible that I can recognize."

"What about the god of the Bible? Do you understand him?"

"From the Muslim eye, Allah is the same god who deals with Moses, who deals with Jesus, who deals with Mohammed. In Hebrew you call him Yahweh, or Elohim. In Arabic we call him Allah."

"So when you read the Bible, your god is there?"

"Yes, because we believe that the creator of all this world is Allah. In the Koran it is mentioned that Allah created the world in seven days. It's the same in the Bible. When I read the Bible I get a certain feeling toward Allah."

"And what is that feeling?"

He thought for a second. "If you are stuck on an island, and you've lost everything, at the end you will feel that the only help will come to you from Allah. That's the feeling I get."

After about an hour we turned east off the highway and ventured across the sand toward one of the most spectacular natural environments I've ever seen. Wadi Rum is one of three dry riverbeds that drip down from the central mountains of Jordan like braids. On a map, the twenty-five-mile-long, two-mile corridor looks similar to the countless wadis we had seen in the Sinai and Negev. What makes Rum so spectacular, "vast, echoing, and godlike," in Lawrence's words, are the granite and sandstone mountains—as high as 2,100 feet—that soar from the sand in endless strata of peanut-butter-colored stone, interrupted with layers of red, purple, and pink. The cliffs have been so softened and shaped by the wind that they look like wet gobs of clay about to be sculpted. They bulge in places, pucker in others, and generally loom so large over the ground, like chubby aunts peering over a crib, that any visitor looking up at them feels diminished, childlike in awe.

As Lawrence, the laureate of Rum, wrote of a journey through the wadi with his bedouin brigade: "The crags were capped in nests of domes, less hotly red than the body of the hill; rather grey and shallow. They gave the finishing semblance of Byzantine architecture to this irresistible place: this processional way greater than imagination. The Arab armies would have been lost in the length and breadth of it, and

within the walls a squadron of aeroplanes could have wheeled in formation. Our little caravan grew self-conscious, and fell dead quiet,
afraid and ashamed to flaunt its smallness in the presence of the stupendous hills."

Even more than that of Moses, the ghost of Lawrence lingers over
this part of Jordan. On our drive, Mahmoud pointed out places associated with Britain's sand prince: here a spring that bore his name, there a
nook where he camped his troops, here a place that David Lean filmed
his 1962 bio-pic. In many ways, the image of Lawrence is more important than the reality. Thomas Edward Lawrence was the second of five
illegitimate sons born to an Irish gentleman and the governess of his
two (legitimate) daughters. Masquerading as "Mr. and Mrs. Lawrence,"
the couple fled Ireland and settled in Oxford, where T.E. (he preferred
the initials) eventually went to university, specializing in medieval architecture. While still a student, Lawrence traveled throughout the Middle
East, surveying Crusader castles like the one in Harran and dabbling in
archaeology. During the war, Lawrence, one of the few British officers
who spoke Arabic, was assigned to do intelligence work in Cairo, eventually tapping Faysal Hussein as the British government's best hope
against the Turks. Soon Lawrence joined Faysal's army as a liaison, and
led it on a spectacular, two-month march through the desert to capture
Aqaba, a feat of myth-making proportions in the Arab world. By the
time Faysal arrived in Damascus, Lawrence had inspired him to liberate
the Arab world.

Or so Lawrence would have us believe. Lawrence's fame arises
mostly from a 330,000-word account of his time with the Arabs, called
The Seven Pillars of Wisdom: A Triumph, of which he published six private copies in 1922. The book contains self-conscious literary prose
coupled with swashbuckling adventure. In 1923, following editing by
George Bernard Shaw, Lawrence printed four hundred additional copies
of the book. After the book was made available to the public in 1935,
Seven Pillars went on to become one of the best-selling books of the
twentieth century and arguably the most influential work written about
the Middle East since the Koran. By the time David Lean turned it into
a gripping, three-hour-and-twenty-six-minute epic, which won seven

Academy Awards, including Best Picture, the image of Lawrence as a heroic figure was already set in stone.

But in more subtle ways, Lawrence is part of a long tradition of Westerners fascinated by Arabs. These Arabists include a long line of authors, adventurers, and rabble-rousers—"sand-mad Britons," as one writer called them. For them, Islam was a dangerous and voluptuous provocation and surviving it was a triumph of virility. Lawrence, an effeminate, five-foot-five intellectual, encapsulated his experience as a sort of sexual conquest, and ultimately turned it into a drama only slightly less grand than the Exodus itself. As a result, just as it is impossible to set foot in the Middle East and not think of Moses, so it is impossible to set foot in the region and not think of Lawrence. If nothing else, he defined a certain romanticism toward the region. In his worldview, the desert is full of mystical, almost frightening aliens—the dark side of civilization—that have to be liberated and integrated into our world before we can become whole ourselves. It's as if we're all split by the division between Abraham's sons, and as the children of Isaac we have a psychological need to confront, unleash, and ultimately make peace with the children of Ishmael.

The parallels between Lawrence's tale and the Exodus are not small. Both involve a pastoral people rising up behind a charismatic leader and conquering the settled world in a sweeping bid for independent nationhood. The differences, though, are important. Lawrence was not dealing with slaves, he was dealing with bedouin. Also, Lawrence was not leading these bedouin on a mission based on the superiority of their god; he was leading them on an anticolonial conquest. Finally, for Lawrence at least, there was an erotic element to his effort. As he wrote in the dedication to *The Seven Pillars of Wisdom:* "I loved you, so I drew these tides of men into my hands and wrote my will across the sky in stars." Its echo of the covenant of Abraham ("I will make your descendants as numerous as the stars") is unmistakable; yet in Lawrence's instance, the "you" is not God, not even the Arab people, but his young male lover.

All of this self-aggrandizement—as well as the homosexuality, and just the fact that he was a Westerner—has made Lawrence a controversial figure in the Arab world. Near the northern entrance of Wadi

Rum, Mahmoud took us to an isolated boulder, about the size of a mobile home, which contained two carved figures about eighteen inches tall. One was clearly an Arab and was inscribed "Prince Abdullah ibn Hussein, 1918," the future king. The other had the familiar square nose of Lawrence. It was inscribed "L the Arab." I asked Mahmoud what he thought of the man.

"Lawrence may have been a good soldier," he said, "but he was not a great man. He was crazy mad for explosives. If you gave him explosives he would blow up any mountain."

"But didn't he help the Arabs?" I said.

"If the British wanted to help the Arabs they would have. They just wanted to help themselves."

"Didn't Lawrence help start Arab nationalism?"

"No. It started with the Nabateans."

Our final stop on our mini-Lawrence tour was a desert mountain at the end of a small ridge. The mountain was divided into a series of vertical strata that look like lady fingers squeezed together around a Bundt cake. Because these colonnades look remarkably like pillars, local bedouin call the mountain "Lawrence," even though there are only five such pillars (and even though the title is never explained in the book). We stopped the car, and I decided to walk across the desert floor to get a closer view. The afternoon was hot, and a small herd of camels grazed nearby. The ground was covered with chips of granite—gray, black, purple, brown. I picked up one and slipped it into my pocket, the first time I had done that since Jebel Musa. As I did, I thought again about Lawrence's legacy and what it said about my own experience in the desert.

For all the lingering fascination with him, few people today hold Lawrence up as a hero worth emulating. One reason may be a largely forgotten part of his story. Lawrence is remembered for his romanticism, for shucking his English khakis and taking up the warrior tradition of his adopted tribe. But by the end of his three-year tenure, Lawrence himself rejects that ideal. As he writes in *Seven Pillars,* "The effort for these years to live in the dress of Arabs, and to imitate their mental foundations, quitted me of my English self." But, he continues, "I could not sincerely take on the Arab skin: it was affectation only. Easily was a man made an infidel, but hardly might he be converted to another faith." This coldhearted reality, not his warm-fuzzy idealism, is Lawrence's true legacy: Not only *can* you go home again; you must.

In this way, I was as much a disciple of Lawrence as of Moses. Few who enter the desert today do so with the notion of leaving themselves behind and becoming somehow bedouin. Though my journey was certainly romantic in its own way, I never suffered delusions nor seriously considered fantasies of "leaving myself behind" and becoming something else entirely. I had traveled too widely and seen too many shallow transformations to put much credence in that. Instead, what I think I was trying to do—and, to an extent, what I think I was doing—was becoming something that I already was: namely, a person with these places living inside me. The desert, as I was discovering, was part of my own geography just as much as my own hometown. And the best way I could explain this feeling to myself was to believe that the desert wasn't a new place for me; it was an old place, a familiar place, that I never quite knew. This was a major revelation: I didn't need to stay here forever to reach some kind of transformation. I was carrying around this place— and perhaps even that transformation—already within me.

That evening we camped on the edge of Wadi Rum before starting the following morning toward Jordan's western border, the Arava Valley, which leads from the Gulf of Aqaba to the Dead Sea along the African rift. It was here, after leaving the Sinai, that the Israelites began their final trek north. We visited several sites associated with the Bible, including Lot's Cave, a grotto that Byzantine travelers identified as the place where Lot convened with his daughters. Today it has the ruins of a church and several mosaics dating from the seventh century C.E. We gave the attendant some baksheesh and hopped over the fence to look around. Later we found him asleep in his shack, cradling a bottle of booze. Given the role of liquor in the place, the scene brought a smile.

After lunch we drove up the sheer face of the rift to the start of the mountains that run along the central spine of Jordan. The terrain shifted rapidly from the melting heat of the valley floor, through a series of jagged mountain teeth along the fault line, to pockets of green along the mountain ridge where olives and figs are joined by oaks, junipers, and cypresses. Because of these stark conditions, few people in history have been brave enough to live here. But many have passed through. This is the start of what Numbers calls the King's Highway, which stretched from the Gulf of Aqaba near Eilat, through the mountain kingdoms of Edom, Moab, and Ammon, before reaching Damascus, where it joined the Via Maris and advanced into Mesopotamia. This is the road Abraham likely took on his way from Harran (though he was farther north); it's also the road Jacob took on his way to and from his grandfather's homeland. Four thousand years later, it's also the road Lawrence and Faysal took on their final run to Damascus. More important for us, it's also the road Moses wanted to take on his trip up from Sinai.

We stopped in a small, mostly abandoned town and took a short hike to a shaded area overlooking the Dead Sea. The sky was pale blue now, and we could see a small herd of goats on a plateau. Some teenage boys crouched behind a rock, looking at the shepherd girls. We watched the scene unfold for a few minutes, then pulled out our Bibles and returned to the story.

After recounting in exacting detail the rebellions that dominate the Israelites' second year in the desert, the Bible is silent on the next thirty-eight years. During this time, members of the first generation presumably are dying, as God had willed following the episode with the spies. New children are born. Miriam dies and is buried. Then, because Moses has concluded that the Israelites will not conquer the Promised Land from the south, he rouses his people and prepares to cross the Jordan and move north. The exact itinerary of the Israelites during this period is almost impossible to decipher; the text appears to repeat itself on some occasions and to contradict itself on others. Kings from one place pop up in another place; nations long since passed suddenly reappear.

But generally speaking, the Israelites proceed as follows. Before setting out, Moses sends messengers to the king of Edom, the southernmost kingdom of Transjordan, which is made up of descendants of

Esau. "Thus says your brother Israel," the messengers say. "You know all the hardships that have befallen us; that our ancestors went down to Egypt, that we dwelt in Egypt a long time, and that the Egyptians dealt harshly with us and our ancestors." Allow us, then, to cross your country, the messengers say. "We will not pass through fields or vineyards, and we will not drink water from wells. We will follow the King's Highway, turning off neither to the right nor to the left until we have crossed your territory." Edom flatly rejects the request. "You shall not pass through us, else we will go out against you with the sword."

With Edom closed off, the Israelites choose an alternate route. First they move eastward across the Negev, where they are threatened by the Canaanite king of Arad, whom they quickly destroy. Next they pass into Jordan just north of the Gulf of Aqaba, near present-day Eilat, at which point they turn north again, skirting Edom to its eastern side. In no time, the Israelites grow ornery again, complaining about the miserable food. God sends fiery serpents to bite them, killing some and wounding others. Moses intercedes, and God instructs him to take a copper serpent and mount it on a pole. The wounded are told they can look at the serpent and recover.

The Israelites then continue north, passing the land of Moab to the land of the Amorites, near modern Amman. The Bible notes in passing that this story is mentioned in the *Book of the Wars of the Lord,* which scholars presume is a lost text describing this part of the journey in more detail. Moses then asks the Amorites for permission to pass through their land, but the Amorites respond by engaging the Israelites in battle. The Israelites win handily and settle the land all the way north to Jabbok. Two and a half tribes will stay here when the rest cross the Jordan and attack Canaan.

What follows is one of the more curious incidents of the Bible, the story of Balaam. Now that the Israelites are camped in the area of modern Jordan, the Moabites, just to the south, grow concerned. The king declares, "Now this horde will lick clean all that is about us as an ox licks up the grass in the field." The king summons a soothsayer named Balaam from along the Euphrates to put a hex on the Israelites. "There is a people that came out of Egypt," the king tells Balaam. "It hides the earth from view, and it is settled next to me. Come then, put a curse upon this people for me, since they are too numerous for me; perhaps I can thus defeat them and drive them out of the land." Balaam asks God for permission to travel to Moab, but God tells him not to go, saying, "You must not curse that people, for they are blessed." The king of Moab sends even more emissaries, and God gives Balaam permission to go, but only if he agrees to follow God's orders.

Once he arrives in Moab, Balaam asks the king to prepare seven altars, with seven bulls and seven rams. Balaam sacrifices the animals and then turns to the Israelites. Instead of a curse, though, Balaam issues a blessing, which he delivers in the form of a poem. "How can I damn whom God has not damned. / How doom when the Lord has not doomed? / As I see them from the mountain tops, / Gaze on them from the heights, / There is a people that dwells apart." The king of Moab is horrified, but, instead of sending Balaam home, the king takes him to another spot to issue his curse. Once again Balaam issues a blessing. Four times the king tries, four times Balaam responds with a message of favor. "God is not mortal to change his mind," Balaam explains. Before leaving, Balaam informs the king that his people will be Israel's next victims.

The story of Balaam is one of the defining events of the Israelites' final years in the desert. Reviewing the event later in the Hebrew Bible, the prophet Micah suggests the episode is a bookend to the liberation from Egypt. At the start of the Exodus, God expresses his devotion to his chosen people by thwarting the king of Egypt; at the end he reinforces his commitment by thwarting the king of Moab. Though the story of Balaam takes up only three chapters in Numbers, some Talmudic scholars thought it should stand on its own, meaning there would be Seven Books of Moses: Genesis, Exodus, Leviticus, Numbers 1–21, Balaam (Numbers 22–24), Numbers 25–36, and Deuteronomy. Either way, by the end of the story, Balaam emerges less as a sorcerer, as he is originally portrayed, and more as a prophet. "A star rises from Jacob," Balaam says, "a meteor comes forth from Israel."

For Avner, the lesson of the story was that God's power is not limited to Israel. "He also controls the destiny of the Amorites, the Moabites, even the Edomites. Balaam foretells their fate as well."

"But Balaam is not an Israelite," I said. "How does he hear the voice of God?"

"The text suggests anyone can hear God. Anyone can follow his commandments. It's the same with the Exodus. Other people join in the Exodus who are not part of the twelve tribes. By accepting the laws, they, too, become part of Israel."

As we were leaving, we noticed a brand-new Toyota Land Rover parked nearby with a family of four enjoying a picnic. Since we had seen few expensive vehicles the entire time we were in Jordan, we were looking curiously at the car, when the father of the family beckoned us over. He was neatly dressed in gray trousers and an Adidas windbreaker. He was from Qatar, he said, and was living in Jordan on a military study program. He asked us where we were from.

Israel and America, we said.

"Ah, you two are always good allies," he said. "Not just military allies, but friends, too."

He asked what we were doing in Jordan and I explained the nature of our project. "But nothing in the Bible takes place here," he said. Sure it does, I said, and showed him various passages in the text. He looked through the book curiously and asked a few questions. After a while he handed it back. "Good luck with your travels," he said. "I hope that we meet again."

"Despite your military studies, may we meet in peace," I said.

"We're all looking for peace," he said, then pointed at my hand. "We've spent too much time fighting ever since the stories in that book."

We drove along the spine of the mountains for a while, toward the place where we would camp for the night. Dusk was setting, and the paved road soon became dirt. As we rose and dipped along the craggy spine, moving gradually higher, the rich blend of trees also gave way to the familiar amalgamation of boulders and desert shrubs, like trail mix sprinkled along the side of the road. There were no other cars on the road, only the occasional bedouin with a camel.

Just after dark, Mahmoud pulled over to greet a bedouin friend in front of his tent. The man, Nissim, insisted we stop for tea, and soon insisted we spend the night. His tent had three rooms and was quilted together out of black goat hair intercut with red-and-gray-striped blankets and the occasional burlap sugar sack. The tent was about fifty feet long, ten feet wide, and faced east. By the time we settled into the southernmost section, designed for guests, and were joined by a few neighbors and teenage boys, this section alone easily accommodated a dozen people. One boy started a campfire out front. A few goats wandered just outside; some camels brayed nearby. The whole place smelled of animal musk, charcoal, and sage. After my encounters with bedouin homes in the Sinai and solar châteaus in the Negev, this was by far the most antiquated lodging I'd seen. Following a few glasses of tea, I asked Nissim why he had chosen to pitch his tent here.

"This is my birthplace," he said. Nissim appeared to be in his thirties and had a serious, focused air to him.

"But why not go to a town?" I asked.

"I prefer to live here in spring and summer. I have goats, it's easy to find space for them."

"How many times a year do you move?"

"It depends on the year. Sometimes we have good rain and I stay in one place. In dry years I sometimes move two or three times in a year. But I prefer here."

"Is there something special about this area?"

"Over there," he said, pointing north toward Petra, "is Wadi Musa," the Valley of Moses. "The prophet Musa passed through there and stuck his stick in the ground and brought water."

"So do you feel more connected to Moses than other prophets because you live here?"

"Since we are Muslim, we believe in all prophets," Nissim said. "But Mohammed is the last prophet, so we feel closer to him."

We had dinner—a platter of barley with vegetables and steaming bread—and afterward I asked him to tell me more about the story of Moses and the spring. Mahmoud was eager to join the conversation, and the two of them described the story as it appears in the Koran. Moses and the Israelites are enslaved in Egypt, when Allah liberates them, leads them across the Red Sea and into the Sinai. Allah gives Moses the Scriptures, but the people rebel and build an idol in the shape of a calf. Later, Allah sends manna and quail for the people to eat. But they still lack for water, so Allah instructs Moses, "Strike the rock with your staff." Moses does, and twelve springs gush forth.

"What happens next?" I said.

"The people drink," Mahmoud said.

"But isn't there a punishment?" I asked.

"What do you mean?"

"Is Moses punished for how he strikes water from the rock? In the Bible, he's not allowed to go to the Promised Land. He has to die in Jordan."

"I don't know this story," Nissim said.

I retrieved the Bible from my bag and read the version of the same story that appears in Numbers 20. After Miriam dies, and before the long series of wars with the Jordanian kingdoms, a mini rebellion occurs in which the people complain about the lack of water. Moses and Aaron make a plea to God, who instructs them, "Take the rod and assemble the community, and before their very eyes order the rock to yield its water. Thus you shall produce water for them from the rock and provide drink for the congregation and their beasts." Moses does as he is told, but instead of speaking to the rock—"ordering" it to yield water— he strikes the rock twice with his rod. Out comes "copious water," and everyone drinks. But God becomes irate and, in a gesture long viewed with horror among commentators and lay readers alike, issues a stern retribution. "Because you did not trust Me enough to affirm My sanctity in the sight of the Israelite people, therefore you shall not lead this congregation into the land that I have given them." Moses thereby learns his fate: He will not set foot in the Promised Land. He, like the people he led out of Egypt, will die in the wilderness.

After I finished the story, Mahmoud, who had been taking notes, asked me a few questions to get the details right. Nissim, meanwhile, wanted to look at my Bible and I handed it across the circle. Several of the teenage boys surged forward to get a closer look. One of them handed me a miniature Koran with well-thumbed pages and a black cloth cover. Here, I thought, was an extraordinary scene: an informal congregation of Muslims and Jews—scholars, shepherds, bedouin, travelers—all sitting around a campfire, beneath a homemade tent, talking, discussing, trading details about the stories of the ancient world.

At least that's what I thought was happening.

After a while I started asking a few more questions of my own. "So this business about talking to the rock versus striking the rock is not mentioned at all in the Koran?" I said.

"No," Mahmoud said.

"And the idea that Moses must die in Jordan. That's not mentioned?"

"No."

"So there's no disappointment?" I said.

"What do you mean, 'disappointment'?"

"Moses doesn't make it to the Promised Land. It's one of the saddest moments in the whole book." I raised my voice in emphasis, and frustration.

Mahmoud seemed a bit confused by my remark. He started fidgeting and glancing at Nissim, who was still playing with my Bible. Mahmoud was uncomfortable, and so was I. There was something missing from our conversation, but I couldn't quite place it.

"Between the Koran and the Bible there is a difference over where Moses died," Mahmoud repeated. "The Koran doesn't say."

"But the difference is bigger than that," I said.

"The main reference to Moses in the Koran—" Mahmoud started to say, but I cut him off.

"I know the story," I said, a bit rudely. "The point I want to make is this: It's not the same Moses. The Moses in the Bible and the Moses in the Koran are different people." Avner, who had been listening nearby, winced.

"You mean not physically, but their meaning?" Mahmoud asked.

"Both," I said. "We think it's the same person, but it's not."

"You'll never make it as a diplomat," Avner remarked dryly.

I knew, under the circumstances, that I should be more gracious, but I couldn't help myself. "I'm basing my opinion on the fact that for Moses in the Bible, the whole objective, the whole point of his life, is to lead the Israelites into the Promised Land. To get them to Israel. Moses in the Koran does not have that. The Promised Land is not even a factor; it's not mentioned. Of course, the Koran doesn't want to glorify the land of Israel. It wants to glorify Mecca and Medina. Therefore, the whole reason Moses lived—according to the Bible—is not mentioned in the Koran. They're the same person, but they have different meanings."

At this point, hearing the slightly frantic edge to my voice, Nissim wanted to know what I was saying, and began conversing with Mahmoud. I took the occasion to step out of the tent. There was a slight chill in the air, and the black bowl of sky was filled with stars as bright as I remembered from my first night in the Sinai. Looking up, I felt more alone than at anytime along our route. An experience that moments earlier seemed so warm and full of possibility suddenly seemed constricting, and cold. We were dealing with stories, passed around campfires not unlike this one, and written down many years later. And yet, in each version of the story, the details were different, therefore the meaning was different, therefore the lessons were different.

For so much of this trip, I realized, I had allowed myself to get caught up in the emotional awakening I had been experiencing. If I could feel a growing openness in myself, if I could sense a similar feeling in Rami, Ofer, Father Justin, and countless other people we met, if I could picture a world full of ecumenical desert people, in touch with their inner selves, riding a wave of sand-hewn memories to international peace and togetherness, then surely it could happen. Surely we could forget the centuries of wars that have been fought over these stories. Surely we could overlook the millennia of bad faith that have been engendered by these stories. Surely we could remove these stories from politics, religion, and geography, and view them instead as a universal sourcebook offering readers a guide to spiritual emancipation and personal fulfillment. Surely, in other words, we could forget the things that drew me into this project—the archaeology and history that firmly anchor them in a time and place—and focus instead on the more universal qualities of reading the book—the internal growth and reaching toward God. Couldn't we?

A few minutes later Avner came out to see how I was doing.

"That was the worst moment of the trip," I said. "It was so exciting sitting around with all those books, but it turned out to be so discouraging."

"But that's the reality of Judaism and Islam," Avner said. "There's almost no commonality. Most Muslims don't know why Jews care about the Holy Land. They don't know that Jews believe it was promised to them."

"So is there any way of reading this conversation as being anything other than depressing?" I said.

"Yesss," Avner said, tentatively. "I suspect if you want to be diplomatic and say, 'Here we at least find the core of the big trouble, and now that we know the problem, maybe we can address it.' "

"But we're talking about different books, different characters, different everything," I said. "We may be people of the Book, but since they're different books, we're different people."

Avner sighed in agreement. "I've been dealing with this for years," he said.

"Part of me wants to run away from what just happened."

"But you can't," he said. "There are other ways to build bridges."

"Maybe. But this is certainly a dagger through any sense of romance I might have been feeling. It's the same thing that happened with Lawrence. When I walked out here I realized, 'This is why he went home. He couldn't bridge the gap.' I finally understood."

"That's clear, even from the movie," Avner said. "The two worlds are not the same."

"The same thing happened with Moses," I said. "Like Lawrence, his role was to get the people out of bondage, but he couldn't lead them all the way to freedom. The people had to do that on their own. And maybe it's not so sad, after all. Maybe it's unavoidable."

"It's a little sad," Avner said.

"But it's God's plan," I said. "And that's the point, I suppose. If we went back in there and wanted to create a happy moment, all we would have to do is turn it to God. That's what the Bible and Koran have in common. It's not the characters. It's not the people. It's God."

"That's what we were discussing after you left," Avner said. We were standing in the open air. Each of us staring straight ahead. There was a certain space between us, and an even greater space between us and them. "Mahmoud said, 'God created everything,' and I agreed. So, in the end, they are the people of God, and so are we. He said it, and I said it, too: 'It's the same God.' "

I looked at him with admiration. He was, indeed, a bridge builder: a man of the desert, not of a nation. "I'd like to believe that," I said. "I really, really would."

2. Half as Old as Time

Waking up in a bedouin tent in the middle of Jordan, twenty miles from the nearest electrical outlet, one hundred miles from the nearest traffic jam, is not as peaceful as it might seem. A goat with a cowbell nibbles on the tent. A camel trips over a guy wire. A handful of shepherd girls, none older than twelve, slip on their sandals and black homemade shawls and chirp with their moms who are packing them lunch. Their brothers snap pieces of wormwood and begin heating the pudgy kettle, which soon emits a growl that seems far more treacherous than tempting. A baby wails. I stick my head out from under my blanket and look at my watch. It's just after 4:00. The monks in Saint Catherine's are still in their beds. The bedouin of Petra are well into their day.

With no choice but to get up, we huddle half-asleep around the campfire for an hour, then decide to begin our morning trek up Jebel Haroun, or Mount Aaron, the holiest site in Petra, where Aaron is said to have died and been buried during the Israelites' final march. Short of a helicopter, or a two-day hike, the only reasonable way to ascend the mountain is by camel, so at just after five we mounted three camels that Mahmoud had engaged from our host. Nissim's camels, it seems, are not unlike Prince Hassan's horses: They suffer from wanderlust. A few weeks earlier, nine camels wandered down the mountain and strolled across the border into Israel, where they promptly disappeared. Nissim mentioned

the problem to Avner as we were leaving, and after an hour of excruci-
ating uphill climbing on a narrow, unkempt path, Avner had an idea.

He drew our camels to a stop at a serrated ledge overlooking the
Dead Sea. The bone-colored rock was so dramatic here, cutting into the
sky like one of those shark-tooth knives that saw through aluminum
cans on late-night infomercials, that you could still feel the force of the
earthquake that caused the great rift twenty-five million years earlier.
Now within earshot of Israel, Avner reached into his knapsack and
pulled out his mobile phone. He punched in Ofer's number in Ezuz and
outlined the plight of the missing camels, being careful to describe their
brand—two horizontal lines and a vertical one like old-fashioned football goalposts. Ofer said he would check into the situation and call back.
Who needs diplomatic immunity, when you have a network of desert
missionaries and access to a cellular phone?

As we continued, I asked Avner about a persistent question I had
read about in discussions of the historical accuracy of the Bible: Were
camels domesticated during the time of the patriarchs? Camels appear
frequently in the Hebrew Bible, surfacing as early as Genesis 12, when
Abraham travels to Egypt during the drought and receives as a gift from
the pharaoh, "sheep, oxen, asses, male and female slaves, she-asses, and
camels." Abraham's servant later takes "ten of his master's camels" on his
trip to Harran to get a wife for Isaac, and Jacob subsequently brings even
more camels back from Harran with his family. William Foxwell
Albright, the archaeologist, was one of the first to conclude that camels
were still wild animals in the Near East during this time of the patriarchs, the early second millennium B.C.E. The earliest inscription that
mentions domesticated camels was not until the eleventh century B.C.E.,
Albright noted, and camel bones were not found in significant numbers
near cities—a sign of their domestication—until centuries later.
Albright insisted that the use of camels in the Pentateuch, including a
reference in Leviticus that prohibits eating camel meat because the animal has no hoofs, was an anachronism.

Avner mentioned that he knew an archaeozoologist, Liora
Horowitz, who was studying the issue and who thought she might be
able to date camel domestication early enough to include the patriarchs.

"We'll have to call her when we get home," he said. "No wait!" Though we were on a particularly tricky bend in the path at the moment, Avner again reached around for his phone, pressed a few numbers of recall, and spoke into the mouthpiece. Then he tossed the phone to me. "Professor Horowitz?!" I said, after juggling the phone in my hands.

I explained my question and she rattled off the results of recent surveys. An article appeared in *Archaeology* a number of years earlier, she said, that cited figurines and camel-hair rope to suggest that camels were domesticated in the Nile Valley as early as 2600 B.C.E. But that data was inconclusive, she said. More recently, she had reviewed all the surveys of second millennium B.C.E. sites in Israel and found no evidence of bones. By contrast, in later periods, the site contained extensive camel remains used in cult sacrifice, suggesting camels had been herded by that time.

"All in all, I'd say there were no domesticated camels from the early second millennium B.C.E.," she said. "Albright is holding up quite well."

I thanked her and tossed the phone back to Avner. Who needs the Internet when you can do research today on camels in the ancient world from the back of a camel on an ancient trail?

We continued for several more hours along a narrow ridge. The mountains were rugged here, though much paler than the ones in Sinai, roughly the color of saltines. The mix of cavernous valleys and ashen cliffs seemed lunar in its barrenness. We would navigate a particularly tight bend, then reach a flat area where we could see Israel to our left and Jebel Haroun up to our right, then descend into a valley where water collected in the rainy season and a shock of pink oleanders lined the ground like a Hawaiian lei on a beach. Then the path would jerk upward, the greenery would disappear, and we'd have to hold on tight.

When the camels needed to climb, they would place their right front foot tentatively on a rock to test its stability, then frantically pedal their back legs like a car stuck in the sand, before lurching forward with a hitch and a groan, and an occasional squeal from their riders. It took such concentration to stay on the saddle, gripping the pommels in front and back, that I began to feel physically drained. All conversation stopped. The only sound I could hear was the gurgling and growling of the camels as they masticated their latest meal. The only smell was from the perspiration that ran down my face, intermingled with the dust that kicked up from the ground and the occasional grassy mulch from my camel's sneeze. All this on a day we were visiting Petra, one of the most romanticized places in the world.

Just the name Petra alone evokes magic, like Xanadu, Shangri-La, or Timbuktu. It's the boutonniere of the Middle East, a shimmering, illusory place, carved out of salmon-colored mountains, where Indiana Jones finds the Holy Grail at the end of *Indiana Jones and the Last Crusade* and where countless generations of European explorers tried but failed to locate its charms. Mention Petra today and people think of the Nabateans, the bedouin tribe from Arabia that hewed its capital in the corkscrew valley and gave Petra its glorious facade. The Nabateans thrived for four hundred years around the time of Christ. The chief source of their livelihood, frankincense, over which they had near monopolistic control, is prominently mentioned in the New Testament, when the Wise Men from the East offer it along with gold and myrrh as a gift to the baby Jesus.

But Petra also has roots in the Old Testament, long before the Nabateans. Because of its strategic location and abundant springs, the city was an important stopover on the King's Highway as early as the second millennium B.C.E. In the Bible, Petra first appears in Numbers 31, when the Israelites are venturing north and slay Rekem, one of the kings of Transjordan. Rekem was the ancient name for Petra, and the king was likely a local chieftain who ruled some of the scattered Edomite population. Later, around 1000 B.C.E., King David occupied Petra in a failed bid to control Edom; his son Solomon consolidated control over the area and diverted Petra's trading profits to his coffers.

This close association with the biblical story has led some to speculate that Petra may have played an even larger role in the history of the Israelites. Before leaving for Jordan, I had gone to visit a colleague of Avner's, Dudu Cohen, an archaeologist, a guide, and a deeply observant Jew who lives with his family in a religious settlement south of Jerusalem. For years Dudu had been carefully constructing a radical theory he had just published in a prominent journal of biblical studies: that Kadesh-barnea, the place where the Israelites lived for thirty-eight of their forty years in the desert, was not Ain el-Qudeirat in northern Sinai, as is popularly believed, but Petra.

The heart of Dudu's theory concerns what the Bible calls the place where the Israelites camped. Sometimes the place is called Kadesh, other times Kadesh-barnea. The popular view holds that these names refer to the same place, but Dudu found evidence suggesting ancient commentators viewed the two as referring to different places. The spy story, for example, is usually associated with Kadesh-barnea, in the wilderness of Paran. The story of Moses striking the rock, by contrast, is associated with Kadesh, in the wilderness of Zin. Paran is generally linked to the Egyptian border, while Zin is connected to the border with Edom.

In addition, some sources directly connected Kadesh with Petra. In Aramaic, the vernacular language of the late first millennium B.C.E., the name Kadesh is translated as Rekem, the same name used for Petra. Also, European travelers who came to the Middle East before the twentieth century, including the Swiss explorer Johann Ludwig Burckhardt, who is credited with "discovering" the place in 1812, believed that Petra was the site of Kadesh. "Plus, it just makes sense," Dudu said. "There is much more water in Petra than in the Sinai. At the time of the Nabateans, thirty thousand people could live there, and nomads require much less water. It easily could have supported the Israelites. Not six hundred thousand, but there probably weren't that many anyway."

So what difference does his theory make to the interpretation of the story?

"For starters, we didn't wander around the desert for forty years," Dudu said. "Sitting in Petra gave us a chance to form an identity. Usually, in sociology, one of the main elements in identifying a nation is territory. That's why we have all the theories that Israel wasn't formed as a nation until the time of David, when the country was unified under a single king. Before that, we were just tribes and didn't have any territory of our own.

"But my theory gives a different perspective," he said. "Slowly, sitting together in Petra, we formed a nation. We built roots. Moses told the story of our history. He planted in people's minds the comments of

God to our patriarchs that we will get the Promised Land. It's ours. God gave it to us. Then, when they moved from there to the border with Canaan, the people were ready. They just waited for the order to cross the Jordan and conquer! And I think that's why the rabbis see that point as a miracle, because the big change had occurred. In Petra we finally overcame the desert and became a unified people."

By late morning, the camel saddle had rubbed off most of the skin from my lower back and inner thigh. I was verging on being in considerable pain by the time we arrived at a resting area just shy of the summit of Jebel Haroun. It was here, in 1812, that Johann Ludwig Burckhardt completed the deception that enabled him to "discover" Petra. Burckhardt, a Swiss-born adventurer, posed as a Muslim—and even learned Arabic—in order to travel through the Middle East, then largely hostile to Europeans. Arriving in Syria in 1810, he was asked about his strange accent. Burckhardt said he was a trader from India and that his mother tongue was Hindustani. Asked to demonstrate, he spoke a guttural concoction of Swiss-German, which seemed to satisfy his hosts.

Two years later he set off for Petra. He couldn't express his desire to search for the lost city, since it would have been interpreted as spying. Also, Muslims were not supposed to be interested in Petra, which was considered the work of infidels. But Burckhardt said he had vowed to sacrifice a goat at Aaron's tomb. When he reached the outskirts of Petra, his guide suggested making the sacrifice there, but Burckhardt wanted to press ahead. They arrived at the entrance to the city, and again the bedouin suggested making the sacrifice. Again Burckhardt demurred. Finally they arrived at the Treasury, Petra's signature structure. Burckhardt was the first Westerner to see the building since the Romans were kicked out almost 1,800 years earlier.

Somehow masking his excitement, Burckhardt managed to describe the building, and even sketch it, all the while concealing his journal underneath his robe. He continued to draw buildings throughout the site. Had his journal been discovered, he surely would have been killed as a spy. As it happens, he spent so much time making drawings that he ran out of time and was forced to sacrifice his goat at the terrace just below the summit of Jebel Haroun.

He clearly was not the only one to use this site for sacrificing. As we left our camels and walked up the final ascent of the mountain, which reminded me of the freestanding peak atop Jebel Musa, we saw dozens of burnt-out fire circles with animal bones scattered around them. Avner identified the bones—goat, sheep, even camels—which clearly had been used in ritual sacrifices by local bedouin. "Do Muslims actually sacrifice camels?" I asked Mahmoud. "Yes," he said, "but rarely. They're very expensive."

About twenty minutes later we arrived at the top of the mountain, where a whitewashed shrine dedicated to Aaron sits atop a bald pate of flesh-colored stone. Holy buildings stood on this site as early as the Byzantine Era, when Christian travelers first associated the mountain with the place of Aaron's death. The current shrine, which dates from 1459, is about the size of a small diner; it's made of stone and topped with a dome that looks like the head of a giant snowman. The building was administered by Greek Christians in the seventh century when the ten-year-old prophet Mohammed passed through on a trip from Mecca to Damascus and climbed Jebel Haroun with his uncle. The guard, a monk named Bahira, prophesied that the boy would change the world. Today's Muslim pilgrims pay homage to the prophet by draping the shrine with green and white pieces of fabric, twined threads, and seashells. These remembrances are considered the Islamic equivalent of lighting a candle to a saint.

We explored the inside of the building, which was dark, bare, and surprisingly cool. A stairway led down into a dank basement, where Aaron is said to be entombed. Two iron gates block the crypt, but we were able to catch a faint glimpse of a large stone tomb.

Back outside, we climbed the narrow stairs to the roof, which had a spectacular view of the surroundings. From here, the true charm of Petra became apparent. The only thing visible for miles in any direction was cluster after cluster of foreboding mountains, each one more parched than the next. In this scene, like a tub of Cracker Jack spilled onto the desert floor, Petra was clearly the prize. The tree-lined valleys around the ancient city looked like mint jelly dripping down a lamb shank. "I'll say this about Dudu Cohen," I said. "I don't know about the historical accuracy of his thesis, but viewed from this location, it makes much more sense for the Israelites to have lived here for thirty-eight years than to have been in Ain el-Qudeirat."

"Certainly for them," Avner said. "It's much nicer."

"It's also better protected. There's plenty of water."

"And the weather is better."

We sat down on the roof and reviewed the story. In Numbers 20, during the Israelites' fortieth year in the desert, after the incident in which Moses and Aaron disobey God's instructions about the rock, God suddenly announces to the brothers: "Let Aaron be gathered to his kin," a biblical euphemism for die. "He is not to enter the land that I have given to the Israelite people, because you disobeyed my command about the waters of Meribah," God says. "Take Aaron and his son Eleazar and bring them up on Mount Hor. Strip Aaron of his vestments and put them on his son Eleazar. Then Aaron shall be gathered unto the dead." Moses does as instructed, and Aaron dies "on the summit of the mountain," a location identified only as being "on the boundary of the land of Edom." The people bewail Aaron for thirty days.

As we were reading, we were joined on the roof by the Muslim guard, who must have been napping when we first arrived. He was from the bedouin tribe around Petra, the Bdul, and worked for the local government. I asked him if he thought Moses had come to this site. "Yes," he said. "With Aaron. According to the books of the Jews, it was 3,200 years ago."

"Do you feel them?" I asked.

"I feel blessed," he said. "When I sleep here, I sleep much better than when I sleep down there." He gestured toward Petra.

"And why is that?"

"This is the best place in the country. The air is good. Aaron is here. I feel safe."

We bid him good-bye and rejoined our camels for the descent into Petra. It didn't take long to realize that while I had twice used a camel to ride *up* a mountain, I had yet to use one to ride down. Riding up uses one set of muscles—the lower back, the inner thigh, the bicep. Riding down uses a different, much more sensitive set—the upper abs, the outer ankle, the tricep—as well as a few body parts I didn't know had feeling, like the coccyx.

The remarkable thing about riding a camel is how much action it requires of the arms, which must work constantly to relieve pressure from every other body part. The right arm grabs the pommel in front to prevent you from falling; the left arm twists around to grab the pommel in back to relieve pressure from your groin. I had read Lawrence said that all bedouin have extensive knowledge of their genealogies. Now I know why. It's impossible to spend eight hours on a camel and not think of your children. As Mahmoud delicately put it after one particularly rocky bend, "I'm glad I have two sons already." It was at that point that I decided to dismount and walk a few steps on my own.

By the time we arrived in the central valley of Petra, Wadi Musa, it was the middle of the afternoon and we were coated in several layers of sweat, camel spittle, and regurgitated sage. I spotted a small spring alongside the path, and we stopped to wash our faces. As we stumbled from there into the main street of the ruined city, I realized that the limp one gets from riding a camel is a lot more twisted than that from riding a horse. All I could think was that eight hours on a camel is like eight hours on a camel—and nothing else. "And to think that the Nabateans arrived in Petra after eight *months* on a camel," Avner said.

Though Petra may have had ancient roots, its glory years didn't begin until the arrival of the Nabateans, one of the fleeting superpowers of the ancient Near East. The Nabateans were a nomadic tribe from the region of Nabatea in the northwest Arabian Desert. In the sixth century B.C.E., when Babylon depopulated the kingdoms of Judah and Israel across the Jordan, the Edomites filtered across the river to take their place. The Nabateans in turn filtered into Edom. Over the next several hundred years, they came to control the major trade route between Mecca and Damascus, as well as the one between Mecca and Gaza, an awesome vise grip on the region. To reflect their power, this previously nomadic people built a capital city in Petra in the fourth century B.C.E. At their peak around the time of Christ, the Nabateans were trading with not only Palestine, Egypt, and Syria but also Greece, Rome, even China.

The Nabateans traded all manner of goods, including animals, spices, iron, copper, fabrics, sugar, medicine, gold, and ivory. But by far their dominant item was frankincense, a product so popular that Avner likened its appeal, and influence, to that of oil in modern life. Frankincense is made from resin extracted from a desert tree of the genus *Boswellia,* which in herbal medicine today is used to treat arthritis, diarrhea, dysentery, pulmonary disease, and ringworm. The process involves cutting trees so their sap comes into contact with oxygen and harden into globules, not unlike what happens with manna, though without the digestion of plant lice.

Frankincense was valued for its smell, which is described as being sweet to the point of intoxicating, but was quite unlike the perfumes of today. For one, it must be burned to produce its smell. In addition, it has sterilizing qualities and was used in healing, preserving food, and protecting against insects. Also, because of its perceived otherworldliness, it was used in religious ceremonies; for example, it covered up the malodor at animal sacrifices. In Exodus, God instructs Moses to mix pure frankincense with several other herbs and use the compound to bless the Tent of Meeting. Frankincense was considered so important that God deemed its use for cultic purposes a capital crime, punishable by death. Other cultures also used it as a palliative to death. Before crucifixion, Roman prisoners (possibly including Christ) were offered wine laced with frankincense as a painkiller. The Roman emperor Nero is said to have burned at his wife's funeral an amount of frankincense equal to the annual production in Arabia.

The reason the Nabateans rode frankincense to the status of regional power is that they figured out how to transport it from deep in the Arabian Desert, the only place on earth where it grows, to the commercial centers along the Mediterranean, where it could be profitably sold. The Nabatean Spice Route was a rarity in the Near East, a homemade route that skirted the fertile areas and thus eluded the larger powers. The two-thousand-mile pathway cut a southeast-northwest line across the desert. Viewed in terms of today's geography, 90 percent was in Saudi Arabia, 6 percent in Jordan, 4 percent in Israel, and the last two miles in Gaza. The journey took three months each way to complete and at its peak involved over one thousand camels, each one carrying as much as five hundred pounds of frankincense. The key to the Spice Route was the Nabatean technique of collecting water in hidden underground cisterns, to be used when the traders arrived. In the Negev, Avner took me to a handful of these caverns, which are still remarkably intact. The Israeli Army trains soldiers for desert survival by dropping them a few miles from the cisterns and instructing them to find the locations. Few ever do.

Because the Spice Route was so complex an undertaking, the previously nomadic Nabateans were forced to undergo a process of civilizing themselves: organizing a security force, collecting and distributing money, building administrative centers. A similar process had occurred in Mesopotamia and Egypt thousands of years earlier when large numbers of tribes shifted from a hunter-gatherer culture to an agricultural one. Here the transition happened again, and the result was Petra, a city that was so spectacular in large part because it was developed by people unaware—and uninfluenced—by traditional urban design. The pyramids of Giza are grander and were built 2,500 years earlier. Jerusalem has a certain timeless aura to it. But Petra takes your breath away.

One reason is the charming oddity of the place. The buildings in Petra are not freestanding but carved out of the side of sheer sandstone cliffs, not unlike the cities I carved out of sandpiles as a child. Because the edifices mostly consist of crypts hewed out of the sides of mountains, with elaborate, Hollywood-back-lot-style facades, the buildings never fell down, like most ancient buildings did. There are dozens still standing today in the one-square-mile area, ranging from tombs that are 150 feet high, to storage rooms no bigger than coffins, to sacred cult sites on mountaintops overlooking it all. There is also an open-air theater and main street from when Rome finally annexed Petra in 106 C.E. Altogether, Petra looks like a shopping center, in which each store has a showier front than its neighbor, and each one is more inviting than the next.

Adding to its allure is that Petra, whose location was unknown for centuries, has become one of the most mythologized cities in recent memory, a real-life Atlantis plucked from obscurity. Also, the cliffs themselves are visually stunning. The rock has been pickled by the wind into a cornucopia of colors: brown, orange, purple, pink. I never wanted to lick a mountain until I went to Petra. Artist Edward Lear walked up the central street in 1858 and described the cliffs as "brilliant and gay beyond my anticipation." Agatha Christie saw the rocks as "blood-red." But the most famous characterization came from John William Burgon, who described the stones in his 1845 poem "Petra" as being "as if by magic grown."

> Not virgin-white like that old Doric shrine,
> Where erst Athena held her rites divine;
> Not saintly-grey, like many a minister fane,
> That crowns the hill and consecrates the plain;
> But rose-red as if the blush of dawn
> That first beheld them were not yet withdrawn;
> The hues of youth upon a brow of woe,
> Which Man deemed old two thousand years ago,
> Match me such a marvel save in Eastern clime,
> A rose-red city half as old as Time.

As it happens, Burgon had never been to Petra when he wrote these oft-quoted lines. When he finally came sixteen years later, he realized his glasses may have been miscolored and wrote abjectly in a letter to his sister, "there is nothing rosy about Petra, by any means."

Burgon's backsliding may have been a bit too steep. If anything, Petra seems to change color every hour of the day, a veritable sundial of shades. In midafternoon, when we arrived, the sun still careened off the top of the mountains and covered much of the central street with sharp-edged shadows, black against the yellow sand. You can see many of Petra's surviving structures from its column-lined central street, which is located at the epicenter of a series of off-shoot canyons that peel off like petals on a morning glory. Petra never contained private homes, or at least they've never been found. Residents are thought to have lived in tents. The city was mostly occupied with administrative buildings, religious sites, and the tombs of nobles and kings. Petra, in that way, is remarkably similar to the pyramids: a paean to national power, a religious zone, but, in its most impressive structures, a graveyard.

We hiked up the so-called East Cliff, a raised plateau just above the central street that looms over the town like the royal box at an opera house. This area contains some of the city's most famous structures, a half-dozen facilities known as the Royal Tombs. Each tomb is named after a prominent architectural detail—the Urn Tomb, the Silk Tomb, the Corinthian Tomb—and consists of a carved exterior masking a hollow cavity about the size of a high school classroom. The facades have been whittled out of the mountain into a series of columns, pediments, and friezes that climb as high as seven or eight stories and can only be described as faux Greek in their style and discombobulated in their effect. The Nabateans are thought to have picked up these and other techniques in their trading with powers around the Mediterranean. All in all, the tombs have the feel of classical temples put together from a kit, not assembled in precisely the right way, and affixed to the front of the mountains to satisfy a newly minted royal class, a few generations out of the desert, and not quite to the point of having set up an art school.

"So why did they care more about building tombs than building houses?" I asked Avner. We had settled on the stoop of one of the tombs, overlooking the fading light in the valley.

"The simple answer is that maybe they considered life after death their normal life. If there is an afterlife, the part of life on earth is very limited. You build pyramids if you're Egyptian. You build *nawamis* if you're a pastoral nomad."

"So if so many Egyptian texts have to do with the afterlife," I said, "and they built the pyramids in 2650 B.C.E.; and if the Nabateans cared so much about the afterlife and they built these enormous tombs in the second century B.C.E.: why doesn't the Pentateuch, which was written halfway between these two times, pay more attention to the afterlife?

The patriarchs are buried in Hebron, but no attention is given to how or why. Miriam, Aaron, and Moses all die in the desert and are buried with no mention of what happened to them."

"Because the Bible deals with life—how to live a holy life, an ethical life, a spiritual life. One of the reasons the Israelites ignored Egyptian influence on death is that the purpose of life in the Pentateuch is largely to serve God, or to have a family that will serve God. There's no mention of an afterlife. Life ceases when you die. And when you die, you stop serving God."

"But God continues."

"That's right. This is a break from other Near Eastern religions. In Egypt, in Petra, the kings become deities themselves. The pyramids, these tombs, are representations of the power of those people after they die."

"But if you're an Israelite—"

"There's only one God. He exists forever. So if you're going to build a temple, you build it to God. You don't build it to yourself."

We climbed down from the Royal Tombs and strolled through the molded canyons toward Petra's most famous site, the Treasury, a two-thousand-year-old architectural masterpiece that would be on any short list of the most beautiful buildings in the world. As visitor Andrew Crichton wrote in 1852, "There is scarcely a building in England of 40 years' standing so fresh and well preserved in its architectural decoration."

Like the tombs, the Treasury, which is believed to have been completed around the first century B.C.E., is not exactly a building, but a carved facade. Its 120-foot-high veneer has columns, pediments, and classical lions that could have come from the Parthenon. But the king's taste was by no means limited to Athens. The Treasury, which is often shown in photographs through a jagged opening in the cliffs, also boasts a reproduction of Isis, the Egyptian goddess, and two large eagles, which represent the chief Nabatean god, Dushara.

"Again, the Nabateans, coming from the desert, had no architecture of their own," Avner said. "Therefore they were very eclectic."

That mix-and-match quality of Nabatean culture is responsible for one of the most notable features of the Treasury, a ten-foot urn at the structure's highest peak whose slender pose reminded me of the statue of Freedom atop the U.S. Capitol. Local bedouin around Petra, unaware of classical history and unable to fathom why anyone would construct such a building, regarded the Treasury as the miraculous creation of the pharaoh, whom they considered the lord of black magic. According to tradition, the pharaoh went in pursuit of Moses and the Israelites after the Exodus and was so burdened by lugging his pharaonic riches and jewels that he constructed the Treasury in a stroke and deposited his loot in the urn, out of reach of human hands. Over the years, local bedouin have spent countless hours, and volumes of ammunition, shooting at the urn as if it were a piñata, trying to dislodge the hidden booty. Their only demonstrable impact has been blasting chunks from the solid stone vessel.

For us, the Treasury had a different meaning. Situated at the entrance to Petra, the Treasury stands as a kind of eternal emblem to the moment of transition when a desert people first becomes settled. As Avner noted, when he described the change the Nabateans underwent: First the tribe of shepherds became traders, then they began to see how much money they could make trading, then they began to travel for months at a time across the desert, then they realized the need to protect their trade routes, then they decided they needed a central power to organize their riches. "Sure enough, in a few years the Nabateans had a king," he said, "and suddenly a society that was built around equal tribes, with people helping one another, now became a stratified society, with nobles, merchants, administrators, and so on. It became like an urban society. That is the same change that the Israelites went through when they came to the Holy Land."

In making that connection—between the transition of the Nabateans in Petra and the transformation of the Israelites in the Promised Land—Avner raised one of the more intriguing, if controversial, subtexts of the final third of the Pentateuch: namely, what were the Israelites really doing during their forty years in the desert?

Answering that question requires a careful reading of Deuteronomy, the final book of the Pentateuch. A common view among biblical scholars is that the first four books of Moses constitute a narrative whole. They are written with a mix of storytelling, genealogies, laws, and poetry. Deuteronomy, by contrast, is written in a dramatically different style: It's a homily, a personal exhortation delivered by Moses to the Israelites on the eve of their entry into the Promised Land. It begins, "These are the words that Moses addressed to all Israel on the other side of the Jordan," and proceeds through a series of speeches in which Moses recounts the Israelites' historic trek and prepares them for the battle to come. While the other four books have an omniscient narrator, this book clearly is in Moses' voice, as he intimately addresses not just his contemporaries but future generations as well. As commentator Joel Rosenberg has noted, Moses, who once defined himself as "not a man of words," suddenly finds his voice, and his voice is remarkably similar to God's.

Most scholars believe that Deuteronomy is a late addition, appended after the first four books were already complete. In this view, the Torah was originally the Tetrateuch and became the Pentateuch only with the addition of the fifth book. As scholar William Hallo has written, "Deuteronomy occupies a unique position in the Hebrew Bible. More nearly than any other biblical book, it can lay claim to having been a book in its own right before it was incorporated into the canon."

If true—and most scholars agree that it is—why was the book added at all? Why not end with Numbers, with the Israelites having finished their trek through the region and prepared to go across the Jordan? This question divides scholars. Some view the speeches in Deuteronomy as a sermon on collective responsibility, others as an elaborate renewal of the covenant, still more as a prophetic foreshadowing of the troubles the Israelites will face in the future. What scholars do agree on is that the central objective of the text is to unify the Israelites in their allegiance to God. As the Hebrew name for the book, *mishne tora,* indicates, Deuteronomy is a "copy of the Torah," a retelling of the law. Accordingly, Moses reviews the Israelites' trek through the wilderness, recapitulates the laws, and generally reminds the Israelites of their responsibilities as a people. In effect, he leads a public reeducation of his people, a mass seminar on the desert floor.

This colloquium is necessary because the population of Israelites preparing to march into the Promised Land has little, if any, knowledge of its own history. None (with the exception of Joshua and Caleb) was present during the Exodus. That population had entirely died off, as God had willed after the rebellion over the spies. Instead, Moses is faced with a band of disparate tribes, each one made up *entirely* of people born in the wilderness. To put this into perspective, a twenty-year-old Israelite on the eve of the conquest would have been born to, say, a twenty-year-old Israelite who was born in the Kadesh-barnea, who in turn was born to, say, a twenty-year-old slave who escaped during the Exodus. That slave, a descendant of one of Jacob's sons, would have been born at least 430 years after the founder of his tribe, who in turn would have been born four generations after Abraham. Based on the Bible's own calendar, it's not unreasonable to assume that the average Israelite listening to Moses' speech in Jordan would have been nearly *eight hundred years* removed from the start of the story, as much time as from today to the reign of Richard the Lion-Hearted. A little review was certainly in order.

It's precisely the nature of that review that makes what the Israelites went through in Jordan analogous to what the Nabateans went through in Jordan. In both cases, a desert people undergoes a transition and starts to become a settled people. The Nabateans, however, never quite made it. They were overrun by the Romans in 106 C.E. and slinked back into obscurity. Why did they fail? "Not enough time," Avner said. "They only had four hundred years. When the Romans came they were not yet ripe."

The Israelites, however, ultimately *were* more successful. They conquered the Promised Land, lived there for five hundred years, were kicked out briefly by the Babylonians in 586 B.C.E., returned for another five hundred years, were kicked out in 70 C.E. for almost *two thousand* years, but returned again in the twentieth century. Why did the Israelites prevail?

"Again, time was a factor," Avner said. "They had long periods of time to develop when nobody interrupted them."

"So if you and I were bedouin now," I said, "and we wanted to transform ourselves into an urban people, what should we do first, and what second?"

"Sorry to be somewhat realistic," Avner said, "but the first thing is an economy. Next, you need an identity. The Nabateans did the first, but they didn't have time to do the second. They didn't even get around to building houses. They were still living in tents."

"The Israelites did number two first," I said, "they developed an identity. And later they developed an economy, but not until after they conquered the land."

"And that's the whole point of the Bible!" Avner said. "It's about building the spiritual unity of the people. That's what they were doing in the desert all those years."

"And that's why they needed Deuteronomy."

"Right. They may not have had the land, but they still transformed themselves into a nation. Moses was telling the people their past, building history into the character of the nation—the DNA you might call it—so that when they conquered the Promised Land, their spiritual unity was already in place."

Now, late in the afternoon, the small viewing area in front of the Treasury was deserted. A bedouin shopkeeper was packing up his kettle; the sun had mostly disappeared. We were bedraggled, having gotten up at 4 A.M., spent eight hours on a camel, and then walked through the ruins. We still had to navigate the mile-long Siq, the twisting, narrow gorge that's the only way in or out of the city that doesn't require going over the mountains. This is the way most visitors arrive in the city. Sort of like the tail on the tadpole of Petra, the

Siq seems like a living organism, twisting one way, then the other. Usually no more than three feet wide, the path, with walls as high as five hundred feet, occasionally widens into a pocket of open air, then narrows again. It was first formed by an earthquake and later deepened by the waters of Wadi Musa. The Nabateans transported water through the Siq through the use of a terra-cotta pipe, which is still visible today.

By far the most magical spot in the Siq is near the end (which for us was near the beginning, since we were coming from inside). After a short walk, we turned to face a dramatic split in the gorge, like a bolt of lightning through the rock. In between the cliffs, the red face of the Treasury appears, like the eager grin of civilization peering through a crack in the desert. The effect is sort of like Jack Nicholson leering through the splintered door in *The Shining*. Instead of fear, though, the reaction one gets is one of awe, tinged with apprehension. Is this civilization triumphing over the desert, or is it the other way around?

"It's like Saint Catherine's," Avner said. "When you stand here and look at the Treasury, it's all square lines and order, but it's in a wilderness that is all about disorder. Some people find it alarming. I find it beautiful."

"So what was it like the first time you came?" I asked.

"I cried," he said. "I knew every millimeter of the place from my studies. Where to go, what to see. I knew it by heart. I came in 1995. Edie"—his Canadian-born wife—"could have come years before with her passport, but she said, 'I'm waiting for you.' And she cried also. Because Petra was, for Israelis, a miracle. Many people had been killed trying to come here over the years. The bedouin would shoot them. We were so close all those years, but we couldn't even see it. And it had so much to say."

"So what does it say to you now?"

"Now I see it as a place of peace. It has to do with mankind. People built this thing. People built Petra. The Nabatean trail goes from Saudi Arabia through Jordan, Israel, and the Palestinian Territories. If we can restore this trail"—as Avner, Rami, and a few others were trying to do, opening it up to cross-border traffic—"we can show that some things in the Middle East are not about religion."

"That leads me to a question I've been waiting to ask you since we started," I said.

"Okaaaay?" Avner said, expectant. We were still staring at the Treasury. The sky had been growing gradually darker in the last half hour, but suddenly the sun must have set, because the blue sliver of sky quickly turned white, then yellow, orange, and peach. It was like watching a bowl of melting Life Savers. And finally, when we didn't think the colors could get any richer, the whole Siq was illuminated in a most pleasant blush the color of rose.

"So why did you come on this trip with me?"

Avner considered the question for a second. His blue eyes twinkled as his lips crept into a grin. His face was burnt with the sun of our morning ride. His hair, unwashed for days like mine, squiggled in a hundred directions. He had that tattered-teddy-bear contentment I had noticed on our first meeting.

"I think you mentioned it once," Avner said. "When I told you I left the Sinai and had to fight to give it back to Egypt, you said, 'You chose to be a prophet and not an archaeologist.' Now that's a big word, 'prophet,' but being an archaeologist can be very narrow. I love archaeology. I love to excavate. Of course," he added, "I hate to *publish*." We both laughed. "But I really love archaeology.

"And yet," he continued, "it's not the only way to engage the ancient world. What I want to do is reach people—to connect the present to the past. I'd hate to be limited to one, very professional, but very narrow-minded way of doing that. I find it much more interesting, for example, and maybe much more important, to try and get the Palestinians and Jordanians and Egyptians and Israelis to cooperate."

"So despite what happened last night in that tent, you believe it can be done?"

"Yes, I do. Last night was not as big a shock to me as to you, because I got that shock years ago. But as I said yesterday, there are other bridges, smaller bridges. More human ones." He paused and seemed to grow almost wistful. "And I guess that's why I decided to come with you," he said. "If you take people, outsiders, and take them on a trip like we have done, you educate them—not just about the Bible, not just about God.

But about tolerance. You link them with other people, and in the end, you open their minds. There's an old saying in the Middle East: With a trail, the best way to keep it alive is to walk on it, because every time you walk on it, you create it again."

For a second neither of us spoke. I thought back on our first meeting at the coffee shop in Jerusalem, and how extraordinarily fortunate I had been to meet him. "I don't think you're crazy at all," he had said when I told him of my idea. "I think it sounds exciting." Perhaps in our own way, we had helped keep the trail alive.

"And there's another thing," Avner said, more puckishly now. "Why would I want to be in a stuffy lecture hall?" He spread his arms, lifted his eyes, and looked around as if he were the luckiest boy alive. "I'd rather be here!"

3. Sunrise in the Palm of the Lord

The last day of our entire journey began, oddly enough, with a car chase. It was just after 8 A.M. on a breezy, summer Sunday in Amman, when we were met in our hotel lobby by the Israeli ambassador to Jordan, Oded Eran, whom Avner had befriended in the course of trying to reopen the Nabatean Spice Trail. Eran was a generous if meticulous man, who scolded us for being five minutes late. Then, gesturing to his entourage of Israeli bodyguards, Jordanian bodyguards, king's policemen, and aides, he invited us into his car, a black, armor-plated BMW 750iL with two-inch-thick windows that Eran, driverless on this morning, wheeled out of the parking lot.

Suddenly we were in the midst of an elaborate, six-vehicle caravan that reminded me of a video game. One car blocked traffic, another rode to our right, another to our left, one in front, another behind. Whenever we would reach an intersection, the cars, which belonged to the special security unit of King Abdullah, would fan out like skaters on a roller-derby rink, executing a moving pick-and-roll that somehow allowed us to pass through without stopping. Turning a corner was even trickier. Several cars would burst into the intersection; we would pull behind them as if going straight; then the cars behind us would quickly make the turn, we would duck in behind them, and the cars that had been leading deftly filled in behind us. I could only imagine how the Israeli ambassador to Egypt ever left home if he was expected to use such intricate precautions in the impassable streets of Cairo.

In our case, the proceedings were made even more complex—and droll—by the presence of Mahmoud, trailing along in our dust-covered jeep, trying to keep pace at the end of the line. Once he got separated from us by a public bus, and I could see him behind us honking, gesticulating, and screaming as if he personally were the linchpin of Middle East peace.

In time we reached our destination, the Ministry of Tourism and Antiquities, and the cars pulled to a stop in rapid succession. One of the king's policemen opened the ambassador's door, and we flitted inside without ever seeming to touch the ground. All of this effort, just for a meeting with the chief of tourism and archaeology, seemed like overkill and struck me as what it must have been like in the days of espio-archaeology, when researchers like Woolley and Lawrence carried the hopes, bona fides, and military aspirations of their entire countries. One could almost hear Agatha Christie, who spent years at digs across the Middle East with her archaeologist husband, chuckling in the background as she answered the frequent request of her sand-jealous friends, a query that later became the title of her autobiography, *Come, Tell Me How You Live.*

"I am thinking," she would often say, "that it's a very happy way to live."

Inside the concrete building, the crowded hallways parted as the entourage made its way to the second floor and quickly disappeared behind the closed doors of the minister. The main purpose of this meeting was to discuss ways in which Israel and Jordan could jointly raise funds abroad to open the Spice Trail. I waited outside with a stern-faced twenty-three-year-old Israeli bodyguard, and when the meeting was over, the ambassador asked the minister if he had a few minutes to speak with me.

Akel Biltaji was the best-dressed person I met in the Middle East, with a hand-tailored, Italian-style taupe herringbone suit, a light blue dress shirt, and an orange silk tie that would have been at home on any European king. His mien was no less regal, with slicked-back gray hair, an ivory smile, and broad-shouldered assurance that no doubt helped him, a Jordanian-born Palestinian, navigate three decades of palace intrigue to assume one of the loftier positions in the kingdom. Over his desk was a beautiful painting of King Abdullah, but on the walls were even larger pictures of Biltaji with various dignitaries, including Pope John Paul II.

"Sit down, what can I do for you?" Biltaji said in Cantabrigian English. In a way I thought it appropriate that at this point in our journey, with the Israelites' battles with the enemy tribes behind them, and their war against the Canaanites ahead of them, we pause for a morning of diplomatic reflection. I feared, however, that Biltaji would be so diplomatic that he wouldn't say anything interesting. I certainly didn't expect him to slap me down.

Taking my cue from the stack of books at his side about the making of *Lawrence of Arabia,* I asked Biltaji what he thought of Lawrence. "Personally, I think he wasn't much of an archaeologist or a spy," he said. "Archaeology, like espionage, is not a science; it's an art, the art of interpretation. I always thought that good archaeologists went in search of the truth, not with the intention of proving something they already believed."

Okay, I suggested, turning the conversation toward archaeology. A new ministry publication I had seen in the lobby discussed over twenty biblical sites in Jordan and said that the Bible was "an excellent tour guide" to the country. I asked Biltaji if he thought these sites could be a source of common ground between Israel and Jordan.

Again his response caught me off guard. "We don't see anybody looking for Jewish connections to the Arabs," he said. "Ishmael was dissected; he was thrown out of the family, simply because his mother was Egyptian. And that's where we feel bitter, and dismayed, that so much injustice was done. Because this kind of injustice continues to separate us as Arabs and Jews, when we should be cousins."

"So do you feel the Bible is hostile to Arabs?" I asked.

"To start, I'm going to quote Hanan Ashrawi"—the Palestinian leader—"when she says, 'God was not in the real estate business. To promise land and give land to begin with is a dangerous thing.'" He then went off into what could only be described as a diatribe, blasting

Israel for "destroying democracy" and "dismaying the world" through its treatment of Palestinians. "If they are so godly, what gives them the authority to strafe people with machine guns?" he asked, apparently rhetorically. "What's happening in Israel is a great distortion to the beauty of the world's Jews, who all along, through persecution, have managed to rise and excel."

I started squirming, but Biltaji showed no signs of letting up. "Palestine is my homeland," he continued. "God must have had a reason to make it the center of his spiritual kingdom. But it's nobody's property, it's God's property. I've always felt comfortable with sharing the best with both sides. That's the spirit of God. When I go sometimes on Fridays to Bethany, to the spot where John baptized Jesus, which Jordanian archaeologists just uncovered and which we're just opening to visitors, I see it bringing peace, not war."

Taking this as a possible olive branch, I asked Biltaji if when he closed his eyes he saw Israeli settlers opening fire, or Christian pilgrims coming to sites like Bethany in Jordan.

"I force myself to see people, carrying the Bible and the Koran, praying their own way."

"You force yourself, or you believe it?"

"I believe it. The Buddhists have a saying: 'Your creator is your own mind.' Your mind is the one who takes you to your god. So before we can make peace, we have to make it in our minds."

Outside in the lobby, Avner was just finishing a call on his cellular phone. Ofer had telephoned during my meeting with Biltaji and announced that he had found Nissim's camels. Avner discussed it with Eran, who turned to Biltaji: Perhaps a special camel crossing could be arranged? "No problem," Biltaji announced, suddenly the peacemaker again. "Just call my assistant and arrange it."

Back in the BMW, I was shaken by my encounter. Biltaji had been so belligerent on the topics of Lawrence and Israel, but he seemed to warm somewhat when the subject turned to pilgrims visiting religious sites. On the one hand, Jordan desperately wanted the hard currency of Western visitors, and it was Biltaji's job to lure them. But there was something else at work. Even a realist like Biltaji admitted that something came over people—came over him—when visiting holy places. I asked Eran if living in Jordan had changed his view of the Bible.

"Basically it has given me a new sense of depth about the Bible," he said. Eran also spoke perfect English, growing out of his time as a diplomat in Washington. "What comes across more than anything is the proximity. Basically, you're looking at one historical unit—fifty miles on either side of the Jordan River—and it's a unique feeling for an ambassador. You're serving in a country that is part of the Bible. Maybe my colleague in Egypt has a similar feeling."

"Egypt is sometimes vilified in the Bible," I mentioned. "How do you feel about Jordan?"

"I think it's a mixed bag," he said. "On the one hand, there are those tribes—the Edomites, the Moabites, the Amorites—that stand in the way of the Israelites on their way to the Promised Land. On the other hand, following the conquest of Canaan, there are times of cooperation between the two sides of the river."

I asked if he thought these tensions affected how contemporary Israelis view Jordan.

"I doubt it. I think most Israelis separate the modern Hashemite Kingdom from Moab and Edom of the past."

"What about the other way around?" I asked. "When you go into meetings here, are you perceived as being the Ambassador of the Bible?"

"There is one question that I'm sure comes to their mind," Eran said. "And that is: 'What is the legitimacy of the claims of the Jews to the Holy Land?' I think most of them challenge this. It's difficult, especially in Jordan, which is sixty percent Palestinian, to reconcile the message of the Bible that Jews are entitled to the Promised Land, with the idea that it came at the expense of sixty percent of the population of Jordan."

"What about the claims of some Israelis that the Promised Land should extend into northern Jordan, since two and a half tribes stayed on this side of the river?"

"There was a member of Knesset [the Israeli parliament] who came to Jordan and stood at the amphitheater in Amman and said, 'My friends, you are standing on the land of the tribe of Reuben.' You can't refute that this appears in the Bible, in Deuteronomy 3. But whether it was appropriate to make this comment at that place is a different issue. There were attempts by these so-called East Bankers in the 1920s and thirties to settle across the river, but I don't think there's a big movement today to make that happen."

I mentioned that one of the things I learned during my trip was that you can't understand the Bible without understanding Mesopotamia or Egypt. Did he think the same applies to Jordan?

"Absolutely."

"So what's the main thing one needs to understand?"

"That these two territories were, in the past, connected. And the same applies to today. These two territories can, as they once did, act as two different entities. Jordan and Israel can survive without each other. But at the end of the day, they are part of a small region, and eventually the movement of people, the movement of trade, will force them to cooperate, as it did two thousand years ago."

Our final stop that morning was the plush mansion of Fawaz Abu Tayeh, perhaps the most colorful diplomat we met. After saying goodbye to Ambassador Eran, we rejoined Mahmoud in our jeep and proceeded across Amman, a city that's easier to define by what it's not than what it is. Amman, like Jordan, is mostly an invention, a city arbitrarily deemed the capital in 1921 that, as a result, has little of the history of Damascus, the beauty of Jerusalem, or the grandeur of Cairo, though it has none of their tiredness, tension, or traffic either. Author Paul Theroux once dismissed it as "repulsively spick-and-span." Though ancient Amman was rarely more than a muddy outpost, the city was briefly freshened up by Alexander the Great's successor, Ptolemy II Philadelphus, who named it Philadelphia. That makes Amman, a place long plagued by earthquakes, refugees, and bedouin rivalries, the original "city of brotherly love."

Insofar as that slogan is true today, Fawaz Abu Tayeh would make an outstanding emissary. Abu Tayeh is the grandson of Ada Abu Tayeh, the bedouin prince who served as Lawrence's chief military officer and who was played in Lean's film by Anthony Quinn. Through a friend, he had agreed to meet us and talk about his family's heritage, and we were shown into an ornate living room, filled with Arabian rugs and European furniture. Abu Tayeh greeted us graciously and offered us Earl Grey tea and cakes. He was tall, with a prominent belly, and was dressed in luxurious white ankle-length robes, a white kaffiyeh, and a purple silk shawl that altogether, he later confided, cost $10,000. "In order to look good in bedouin clothing," he said, "you need to be brown and tall."

Abu Tayeh was born in Amman in 1933, studied law at Jordan University, and later received a master's degree in politics from Oxford, a poetic turnabout considering that Lawrence had come from Oxford to lead his grandfather into power. For twenty years Abu Tayeh served as the chief of royal protocol for King Hussein and was later rewarded with ambassadorships to Romania and Bulgaria. On his wall (like Biltaji's) were oversized photographs of him with assorted luminaries: Alexander Haig, Barry Goldwater, Helmut Kohl, Margaret Thatcher, Queen Elizabeth II. Power is etched grandly in Amman's salons.

Befitting his status, Abu Tayeh was diplomatic—and noncommittal—when I asked him about the remarkable rise of the Hashemite family from Arabian tribe to leaders of a nation. "We are open. We are proud of our history. We are proud of our goals," he said.

He was a bit more forthcoming when I asked about the role of his grandfather in this story. "My grandfather was the most famous warrior of the desert," he said. "When Ada Abu Tayeh met Faysal Hussein, Lawrence of Arabia said, 'Now I know the Arab Revolt will succeed. When the prophet—Faysal—meets the fighter—Abu Tayeh—this is what the Arabs need.'"

He was downright charitable on the subject of Lawrence. "When it comes to Lawrence, as a person, my opinion is always positive, never negative," he said. "We consider him a great man, a great help. As a young British officer, to endure the difficult life of the desert, Lawrence must have been a great admirer of the Arab cause."

The conversation went on like this for half an hour, and I began thinking of ways to extract myself, when, apropos of nothing, I asked Abu Tayeh, "What do you think of the desert?"

The change that came over him was instantaneous. He suddenly seemed to shuck his diplomatic reserve and speak to me like a friend. "The desert is a way of life!" he said, his eyes brightening. "The Jewish tribes, led by Moses, came from the most advanced civilization, in Egypt. They crossed the desert to the Promised Land, where they civilized again. But during their journey in between they were bedouin. And look what happened to them. The desert, because of its uncertainty, forces you to feel more attached to the higher power."

"So can someone like me, who was not born in that world, feel that attachment?" I asked.

"I don't know why not," he said, now openly giggling. "I wasn't born in the desert, and I feel the same!" He leaned forward, as if in confession. "I'm not a specialist in this," he said, "but when you go to the mountains along the Jordan Valley, if you know the Bible, and if you leave the roads behind and walk two or three miles by yourself, you expect Moses to come looking for you!

"I've been to Petra a hundred times," he continued. "But this year, for the first time, I walked up Jebel Haroun. And it was such an experience. I hiked seven hours, and when I got near Haroun mountain I got confused. I could not see the top of the mountain. And if you go the wrong way, you're lost. All of a sudden a man appeared, a bedouin. He was eighty-one years old. I said, 'How long to Jebel Haroun?' He said, 'I will go with you.' I said, 'You are a great man.' And he said, 'No, I am a servant of our master Haroun.'

"And he walked in front of me, for one hour and thirty minutes, until we got there. I reached what I thought was the top of the mountain, but I was not there yet. I had to walk up another twenty minutes. If you have disease, or sickness, or any psychological problem, you will never do it! And once I got there I went inside the chapel, I went down the stairs and saw the real tomb where Haroun is located, and then I went up on the roof and looked over the land. It was the best experience of my life.

"And before I left," Abu Tayeh continued, "I read two things: the Koran and the Bible."

"Really?" I said. "So what did you learn?"

"I learned that this shrine is there as a symbol, to remind us that we belong to the same tradition. The mentality of our people may have changed, but we have the same roots. There's no reason we can't get along."

By the time he finished his story, the entire room had been transformed. It went from being a chilly diplomatic parlor to my home away from home. Within minutes Abu Tayeh was giving us a private tour and showing us a signed copy of one of the original editions of *The Seven Pillars of Wisdom*. He summoned his college-age son from his room and asked him to bring out some old family photos. Finally he called back to the kitchen and ordered up an impromptu feast of chicken, rice, yogurt, and sweet Arab *knafi* cake, which we shared with neighbors and ate with our hands while drinking toasts of alcohol-free wine in the most lavish meal we ate on our entire journey. All this happened with so little effort, and so much affection, that when Abu Tayeh ushered us to the door of our jeep and bid us good-bye with a hug and smile, I knew that the desert had served up an antidote to our clash in Nissim's tent and to my meeting with Biltaji. I knew that the openness of the place had triumphed over the hostility.

It was almost 2 P.M. by the time we left Abu Tayeh's house and began our drive southeast of Amman toward Ma'daba, a small town that houses the most famous mosaic map of the ancient world. This part of the King's Highway shows how pleasant the Middle East could be with a little more rain and a lot less diesel exhaust. The hills are gentle with an occasional mountain stream that spawns meandering banks of green that could almost be in Switzerland. The only thing missing are cows. There is another similarity with the Alps, though. Occasionally one

hears the shrill cry of bedouin tongues, a high-pitched, quavering ulu-
lation that if it moved deeper into the throat and took on a bit more
melody would sound exactly like a yodel.

Since this is the Middle East, however, the verdant pastures quickly
give way to dust-infested towns crowded with onion stands and pita
vendors. Ma'daba, located about fifty miles southeast of the capital, is
one such city. Once part of the kingdom of Moab, Ma'daba is mentioned in Numbers 21 as a place the Israelites destroyed on their bloody
trip north. The city continued to be a pawn for the next millennium,
switching from Israelite hands back to Moabite, from Hellenistic to
Nabatean. By the first millennium C.E., Christianity took hold, leaving
the city its richest legacy: dozens of Byzantine mosaics.

We parked and entered the modest Saint George's Church, a whitewashed Greek Orthodox facility with several brass lanterns dripping
from the ceiling and a few wooden icons hanging from the walls. The
church reminded me of Saint Catherine's, but was smaller and less
ornate. In 1976, a worshiper noticed that one of the icons, depicting the
Virgin Mary, had suddenly grown a third hand, which was blue, and
which had been invisible to congregants only minutes earlier. The protuberance was declared to be a miracle, and soon drew visitors from
around the world.

The real attraction in Saint George's, however, is its mosaic map, dating from the sixth century C.E., which is considered one of the oldest
existing depictions of the Holy Land. Spread out on the floor in incomplete patches that collectively are about the size and shape of the stain
that would result from spilling a gallon of paint on the floor, the mosaic
represents only a fragment of the original, which stretched fifteen feet
by forty-five feet and included over two million tiles. Uncovered when
the church was reconstructed in 1884, the map depicts over 150 biblical
sites across the Near East, from Egypt to Lebanon.

Oriented to the east, as if the viewer is standing in the Mediterranean looking toward the Jordan River, the map is focused around
Jerusalem, labeled the "center of the world" and portrayed in vivid red,
yellow, brown, and white tiles. The map is so precise that it depicts the
Church of the Holy Sepulcher in three dimensions, as if done by

Picasso in his cubist phase. Jericho, the "city of palms," is surrounded by palms, and Hebron shows the Cave of the Patriarchs. There are even a few playful asides. At the mouth of the Dead Sea, one fish from the Jordan swims eagerly toward the sea, while another swims even more eagerly *away* from the sea, apparently desperate to flee the salt.

I was struck by the number of places we had visited that were represented on the map, including Nablus, Goshen, Gaza, the Sinai, the Negev, even Edom and Moab. "We didn't have to make our trip," I joked to Avner. "We could have just come here."

"In fact, this was probably put here originally to help guide pilgrims," he said.

As we were leaving, we ran into a bookish-looking American man in his forties, dressed in a khaki shirt and straw hat, who we guessed was an archaeologist. He was, as well as a pastor. Doug Clark was a thin, fair-haired native of Washington State who had been coming to Jordan for twenty-five years in his capacity as a professor of biblical studies and archaeology at the School of Theology at Walla Walla College. A passionate excavator of ancient sites and an ordained Seventh-Day Adventist pastor, Doug seemed to embody all the tensions—between science and religion, between history and faith—that characterized so many conversations along our route. As we sat in a pew, I asked how he reconciled his work as an archaeologist with his beliefs.

"I guess I have come to terms personally with the Bible, a book which is precious to me," he said, "so that I don't have to lock in every story as being factual. My own sense of Scripture is that I believe some kind of divine activity is behind the Bible, but I don't assume that every detail in the story is true. It can't be. But I don't believe the details are important. I believe the lessons are important."

"So as a person of the Bible, do you wish you never encountered archaeology?"

"I remember the first time I came to Jordan to dig," he said. "It was 1973, and this man, who must have been sixty and had nothing to do with archaeology, said to me, 'Be very careful about archaeology.' I have applied that a number of times since. I think that if one is honest with the archaeological data, one will confront issues and have a crisis of faith. And I had my crisis of faith.

"But"—and his voice lifted here—"I think anyone who has a wish to be faithful and honest will have a crisis of faith. Still, I think that crisis has made my faith stronger. It's just no longer rooted in the same way. I'm not dependent on factuality in everything. I can look back and say, 'Okay, so it didn't happen that way. So there weren't two million people in the Exodus.' But I still have a sense that historically, archaeologically, we can see the larger elements of the story."

"So has coming here enhanced your faith?"

"It's been very much an enhancement," he said. "I grew up in a tradition in which the earth was only six thousand years old, but I was working in a site today that's 250,000 years old. So on the one hand I continue to grow in my awareness of the facts, and I'm enamored by that. On the other hand, to visit places like Ma'daba, or Nebo, is a devotional experience. I continue to be touched by the fact that somehow God chose to interact with human beings in this place. I don't know how he chose it, but he did.

"Take Mount Nebo," he continued. "Three days ago I got an e-mail from one of my friends at home; her daughter had been murdered. So I went to Mount Nebo the next day. I just sat there. I wanted to think about the Promised Land. I wanted to look at Jericho. And when you think about Moses on that spot, about God choosing to make a connection with human beings there, about the Israelites on the verge of achieving their destiny—that, for me, is worship."

By the time we made it back to our jeep and turned eastward it was late afternoon and the sun was starting to fade. Instead of the glorious reds and pinks of Petra, dusk was mostly grayish here, the color of concrete. The road slowly climbed through a series of villages. We were moving westward through the Jordanian mountains, which reached their peaks and then collapsed into the Rift Valley, meaning, as a geographical matter, that the mountains were far steeper on their western side than their eastern. We were in a temperate zone, and in what seemed a fitting ode to a place of ending, the terrain had many of the topographical elements we had seen across our route: the medieval thatched roofs and wooden carts of eastern Turkey; the pine trees and sage bushes of the Jerusalem hills; the craggy rocks and sandy soil of the Negev. And, as in the Sinai, everywhere the sense of drama: big boulders, big mountains, big sky.

Eventually we climbed our way to the series of peaks collectively referred to as Mount Nebo, the single most important biblical site in Jordan and, after Ararat and Sinai, the third emblematic mountain of the Pentateuch. In Deuteronomy 32, after Moses delivers a passionate speech to the Israelites, God tells him, "Ascend these heights of Abarim," the biblical name for the Jordan hills, "to Mount Nebo, which is in the land of Moab facing Jericho, and view the land of Canaan which I am giving the Israelites as their holding. You shall die on the mountain that you are about to ascend, and shall be gathered to your kin, as your brother Aaron died on Mount Hor and was gathered to his kin." God reminds Moses of the reason, saying it's because "you broke faith with Me among the Israelite people," at the waters of Meribath-kadesh, then adds: "You may view the land from a distance, but you shall not enter it."

Like Mount Ararat, the mountain now called Nebo has a natural claim to its identity: At 2,540 feet, it's the tallest in the area, though it's only a third as tall as Jebel Musa and an eighth as tall as Ararat. The mountain actually consists of a number of peaks, the two tallest being Siyagah and el Mukhayyat. Though Siyagah is slightly lower, it's also flatter, and holy buildings have existed on it since the first millennium B.C.E. The first Christian building was erected in 394 C.E. and was later expanded to include a church and a monastery, which was abandoned in 1564. In 1933, the ruined site was purchased by the Franciscans, who excavated and restored the basilica and monastery, both of which still function today.

The front gate to the Franciscan facility was closed when we arrived, so we walked along the southern side and rang the private bell of the proprietor. A crotchety Italian man in his seventies opened the door. "Garbo" was the caretaker hired by the Franciscans, and we'd been given his name by an archaeologist in Amman. We explained what we were doing and asked if he would let us spend the last night of our journey on

Mount Nebo, so we could see sunrise from the spot where Moses is said to have died. Garbo grumbled a few minutes as he mulled our request. He asked if we had a letter from the chief archaeologist of Mount Nebo; we didn't. He asked if we were Catholic. Finally, citing regulations, he politely turned us down, but said that if we returned at 5 A.M. he would personally open the gate for us. He gestured to the neighboring peak, el Mukhayyat, and implied that we should sleep there. He knew it was illegal to spend the night on the mountain. Mahmoud also knew it was illegal, and advised against it. Even Avner's wife, Edie, knew it was illegal. Before we left she had said she might not be willing to bail us out if we got arrested. "I've got better things to do with my money," she said.

We stayed anyway. We drove on the dirt road that circled the bald peak of el Mukhayyat until we found a gravelly area flat enough to sleep on. We doubled back to one of the villages, bought a few bags of provisions—bread, cheese, tuna, honey, even orange juice—as well as two bedouin mattresses wrapped in purple flowery fabric. Back at the site, we gathered dried branches of wormwood and sagebrush in case we wanted a fire. We bid good-bye to Mahmoud, who agreed to pick us up at the monastery around 8 A.M., and settled into our jerry-built home.

Nebo is located on a geological seam. Behind us were the central mountains of Jordan, followed by the eastern desert, then the vast deserts of Saudi Arabia and Iraq, like two coattails that never end. In front of us was the precipitous drop-off of the Rift Valley, followed by the Judean hills of central Israel. From our vantage point, we had a complete, 180-degree panorama of the misty infinity of the biblical Promised Land. At this hour, with the sun already set, the dark screen of dust settling over the horizon had the density of steel wool. To the left was the Dead Sea; to the right the huddled lights of Jericho. Jerusalem, in between, was invisible. Nothing seemed to be moving, but there were sounds of life: donkeys braying, motorbikes sputtering, wind blowing, birds chirping.

We grew nostalgic. Almost two years had passed since I first met Avner, and we began recalling various events. Remember finding those quail eggs in the Sinai? Can you believe they have e-mail at Saint Catherine's? Do you think Parachute *really* found Noah's ark? A second telling, our own private Deuteronomy.

As we talked, we drifted into a discussion of what we'd learned. Perhaps the most striking thing we gleaned from retracing the Five Books of Moses was not all that different from what had originally propelled me on this trip: The Bible is not an abstraction in the Middle East, nor even just a book; it's a living, breathing entity, undiminished by the passage of time. If anything, the Bible has been elevated to that rare stature of being indefinitely immediate. That's a principal reason few people ultimately care when the Bible was written; the text is forever applicable. It's always now.

This ability of the Bible to continually reinvent itself is matched only by its ability to make itself relevant to anyone who encounters it. Probably the most surprising thing about our trip is that in every place we went—"three continents, five countries, four war zones," I used to joke—we asked everybody basically the same question: "What does the Bible mean to you?" And *everybody* had an answer. Every single person had a way to relate to the story, whether it was a Kurdish freedom fighter in Dogubayazit, a Jewish settler on the West Bank, a Muslim archaeologist in Cairo, a bedouin shepherd in the Sinai, a Palestinian ambassador in Amman. In all of our travels, I never entered a room in which someone didn't have a story, a theory, or a question about the text. An eight-year-old Jerusalemite wondered whether the reeds I brought back from Egypt were papyrus or bulrushes (they were bulrushes). A fiftysomething lawyer asked whether Petra could be the place Lot fled after leaving Sodom (unlikely). A forty-year-old priest wanted to know if the desert can truly be a spiritual place (absolutely).

This chameleon-like quality is what makes the Bible so vital. It's an organism so universal it has the ability to engage its human interlocutors in whatever form they desire—geological, ecological, zoological, philological, psychological, astrological, theological, illogical. It can even regenerate itself in locations where it's been dead for years, or even centuries, as happened when Byzantine travelers first came to the Sinai in the fourth century C.E., or when large numbers of Jews arrived in Israel in the twentieth century. Put tautologically: The Bible lives because it never dies. As a rabbi friend of mine said, it's like a fungus that can live underground for long periods then pop up and thrive wherever it appears.

Though my friend quickly regretted his remark, he actually made a significant point. Easily the most impressive thing I learned during my trip was that the Bible's ability to be relevant to contemporary life was by no means guaranteed. If anything, over the last two hundred years it has undergone the most concentrated and ruthless academic scrutiny that any written work has ever faced. This scientific interrogation, from every conceivable corner—archaeology, history, physics, metaphysics, linguistics, anthropology—was designed, in many cases, to undermine the Bible, to destroy its credibility. But in every case (at least the ones involving historical events, after the primeval stories of Creation), the Bible not only withstood the inquisition but came out stronger, with its integrity intact, and its nuances more on display. This doesn't mean that the stories are true, but it does mean that they're true to their era. The Bible lives today not because it's untouchable but precisely because it *has* been touched—it has been challenged—and it remains undefeated.

This remarkable ability of the Bible to thrive, even in a world dominated by skepticism and science, came home to me during a meeting I had just before leaving for Jordan. I went to see Israel Hershkovitz, a professor of anatomy and anthropology at Tel Aviv University, who was Avner's deputy in the Sinai and now studies ancient skeletons. I was hoping to find out once and for all whether the attachment to the land I first felt in Turkey might be in my DNA or whether it was more likely in my mind. Israel was a warm, messy-haired man like Avner, who invited me into his laboratory, which was lined from floor to ceiling with hundreds of skulls from the ancient world, like some creepy vision out of Darwin's, or maybe Frankenstein's, laboratory. Seated in front of his collection, Israel looked like one of those experts who appear on *National Geographic* specials nodding gravely.

He conceded that certain aspects of the story were inconsistent with current knowledge: that humans could live to be six hundred years old, that the world was created 5,700 years ago, that all humans were descended from one couple. He viewed these as narrative devices. "If you take a group of people, and the group is very large, the only way to keep the people together, working toward the same goal, is to say, 'We all came from the same forefathers.' "

But otherwise, he was a devotee of the Bible. He read it every day to his daughter, he said, and believed it captured larger truths about the ancient world: foremost among them, the power of the desert. "It makes sense to me that the desert is where most of the great religions were born," he said. "More than any other place, it gives you time for thinking about spiritual things."

"But is there a physiological reason for that connection?" I asked. I then outlined for him the somewhat eccentric idea I had been developing. If, as scientists say, human beings first evolved in Africa, and if, as he confirmed, they spread out to the rest of the world over the land bridge of the Middle East, and if, as he mentioned, the three monotheistic religions that sprung from that bridge all have at their heart the story of human beings finding God in the desert, is it possible that humans somehow developed in themselves a physical attachment to the deserts of the Middle East, their earliest home?

"In a way, yes," Israel said. "Because if we take ourselves back eleven thousand years or so, men were basically hunter-gatherers. Then we had the agricultural revolution, and at that point there was a split. Most people became farmers and developed a food-producing economy. About ninety percent did that. But about ten percent didn't, they were pushed aside. They developed a lifestyle that was in between the nomadic lives of their ancestors and the settled lives of the farmers."

"So some people can have an attachment to the desert but not *everyone* has to have it?"

"Absolutely. We know now that genes have the ability to store ancestral memories. And these can survive for hundreds of years. The Jewish people, for example, are very stubborn. To keep up with their religion for all those years in exile, first in Babylon, then in the diaspora, reminds me of a very special people: the bedouin. You give up a lot, you live in marginal areas, you don't enjoy all the benefits of life. But you preserve your identity."

"So to bring this to a personal level, when I come to this part of the world and have a personal reaction, 'This is where I feel at home,' is it possible that I'm discovering something that was already within me?"

"I think so. Everybody discovers sooner or later where they fit into the spectrum. I always say to Avner, if Sadat had not come to Jerusalem and made peace, I would probably have stayed in Sinai with Avner for the rest of our lives. It was quite a hard life. It's not like you could go to a restaurant, or watch a movie. We were basically by ourselves. But we were happy."

I asked him where God fit into his formulation.

"I believe in God," he said.

I indicated surprise. "So where is your God?" I said.

"God is everywhere, everyplace," he said. "The problem with God is that what the early Israelites meant by God in the Bible is very different from what present-day religious people mean when they say God. If you talk with the bedouin about their religion, they have holy places and holy mountains. The early Israelites were much closer to the bedouin in that regard."

"So what is God then?"

"I don't know," he said. "But I know that when you go certain places you feel him, and you become a better person. When I go into the desert I become a better person."

"And that's not incompatible with what you know about science?"

"Absolutely not. Science is never going to prove the divine, but it's never going to disprove it either. We explain many things, but we can't explain what's inside the human soul. That's God."

"What about the Bible?" I mentioned. "Is that part of your under-standing?"

"Yes. Because I can't always go to the desert, I can't always take my children there. But I can read the stories. The way I see it, if you read the book, you also become a better person."

"So you're saying that the desert helps you to do that, and the Bible helps you to do that?"

"Yes, the desert and the Bible. They're partners. They're good part-ners."

I repeated this story to Avner while we were sitting on the mountain. We had begun talking about the relationship between human evolution and the Bible, a conversation we had started in the Sinai. Night had fallen over the Holy Land, revealing a full constellation of sky, the color of onyx. Jupiter was directly in front of us, Avner pointed out, Mars to our left. The crescent moon was resting on its rounded bottom, an empty candy dish. The sky seemed so close that the stars appeared as if they could be plucked from their positions and placed somewhere else.

Avner emphasized that in nature, new species develop in response to evolutionary pressure. The giraffe needed to eat the leaves of trees, for example, so it developed a long neck. Humans, however, developed a complex brain, which gave us the ability to change the environment to suit our needs. "Here we find ourselves in a sunny place," Avner said, "but instead of waiting for all the people with light skin to die off and all the people with dark skin to survive, we put on creams to protect ourselves. It's the same with the sweet tooth, the seeking of deep-fried foods and meat. These were designed for the time when people could hardly get food and they needed to store extra fat in their bodies. But things change, and now we have access to more food. We all know it would be better not to eat too much red meat and sweets, but we love them. So instead of curbing our appetite, we developed medicines and surgical procedures like bypass.

"What I'm trying to say," he continued, "is that in humans, evolution now involves creating behavior patterns that we pass from generation to generation. Our genes haven't changed that much since neolithic times. And that collection of behavior patterns is culture. Culture is the way that a group of people develop together in order to survive, to maintain their way of life.

"And when we talk about culture," he added, "it's like talking about a different species of wildlife. That's the way this group of people deal with the environment. Therefore, being a Palestinian, or an Israeli, or an Edomite, is not some collection of crazy things. It is the essence of being."

"So what you're suggesting," I said, "is that this attachment to the desert I feel is probably not in my physical DNA?"

"No, I don't think so. I think it's in your cultural DNA—as a Westerner, a member of the Judeo-Christian world."

"If that's the case, then presumably the reason it got there is that this"—I tapped my Bible—"is one of the greatest sources of cultural DNA ever invented."

"I agree," he said. "In fact, I agree even more after our travels."

"What do you mean?"

"I would have agreed before we worked together, but now it's become so much more solid in my understanding, and my feelings." The Hebrew Bible, he continued, is clearly the most important document of the ancient Near East. It's important because so many other documents—the Prophets, the Gospels, the Koran—grew out of it. But it's also important because it incorporates so many elements from documents that *preceded* it. "There are countless ideas in the Bible that cross borders and civilizations—Creation, the Flood, the idea of a contract between humans and God—which the text captures perfectly because it draws from so many different cultures."

"So let me ask you what I asked Professor Malamat," I said. "When you think of the Bible, what do you think of?"

"I think of creation. I don't think of written material at all. These are stories that were crystallized over time, the deepest creativity of a certain culture. If the Bible comes from people, and not from God, as I believe it does, then it's the essence of being human. It's the story of the creation of a people. I don't know of any other created thing that has had such lasting impact, and I wonder, I still wonder, why the Bible is greater than the collected works of Mozart, or Shakespeare, or Greek mythology?"

We took up that question. We agreed that the Bible shares with those works the ability to appeal to almost anyone. If you're a woman who can't have a baby, you can relate to it. If you're a brother who fights with your brother, you can relate to it. If you're a person who works your whole life toward a dream and are denied it, you can relate to it. Also, the Bible, like Beethoven's Fifth Symphony or the Mona Lisa, is infinitely complex and infinitely simple. You can read it as a story, or you can read it as a philosophical tract.

But therein also lies a difference. Unlike most works of art, the Bible is ultimately about the relationship between people and God. It shares that subject matter with Greek mythology, of course, as well as with other ancient religions that have long since died out. So why did biblical religion survive? One answer seems to be the abstract nature of God, his ability to be everywhere, not just on top of Mount Olympus, say, tinkering with events on earth. "In Greek mythology, you have *moira,* fate," Avner said. "You're born with everything already written among the gods. You cannot change things.

"With monotheism," he continued, "God is the deity, but humans can choose whether they follow him or not. As human beings, we are responsible for our own actions. We can go one way, or the other. But the right way is the moral way."

"So if what you're saying is correct," I said, "then the great irony of this story is that for all that's written down, the most important thing about the Bible is *not* what's written."

"Because it's written by each individual who encounters the text."

"Each reader."

"That's right. We take what's written, ask questions, and struggle for answers."

"We 'go forth.' "

"And it's that process," Avner said, "that longing, that desire to touch the untouchable . . ."

"That takes us to God," I said.

He grinned. "Where else could it lead?"

Midnight was nearing by the time we pulled out our Bibles to read Moses' valedictory speech. A slight chill filled the air, and we slipped into our sleeping bags. We decided not to build a fire for fear of drawing attention to ourselves, and used flashlights to read. Occasionally the wind would howl, or a tuft of sagebrush would blow in front of us, and we'd stop: We'd been discovered! But then nothing would happen, we'd relax, and return to our books.

While Deuteronomy unfolds as a sort of *Reader's Digest* condensation of the preceding four books, the language is different, more sanctified. The tone would be familiar to anyone who attends religious services today. As Moses says in Deuteronomy 5, "Hear, O Israel, the laws and rules that I proclaim you this day! Study them and observe them faithfully!" What emerges is a portrait of an inextricable bond between the people of Israel and God. As commentator Everett Fox observes, every act that Israel performs as a community, and every one done by its individuals, is to be seen in the light of God's moral and ethical code. "Breaking one of God's rules means not merely a violation of a statute but an affront to the suzerain, the sovereign Lord, and thus a grave risk to society's well-being and even to its very existence."

Moses, in his final oration, emphasizes this blunt choice between right and wrong. "I set before you this day life and prosperity, death and adversity," he says in Deuteronomy 30. On the one hand, if the people love God and walk in his ways, they will thrive in the land they are about to invade. But if they turn to other gods, he says, they shall certainly perish. "Choose life," Moses says, "by loving the Lord your God, heeding His commands, and holding fast to him."

In Deuteronomy 31 Moses then publicly blesses Joshua, his successor. "Be strong and resolute, for it is you who shall go with this people into the land that the Lord swore to their fathers to give them, and it is you who shall apportion it to them. And the Lord Himself will go before you." At this point, Moses and Joshua enter the Tent of Meeting, where God issues a dire prediction: Israel will, indeed, go astray in the new land. "They will forsake Me and break My covenant," God says. "Then My anger will flare up against them, and I will abandon them."

God instructs Moses to write a poem and teach it to Israel, in order that they will not forget him. "Give ear, O heavens, let me speak," the poem begins, invoking the most sacred ingredient of the desert, water. "Let the earth hear the words I utter! / May my discourse come down as the rain, / My speech distill as the dew." The poem goes on to predict the ultimate rebellion by the people against God, but says, in the end, that God will not forsake Israel. "For the Lord will vindicate His people / And take revenge for His servants."

"So after all their time in the desert," I said, "the Israelites still haven't learned their lesson?"

"Monotheism, as we saw, is not a straight path," Avner said.

"But what Moses seems to be saying is that it's not enough just for individuals to have a connection to God. The entire *community* must have a relationship with God."

"It's like Rami said back in the Negev," Avner said. " 'You can't survive by yourself in the desert, you have to come together.' "

As he spoke I heard a rustling over the hill. "Do you hear something?" I said. He listened for a few seconds. "Probably just the wind," he said. "Okay," I agreed, and we chuckled.

I returned to the topic. "It can be beneficial to be with people who share your beliefs. But it can also be destructive. Look how many people died so far in the Five Books, and look how many people are going to die in the conquest. Culture may be beautiful, but it's also deadly."

"That's because culture is like creating a new species," Avner said. "And species fight for their territory, for their resources, for their existence."

"God's the same way," I said. "According to the story, he's beautiful, but deadly, too."

"And people are made in God's image."

As he said that, I heard another sound. This time Avner heard it, too. We sat upright and listened toward the wind. Several seconds passed, then two dark shadows emerged over the hill and began striding in our direction. We didn't move. It didn't take long for the figures to reach us. Two broad-shouldered men appeared, each wearing a dark shirt and trousers, a cap, and boots, and each carrying a gun. They greeted us in English. We greeted them back.

What followed was a typical bedouin meeting scene. We invited them to sit down. They did. We offered them something to drink. They accepted. No one said anything for a few minutes. Finally, the taller of the two men, with a mustache, lifted his head, smiled, and announced, "We are from the police. You are not supposed to be here. You know it. We know it. What are we going to do about it?"

If nothing else, he was admirably polite.

"This is a very dangerous area," he continued. "There are smugglers who could shoot you, or hyenas who could eat you. We are concerned about your safety and security. Do you understand?"

"We understand," Avner said.

"So what do you want to do now?" the man asked.

"I want to tell you why we are here," Avner said. He then proceeded through a gentle recitation of our reasons for being on Mount Nebo. We had been working together for several years, he said, on a project retracing the Bible through the Middle East. We had been to Turkey, Israel, the Palestinian Territories, Egypt, the Sinai, and now Jordan.

"You are Israeli?" the man asked.

"And American," I said.

"You are welcome," the man said.

We had visited many places, Avner continued. We had interviewed many people. And this was the last night of our journey and we wanted to end where Moses ended, on top of Mount Nebo. The man seemed not to understand what Avner had said. "You have been where?" he wanted to know. "Doing what?" "The Bible?" he repeated, in a manner that indicated he didn't know what that was. "One of the holy books," I said. "And you are *writing* a book?" he repeated. "Yes," I said. "And your book is going to *replace* the Bible?" he asked. The conversation was not going well.

After a while he began going through our bags, looking at my notebooks and camera, our maps and dirty clothes. He looked at my passport with its many stamps from around the Middle East. Finally he seemed to understand. "I think your work is very important," he said. "I think I will ask my supervisor to let you stay here for the night." Thank you, we said. Thank you. "Why don't you just pack up your belongings and we'll drive down to the jail in Ma'daba and ask his permission?" My heart sank. Even if we did get our approval, our chances of getting them to drive us back to the mountain by sunrise seemed slight.

"Perhaps you and I can drive there," I said cheerily, "and the other two can stay here with our belongings." He didn't like that idea. "I'm afraid—" At this point, the other officer began speaking to his partner in

Arabic. It was clear he was arguing our case. Finally, the two men stood up. "You have been traveling for years," the first man said. "You are working very hard. We would feel bad if we interrupted your work. Bad for ourselves, bad for our country. We will drive back to Ma'daba and ask our supervisor to help you.

"But this place is unsafe," he continued. "There are smugglers who could shoot you, and hyenas who could eat you. So we will send two officers to protect you. They will have guns." Thank you, we said. We understand. "And will you be one of those officers?" I asked the man. "No, I have to work in the morning," he said. "If I could, I would like to come back. Because this is a very special place."

After they left, we sat in shocked silence for a while. Ten minutes passed, then twenty. We could no longer hear them or their car. Had they really driven back to Ma'daba? Were they really going to send officers to guard us? We were afraid to sleep, having assured them we had no intention of doing so. We'd just be talking. Also, there was the matter of the smugglers. Seemed unlikely, but we didn't know.

An hour passed with still no sign. The moon was over Jerusalem now. It had turned the color of cantaloupe. Avner began drifting off and in a few minutes was sound asleep. It was after 2 A.M. by now and we were due at the monastery by five. I lay down to sleep, but kept thinking of the imminent arrival of our guards. I felt partly agitated by the thought of their returning, partly comforted. Either way, I was unable to sleep. My mind drifted to our earlier conversation about the nature of God.

When I first started out on this journey, I convinced myself that this trip was not about me and my spirit, or me and my God. It didn't take long for me to realize that that idea was self-protective folly. It would be impossible to do what we did—to spend so much time visiting biblical sites, and so much time reading the Bible—and not come face-to-face with questions of faith and divinity. If anything, these issues emerged from our earliest days in Turkey and continued until the end, forming an emotional undercurrent to the trip. This undercurrent grew out of a series of unexpected moments: driving across the plains of Mesopotamia to Harran, riding a horse with Yehuda Avni in the Galilee, floating in the rowboat on Lake Timsah, sitting alongside the burning bush in Sinai. I began to realize that this set of experiences—this thread of personal moments—had calmed me in ways I hadn't anticipated, had prepared me somehow for tests I had yet to face in my life. Above all, I felt a deep sense of peace from having spent so long in the presence of such elemental ideas—land, water, walking, family, nation, and, yes, God.

But were experiencing those feelings enough for me to know that I had encountered God? One monumental problem I faced in trying to answer that question is that God in the Bible is such a variable character—here an angel, there a visitor, here a warrior, there a gentle provider, here a wrathful tyrant, there a bestower of life. And that's just in the Five Books, before the rest of the Hebrew Bible, the New Testament, the Talmud, the Koran, and the writings of countless philosophers, physicists, gurus, rabbis, pastors, and priests. I had grown up with the inescapable question "Do you believe in God?" Now I realized that the question was merely a beginning. "Do you believe in God?" must be followed immediately by "Which version of God?" The creator God of Genesis, the destroyer God of Numbers, the Christian God of Saint Catherine's, the Muslim God of Jebel Haroun, the deeply personal God that Doug Clark found on Mount Nebo. Could it be that spending several years in the birthplace of the word of God might bring you no closer to God himself because words are inadequate to the task?

The answer to that question, I believe, is yes and no. When I set out on this trip, I basically believed there was a unified notion of God and that I either shared it or didn't. This journey would plant me squarely in that spot, or it wouldn't. What I didn't expect is that the journey would do something else entirely. First, it showed me that there is no single place, no such thing as an accepted notion of God. If anything, admitting that I didn't know what God was, but that I was consumed by doubt and fascination on the matter, brought me into line with a rich theological tradition. For many, doubt is a prerequisite for faith. As Gregory of Nyssa, a fourth-century C.E. bishop, wrote in his *Life of Moses:* "The true vision and the knowledge of what we seek consists precisely in *not* seeing, in an awareness that our goal transcends all knowledge and is everywhere cut from us by the darkness of incomprehensibility." What Gregory recommended was doing what Abraham and Moses had done: realize that we could not *see* God intellectually but that if we let ourselves be enveloped in, say, the cloud that descended upon Mount Sinai, we could *feel* his presence.

That leads to the second, and more profound, change the journey brought about in me. It allowed me to turn off my mind occasionally and open myself up to feelings—spiritual, emotional, divine, even imaginary—that might innately connect me to the world. In effect, it uprooted me from some of my rational instincts, then rerooted me to many of the nonrational elements in the world. After months of traveling around the Middle East, I felt newly aware of the emotional power of certain places, the essential meridians of history that exist just underneath the topsoil, waiting for someone to kick up the dust and lie down on top of them. This feeling was embodied in a quote I found in Bruce Chatwin's *Songlines*. "You cannot travel on the path before you have become the Path itself." The quote was from the Buddha, but it could easily have come from any of the theologians I'd read, or even Deuteronomy, in which God advises the Israelites to celebrate Passover as if each celebrant had personally come out of Egypt. God's lesson here is clear: only by entering the story ourselves can we truly understand its meaning.

So what does entering the story have to tell us? For starters, it tells us that the land is central to the Israelites and to their experience of God. I had read hundreds of theories about the meaning of the Israelites' journey, but none prepared me fully for the one overwhelming reality that emerged from retracing their route: its geographic equilibrium, its symmetry. It began in one corner of the ancient world, Mesopotamia; it continued down the central corridor, Canaan; it waylaid in the opposite corner, Egypt; it wandered for years in the desert; then returned, in the end, to the heart of the region. And not just the geographic heart, also the heart of trade, travel, conflict, and cultural exchange. The Fertile Crescent, the Via Maris, the King's Highway, the Rift Valley, even the Continental Divide all pass directly through the biblical Promised Land.

This sense of centrality—of crossroads—is perfectly captured in the text, which is a paean to taking elements from one culture, mixing them with ingredients from another culture, and creating a greater whole. The Bible may be the greatest melting pot ever forged. Indeed, it survives, I believe, in large measure, because it incorporates spiritual components taken from civilizations all across the region. If the Israelites had begun in Mesopotamia and then promptly captured the Promised Land, their journey—and their faith—would have seemed somehow incomplete. If they had begun as slaves in Egypt and then swiftly conquered Canaan, their trip—and their belief system—would have seemed somehow less monumental, less tested. Ultimately, it is the essential pan–Near Eastern nature of their travels that makes their story—and their religion—stand so well across time and place. They covered every inch of the ancient Near East and faced every imaginable threat to their existence—infertility, famine, slavery, war, starvation, mass death—and still they came out believing in their abstract, universal God.

For me, the feeling that emerged at the end of traversing that itinerary was one of profound stability and composure. As a veteran traveler, I had always believed that I left a bit of me wherever I went. I also believed that I took a bit of every place with me. I never felt that more than with this trip. It was as if the act of touching these places, walking these roads, and asking these questions had added another column to my being. And the only possible explanation I could find for that feeling was that a spirit existed in many of the places I visited, and a spirit existed in me, and the two had somehow met in the course of my travels. It's as if the godliness of the land and the godliness of my being had fused.

Recognizing that continuity was the biggest revelation—and the biggest joy—of my trip, I was fascinated to discover that Saint Augustine, in one of the more famous depictions of spiritual rebirth, described his moment of revelation as taking him not out of his body but deeper inside it, into a complex topography that he never knew existed. And the place he visited was not the Promised Land, not a mountaintop, not the desert. The place was his own imagination—his own memory—and its breadth and richness filled him with astonishment. "It was an awe-inspiring mystery," he wrote in *City of God,* "an unfathomable world of images, presences of our past and countless plains, caverns and caves."

To me, the most fascinating thing about encountering that mystery was what Augustine himself had described: the feeling that I was *recovering* it, not *discovering* it. The inchoate belief that the feeling was somehow in me already and that this trip, this route, this dirt, somehow brought it out of me. In the end, I believe the essential spirit that animates those places also animates me. If that spirit is God, then I found God in the course of my journey. If that spirit is life, then I found life. If that spirit is awe, then I found awe. Part of me suspects it's all three, and that none can exist without the other. Either way, what I know for sure is that all I had to do to discover that spirit—and the resulting feeling of humility and appreciation—was not to look or listen or taste or feel. All I had to do was *remember,* for what I was looking for I somehow already knew.

In coming to that conclusion I returned to the essential triad at the heart of the Bible: the people, the land, and God. I had gone to the land, I had encountered a spirit, and in so doing I had become more human. That equation drew me back to one of the defining moments of the Pentateuch, Jacob's wrestling with the messenger of God in the valley of Jabbok, just north of Nebo. At first Jacob doesn't know who the messenger is. They wrestle, they struggle, one seems to be winning, then the other, until finally Jacob is scarred. The scar, significantly, does not end up on Jacob's hand, nor on his head, his heart, or his eyes. Humans experience God, the text seems to be saying, not by touching him, imagining him, feeling him, or seeing him. Jacob is scarred on his leg, for the essential way humans experience God, the text suggests, is by walking with him.

This realization marked my closest bond with the Bible. Jacob, more than any other character, embodies the geographical breadth of the Five Books of Moses: He is born in the Promised Land, journeys back to Harran, returns to Canaan, travels to Egypt, and is eventually brought home to the land that bears his name. Like Jacob, I felt as if I had touched the two arms of the Fertile Crescent and engaged in a struggle that I never set out to have. There were times when I felt I was winning that struggle, that I was close to getting my mind around the puzzle of God. I was *this* close to an answer. But then, just as quickly, that feeling would go away, and I'd be overcome by waves of ignorance and opaqueness. I was defeated by unknowingness and the limits of my own imagination.

Ultimately, rather than try to win this struggle, or succumb to this struggle, I realized that the struggle itself was the goal. I had, like Jacob, wrestled with an adversary I never saw, whose name I never learned, but whose presence I deeply felt. I had, to use the words of Genesis, "striven with God," the original meaning of *Israel* and the name given to all his descendants. After all my travels, I had reached the destination that the Five Books, at least, may have intended all along. I had reached the Promised Land—Israel—the place where one strives with God.

Back on the mountain, I was tossing in my bag. Why was I sweating? Had I fallen asleep? I lifted my head. The panorama had changed. The moon was brighter than it had been all night, and the stars more vivid. All trace of haze was gone and the entire landscape was brilliantly illuminated. I could see palm fronds in Jericho, and streetlights in Jerusalem. The moon glanced off the smooth surface of the Dead Sea as if it were a silver serving tray.

There was another change from earlier: A strong wind was now blowing from the east. It was a tenacious wind, with broad fingers, that seemed intent on pushing me down the hill. It reminded me of my first night in the Sinai, when the wind wrapped around my arms, filled my ears, and made me feel alone. I held up my hand to feel the force, then stuck out my index finger to see if I could block out the lights of Jerusalem. I could. The image of Moses reaching out to touch the Promised Land came to mind, followed closely by Lot's wife, with her finger outstretched, locked in salt. Moving in and out of sleep by now, I could feel a host of images ricocheting around my head: salt fingers, salt sea, frozen arms, orange moon, rising sun, Dome of the Rock, Mount of Olives, Jerusalem, Jericho, Jordan. *Jordan.*

Guards!

Were they coming? I sat up. Avner was still asleep. There were sounds from over the hill, but no movement. We were being watched, though, I could tell. I lay back down to sleep but squirmed with a mix of unease and anticipation. Finally I succumbed to the emotion and sat up on the mattress. The first hint of light appeared behind me. It was 3:30. As soon as the sky showed signs of gray, the haze began to return. The palm trees and buildings gradually began to disappear. The street-lights dimmed. Soon there was no horizon.

The wind, which had been gaining steadily, was now whipping past me with greater speed. It was blowing with a force unimaginable even a few minutes earlier. I began to estimate its strength—forty miles per hour, fifty. The wind was cooler than before, and its force had a chilling effect that began at the lower part of my back and spread across my shoulders to the tips of my fingers. I felt completely exposed, as if my skin were being pulled from my body. It was as if the wind was going to reach under my legs, lift me off the mountain, and toss me into the valley.

Looking around, I realized what was happening. The world had entered a state of transition. It was fulfilling its diurnal ritual, creating itself anew. And though I had witnessed many dawns in my life, this time I experienced something I had never felt before: the exact moment when one day ends and another begins. It was as if the wind was blow-ing so hard it had pushed a new day into existence.

And in the limen of that dawn, I had undergone a transition along with the place. I had slid, unawares, into tomorrow. Looking below, I saw the change instantly. The clear vision and sparkling lights of the evening were now completely awash in haze. Jerusalem had disappeared. Jericho was a fog. The Dead Sea was gone. A sparrow chirped furiously, as if struggling to be heard. There was chaos in the air, but also familiarity, as if everything knew what to do to get ready for morning. And in that dream-addled state, I suddenly realized the power of creation. There was something exhilarating about the moment: I felt directed. There was something destructive about it, too: I felt disconnected from my past. But above all, there was something cleansing about it, as if someone had slid a pipe cleaner through my being and emptied everything out.

And suddenly all the ideas I had been contemplating—my identity, the land, time, God—came together in a flash. And that flash created an energy that seemed to exist outside of time, but that, in its own way, seemed to mark a restarting of time. And without verbalizing it, without even understanding it, I knew that this moment—as light and ineffable as it was—would always be an anchor for me. This would be my beginning. I was new. I was clean.

I was day.

It was the alarm clock that brought me back to earth. At 4:30 it sounded, waking Avner and reminding us that we hoped to be at the monastery by five. Avner took a bottle of water and stumbled down the hill to wash. He left a carton of orange juice on his mattress as a weight. As soon as he disappeared, however, the wind prevailed, sucking his mattress, his sleeping bag, and the carton of juice into the air. Panicked, I jumped from my bag and, before realizing that I was in my underwear and bare feet, went sprinting after the bag. This was a bad idea. First, I was now running around Mount Nebo with no clothes on, a sure invitation for smugglers or hyenas. Second, my feet could not handle the sharp rocks and sage. And third, *my* sleeping bag and mattress soon joined the others, raining down in a shower of foam and 100 percent artificial juice.

Avner returned just in time to witness my immersion. We laughed, hurriedly packed, then set off down the hill toward the monastery. Along the way, we talked about our visitors. Had they really come at all? Or had we made the whole thing up? Given my hallucinatory night, if Avner hadn't been there, I might have thought the whole episode a chimera. We did agree, though, that the only reason they allowed us to stay was the nature of our trip. "Maybe they were sent to make us feel special," Avner said. "If we hadn't traveled the entire route, we would have been arrested."

A few minutes later we arrived at the monastery, and Garbo appeared to let us in. He was wearing a gardener's floppy cap, and I now noticed that he had alternating teeth on his upper and lower gums. "The desert wind is strong this morning," he said, adding that forecasters were predicting that down in the valley the temperature would reach 50 degrees Celsius, or 120 Fahrenheit.

Garbo invited us to his patio for a cup of coffee. On the way, he moved a hose from the flower bed to a baby olive tree. "Why didn't Moses strike the rock here," he said despairingly. "We need the water." On the wall above the tree was a poster of Michelangelo's *Moses*.

We stayed for a few minutes, then walked the short distance to the garden in front of the church. A few stone benches lined the paths, along with cypress trees planted by the Franciscans. We settled underneath a fifteen-foot-high red iron cross, entwined with a serpent, that was designed to replicate the copper snake Moses erects on a pole in Numbers 21. After all our discussion about seeing sunrise, we could see nothing. The desert wind had blown with such fury overnight that it fussed up an even thicker cloud of dust, which obscured not only the sun, but also the sky, the horizon, and most of the landscape we had seen overnight. Looking toward the Holy Land was like staring into a plate of grits. There was a faint hint of yellow, but basically the panorama was mealy and white. I thought back on the sunrise of our first morning on the Euphrates, but there was no chance that the sun would break through here. If anything, the haze would only get worse. I realized again how special our overnight view had been, our own private screening.

We pulled out our Bibles for the final time. In Deuteronomy 34, the last of the Pentateuch's 187 chapters, Moses goes up from the plains of Moab to Mount Nebo, the peak "across from Jericho." There God gives him a private tour of the Promised Land. God moves methodically, starting first with the northern area, around the Sea of Galilee, then to the Mediterranean coast and the Negev. He ends with the area closest to Moses, along the Jordan.

"This is the land of which I swore to Abraham, Isaac, and Jacob," God says. He then reminds Moses: "I have let you see it with your own eyes, but you shall not cross there." Moses, the "servant of the Lord," then dies on Mount Nebo. God buries him in the valley down below, with the text observing, "and no one knows his burial place to this day." Moses is 120 years old when he dies, but "his eyes were undimmed and his vigor unabated." The Israelites bemoan him for thirty days.

The death of Moses is one of the most poignant passages in the entire Hebrew Bible. It seems impossibly sad that Moses could lead the Israelites out of Egypt, direct them for forty years in the desert, beat back their many rebellions, only to be stopped just inches from the Promised Land. "It's a tragedy," Oded Eran had said earlier. "Moses leads the people from bondage, he resists their pleas to return to the fleshpots, he survives the crisis of the doubting nation. He goes through all this, and he gets two feet, two *minutes,* from the goal, and God says, 'Sorry, you're not going in!' It's as if you said to Nelson Mandela, 'You fought for the people, you led the people, but we won't make you president. You belonged to the previous generation.' It's unfair!"

Avner agreed, pointing to a passage in Deuteronomy 3 in which Moses begs God to change his mind. "You whose powerful deeds no god in heaven or on earth can equal!" Moses says. "Let me, I pray, cross over and see the good land on the other side of the Jordan." But God snaps back. "Enough! Never speak to Me of this matter again!" Surely this exchange proves Moses' anguish, Avner said.

While there is certainly a personal tragedy inherent in these passages, there is also, I came to believe, a personal triumph for Moses. This triumph is hinted at in the unusual comprehensiveness of Moses' final tour. Simply put: It would be impossible, even on the clearest day (or the clearest night), for a person to see everything from Mount Nebo that the text says Moses sees. David Faiman, the physicist from Sdeh Boker, actually did a mathematical calculation to prove that based on the curvature of the earth, the speed of light, and the strength of the human eye, no person could ever see the Galilee, the Mediterranean, or the Negev from Mount Nebo.

Also, the text doesn't actually end with Moses' death. It ends with a poignant eulogy of the great leader. The last three of the Pentateuch's 5,845 verses declare: "Never again did there arise in Israel a prophet like Moses—whom the Lord singled out, face to face, for the various signs and portents that the Lord sent him to display in the land of Egypt, against Pharaoh and all his courtiers and his whole country, and for all the great might and awesome power that Moses displayed before Israel." The Pentateuch doesn't end by emphasizing Moses' tragedy. It ends by emphasizing his uniqueness and his unique relationship with the divine.

This prompted the last—and most unexpected—observation of our trip. The actual physical dimensions of the Promised Land matter far less at this moment than its spiritual dimensions. After hundreds of years in which the land has been the driving force in the story, it now assumes a metaphoric role. Surely, for the Israelites, the Promised Land is still their destination. For Moses, too, the Promised Land is still a dream, and he was no doubt deeply disappointed that he didn't get to achieve it.

But at the end, his tragedy is ameliorated by his ability to see what no one else sees. Denied entry, Moses actually gets more: He gets prophetic vision, personally granted to him by God. The Israelites will get the land, but they will continue to struggle with God. Their leader, however, has fulfillment. And he reaches this pinnacle not by looking out from the mountain. For looking out will not show him what he sees. The only way for Moses to see the complete dimensions—the full glory—of the Promised Land is by looking inward, toward his own internal geography, the true reflection of divine glory. Moses may not get the land, but he gets the promise. This is the lesson of Mount Nebo and the poetic twist at the end of the Five Books that help make them such a hymn: The land alone is not the destination; the destination is the place where human beings live in consort with the divine. Ultimately, it doesn't matter that what the Bible describes is impossible to see. It doesn't matter because Moses wasn't seeing as we do. At the end, he wasn't even looking at the land. He was looking where we *should* look. He was looking at God.

And the People Believed

Fred Benjamin gave the tour that inspired this project and was a source of wisdom throughout its completion. Laura Benjamin was a loyal, enthusiastic companion—and a good friend. Thank you also to Yael and Noah Benjamin.

This book, obviously, is a tribute to the wisdom, experience, and good humor of Avner Goren. I would also like to express my deepest appreciation to Edith Sabbagh, who sent us off with best wishes and welcomed us home with open arms. I am indebted to the dozens of people who appear by name in this book, many of whom discussed extremely private matters with openness and insight. Thanks also to Ahmed Ali, Avi Armoni, Zvika Bar-or, Bezalel Cohen, Trude Dhotan, Ilan Stein, Jane Taylor, and Linda and Donald Zisquit.

David Black is my friend and agent, and the most devoted of partners. I feel fortunate to be surrounded by such warm, supportive colleagues: Susan Raihofer, Gary Morris, Joy Tutela.

Trish Grader believed passionately in this project from the moment she heard of it, and escorted it gracefully through every stage, improving it greatly along the way. At Morrow/HarperCollins, I am deeply thankful for the support of Cathy Hemming, Michael Morrison, Lisa Gallagher, and Dee Dee DeBartlo. Thanks to Sarah Durand for all her hard work, and a special word of appreciation to Lou Aronica for his commitment.

I am blessed with good friends and tough, generous editors. Everlasting thanks to Karen Essex, Karen Lehrman, and Joe Weisberg. Amy Stevens read several versions of this book, improving each one—and me—along the way. Max Stier accompanied me on an early, exploratory mission, and made the idea seem worthwhile. Doug Frantz gave me a push when I needed it. Linda Rottenberg provided daily, inspirational support. Beth Middleworth is a talented and extremely accommodating designer. Lynn Goldberg and Camille McDuffie are old friends and true professionals. For their love, patience, and occasional prodding, thanks to Andy Cowan and Deena Margolis, Justin Castillo, Susan Chumsky, Jane von Mehren and Ken Diamond, Jan and Gordon Franz, James Hunter, Beverly Keel, Jessica Korn, Dana Sade, Lauren Schneider, David Shenk, Ben Sherwood, Jeff Shumlin, Devon Spurgeon, Rob Tannenbaum, and Teresa Tritch.

My parents read early drafts of this book and gave valuable comments and even more valuable heartfelt enthusiasm. My brother, Andrew, continues to be my most acute critic and trusted collaborator. A few days after I returned from Mount Nebo, my sister, Cari, gave birth to her first son, Max. May this book stand as a tribute to her and to the hope that her descendants—and *his* descendants—will be as numerous as the stars.

Take These Words

One of the many pleasures of spending so much time around the Bible was sampling the extensive literature on life in the biblical world. My research, while comprehensive, was in no way definitive. Instead, I tried to read as widely as possible and seek out experts who might further guide me. In lieu of footnotes I have decided to include detailed source notes, with particular attention to books that I found most helpful or that might be of interest to those curious about further study.

First a few words on fundamentals. English translations of the Bible vary in style, substance, and purpose. For the sake of consistency, all quotations in the text come from *The Torah: A Modern Commentary* (New York, 1981), edited by W. Gunther Plaut. Another superb translation is *The Five Books of Moses* (New York, 1995) by Everett Fox. I also consulted the Revised Standard Version, the New International Version, the King James Version, and one by the Jewish Publication Society. Robert Alter, author of *The Art of Biblical Narrative,* has made an artful translation of his own, called *Genesis.*

In keeping with long-standing academic custom and recent trends in popular writing, the nonsectarian terms B.C.E. (Before the Common Era) and C.E. (Common Era) are used throughout the book in lieu of the terms B.C. and A.D.

The most authoritative guide to understanding the Bible is the *Anchor Bible Dictionary* (New York, 1992), a six-volume reference book that was never out of arm's reach. Other thorough reference books I consulted frequently include *The Oxford Companion to the Bible*, *The Cambridge Companion to the Bible*, and the *Lutterworth Dictionary of the Bible*. Rabbi Joseph Telushkin's *Biblical Literacy* is a delightful—and highly readable—one-volume resource.

INTRODUCTION

The early history of the Fertile Crescent is discussed in many places, including, most recently, Jared Diamond's *Guns, Germs, and Steel* and Robert Wright's *Nonzero*. The relations between the stories of Genesis and Mesopotamia are examined in Thorkild Jacobsen's *The Treasures of Darkness*, O. R. Gurney's *The Hittites*, Samuel Noah Kramer's *The Sumerians*, and Nahum Sarna's *Understanding Genesis*. The history of Noah's ark is the subject of *The Incredible Discovery of Noah's Ark* by Charles Sellier and David Balsiger and *Noah's Flood* by William Ryan and Walter Pitman.

BOOK I

The historical roots of the patriarchal narratives are discussed in E. A. Speiser's *Genesis*, John Bright's *A History of Israel*, and Susan Niditch's *Ancient Israelite Religion*. Many of the extrabiblical legends of the patriarchs are gathered in Louis Ginzberg's *The Legends of the Jews* (the first three of seven volumes), Angelo Rappoport's *Ancient Israel* (two volumes), and the writings of Josephus, gathered in *The Works of Josephus*, translated by William Whiston. Popular retellings of the stories appear in Chaim Potok's *Wanderings* and Thomas Cahill's *The Gifts of the Jews*.

Two extraordinary books of contemporary commentary on the Bible stand out as exemplary works of popular scholarship: The first is Jack Miles's breathtakingly original *God: A Biography*; the second is James Kugel's monumental *The Bible as It Was*. I have benefited immensely from both, and highly recommend them.

The question of the Bible's authorship is examined in Harold Bloom's *The Book of J* and Richard Elliott Friedman's highly accessible *Who Wrote the Bible?* The history of biblical archaeology is told thoroughly in P. R. S. Moorey's *A Century of Biblical Archaeology*, Moshe

Pearlman's *Digging up the Bible,* and Neil Asher Silberman's masterly *Digging for God & Country.* Silberman is also the author of *A Prophet from Amongst You: The Life of Yigael Yadin;* Leona Glidden Running and David Noel Freedman are authors of *William Foxwell Albright: A Twentieth-Century Genius.* Other scholarly books on archaeology I consulted include *Archaeology of the Land of the Bible* by Amihai Mazar and *The Oxford Companion to Archaeology,* edited by Brian Fagan. Easily the most popular book ever on biblical archaeology is Werner Keller's *The Bible as History,* which is still in print today in English. It has a companion, *The Bible as History in Pictures* (New York, 1963).

BOOK II

T. G. H. James has written several landmark histories of ancient Egypt, including *An Introduction to Ancient Egypt* and *Ancient Egypt.* I also consulted Barbara Mertz's *Temples, Tombs, and Hieroglyphs* and Emil Ludwig's magisterial *The Nile,* the kind of ornate history that is rarely written today. I also highly recommend Alan Moorehead's *The White Nile* and *The Blue Nile.*

The subject of Egypt's relationship with the Bible is addressed in Donald Redford's powerful and comprehensive *Egypt, Canaan, and Israel in Ancient Times,* as well as in his biography *Akhenaten: The Heretic King.* Other books that explore the relationship between Egypt and the Bible include James Hoffmeier's *Israel in Egypt,* David Rohl's *Pharaoh's and Kings,* Ian Wilson's *Exodus: The True Story,* and Sigmund Freud's *Moses and Monotheism.*

The story of Joseph in Egypt is retold in Thomas Mann's four novels, *Joseph and His Brothers, Young Joseph, Joseph in Egypt,* and *Joseph the Provider.* Though these books are hard to find, they are, to my mind, unrivaled acts of imagination and prose.

BOOK III

The best single book I found on the Sinai, Saint Catherine's, and Jebel Musa is *Mount Sinai* by Joseph Hobbs. *Exploring Exodus* continues the tradition of detailed examination of history, the natural world, and the text that Nahum Sarna initiated with Genesis. Jonathan Kirsch's biography *Moses* follows a similar pattern, with thoughtful literary analysis as well.

Other books I consulted include *Sinai* by Burton Bernstein, *Guide to Exploration of the Sinai* by Alberto Siliotti, and *Sinai: The Exodus Trip* by Mario Vinei. On the subject of early monasticism, I highly recommend *The Wisdom of the Desert* by Thomas Merton, an elegant and inspiring book.

BOOK IV

There are many contemporary histories of Israel. Two I have enjoyed and consulted frequently are *The Siege* by Conor Cruise O'Brien and *A History of Israel* by Howard Sachar. A broader history of the entire region is *The Middle East* by Bernard Lewis. The relationship between Israel and Britain, with particular focus on the Bible, is treated in Barbara Tuchman's graceful *Bible and Sword*.

BOOK V

The defining piece of adventure writing about the Middle East remains *The Seven Pillars of Wisdom* by T. E. Lawrence. Other masterworks in this field include Sir Richard Francis Burton's *Narrative of a Pilgrimage to Mecca and Medina,* Charles Doughty's *Travels in Arabia Deserta,* and John Lloyd Stephen's *Incidents of Travel in Egypt, Arabia, Petraea, and the Holy Land,* each of which is fascinating, if only in pieces. The collective impact of these writings is brilliantly illuminated in the opening chapters of Robert Kaplan's *The Arabists.*

Two pieces of contemporary travel writing, William Dalrymple's *From the Holy Mountain* and Bruce Chatwin's *Songlines,* are sterling examples of how to mix the sacred and the profane into compelling personal narratives.

I benefited from a number of books on Petra and contemporary Jordan, including *The Art of Jordan,* edited by Piotr Beinkowsky, *Petra* by Iain Browning, and *Petra* by Jane Taylor. The same applies to *The JPS Commentary on Numbers* by Jacob Milgrom and *Moses and the Deuteronomist* by Robert Polzin.

I would also like to recommend a number of novels I read that relate directly, or in part, to life in the Middle East, or the desert: *The Sheltering Sky* by Paul Bowles, *Damascus Gate* by Robert Stone, and the incomparable *Quarantine* by Jim Crace.

The Internet has proved to be fertile territory for information about the Bible. There are newsgroups available for Bible research at alt.christnet.bible and soc.culture.jewish. Recent archives for the extraordinary magazine *Biblical Archaeology Review,* the international standard-bearer of the field, can be found at www.bib-arch.org. The on-line search Bible I used most frequently contains the King James translation as well as the Revised Standard Version. It can be found at http://etext.virginia.edu/frames/bibleframe.html.

In the spirit of keeping this ongoing conversation about the Bible alive, and in an effort to provide further help for those interested in visiting some (or all) of the sites described in this book, I have a started an on-line site of my own, www.walkingthebible.com. E-mail inquiries to me, or to Avner, are welcome at that site. The forum for discussing the biblical stories may have changed dramatically over time, but, as I believe our journey made clear, the desire of people around the world to connect themselves to these stories remains as strong—and as passionate—as ever.

Index

P.S.

Insights,
Interviews
& More . . .

Meet **Bruce Feiler**

Jim Coane

BRUCE FEILER is one of America's most thoughtful and popular voices on contemporary life. He writes the "This Life" column about today's families for the Sunday *New York Times* and is the author of six consecutive *New York Times* bestsellers, including *Walking the Bible* and *The Council of Dads.* He is the writer/presenter of the PBS series *Walking the Bible* and *Sacred Journeys with Bruce Feiler.* His latest book, *The Secrets of Happy Families,* is a bold playbook for families today. It collects best practices for modern-day parents from some of the country's most creative minds, including top designers in Silicon Valley, elite peace negotiators, the creators of *Modern Family,* and the Green Berets. The book was a top 5 *New York Times* bestseller.

His previous book, *The Council of Dads,* is the international sensation that describes how, faced with one of life's greatest challenges, he asked six friends to form a support group for his young daughters. The book was profiled in *People* magazine, *USA Today, Time*, and the *Washington Post,* and was the subject of a one-hour documentary on CNN hosted by Dr. Sanjay Gupta. Bruce was named "Father of the Year" by the National Fatherhood Initiative.

Since 2001, Bruce has been one of the country's preeminent thinkers, writers, and speakers about the role of religion in contemporary life. *Walking the Bible* describes his perilous, 10,000-mile journey retracing the Five Books of Moses through the desert. The book was hailed as an "instant classic" by the *Washington Post* and "thoughtful, informed, and perceptive" by the *New York Times*. It spent more than a year and a half on the *New York Times* bestseller list, has been translated into fifteen languages, and is the subject of a children's book, a photography book, and a miniseries on PBS.

Abraham recounts his personal search for the shared ancestor of Jews, Christians, and Muslims. "Exquisitely written," wrote the *Boston Globe*, "100 percent engaging." The book was featured on the cover of *Time*, debuted in the top 5 of the *New York Times* bestseller list, and inspired thousands of grassroots interfaith discussions around the world.

Where God was Born describes his yearlong trek visiting biblical sites through the front lines of Israel, Iraq, and Iran. "Bruce Feiler is a real-life Indiana Jones," wrote the *Atlanta Journal-Constitution*. *America's Prophet* is the groundbreaking story of the influence of Moses on American history. Both were top 10 bestsellers.

Bruce Feiler has written for numerous publications, including *The New Yorker, New York Times Magazine*, and *Gourmet*, where he won three James Beard Awards. He is also a frequent contributor to NPR, ABC, NBC, CBS, CNN, and Fox News. A former circus clown, he has been the subject of Jay Leno jokes and a *Jeopardy!* question, and his face appears on a postage stamp in the Grenadines.

A native of Savannah, Georgia, Bruce lives in Brooklyn with his wife, Linda Rottenberg, and their identical twin daughters. ◁

A Conversation with
Bruce Feiler

Bruce Feiler reprised his travels through the Holy Land that led to Walking the Bible—*this time he took along a documentary film crew. In this interview, Feiler discusses the experience of filming a documentary based on his bestselling book.*

How did the experience of filming the PBS documentary of Walking the Bible *differ from the writing of the book?*

There were a lot more people along for the ride. The first time we made this journey we were alone, both in how we traveled and in the sense that I, at least, was on unfamiliar territory. This time we went with a crew that ranged from five to ten people with almost fifty pieces of luggage for equipment. One consequence is that time moves slower, as getting that equipment into the pharaoh's tombs or to the top of Mount Sinai takes much longer. The enormous upside is that TV cameras unlock a lot of doors, so we got to see a number of places—the slopes of Mount Ararat and the tops of the pyramids, for example—that mere mortals are not usually allowed to go.

When you returned to these biblical sites for the documentary, did you see anything you hadn't noticed before?

A lot more sunrises! TV crews never sleep in. Seriously, as a writer, I spend a lot of time trying to think of words to describe the physical appearance of a place. This was particularly challenging while spending so much time in the desert. The director of the documentary, David Wallace; the cameraman, Peter Harvey; and the sound recordist, Mick Duffield; are all British, all true masters at painting the most beautiful images with the camera. And the fact that the documentary was shot in high-definition, one of the first in the region, makes the pictures all the more extraordinary. So I spent less time trying to describe pure landscape, and more time noticing the details of everyday life—milking a water buffalo, pulling water for a camel from a well, and climbing the trunk of a date palm with your hands—all of which we filmed.

Can you tell us what we'll see you doing in the documentary?

The documentary is extremely adventurous. With Parachute, we climbed halfway up Mount Ararat looking for Noah's ark; with Avner, I hiked up to the top of one of the salt pillars in Sodom and Gomorrah; with Father Justin, I ventured to the top of Mount Sinai and witnessed an extraordinary ritual at the summit. I got to see the mummy of a pharaoh and learn how Jacob and Joseph might have been embalmed; I nearly broke my neck galloping in front of the pyramids on a runaway horse; and I witnessed what is surely the most beautiful scenery I've ever seen: Wadi Rum from a helicopter.

Did the filming of the documentary change your views about the role of religion in our lives today? ▶

> " I spent less time trying to describe pure landscape, and more time noticing the details of everyday life— milking a water buffalo, pulling water for a camel from a well, and climbing the trunk of a date palm with your hands—all of which we filmed. "

A Conversation with Bruce Feiler *(continued)*

It reminded me anew that away from the sometimes bloody, sectarian battles over theology that dominate many institutions, religion is a much broader, more humane enterprise. In the desert, people long for meaning, and the biblical stories have endured because they build connections—both people to people, and people to God.

Did you have any daredevil moments while filming the documentary?

> By far the most difficult and stressful thing I did was climb one of the pyramids at Giza.

By far the most difficult and stressful thing I did was climb one of the pyramids at Giza. Visitors have been forbidden to climb the pyramids for a number of decades, because a handful of people died every year. The stones are very high (at least four or five feet), they easily crumble, and the vertigo is intense. The experience was almost like climbing a sheer wall, requiring hand grips, tiny foot holds, and intense concentration. And you couldn't look down or admire the view or you'd risk getting wobbly knees. After about forty minutes, I reached the top. I pumped my hands so high you would have thought I had run a marathon. Then I looked over the edge: "You mean I have to go down!"

An Excerpt from
Where God Was Born: A Daring Adventure Through the Bible's Greatest Stories

Where God Was Born *is the long-awaited sequel to* Walking the Bible. *This new book continues Bruce Feiler's biblical adventures through the second half of the Hebrew Bible, including the stories of Joshua, David, and Solomon, the destruction of Jerusalem, the exile in Babylon, and the return to the land of Israel. Both a heart-racing adventure and a deeply personal quest,* Where God Was Born *recounts Feiler's ten-thousand-mile journey through Israel, Iraq, and Iran, visiting archaeological sites unseen for decades and uncovering new information about the untold links among Judaism, Christianity, and Islam.* Where God Was Born *is a powerful and inspiring story that will forever change how we view our world, our future, and ourselves.*

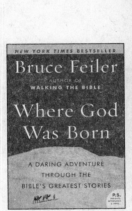

....

I FEEL THE TENSION before I know its source. My legs begin to quiver, then shake. Soon my whole body is quaking with vibration, or is it fear? Up above, the whir begins to build into a thudding bass beat. Cold air blows through the cracks and up my spine. I'm shivering. My feet are trembling. "Are you ready?" The sound in my ears is crackling, and a bit wicked. I nod. Within seconds, the shaking becomes overwhelming, the thumping dense, and the pull so strong it seems ready to suck my head off. I feel as if ▶

An Excerpt *(continued)*

I'm in a full-body migraine. And then, just as suddenly, quiet. The sound dissolves, my body relaxes. I'm in the air, in a war. I'm at peace.

The helicopter pauses for a second, then accelerates into a gentle glide. Down below, the landing pad disappears, and rows of orange and avocado trees poke up toward the sky. I see the hairs on a donkey's ears. Our nose is tipped, we're flying, yet we're not moving very quickly. Lifting off in a helicopter is like drifting off to sleep: You leave one realm and shift into another; the features seem dreamily unfamiliar; you want to touch what you see, but you can't.

We bank toward the Mediterranean. Voices in my headphones interrupt. *"This is the Air Force. Identify yourself! Do you have permission to be here?"* Boaz, the pilot, smiles. He's anticipated this. He's flown in every war the State of Israel has fought for the previous thirty years. When I asked him what his most dangerous mission was, he thought for a second, then replied, "I once flew seven and a half hours from Israel into enemy territory on a secret mission." I raised my eyebrows; that's halfway to Iran, or Libya.

"Were you part of the mission that destroyed the nuclear plant in Iraq?"

He smiled. "Let's just say I was in the Middle East."

Boaz replied to air traffic control with a mixture of authority and evasion. We did have permission, garnered over the preceding six months, from three government agencies. The night before a suicide bomber had killed seven soldiers in Tel Aviv, and the Israeli Defense Forces (IDF) rescinded its green light. Boaz had to scramble to find a general to overturn

> 66 Lifting off in a helicopter is like drifting off to sleep: You leave one realm and shift into another; the features seem dreamily unfamiliar; you want to touch what you see, but you can't. 99

the decision. This morning, after we boarded the McDonnell Douglas MD-500, storm clouds descended, limiting visibility above 1,000 feet. We were forced to cancel. An hour later, visibility lifted. "There are always risks with flying," Boaz said. We dashed to the landing pad.

Weather was the least of our risks. War was raging—between the Israelis and the Palestinians, between a fragile coalition and Iraq, between the pluralist West and Islamic extremism. Ripples were reverberating around the globe—in Iran, Saudi Arabia, Yemen, Kenya, Morocco, Indonesia, and, yes, the United States. The Cradle of Civilization—the tiny, fertile crescent of land that stretched from Mesopotamia to North Africa—had once more seized control of the world's destiny and the future of civilization seemed to be at stake.

And so, I thought, what better way to confront my doubts about religion and consider the future of faith than to travel to the land where God was born? And, again, what better guide to read along the way than the text that defines identity for half the world's believers?

I would journey to the flashpoints in the new world war over God—Israel, Iraq, and Iran—and bring along my Bible. And I would begin my quest with the second half of the Hebrew Bible, at the moment when the children of Israel, sprung from Adam and Eve, descended from Abraham, and freed by Moses, face their harshest challenge. "Conquer the Promised Land," God says to Joshua, Moses's successor, at the start of the books of the Prophets. "Seize the future for yourselves—and for me." ▶

> "Weather was the least of our risks. War was raging—between the Israelis and the Palestinians, between a fragile coalition and Iraq, between the pluralist West and Islamic extremism."

An Excerpt *(continued)*

After twenty minutes we approached an isolated landing strip just north of Ben Gurion International Airport. A silvery mist hung low over the Mediterranean, a few miles to the west. Shallow waves unfolded onto the narrow beaches. Palm trees, like artichokes on sticks, bent in all directions. As we hovered, a man strode out of a small building onto the black tarmac. He directed Boaz to his preferred spot, and, as the blades spun, he bent and scampered toward the door.

Yoram Yair is that rare individual known only by his nickname. For months afterward, when I told Israelis (and Palestinians) I had gone on a military tour of the Israelite conquest of the Promised Land with one of the most decorated generals in the history of the country, a man who had been the first Israeli to penetrate the Sinai during the Six Day War, the last to hold the Golan Heights during the Syrian offensive of the Yom Kippur War, and the one who led an amphibious landing closest to Beirut during the Lebanon War, they all said, *"Yaya!*? What's he like?"

A rock. As he boarded the helicopter and greeted us all crisply, yet warmly, he evinced an unimpeachable stableness and sureness of gesture—firm handshake, steady stare, was that a twinkle? —that made us instantly trust him.

Yaya was wearing white boaters, navy khakis, and a pink and green Hawaiian shirt unbuttoned to his chest. He had a silver Brylcreemed pompadour that, despite the wind, came to a perfect nest above his forehead, causing me to spend the next few hours wondering how he kept it in place in a foxhole. Altogether with his leathery skin and avuncular matte of gray chest hair, he

> " He had a silver Brylcreemed pompadour that, despite the wind, came to a perfect nest above his forehead, causing me to spend the next few hours wondering how he kept it in place in a foxhole. "

reminded me of my Uncle Bubba walking the strip on Miami Beach.

"I will try to be very modest, but maybe there are another five generals in the world today, alive, who have similar combat experience," Yaya said. "Unfortunately for normal human beings, but fortunately for a military person, I fought in four wars, and in each of those wars, I was in a commanding position. You can't see it, but my body is full of shrapnel."

"So during these times," I said, "did you ever turn to the Bible for inspiration?"

"Ever since I was a child," he said, "I liked very much the Bible—the story, the heritage, the connection to the land. When I was a young officer, whenever we trained, I always asked one of the soldiers to prepare something about the place. Every Israeli commander will tell you that part of our mission is education. Not just about weapon systems, but about values and ethics.

"And I'll tell you," he continued. "The best thing about the Bible is what it teaches about community. Take Moses: When he leads the Israelites out of Egypt, he does what all good leaders should do, first he sets a goal. Then he builds tactics. But before they leave, he asks his people to do a difficult thing: to put blood on the doorposts. Is this for God? Nonsense. God doesn't need signs. Moses does this because he wants the people to develop a strong identity."

I had sought a warrior to take me on my tour. Had I found something more?

"And what about Joshua," I said. "What does his story tell you about values?"

He raised his eyebrows. "Let's go," he said. "I'll show you." 〜

Have You Read?
More by Bruce Feiler

THE SECRETS OF HAPPY FAMILIES

- Don't worry about family dinner.
- Let your kids pick their punishments.
- Ditch the sex talk.
- Cancel date night.

These are just a few of the surprising ideas in this first-of-its-kind, bold playbook for families today. Bestselling author and *New York Times* family columnist Bruce Feiler found himself squeezed between aging parents and rising children.

He set out on a three-year journey to find the smartest ideas, cutting-edge research, and novel solutions to make his family happier. Instead of the usual psychologists and family "experts," he sought out the most creative minds from Silicon Valley to the country's top negotiators, from the set of *Modern Family* to the Green Berets, and asked what team-building exercises and problem-solving techniques they use with their families. Feiler then tested these ideas with his own wife and kids. The result is a fun, completely original look at how families can draw closer together, complete with 200 never-before-seen best practices.

Feiler's life-changing discoveries include: A radical plan that can reshape your family in twenty minutes a week; Warren Buffett's guide for setting an allowance; and the Harvard handbook for resolving conflict. *The Secrets of Happy Families* is a timely, counterintuitive book that answers the questions countless parents are asking: How do we manage the chaos of our lives? How do we teach our kids values? How do we make our family happier?

Written in a charming, accessible style, *The Secrets of Happy Families* is smart, funny, and fresh, and will forever change how your family lives every day.

"The best book I've read about how to transform families. . . . Run, don't walk, to get a copy."   —Washington Post Writers Group

THE COUNCIL OF DADS

When Bruce Feiler was diagnosed with cancer in 2008, he instantly worried what his daughters' lives would be like with him not around: "Would they wonder who I was? Would they wonder what I thought? Would they lack for my approval, my discipline, my voice?" *The Council of Dads* is the inspiring story of what happened after he decided how to give his daughters that voice. Bruce reached out to six men from all the passages in his life and asked them to be present in his daughters' lives. And he would call this group "The Council of Dads." This is a touching, funny, and ultimately deeply moving book on how to live life, how the human spirit can respond to adversity, and how to deepen and cherish the friendships that enrich our lives.

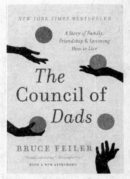

"*The Council of Dads* . . . reminds us of which values we value most, and helps us make sure we transmit them."   —*Time*

AMERICA'S PROPHET

For four hundred years, one figure has inspired more Americans than any other. His name is Moses. Traveling through touchstones in American history, bestselling author Bruce Feiler traces

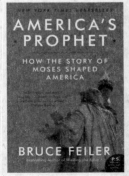

the biblical prophet's influence from the *Mayflower* through today. Meticulously researched and highly readable, *America's Prophet* is a thrilling, original work of history that will forever change how we view America, our faith, and our future.

"Audacious. . . . Classically Feiler."

—*USA Today*

ABRAHAM

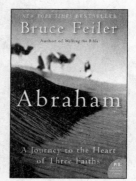

Both immediate and timeless, *Abraham* tells the powerful story of one man's search for the shared ancestor of Judaism, Christianity, and Islam. Traveling through war zones, braving violence at religious sites, and seeking out faith leaders, Bruce Feiler uncovers the defining yet divisive role that Abraham plays for half the world's believers. Provocative and uplifting, *Abraham* offers a thoughtful and inspiring vision of unity that redefines what we think about our neighbors, our future, and ourselves.

"An exquisitely written journey."

—*Boston Globe*

WALKING THE BIBLE: A PHOTOGRAPHIC JOURNEY

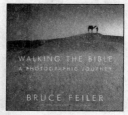

Featuring Bruce Feiler's own photography as well as his selections from professional collections, *Walking the Bible: A Photographic Journey* brings together breathtaking vistas, intimate portraits, and fascinating panoramas, providing firsthand access to the inscrutable land where three of the world's great religions were born—and finally puts a face on the stories that have long inspired the human spirit.

"Beautifully depicts the dramatic land that gave birth to three of the world's great religions." —*USA Today*

DREAMING OUT LOUD

Country music has exploded across the United States and undergone a sweeping revolution, transforming the once ridiculed world of Nashville into an unlikely focal point of American pop culture. In writing this fascinating book, Feiler was granted unprecedented access to the private moments of the revolution. Here is the acclaimed report: a chronicle of the genre's biggest stars as they changed the face of American music. With intimate portraits of Garth Brooks, Wynonna Judd, and Wade Hayes, Feiler has written the defining book on the new Nashville.

"Penetrating and insightful." —Elvis Mitchell, *New York Times*

UNDER THE BIG TOP

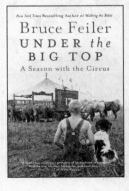

It's every child's dream: to run away and join the circus. Feiler did just that, joining the Clyde Beatty–Cole Bros. Circus as a clown for one year. This is the story of that crazy, chaotic, heartbreaking ride, a book that will remind you of how dreams can go horribly wrong—and then miraculously come true.

"A stunning collective portrait." —*The New Yorker*

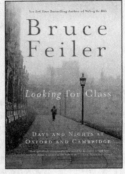

Discover great
authors, exclusive offers,
and more at hc.com.

Have You Read? *(continued)*

LOOKING FOR CLASS

An irresistible, entertaining peek into
the privileged realm of Wordsworth and
Wodehouse, Chelsea Clinton and Hugh
Grant, *Looking for Class* offers a hilarious
account of Feiler's year at Britain's most
exclusive universities, Oxford and
Cambridge—the garden parties and
formal balls, the high-minded debates
and drinking Olympics—and gives us
a eye-opening view of the often
romanticized but rarely seen British
upper class.

"A trenchant, witty, and engaging critique of
the English establishment."
—*San Francisco Chronicle*

LEARNING TO BOW

Feiler's first book, *Learning to Bow*, is
one of the funniest, liveliest, and most
insightful books ever written about the
clash of cultures between America and
Japan. With warmth and candor, Feiler
recounts the year he spent as a teacher in
a small rural Japanese town. Beginning
with a ritual outdoor bath and
culminating in an all-night trek to the
top of Mount Fuji, Feiler teaches his
students about American culture, while
they teach him everything from how to
properly address an envelope to how to
date a Japanese girl.

"Incisive, often hilarious, and presents
a rounded portrait of the modern
Japanese."
—*USA Today*

BOOKS BY BRUCE FEILER

WALKING THE BIBLE A Journey by Land Through the Five Books of Moses

To tie in to the six-part PBS series *Sacred Journeys with Bruce Feiler*, a reissue of the classic *New York Times* bestseller.

"Thoughtful, informed and perceptive." —*New York Times*

THE SECRETS OF HAPPY FAMILIES
Improve Your Mornings, Tell Your Family History, Fight Smarter, Go Out and Play, and Much More

"The best book I've read about how to transform families." —The Washington Post Writers Group

THE COUNCIL OF DADS A Story of Family, Friendship, and Learning How to Live

"Reminds us which values we value most and helps us make sure we transmit them." —*Time*

AMERICA'S PROPHET How the Story of Moses Shaped America

"This is one of the most original, intelligent, and endlessly fascinating books I have read in years." —Simon Winchester

WHERE GOD WAS BORN A Daring Adventure Through the Bible's Greatest Stories

"Another absorbing blend of travelogue, history, Bible commentary, memoir, current events, and passionate preaching." —*Publishers Weekly*

ABRAHAM A Journey to the Heart of Three Faiths

"A winning mix of insight, passion, and historical research." · —*Christian Science Monitor*

DREAMING OUT LOUD
Garth Brooks, Wynonna Judd, Wade Hayes, and the Changing Face of Nashville

"Well-written and meticulously researched . . . Essential reading for anyone who cares about American music." —*Washington Post*

LEARNING TO BOW Inside the Heart of Japan

"A refreshingly original look at Japan." —*Atlanta Journal-Constitution*

LOOKING FOR CLASS Days and Nights at Oxford and Cambridge

"Full of companionable characters, solid information, and wit." —Scott Turow

UNDER THE BIG TOP A Season with the Circus

"A colorful, sometimes unsettling pageant of circus life." —*Entertainment Weekly*

Titles available in Paperback and e-Book